HAYNES MAX POWER Peugeot

# 206

The definitive guide to **modifying**
by **Richard Nicholls**

HAYNES MAX POWER Peugeot

# 206

The definitive guide to **modifying**

by **Richard Nicholls**

Haynes Publishing

ISBN 1 84425 077 6

Printed by **J H Haynes & Co Ltd,**
Sparkford, Yeovil, Somerset BA22 7JJ, UK.

Tel: 01963 442030 Fax: 01963 440001
Int. tel: +44 1963 442030 Fax: +44 1963 440001
E-mail: sales@haynes.co.uk
Web site: www.haynes.co.uk

**Haynes North America, Inc**
861 Lawrence Drive, Newbury Park, California 91320, USA

**Editions Haynes**
4, Rue de l'Abreuvoir
92415 COURBEVOIE CEDEX, France

**Haynes Publishing Nordiska AB**
Box 1504, 751 45 UPPSALA, Sweden

# It **wasn't my idea** guv'nor!

**1** Advice on safety procedures and precautions is contained throughout this manual, and more specifically on page 170. You are strongly recommended to note these comments, and to pay close attention to any instructions that may be given by the parts supplier.

**2** J H Haynes recommends that vehicle customisation should only be undertaken by individuals with experience of vehicle mechanics; if you are unsure as to how to go about the customisation, advice should be sought from a competent and experienced individual. Any queries regarding customisation should be addressed to the product manufacturer concerned, and not to J H Haynes, nor the vehicle manufacturer.

**3** The instructions in this manual are followed at the risk of the reader who remains fully and solely responsible for the safety, roadworthiness and legality of his/her vehicle. Thus J H Haynes are giving only non-specific advice in this respect.

**4** When modifying a car it is important to bear in mind the legal responsibilities placed on the owners, driver and modifiers of cars, including, but not limited to, the Road Traffic Act 1988. IN PARTICULAR, IT IS AN OFFENCE TO DRIVE ON A PUBLIC ROAD A VEHICLE WHICH IS NOT INSURED OR WHICH DOES NOT COMPLY WITH THE CONSTRUCTION AND USE REGULATIONS, OR WHICH IS DANGEROUS AND MAY CAUSE INJURY TO ANY PERSON, OR WHICH DOES NOT HOLD A CURRENT MOT CERTIFICATE OR DISPLAY A VALID TAX DISC.

**5** The safety of any alteration and its compliance with construction and use regulations should be checked before a modified vehicle is sold as it may be an offence to sell a vehicle which is not roadworthy.

**6** Any advice provided is correct to the best of our knowledge at the time of publication, but the reader should pay particular attention to any changes of specification to the vehicles, or parts, which can occur without notice.

**7** Alterations to vehicles should be disclosed to insurers and licensing authorities, and legal advice taken from the police, vehicle testing centres, or appropriate regulatory bodies.

**8** The vehicle has been chosen for this project as it is one of those most widely customised by its owners, and readers should not assume that the vehicle manufacturers have given their approval to the modifications.

**9** Neither J H Haynes nor the manufacturers give any warranty as to the safety of a vehicle after alterations, such as those contained in this book, have been made. J H Haynes will not accept liability for any economic loss, damage to property or death and personal injury arising from use of this manual other than in respect of injury or death resulting directly from J H Haynes' negligence.

# Contents





## 01 Haynes Max Power

## 02 Buyer's guide

## 03 Insurance

## 08 Suspension

## 09 Brakes

## 10 Interiors

## Security

04



## Body styling

05



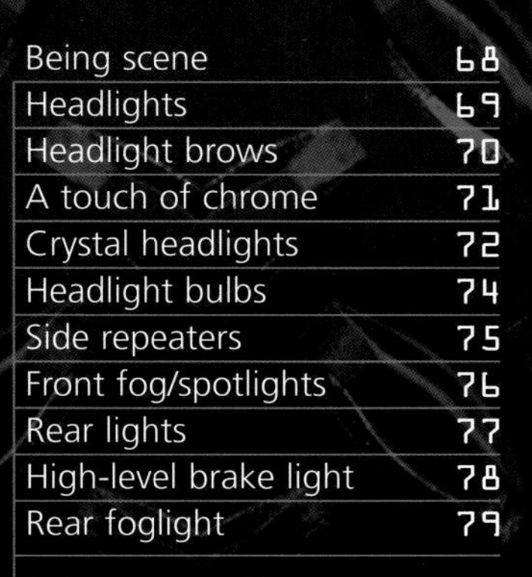

## Lights & bulbs

06



## Wheels & tyres

07



11

## ICE

12

## Engines

13

## Exhausts

14

## Reference

# Haynes Max Power

## What's that then?

Haynes Publishing have, for more than forty years, been helping people keep their cars on the roads in countries all over the world by publishing maintenance manuals. Chances are you've either got one of them yourself or you know somebody who has.

"Lights & bulbs" includes fitting smoked lights, [illegible] [illegible] etc

## Before

## After

Remember what it feels like on your birthday, or at Christmas, when you're faced by a pile of pressies? So do we, that gnawing feeling in your gut, what's in them? What did I get? Take that feeling and multiply it by twelve, that's how we felt when we started this project. When we decided that it was time to try something new, we couldn't wait. Because the same theories apply to modifying your car as servicing it, we reckoned we'd better get on and do it ourselves. We don't pay other people to do it for us, and we get the same dodgy instructions with kit as everybody else.

So if you've ever wondered how to fit a universal door mirror properly, smooth a tailgate or just bolt a seat in, this book is for you.

We've picked up a skip full of tips along the way, and they're all here for you to use. We haven't tried to set any trends, but we've covered every possible process we think you'll need. So where we've tinted a front door window, the same rules apply to a rear one, job done.

If you look in the magazines and want some of that, join us, 'cos so do we, and we'll show you how to get it.

## Keeping it real

Modifying a car is not without its problems in the 'real world', as opposed to the seemingly fantasy world of the glossy mags. For instance, it's pretty silly to spend hours fitting illegal window tints or smoked lights if you get pulled the first time you're out afterwards. Of course, you can get pulled for all sorts of reasons (and just driving a modified car is reason enough sometimes), but keeping the car actually legal is one of the 'hidden' challenges with modifying. Throughout the book, our tips should give all the help you need to at least appear to be on the right side of the law. The annual MOT test is another favourite time for your mods to get panned, and again, we aim to give you all the help necessary to ensure at least that what you've changed doesn't lead to a fail.

Security is another major issue with a tweaked motor, and the perils of insurance cannot be taken lightly, either. We aim to give down-to-earth advice to help you keep the car in the first place, and to help you in not upsetting your insurers too much if the worst happens.

## A word about fashion

In producing this book, we're aware that fashions change. What we show being fitted to our car might well be hideously out of date in 6 months time, or might not be your thing in the first place! Also, some of the stuff we've acquired from our various suppliers may no longer be available by the time you read this. We hope that, despite this, our approach of showing you step-by-step how to fit the various parts will mean that, even if the parts change slightly, the procedures we show for fitting will still be valid.

Our main project car was a 1.6 XS, 1999 V reg.

"Wheels & tyres" takes a detailed look at all the options

"Body styling" shows you how to fit universal mirrors to full body kits

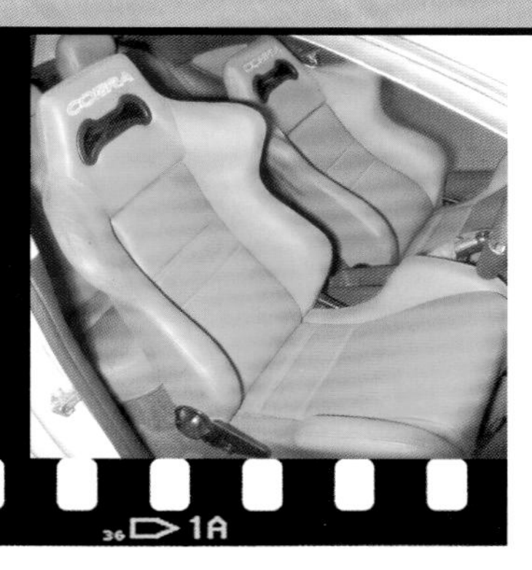


"Interiors" includes seats, painting trim, gear knobs and loads more

# Peugeot 206 – **we're lovin' it**

If you're a car maker, having huge gaps in your model range is not good. Peugeot found this out the hard way, when the old 205 died in 1996, leaving only the baby 106 and the grown-up 306 behind. Took them another two years to plug the gap, but when the 206 landed in late 1998, it was worth the wait. "Stop liking, start loving" was the tag line, and our steamy affair with Peugeot's pert new babe still

**hasn't come up for air. Those saucy Frenchies have never been slow in the lurve department, so it was no surprise to find them tickling our erogenous zones once again in 1999, with the arrival of the 2.0 litre GTI. And now we've got the "Play away from home" GTI 180. Phew. Steady on - we're only flesh and blood!**

For those of you who've been living in a cave these past few years, the 206 is the latest in a long line of tidy-looking Peugeot hatches, and it's sold here and in Europe by the bucketload. Some suggested Peugeot had cribbed the 206 front end look from Ford's wedgy Focus, but whatever - the rest of the car's definitely all their own work, and deserves its success. It's a big hit with young people in parts of India, too. Or so we believe...

With the 106 and 306 already showing up in numbers at cruises, the success of the 206 as a top modded motor was a no-brainer, and it's getting bigger on the scene all the time. About the only thing the car doesn't have going for it is the interior, but it looks so sweet outside, this hardly matters - and who says it has to stay standard? With a growing choice of excellent bodykits, crystal lights everywhere you look, and big-rim-friendly arches, this thing with the 206 ain't gonna be no one-night stand.

02



# Buyer's guide

## What to buy

The main reason for buying a 206, of course, is the styling. May not be to everyone's taste, but its wedgy curviness is pretty radical, with some great design features such as the steeply raked screen, nicely-shaped lights front and rear, plus the deep-skirted bumpers. Plenty of room for big rims in those arches, too. Providing you can resist the GTIs, insurance is pretty cheap, with the still-desirable 1.6 models no higher than Group 8, and the pokey D-Turbos in Group 5. As you'd kinda hope, there's more room inside than the baby 106, and it's pretty well screwed together.

Any bad news, then? Well, this is one car you really should try before you buy. The driving position is not big-person friendly, with limited legroom and rather awkward pedals. And while the interior's quality-built, quality-looking it ain't, with some fairly unpleasant textures on the dash itself. Only our opinion - if you love it enough, you'll forgive it. Finally, make sure you're not buying a 5-door before you set out after your dream 206 (if the advert doesn't say - ask), as we suspect you won't see too many 5-doors featured in the mags. As for the 5-door SW (Sport Wagon) - well, they got it half-right. It's a Wagon.

## Keeping it real

At the budget end of the 206 range, what do we get? Well, the L and Style trim levels don't exactly get you much kit to shout about (apart from power steering), and only come with the rather weedy 1.1 litre engine (Group 3 insurance). The minimum spec you should aim for is the LX, which adds electric windows, remote locking, and often air conditioning. Most LX models you'll be offered have the more effective 1.4 engine, with 75 bhp and Group 4 insurance, but the 8-valve 1.6 engine has 90 bhp and is only one group higher. The GLX has luxuries such as electric mirrors, front fogs, and rear

headrests - more usefully, it features an ultrasonic alarm and 6-disc CD. The "Roland Garros" is the real luxury deal, with full leather seats, but it only comes in a 5-door.

For something a little sportier, try the 1.4 Quiksilver, with air con, sports seats and ally trim. Only available as a 3-door, but colour choice is limited to one (we think you can guess). Another sports bargain is the 1.6 XS, with the 90-brake 8-valve engine and Group 5 insurance, it offers something close to a GTI for lots less dosh. We hear the engine responds well to intake and exhaust mods, too (essentially, it's the same engine as the Saxo VTR). The XSi model (which replaced the XS late in 2000) has a 16-valve 1.6 unit, packing 110 bhp, but insurance is Group 8 - do you reckon it's worth the extra?

## Cheap insurance is for wimps

The 2.0-litre GTI is obviously the Daddy, and definitely one for the enthusiasts. Awesome performance throughout, and especially quick when modded. If Group 14 insurance doesn't scare you off, go for it. For the really brave amongst you with plenty of no-claims (or rich parents?), the GTI 180 is the ultimate 206-sized thrill - and it'd flippin' better be worth those Group 17 premiums, too. The GTIs feature ABS with discs all round, flared front arches, digital air con, leather/alcantara trim, and a CD changer.

## Diesel do nicely

Awesome fuel economy's hardly very cool, and there's no getting away from the tickover rattle, but hang on - there could be more to this diesel thing than you think. The 206 D Turbo is actually a sporty XS with a 2.0 litre HDi diesel under the hood, so the look's there. What about the engine? Well, the diesel's good for 90 bhp (like the XS), and it's in Group 5. The big news is the diesel's extra turbo torque, which slings you down the road with its midrange muscle. Give one a try. And don't forget, turbo-diesels are very chippable these days. Avoid the old-school, non-turbo 1.9 diesel 206s if you want any sort of cred, though. The 2002-onwards 1.4 HDi engine might be worth a look, but with only 67 bhp, it's never going to match its 2.0 litre big brother for poke.

## Hairdressers only

Finally, there's the drop-top CC models, available with the 2.0 litre GTI motor, or the 1.6 from the XSi (for those who don't want to mess up their hair as much). Very nice. Lovely. Any other comments we might make about these models would have too-sexist overtones, so we'll leave it there.

# Don't buy a dog

**No-one's accusing the 206 of being a girly car, but they are popular with those of the female persuasion.**

If you can find a one-lady-owner 206, used only as a second car, you could be in for a major bargain. It's been years since you had to worry about a Peugeot going rusty, and flimsy French build quality is also a thing of the past. So nothing ever goes wrong? Don't be silly.

No, they don't rust, but 206s sometimes suffer from other problems caused by the elements. First is the central locking, which can play up big-time, through water getting into the locks - ask the seller if there's been any problem, and check the reaction you get. Some 206s suffer from water getting inside, through the bonnet vent, resulting in wet carpets and misting-up. Last on the list of weather-related woes - gearbox problems can result from the car being driven through deep floodwater.

Models with the 1.4 engine can suffer from throttle problems causing sudden power loss, or maybe dodgy engine mountings (check for excessive engine movement, or strange clonking noises on the test drive). Any misfiring on a 1.1 litre model could spell expensive problems with the ignition system.

Any clonking noises over bumps will either mean worn bottom balljoints or anti-roll bar drop links (£50+ per side). On GTIs, check the condition of the exhaust - there's been suggestions that even genuine Peugeot items don't last long. On models from 2001, check the indicator stalk carefully, as they seem to seize up, and then get broken when owners force them. Lastly, it's worth getting your jeans dirty to check the spare wheel's actually where it should be, under the back of the car - especially on a car with alloys, they're known to go missing in the night.

All 206s have a camshaft drivebelt (cambelt, or timing belt) which is made of reinforced rubber. The belt deteriorates with age, and for safety's sake, a new one should be fitted every 3 years or 36000 miles, especially if the engine gets a regular caning. If the belt snaps, the engine could be wrecked. Finished. Ruined. Knackered. It's not too bad a DIY job if you're confident under the hood, or budget for a garage bill around the £80 mark. Ask for a new tensioner/pulleys at the same time.

## General stuff

Usually, it's far better to buy your 206 privately, as long as you know what you're doing. Dealers have to make a living, but sometimes all you'll get for the extra money is a full valet and some degree of comeback if the car's a hound. Buying privately, you get to meet the owner, gaining you valuable clues about how the car's been treated.

Everyone's nervous when buying a car, but don't ignore your 'gut feelings' at first sight, or when meeting the owner. Don't make the mistake of deciding to buy the car *before you've even seen it* - too many people make up their minds before setting out, and blindly ignore all the warning signs. Remember, there *are* other cars, and you *can* walk away! Think of a good excuse before you set out.

Take someone who 'knows a bit about cars' along with you - preferably, try and find someone who's either got a 206, or who's had one in the past.

Never buy a car in the dark, or when it's raining. If you do have to view any car in these conditions, agree not to hand over any major money until you've seen it in daylight, and when the paintwork's dry (dull, faded paint, or metallic paint that's lost its lacquer, will appear to be shiny in the rain).

Check the mileages and dates shown on the receipts and MoTs follow a pattern indicating normal use, with no gaps in the dates, and no sudden drop in the mileage between MoTs (which might suggest 'clocking'). If you're presented with a sheaf of paperwork, it's worth going through it - maybe the car's had a history of problems, or maybe it's just had some nice new parts fitted (like a clutch, starter motor or alternator, for instance).

Check the chassis number (VIN number) and engine number on the registration document and on the car. Any sign of welding near one of these numbers is suspicious - to disguise the real number, a thief will run a line of weld over the old number, grind it flat, then stamp in a new number. Other scams include cutting the section of bodywork with the numbers on from another car, then cutting and welding this section into place. The VIN number is stamped into the rear edge of the boot floor (open the tailgate), on the VIN plate inside the boot at the very back, and is visible just above the passenger wiper arm.

The engine number is stamped into the front or the side of the engine block, at the transmission end - shouldn't be difficult to spot. If the number's been removed, or if there's anything suspicious about it, you could be buying trouble.

Check the registration document (V5) very carefully - all the details should match the car. Never buy a car without seeing the V5 - accept no excuses on this point. If buying privately, make sure it's definitely the owner's name and address printed on it - if not, be very careful! If buying from a dealer, note the name and address, and try to contact the previous owner to confirm mileage, etc, before handing over more than a deposit. The car shouldn't

### Tricks 'n' tips

*Tyres can be a giveaway to a car maintained on a shoestring - four different makes of tyre, especially cheap brands, can indicate a penny-pinching attitude which won't have done the rest of the car any favours.*

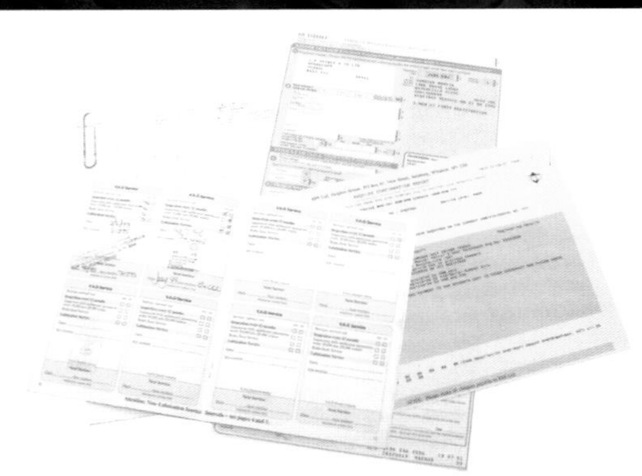

### Full service history (fsh)

*Is there any service history? If so, this is good, but study the service book carefully:*

- **a** *Which garage has done the servicing? Is it a proper dealer, or a backstreet bodger? Do you know the garage, and if so, would you use it?*
- **b** *Do the mileages show a nice even progression, or are there huge gaps? Check the dates too.*
- **c** *Does it look as if the stamps are authentic? Do the oldest ones look old, or could this 'service history' have been created last week, to make the car look good?*
- **d** *When was the last service, and what exactly was carried out? When was the cambelt last changed? Has the owner got receipts for any of this servicing work?*

*One sign of a genuine car is a good batch of old MOTs, and as many receipts as possible - even if they're for fairly irrelevant things like tyres.*

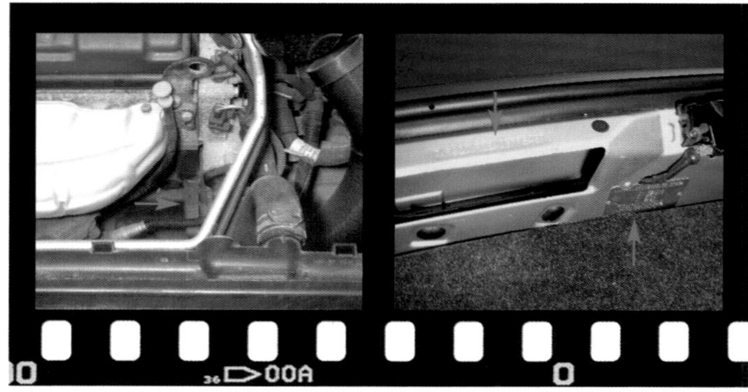

The engine number is stamped into the end of the engine block . . .

. . . and the VIN is stamped into the rear edge of the boot floor - the VIN plate is also in the boot.

have had many previous owners - otherwise, it may mean the car is trouble, so checking its owner history is more important.

While the trim on a 206 is quite durable, it should still be obvious whether the car's been abused over a long period, or whether the mileage showing is genuine or not (shiny steering wheels, worn carpets and pedals are a good place to start checking if you're suspicious). Okay, so you may be planning to junk most of the interior at some point, but why should you pay over the odds for a tat car which the owner hasn't given a stuff about?

Although you may feel a bit stupid doing it, check simple things too, like making sure the windows and sunroof open and shut, and that all the doors and tailgate can be locked (if a lock's been replaced, ask why). Check all the basic electrical equipment - lights, front and rear wipers, heated rear window, heater fan; it's amazing how often these things are taken for granted by buyers! If your chosen 206 already has alloys fitted, does it have locking wheel bolts? Where's the key? What about the code and removal tools for the stereo?

Is the catalytic converter ('cat') working? This is a wickedly expensive part to replace - the best way to ensure at least one year's grace is to only buy a car with a full MoT (the cat is checked during the emissions test). Many 206 modifiers remove the cat altogether (by fitting a de-cat pipe), which is great for performance, but means the car's illegal to use on the road.

## Look closer

Don't take anything at face value. Even a fully-stamped service book only tells half the story of how your chosen 206 has been treated. Does the owner look bright enough to even know what a dipstick is, never mind how to check the oil level between services?

Check for signs of accident damage, especially at the front end. Ask if it's ever been in a shunt - if the seller says no, but there's paint overspray under the bonnet, what's going on? Also check for paint overspray on the window rubbers, light units and bumpers/trim. Look at the car side-on - are there any mis-matched panels? With the bonnet open, check that the headlight rear shells are the same colour - mis-matched or new-looking ones merit an explanation from the seller. Does the front number plate carry details of the supplying garage, like the back one? If not, why has a new plate been fitted?

Check the glass (and even the head and tail lights) for etched-in registration numbers - are they all the same, and does it match the car's actual registration? A windscreen could've been innocently replaced, but new side glass indicates a break-in at least - is the car a 'stolen/recovered' (joyridden) example? Find the chassis and engine numbers, as described earlier in this Section, and satisfy yourself that they're genuine - check them against the registration document. An HPI check (or similar) is worthwhile, but even this won't tell you everything. If you're in doubt, or if the answers to your questions don't ring true, walk away. Make any excuse you like.

The 206 has a decent immobiliser as standard, but there's no harm fitting a good ultrasonic alarm on top (if it hasn't already got one) - might even be worth a bit of insurance discount. Make sure that any aftermarket alarm actually works, that it looks properly installed, with no stray wires hanging out, and that you get the Thatcham certificate or other paperwork to go with it. If possible, it's worth finding out exactly how it's been wired in - if it goes wrong later, you could be stranded with no chance of disabling the system to get you home.

## Model history

**Note:** *As usual, there's plenty of "special edition" 206 models. Don't pay over the odds for a special edition, unless it's really got some extra kit you actually want.*

**October 1998 (S reg)** - 206 range introduced in the UK. 3-door and 5-door hatchbacks, 1.1, 1.4 and 1.6 litre petrol engines, 1.9 litre non-turbo diesel. Trim levels - L, LX, GLX.

**February 1999 (S reg)** - Roland Garros models introduced, initially as a 1.4 litre-only, later with the 1.6 litre engine. Luxury spec, with full leather sports seats, coloured dials, climate control, alloys, front fogs. 5-door hatchback only.

**June 1999 (T reg)** - 2.0 litre GTI introduced. 3-door only, 137 bhp 16-valve engine, 15-inch alloys, ABS with four-wheel disc brakes. Sports seats, leather trim. Grand Tourisme limited edition model also introduced, as GTI but in silver only, with 16-inch 9-spoke alloys and luxury equipment.

**December 1999 (V reg)** - 2.0 litre HDi turbo-diesel models introduced.

**May 2000 (W reg)** - 1.1, 1.4, 1.9D and 2.0 HDi Look special editions introduced, with air con or electric sunroof, velour trim, body colour bumper apron, and choice of metallic paint shades or solid red, white, green, black or blue. Base L models replaced with Style.

**June 2000 (W reg)** - Minor changes across the range. Heated electric mirrors (LX), three rear seat belts (LX/GLX/Roland Garros), three fold-over rear head restraints (LX/GLX). ABS standard on Roland Garros.

**October 2000 (X reg)** - 1.6 XSi introduced, replacing 1.6 XS, but with 16-valve 110bhp engine. 206 CC (Coupe Cabriolet) introduced, with 2.0 litre engine from GTI (later also with new 1.6 XSi engine).

**December 2000 (X reg)** - Quiksilver introduced, with 1.4 litre engine, air con, sports interior. Style models gain passenger airbag, GLX gains climate control, GTI gains side airbags.

**June 2001 (Y reg)** - More Look special editions, based on 1.1 Style, but with air con, sports seats, ally interior trim and metallic paint.

**January 2002 (51 reg)** - 1.4 litre HDi diesel engine introduced, with 67 bhp.

**May 2002 (02 reg)** - SW 5-door estate models introduced. 1.4 Look special edition with air con, Silver and Black limited edition CC models introduced.

**August 2003 (03 reg)** - GTI 180 introduced. 2.0 litre engine with variable valve timing giving 180 bhp, 17-inch alloys, twin tailpipes, racing seats, leather-trimmed dash.

### Performance figures

| | 0-60 (sec) | Top speed (mph) |
|---|---|---|
| 1.1 LX | 14.4 | 95 |
| 1.4 LX | 12.5 | 103 |
| 1.6 XS | 11.3 | 112 |
| 1.6 XSi | 9.5 | 123 |
| 2.0 GTI | 7.6 | 124 |
| GTI 180 | 7.4 | 132 |
| 1.4 HDi | 13.9 | 104 |
| 1.9 D | 15.7 | 99 |
| 2.0 HDi | 12.0 | 112 |

# Insurance
## A necessary evil

**Ah, insurance - loads of money, and all you get's a piece of paper you're not supposed to use! Of course, you must have insurance - you're illegal on the road without it, and you won't be able to get the car taxed, either. If you're ever caught driving without insurance, you'll have great trouble ever getting insurance again - insurance companies regard this offence nearly as seriously as drink-driving, so don't do it!**

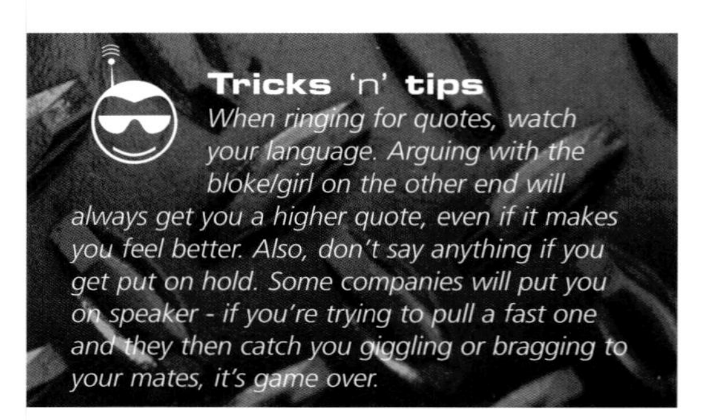

**Tricks 'n' tips**

*When ringing for quotes, watch your language. Arguing with the bloke/girl on the other end will always get you a higher quote, even if it makes you feel better. Also, don't say anything if you get put on hold. Some companies will put you on speaker - if you're trying to pull a fast one and they then catch you giggling or bragging to your mates, it's game over.*

The way insurance companies work out premiums and assess risks is a mystery to most of us. In general, the smaller the engine you have in your 206, the less you'll pay. However, if one company's had a lot of claims on 206s in the past, the GTI factor might 'unfairly' influence the premiums of lesser Pugs, too (this is why it's important to shop around). An 'insurance-friendly' 1.4 or 1.6 should be a good bet for a sensible premium, but remember that insurance companies aren't stupid - if you swap in that GTI engine and turn your LX into a rocket, they may well 'load' the premium to GTI level (and that's at least Group 14). Insurance is a game you can't win, but you must play.

If your annual premium seems like the national debt of a small African country (and whose isn't!), always ring as many brokers and get as many quotes as you possibly can. Yes, there's loads better ways to spend an evening/afternoon than answering the same twenty questions over and over again, but you never know what the next quote will be. A few extra minutes spent on the phone (or on the 'net) once a year may result in an extra few hundred quid in your back pocket. Well, you live in hope don't you!

With modified cars, insurance becomes even more of a problem. By putting on all the alloys, trick body kits, nice interiors, big ICE, you're making the car much more of a target for thieves (yes, ok, we know you know this). The point is, the insurance companies know this too, and they don't want to be paying out for the car, plus all the money you've spent on it, should it go missing. There is a temptation 'not to tell the insurance' about the mods you've made. Let's deal with this right now. Our experience has been that, while it can be painful, honesty is best. Generally, the insurance company line is: '...thanks for telling us - we won't put the car 'up a group' (ie charge you more), but we also won't cover the extra cost of your alloy wheels/body kit/tasty seats in the event of any claim...'. This is fair enough - in other words, if your car goes missing, you get paid out, based on a standard car, minus all the goodies. If you particularly want all the extras covered, you might have a long hard search - most companies only offer 'modified for standard' policies. There are specialist insurers who are more friendly towards fully-loaded cars, but even they won't actually cover the cost of replacement goodies.

### What type of cover, Sir?

For most of us, cost means there's only one option - TPF&T (third party, fire and theft). Fully-comp insurance is an unattainable dream for most people until they reach the 'magic' age of 25, but what's the real story?

**Third Party only**

*The most basic cover you can get. Basically covers you for damage to other people's cars or property, and for personal injury claims. Virtually no cover for your own stuff, beyond what you get if you take the optional 'legal protection' cover.*

**Third Party, Fire and Theft**

*As above, with cover for fire and theft, of course! Better, but not much better. This is really only cover in the event of a 'total loss', if your car goes missing or goes up in smoke. Still no cover for your car if you stack it into a tree, or if someone breaks in and pinches your stereo (check your policy small-print).*

**Fully-comprehensive**

*In theory at least, covers you for any loss or damage. Will cover the cost of repairing or replacing your car, often with discounted windscreen cover and other benefits. If you lose control of the car on an icy road (arguably, not your fault) you get paid. If someone pinches your wheels and drops the car on the floor, you get paid - at least for the damage done to the underside, and for standard wheels and tyres. Most policies include provision of a hire car after a shunt, which is pretty useful. Some offer cheap breakdown cover packages in with the main policy. With a fully-comp policy, you can 'protect' your no-claims bonus for a small fee so you don't automatically lose all those hard-earned years' worth of discount if you prang it (generally, you can only do this on fully-comp).*

*All this extra cover costs, obviously, but how much? You might be surprised what the actual difference is. Think about it, anyway - it's got to be worth a couple of hundred quid more to go fully-comp, if your car's worth into four figures, surely?*

### Valuing your car

When your insurance pays out in the event of a total loss or write-off, they base their offer on the current market value of an identical standard model to yours (less your excess). The only way you'll get more than the average amount is to prove your 206 is in above-average nick (with photos?) or that the mileage was especially low for the year.

With this in mind, don't bother over-valuing your 206 in the hope you'll get more in the event of a claim - you won't! The only way to do this is to seek out an 'agreed-value' deal, which you can usually only get on classic-car policies (with these, the car's value is agreed in advance between you, not worked out later by the company with you having no say in it). By over-valuing your 206, you could be increasing your premium without gaining any benefit - sound smart to you?

Equally though, don't under-value, in the hope you'll get a reduction in premium. You won't, and if there's a total loss claim, you won't get any more than your under-valued amount, no matter how loudly you complain.

Work on what you paid for the car, backed up with the sort of prices you see for similar cars in the ads (or use a secondhand car price guide). Add no more than 10% for the sake of optimism (or add on your policy excess), and that's it.

### Your car? Or your Dad's?

Insurance really costs when you're the wrong side of 25. Ever been tempted to tell your insurance that your full-on sorted 206 belongs to your Dad (old insurance-friendly person), then get him to insure it, with you as a named driver? Oh dear. This idea (known as 'fronting') is so old, it's grown a long white beard. And it sucks, too. First of all, insurance companies aren't stupid. They know your Dad (or your Mum, or old Uncle Bert) isn't likely to be running around in a kid's pocket-rocket, and they treat any young 'named driver' application with great suspicion. Even if they do take your money, don't imagine they've been suckered. In the event of a claim, they'll look into everything very carefully, and will ask lots of awkward questions. If you get caught out in the lie, they've taken your money, and you've got no insurance - who's been suckered now?

This dubious practice also does you no favours in future years. All the time you're living the lie, you're not building up any no-claims bonus of your own - you're just delaying the pain 'til later, and without having real cover in the meantime.

## 'Legit' ways to limit your premium

If you do enough ringing around for quotes, you'll soon learn what the 'right answers' to some of the questions are - even if you can't actually give them (don't tell lies to your insurance company). Mind you, with a little thought, you can start to play their game and win - try these:

**Volunteer to increase your excess**. The 'excess' is put there to stop people claiming for piddling little amounts - when they pay out, it's always the repair/replacement cost MINUS whatever the 'excess' is. So, for instance, if you've got a £200 theft excess, it means you'll automatically get £200 less than the agreed value of your car, should it be stolen. Most policies have 'compulsory' excess amounts, which you can do nothing about. By increasing excesses voluntarily, you're limiting the amount you'll get still further. Insurance companies like this, and should reduce your premium in return - but this only goes so far, so ask what the effect of different voluntary excesses will be. Don't increase your excess too far, or you'll get paid nowt if you claim!

**Limit your mileage**. Most companies offer a small discount if you only cover a small annual mileage. To get any meaningful reduction, the mileage has to be a lot less than 10,000 per year. Few companies, though, ever ask what the car's current mileage is - so how are they gonna know if you've gone over your self-imposed limit?

**Make yourself the only driver**. Pretty self-explanatory. The more people who drive your car, the greater the risk to the company, and a car's owner will always drive more carefully (it's their money that bought it) than any named driver. If you've built up 2 years' worth of no-claims, but your partner hasn't, putting them on your insurance will bump it up, due to their relative inexperience.

**Get a garage - and use it**. Where you park can have a big effect on your premium. Parking it on the street is the worst. Park off the road (on a driveway) when you're at home. The best thing is to have a garage of your own (don't pretend you use your Dad's garage) - see if you can rent one locally, even if it means walking a few hundred yards. If you're a student living away from home, tell your company where the car will be parked during term-time - if you're at Uni in London, this is a bigger risk than living at home 'in the country', and vice-versa.

**Fit an approved alarm or immobiliser**. See if you can get a list from your company of all their approved security devices, and fit whatever you can afford. Not all companies approve the same kit, so it might even be worth contacting more than one company for advice. Any device with a Thatcham or Sold Secure rating should be recognised. In some cases, the discounts offered are not that great any more - but an alarm is still a nice way to get peace of mind.

**Build up your no-claims bonus**. You'll only do this by owning and insuring a car in your own name, and then not making any claims. Simple really. One rather immoral (but not actually illegal) dodge is to buy an old banger, insure it cheap, then never drive it. You'll need to keep it fully road-legal (with tax, MOT) if you park it on the road. For every year you do this, you'll build up another year of NCB.

**Hang onto your no-claims bonus**. Obviously, the less you claim, the less your insurance will cost. If something happens to your car, don't be in too big a hurry to make a claim before you've thought it all through. How much will it cost to fix? How much is your excess? How much will your renewal premium be, next year? If you have a big enough accident which you're sure isn't your fault, ring your company, but make it quite clear you're NOT claiming yet - just informing them of the accident. It should be down to the other driver's insurance to pay. You don't always lose all your no-claims, either, even if it was your fault - depends how many years you've built up. Once you've got a few years, ask whether you can 'protect' your no-claims.

**Avoid speed cameras and The Law**. Yes, okay, easier said than done! But anything less than a clean licence is not good from the insurance perspective. One SP30 won't hurt much, but the second strike will, so take it easy. Don't get caught on traffic-light cameras, either - just one is a major no-no.

# Insurance-friendly mods?

Insurers don't like any changes from standard, but some things you'll do are worse from their viewpoint than others. The guidelines below are just that - for guidance. No two companies will have the same outlook, and your own circumstances will play a big part too.

***Golden Rule Number One:*** *If in doubt, declare everything. Insurance companies are legally entitled to dispute any claim if the car is found to be non-standard in any way.*

***Golden Rule Number Two:*** *Before you spend huge money modifying the car, ring your insurance, and ask them how it will affect things.*

**Body mods** – Even a tiny rear spoiler could be classed as a 'bodykit' (yes, it's daft, but that's how it is). Anything which alters the exterior appearance should be declared. As long as the mods don't include a radical full-on bodykit, the jump in premium should be fairly small. Any genuine Peugeot add-ons (GTI bumpers, arch extensions) might not cost at all - bonus.

**Brakes** – The companies view brake mods as tampering with safety-related kit, and modifying the brakes implies that you drive fast and hard. You might get away with standard-sized grooved/drilled discs and pads, but fitting bigger discs and replacement calipers will prove expensive.

**Engine mods** – 'Mild' mods such as induction kits and exhausts don't give much more power, so don't generally hurt. But 'chipping' your 206 will lead to drastic rises in premiums, or a complete refusal of cover. With complete engine transplants, you'll be required to give an engineer's report, and to get your wad out.

**Interior mods** – Don't assume that tarting up the inside won't interest the insurance company. By making any part of the car more attractive, you're also attracting the crims. Cars get trashed for parts, as often as not - and your racing seats and sexy steering wheel could be worth major money. Still, the effect on premiums shouldn't be too great, especially if you've got an approved alarm..

**Lights** – Change the car's appearance, and are safety-related. You'll probably get asked for lots of details, but as long as you've kept it sensible (and legal, as far as possible), the effect on your wallet shouldn't be too harsh.

**Security** – Make sure you mention all security stuff - alarms, immobilisers (including mechanical devices), locking wheel nuts, large Alsatian in the back seat... But - don't over-sell the car. Tell the truth, in other words. If you've got a steering wheel lock, do you always fit it? If you didn't when your car went missing, you're in trouble. Don't say you've got a Cat 1 alarm if it really came from Argos, and don't tell them you garage the car at night if it's stuck out in the road.

**Suspension** – Changes the car's appearance, and is safety-related. Some enlightened companies once took the view that modded suspension helps the car corner better, so it's safer. Drops of only 30 to 40 mm shouldn't mean bigger premiums.

**Wheels** – Very appearance-altering, and very nickable. At least show some responsibility by fitting some locking nuts/bolts and an approved alarm. Quite likely to attract a low-to-moderate rise in premium, which still won't cover your wheels properly - you could arrange separate cover for your wheels, then at least you'll get paid. Some companies may ask for a photo of the car with the wheels on.

### And finally - a new nightmare

Not telling the insurance the whole truth gets a little tricky when you make a claim. If the insurance assessor comes to check your bent/burnt/stolen-and-recovered 'standard' 206, and finds he's looking at a vehicle fitted with trick alloys/bodykit/radical interior, no way will he turn a blind eye. Has the car got an MoT? Oh, and did you declare those points on your licence? No? You're then very much at the mercy of your insurer, especially if they can prove any mods contributed to the claim. At best, you'll have a long-drawn-out battle with your insurer to get a part-payout, and at worst they'll just refuse to get involved at all.

One more thing - *be careful what you hit*. If your insurance is declared void, they won't pay out for the repairs to the other car you smacked into, or for that lamp-post you knocked down (several hundred quid, actually). And then there's the personal injury claims - if your insurance company disowns you, it'll be you who has to foot the bill. Even sprains and bruises can warrant claims, and more serious injuries can result in claims running into lots of zeroes! Without insurance cover, **you'll** have to pay. Probably for a long, long time. Think about it, and we won't see you in court.

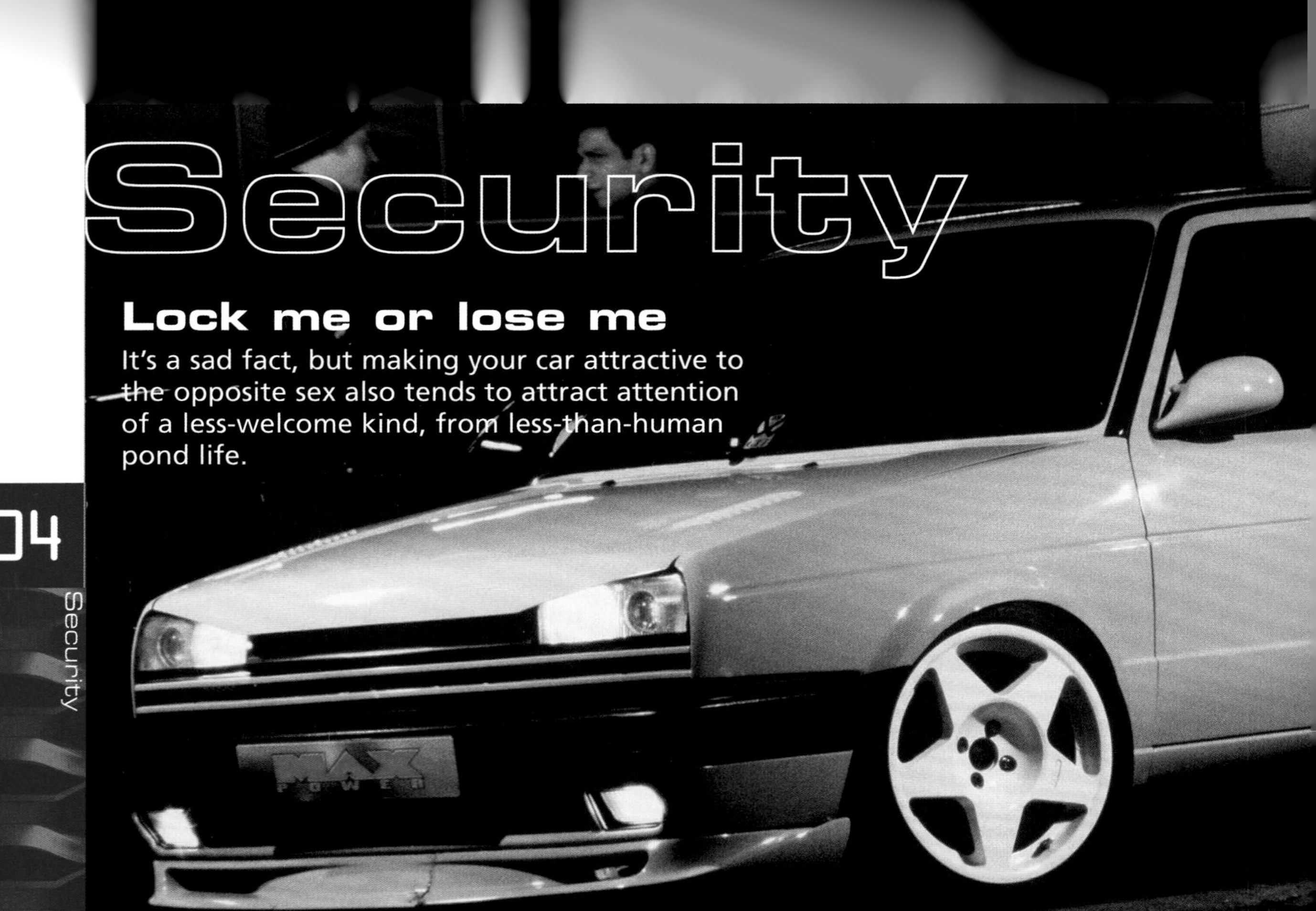


# Security

## Lock me or lose me

It's a sad fact, but making your car attractive to the opposite sex also tends to attract attention of a less-welcome kind, from less-than-human pond life.

### Avoiding trouble

Now come on - you're modifying your car to look cool and to be seen in. Not a problem - but be careful where you choose to show your car off, and who to. Be especially discreet, the nearer you get to home - *turn your system down* before you turn into your road, for instance, or you'll draw unwelcome attention to where that car with the loud stereo's parked at night.

Without being too paranoid, watch for anyone following you home. At night, if the car behind switches its lights off, be worried. If you suspect this is happening, do not drive home - choose well-lit public places until they give up. Believe us - it happens.

If you're going out, think about where you're parking - well-lit and well-populated is good. Thieves hate light being on them, so don't make it easy by parking somewhere dark - think about this if you park up in daylight, knowing you won't be back 'til late.

Hands up, who doesn't lock their car when they get petrol? Your insurance company has a term for this, and it's 'contributory negligence'. In English, this means you won't get a penny if your car goes missing when you haven't locked it.

If you're lucky enough to have a garage, use it. On up-and-over garage doors, fit extra security like a padlock and ground anchor.

A clever thief will watch your movements and habits over several days before trying your car. Has it got an alarm, and do you always set it? Do you only fit your steering wheel lock when you feel like it? Do you always park in the same place, and is the car hidden from the house or from the road? Don't make his life easier. Ask yourself how you'd nick your car...

### A word about your stereo

From the moment you bolt on those nice alloys, it's taken as read that you've also got stereo gear that's worth nicking - and the thieves know it. All the discreet installation in the world isn't going to deter them from finding out what's inside that nice motor.

Please don't advertise your love of ICE around your car. Your nice stereo gear will fit other cars too, and can be ripped out in nothing flat. You may be very proud of your ICE install, but nothing is more of an 'invite' than a huge ICE sticker or sunstrip. If you've fitted one just to look cool, replace it now with something less provocative - seriously. Your set might not actually be very expensive, but you could still lose a side window for advertising something better.

You'll have got a CD player, obviously, but don't leave discs or empty CD cases lying around inside the car. A nice pair of 6x9s in full view on the back shelf is an invite to having your rear window smashed - stealth shelf, anyone? When you're fitting your system, give some thought to the clues you could accidentally leave in plain view. Oxygen-free speaker cable is great stuff, but it's also a bit bright against dark carpets, and is all the clue necessary that you're serious about your tunes. Hide amps and CD changers under your front seats.

Most modern sets are face-off or MASK, so if they've got security features like this, use them - take your faceplate off when you leave the car, and take it with you rather than leaving it in the door pocket or glovebox (the first places a thief will look).

### Things that go beep in the night

Unless your insurance company demands it up front, fitting an alarm is something generally done as an after-thought. We know alarms aren't exactly sexy, but don't skimp - an alarm may never be put to the test, but if it is, you'll be glad you spent wisely...

The simplest first step to car security is to fake it. Tacky *'This car is fitted with an alarm'* stickers won't fool anyone, but if you want cheap, just fit a flashing LED. We know it's not the real thing, but everyone else will think you've got a posh alarm. An LED is cheap to buy and easy to fit, and can be rigged to a discreet switch inside the car.

Don't overlook the value of so-called 'manual' immobilisers, such as steering wheel locking bars and gear-to-handbrake lever locks. These can be a worthwhile deterrent - a thief not specifically after your car may move on to an easier target. Some of the items offered may be 'Sold Secure' or Thatcham Cat 3, accolades well worth checking out, since it means they've withstood a full-on brute-force attack for a useful length of time.

The only way to combat the more determined thief is to go for a well-specified and intelligently-installed alarm. Immobilisers alone have their place, but sadly, even a pro-fitted immobiliser on its own won't stop someone pinching your wheels, or having it away with the stereo gear. Neither, incidentally, will a cheap alarm - you have to know how the thieves operate to stand any chance defeating them. Any alarm you fit yourself probably won't gain you any insurance discount, but it will give you peace of mind, and DIY means you can do a real trick installation, to make it very hard work for the gyppos.

Finally, one other scam which you might fall victim to. If you find your alarm is suddenly going off a lot at night, when previously it had been well-behaved, don't ignore the problem. It's an old trick for a thief to deliberately set off your alarm several times, each time hiding round the corner when you come out to investigate, then to wait until the fifth or sixth time when you don't reset it (in disgust), leaving him a clear run. If your alarm does keep false-alarming without outside assistance, find out the cause quickly, or your neighbours will quickly become 'deaf' to it.

### Thatcham categories and meanings:

1. **Cat 1.** For alarms and electronic immobilisers.
2. **Cat 2.** For electronic immobilisers only.
3. **Cat 2-1.** Electronic immobilisers which can be upgraded to Cat 1 alarms later.
4. **Cat 3**. Mechanical immobilisers, eg snap-off steering wheels, locking wheel bolts, window film, steering wheel locks/covers.
5. **Q-class.** Tracking devices.

### Other alarm features

**Two-stage anti-shock** - means that the alarm shouldn't go off, just because the neighbour's cat jumps on your car roof, or because Little Johnny punts his football into your car. Alarm will only sound after a major shock, or after repeated shocks are detected.

**Anti-tilt** - detects any attempt to lift or jack up the car, preventing any attempt to pinch alloys. Very unpopular with thieves, as it makes the alarm very sensitive (much more so than anti-shock). Alarm may sound if car is parked outside in stormy conditions (but not if your suspension's rock-hard!).

**Anti-hijack** - immobiliser with built-in delay. If your motor gets hijacked, the neanderthals responsible will only get so far down the road before the engine cuts out.

**Rolling code** - reduces the chance of your alarm remote control signal from being 'grabbed' by special electronic equipment.

**Total closure** - module which connects to electric windows/sunroof and central locking, which closes all items when alarm is set. Alarms like this often have other nifty features such as remote boot opening.

**Pager control** - yes, really - your alarm can be set to send a message to your pager (why not your mobile?) if your car gets tampered with.

**Current-sensing disable** - very useful feature on some cars which have a cooling fan which can cut in after the ignition is switched off. Without this feature, your alarm will be triggered every time you leave it parked after a long run - very annoying.

**Volumetric-sensing disable** - allows you to manually disable the interior ultrasonics, leaving the rest of the alarm features active. Useful if you want to leave the sunroof open in hot weather - if a fly gets in the car, the alarm would otherwise be going off constantly.

**Talking alarms** - no, please, please no. Very annoying, and all that'll happen is you'll attract crowds of kids daring each other to set it off again. Unfortunately, these are becoming more popular, with some offering the facility to record your own message!

## The knowledge

**What people often fail to realise (at least, until it happens to them) is the level of violence and destruction which thieves will employ to get your stuff - this goes way beyond breaking a window.**

It comes as a major shock to most people when they discover the serious kinds of tools (weapons) at many professional thieves' disposal, and how brutally your lovingly-polished car will be attacked. Many people think, for instance, that it's their whole car they're after, whereas it's really only the parts they want, and they don't care how they get them (this means that these parts are still attractive, even when fitted to a basic car which has yet to be fully modded). Obviously, taking the whole car then gives the option of hiding it to strip at leisure, but it won't always be the option chosen, and you could wake up one morning to a well-mangled wreck outside.

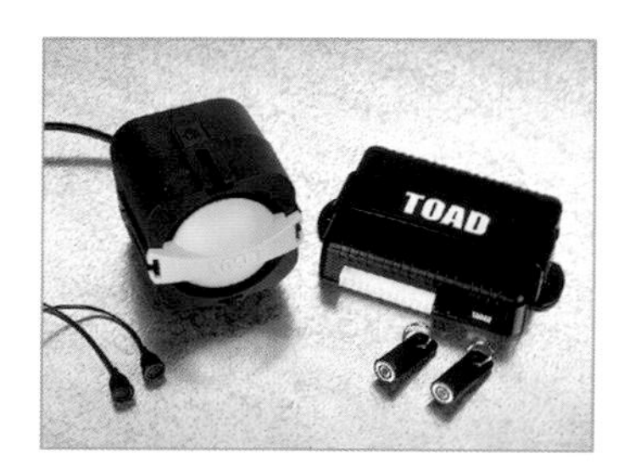

**Attack 1** The first option to any thief is to smash glass - typically, the toughened-glass side windows, which will shatter, unlike the windscreen. Unfortunately for the thief, this makes a loud noise (not good), but is a quick and easy way in. The reason for taking this approach is that a basic car alarm will only go off if the doors are opened (voltage-drop alarm) - provided the doors aren't opened, the alarm won't go off.

**Response 1** A more sophisticated alarm will feature shock sensing (which will be set off by the impact on the glass), and better still, ultrasonic sensing, which will be triggered by the brick coming in through the broken window.

**Response 2** This kind of attack can also be stopped by applying security film to the inside of the glass, which holds it all together and prevents easy entry.

**Attack 2** An alternative to smashing the glass is to pry open the door using a crowbar - this attack involves literally folding open the door's window frame by prising from the top corner. The glass will still shatter, but as long as the door stays shut, a voltage-drop alarm won't be triggered.

**Response** This method might not be defeated by a shock-sensing alarm, but an ultrasonic unit would pick it up. Incidentally, another bonus with ultrasonic alarms is that the sensors are visible from outside - and act as a deterrent.

**Attack 3** The next line of attack is to disable the alarm. The commonest way to kill the alarm is either to cut the wiring to the alarm itself, or to disconnect the battery, 'safely' hidden away under the bonnet. And just how strong is a bonnet? Not strong enough to resist being crowbarred open, which is exactly what happens.

**Response 1** If your alarm has extra pin-switches, be sure to fit one to the bonnet, and fit it in the bonnet channel next to the battery, so that it'll set off the alarm if the bonnet is prised up. Also make sure that the wire to the pin-switch cannot be cut easily though a partly-open bonnet.

**Response 2** Make sure that the alarm module is well-hidden, and cannot be got at from underneath the car.

**Response 3** Make the alarm power supply connection somewhere less obvious than directly at the battery terminal - any thief who knows his stuff will immediately cut any 'spare' red wires at the battery. Try taking power from the fusebox, or if you must source it under the bonnet, trace the large red battery lead to the starter motor connections, and tap into the power there.

**Response 4** Always disguise the new alarm wiring, by using black insulating tape to wrap it to the existing wiring loom. Tidying up in this way also helps to ensure the wires can't get trapped, cut, melted, or accidentally ripped out - any of which could leave you with an alarm siren which won't switch off, or an immobiliser you can't disable.

**Response 5** An alarm which has a 'battery back-up' facility is a real kiss of death to the average thief's chances. Even if he's successfully crowbarred your bonnet and snipped the battery connections, the alarm will still go off, powered by a separate battery of its own. A Cat 1 alarm has to have battery back-up.

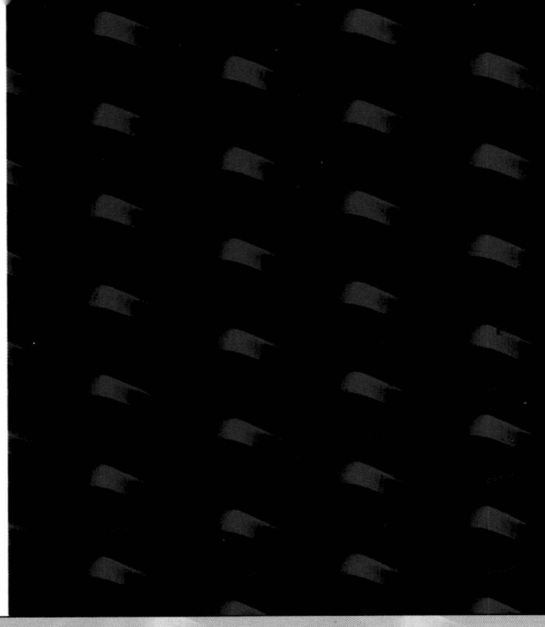



# Fitting a basic **LED**

All you need for this is a permanent live feed, an earth, a switch if you want to be able to turn it on/off, and the flashing LED itself (very cheap, from any car accessory shop).

An LED draws very little current, so you'll be quite safe tapping into almost any live feed you fancy. If you've wired in your ICE, take a live feed from the permanent (radio memory supply) wire at the back of your head unit, or have a delve into the back of the fusebox with your test light. An earth can easily be tapped again from your head unit, or you can make one almost anywhere on the metal body of the car, by drilling a small hole, fitting a self-tapping screw, then wrapping the bared end of wire around and tightening it.

The best and easiest place to mount an LED is into one of the many blank switches the makers seem to love fitting. The blank switch is easily pried out, and a hole can then be drilled to take the LED (which usually comes in a separate little holder). Feed the LED wiring down behind the dashboard to where you've tapped your live and earth, taking care not to trap it anywhere, nor to accidentally wrap it around any moving parts.

Connect your live to the LED red wire, then rig your earth to one side of the switch, and connect the LED black wire to the other switch terminal. You should now have a switchable LED! Tidy up the wiring, and mount the switch somewhere discreet, but where you can still get at it. Switch on when you leave the car, and it looks as if you've got some sort of alarm - better than nothing!

# Wiring basics

With your wires identified, how to tap into them? Before we even get that far, is that wire you're planning on playing with live?

Switch off the ignition at least - and ideally disconnect the battery before you do anything else. On cars with airbags, don't go tapping into any of the airbag wiring, which is usually bright yellow. With that cleared up, how were you planning on joining the old and new wires together?

**Here's our advice:**

**Soldering** - avoids cutting through your chosen wire - strip away a short section of insulation, wrap your new wire around the bared section, then apply solder to secure it. If you're a bit new to soldering, practice on a few offcuts of wire first - it ain't rocket science! Re-insulate the soldered connection afterwards, with tape or heatshrink tube.

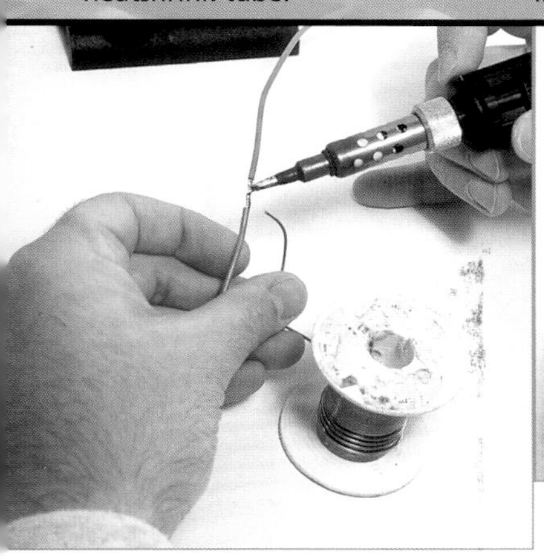

**Bullet connectors** - cut and strip the end of your chosen wire, wrap your new one to it, push both into one half of the bullet. Connect the other end of your victim wire to the other bullet, and connect together. Always use the 'female' half on any live feed - it'll be safer if you disconnect it than a male bullet, which could touch bare metal and send your motor up in smoke.

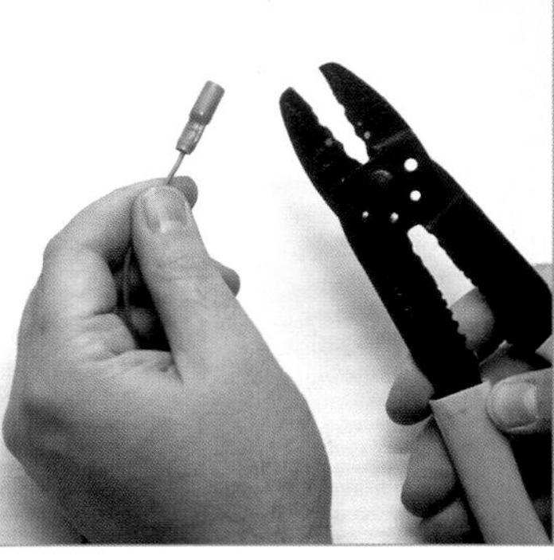

**Block connectors** - so easy to use. Just remember that the wires can come adrift if the screws aren't really tight, and don't get too ambitious about how many wires you can stuff in one hole (block connectors, like bullets, are available in several sizes). Steer clear of connectors like the one below - they're convenient, but they can give rise to problems.

With any of these options, always insulate around your connection - especially when soldering, or you'll be leaving bare metal exposed. Remember that you'll probably be shoving all the wires up into the dark recesses of the under-dash area - by the time the wires are nice and kinked/squashed together, that tiny bit of protruding wire might just touch that bit of metal bodywork, and that'll be a fire...

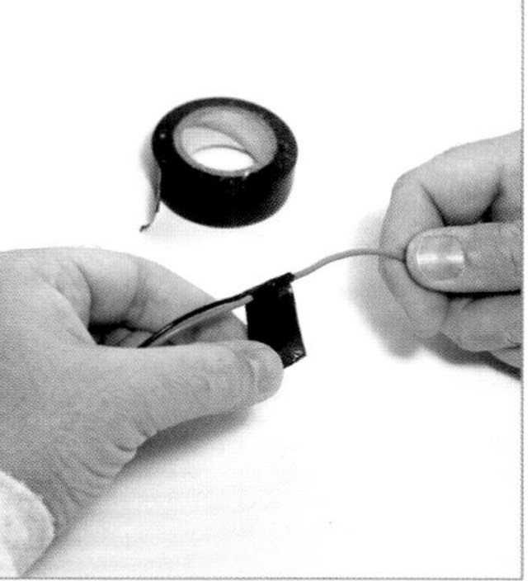

# Alarm fitting

Security

**All 206s have an immobiliser, but only the higher-spec models got an alarm. Our 206 had a pretty decent alarm on it already, so we decided not to mess with it. And that, in a way, is your first lesson in alarms - if you're thinking of fitting one to a car that's already got one, be prepared for some nasty surprises when you dive behind the dash. How the heck have they wired this in? Will chopping that wire mean the car won't start? If it looks a mess behind there, it's best to leave it - and then hope it never goes wrong.**

If your 206 is still a virgin in the aftermarket alarm sense, things are a bit easier. Here's a few tips to successful alarm fitting which we've picked up on our other project cars.

Disconnect the battery negative lead, and move the lead away from the battery, or you'll be blowing fuses and your new alarm will go mental the minute it's rigged up. Decide where you're going to mount the alarm/siren. Choose somewhere not easily reached from underneath, for a start, and if you can, pick a location away from where you'll be topping up washers, oil or coolant - fluids and alarm modules don't mix.

Now there's wires to play with. Most of them should go thorough into the car, but not all - check your alarm's instructions. You've probably got a bonnet pin switch and an earth wire which can stay in the engine bay. The rest? Get out the electrical tape, and wrap that bunch of wires into a neat loom, to go inside. On our 206, removing the glovebox gave us access to a plastic bulkhead panel right behind one of the suspension struts - making a new wiring hole was easy after that. Don't forget to use a rubber grommet on any sharp-edged hole with a wire passing through.

The bonnet pin switch should be close to the battery, but it must hit a 'good' (flat) spot on the bonnet - getting this right can be tricky. Partly shut the bonnet, and peer through the gap, or

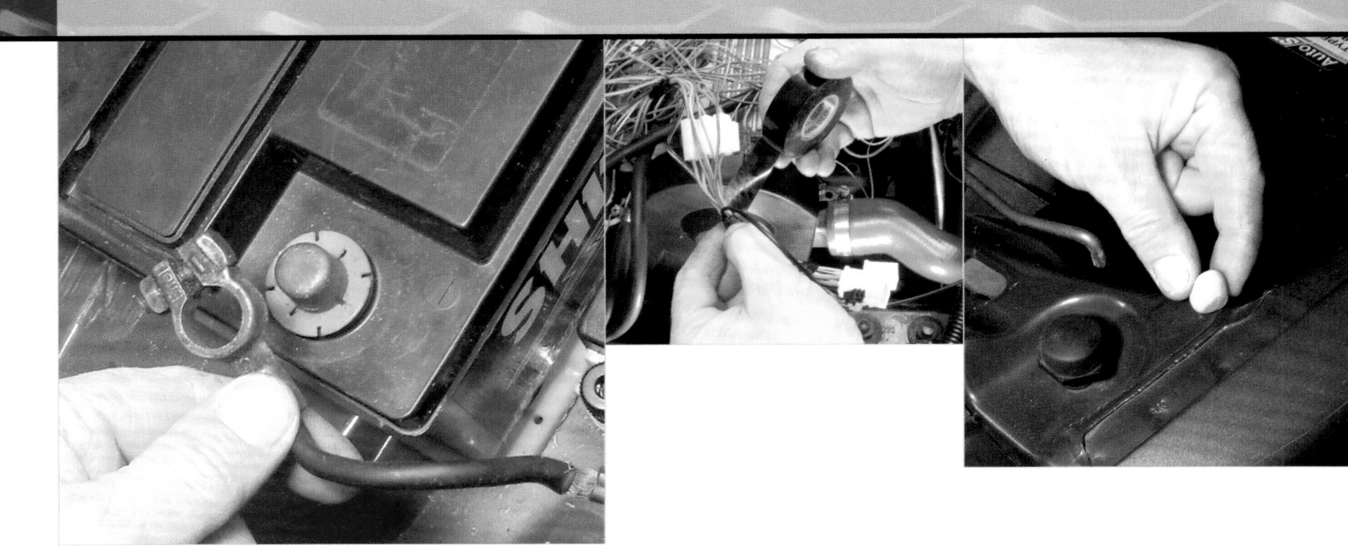

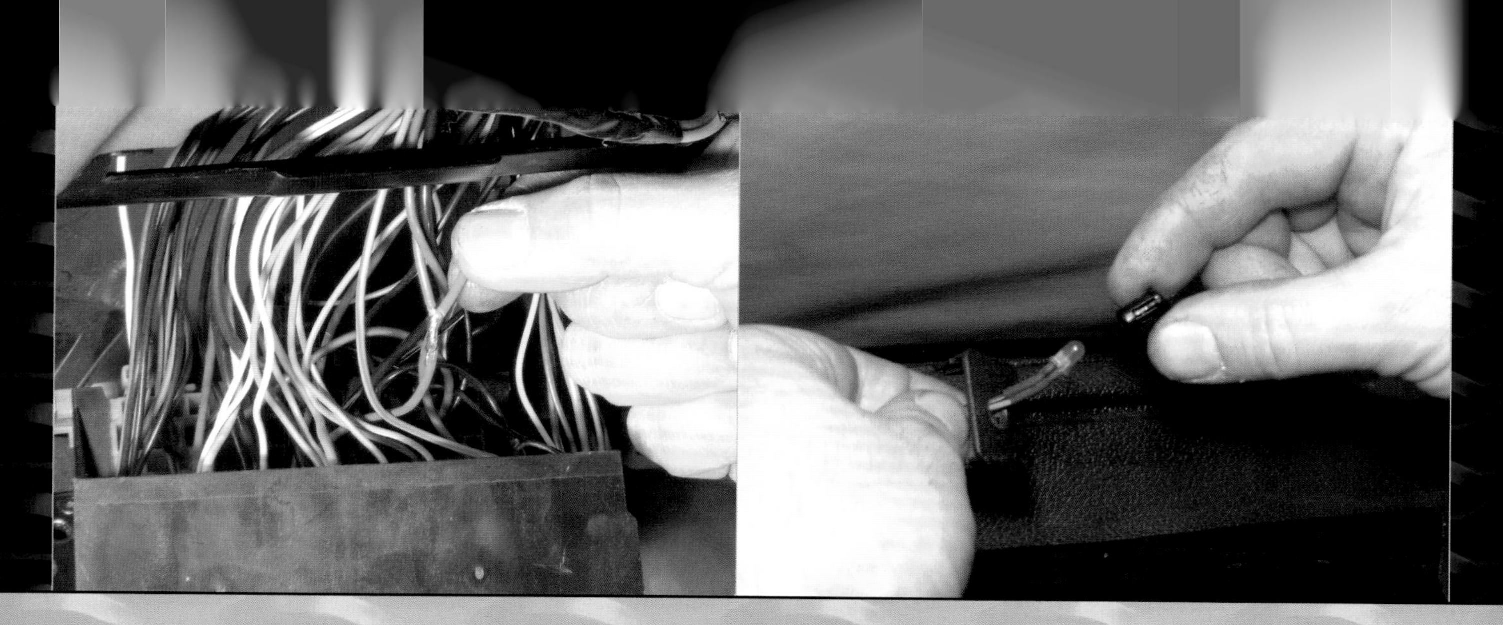

> **Tricks 'n' tips**
>
> *Don't assume you'll automatically be able to close the bonnet fully, when you first fit your pin switch - the plunger might be too long, and you'll bust the switch if you force the bonnet shut. Also, check that the switch plunger can be pushed fully down, without catching on any other vital components. If the bonnet opens much before the switch works, you'll be giving access which the crims can exploit. Just trim off some of the plastic switch plunger until all's well - trimming the pin switch down will make it 'go off' sooner, but only take off a little plastic at a time, then re-test. If you go too far when trimming down a pin switch, you can sometimes rescue the situation by screwing a little self-tapping screw into the top of the plunger. You can then 'adjust' the length of the plunger at will. The proper answer, though, is to buy a new switch.*

experiment by placing a lump of Blu-tac on the bonnet, then close it and see where the lump sticks.

Tapping into the car's wiring - always makes the less-experienced Maxer a tad nervous. Will I mess up something else by chopping in my alarm wires? The trick we use is not to cut through any of the standard wiring if we can help it. Instead, once you've identified the wire you need to join onto (like an ignition live, say), just carefully strip off a little of the plastic insulation so part of the wire's bare, then wrap the bared end of your new wire around it, and secure with a little solder (finish off with a little insulating tape). That way, whatever circuit you've tapped into should still work afterwards. Arm yourself with the Haynes manual wiring diagrams to help track down those pesky wires.

The only other bit to worry about is drilling a hole somewhere on your dash for the alarm LED. The best place for one of these is in a blank switch (there usually is one, even on a top-spec 206) - the blank can be prised out, making feeding the LED wire up through a bit easier, and it'll be in a good prominent place on the dash, so the pikeys can't miss it.

So come on - does it work? Most alarms require you to 'programme in' the remotes before they'll work. Test all the alarm features in turn, remembering to allow enough time for the alarm to arm itself (usually about 30 seconds). When you test it for the first time, don't forget to either shut the bonnet completely, or do like us, and hold the bonnet pin switch down. Our way, you can pull out the alarm fuses and shut it up, if something goes wrong!

Set the anti-shock sensitivity with a thought to where you live and park - will it be set off every night by the neighbour's cat, or by kids playing football? Finally, and most important of all - next time you park up, remember to set it!

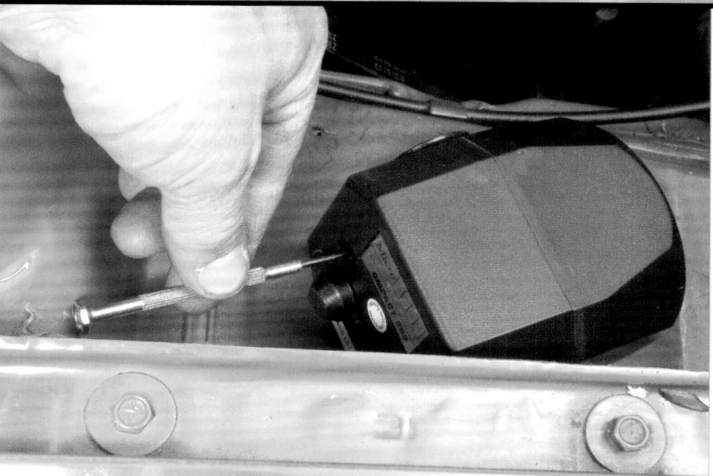

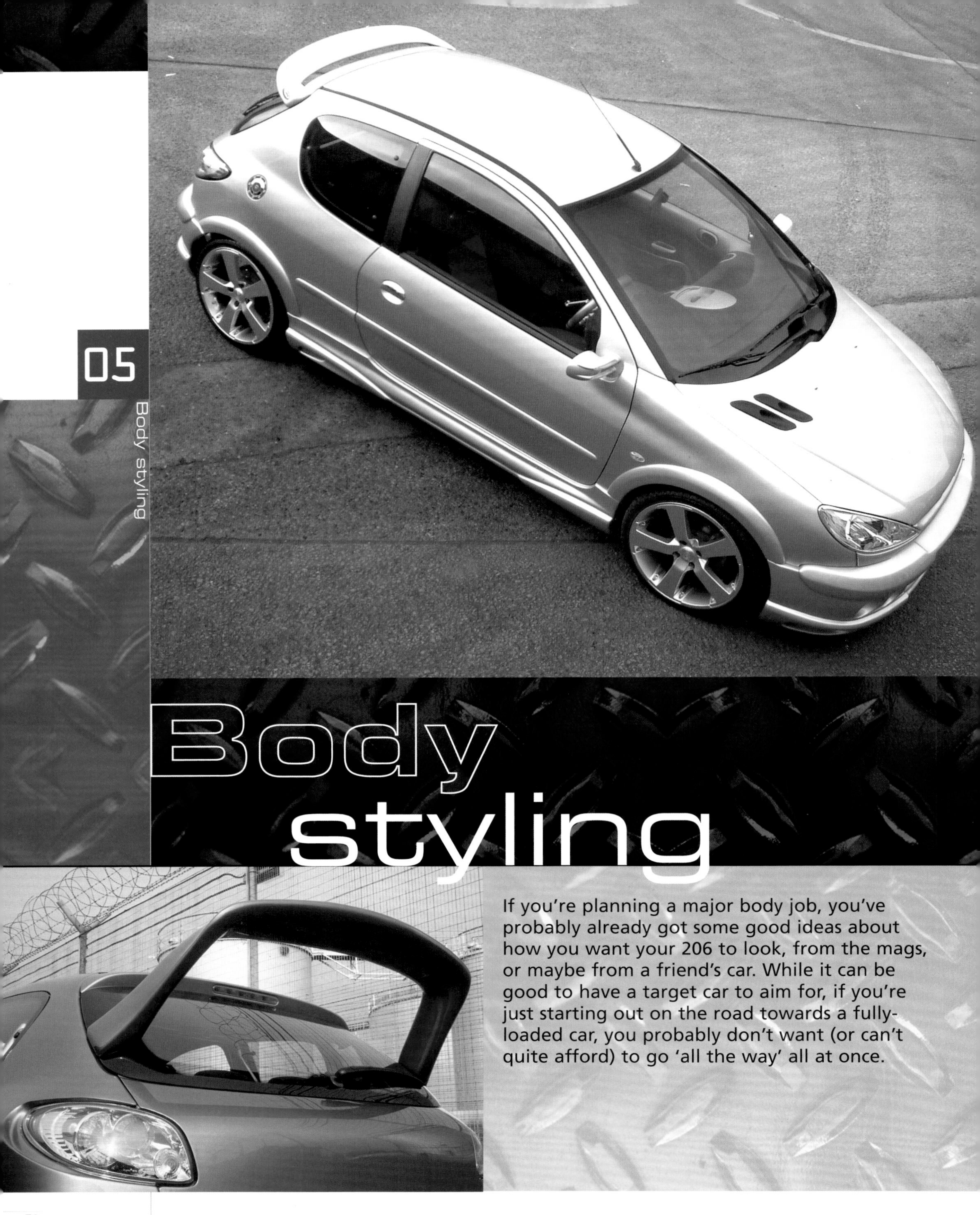

05

Body styling

# Body styling

If you're planning a major body job, you've probably already got some good ideas about how you want your 206 to look, from the mags, or maybe from a friend's car. While it can be good to have a target car to aim for, if you're just starting out on the road towards a fully-loaded car, you probably don't want (or can't quite afford) to go 'all the way' all at once.

If you're new to the world of modifying, it's a good idea to start with smaller jobs, and work up to the full body kit gradually, as your skills increase; spending loads on a body kit is a pretty lame idea if you then make a mess of fitting it! There's plenty of small ways to improve the look of your 206, which don't cost much, and which are simple enough to fit; start with some of these before you go too mad!

One golden rule with any body mods is to plan what you're going to do, and don't rush it. It's better that the car looks a bit stupid for a week (because you couldn't get something finished) than to rush a job and have the car look stupid forever. Do half the job properly instead of messing up all of it. Try and think the jobs through - plan each stage. Have you got all the tools, screws or whatever before you start, or will you have to break off halfway through? If you get stuck, is there someone you can get to help, or have they gone off for the weekend? Above all, if something goes wrong - don't panic - a calm approach will prove to be a huge bonus (that job doesn't have to be done today, does it?).

If a piece of trim won't come off, don't force it. If something feels like it's going to break, it probably will - stop and consider whether to go on and break it, or try another approach. You could even try the Haynes manual... Especially on an older car, things either never come off as easily as you think, or else have already been off so many times that they either break or won't fit back on properly. While we'd all like to do a perfect job every time, working on an older car will, sooner or later, teach you the fine art of 'bodging' (finding valid alternative ways of fixing things!). Don't assume you'll have to bodge something back on, every time - if a trim clip breaks when you take something off, it might be easier and cheaper than you think to simply go to your Peugeot dealer, and buy a new clip (remember, even Peugeot mechanics break things from time to time, so they will keep these things in stock!).

# Mirror, mirror

**Mirrors are another simple to fit, must-have accessory. The DTM or M3-style door mirrors are well established on the modified car circuit, but there are lots of variations of mirror styles and finishes, so finding some you like won't be hard.**

If you want to be just a little different, try some 'California' mirrors. The trouble with being different is it's always more work - California mirrors are 'universal fit', meaning you have to make them fit your car. You bought a 206 'cause it's a popular car, so why make life difficult? Buy some 206 mirrors (or at least some 206 mirror bases), and your new mirrors could be fitted in minutes.

There's more to mirrors than just looks, though - some have toys attached. Like side repeater lights (in a Merc stylee) or thumb switches for releasing your de-locked, de-handled doors. We want some of that.

Visiting the French Salon du Tuning show was a very bad move for us - we saw a set of Planet Line mirrors (for a Golf) and fell in love. Suddenly, we didn't care what it would take to get them on our 206 - we had to have them. Everyone said they'd be no good for us, they're meant for another. Not wanting to let our love affair die for so simple a reason, we put Kevin from Avon Custom on the task of making these mirrors fit.

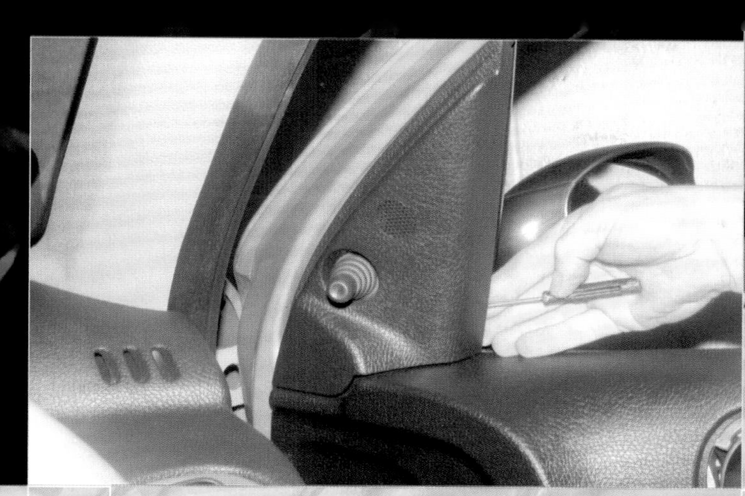

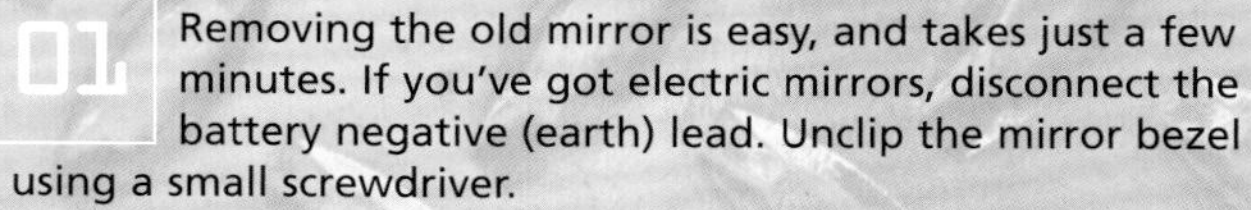

01 Removing the old mirror is easy, and takes just a few minutes. If you've got electric mirrors, disconnect the battery negative (earth) lead. Unclip the mirror bezel using a small screwdriver.

02 Remove the three mirror mounting screws from inside, while holding the mirror from outside. Is it seven years' bad luck for breaking a mirror? Or is that for walking under a ladder?

## **French** Golf **mirrors???**

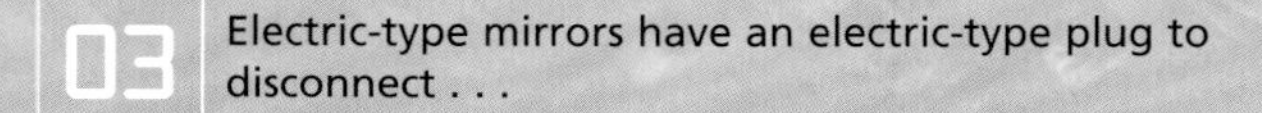

03 Electric-type mirrors have an electric-type plug to disconnect . . .

04 . . . and then those mirrors are free! Hang onto them if the car's going back to standard before you sell it on.

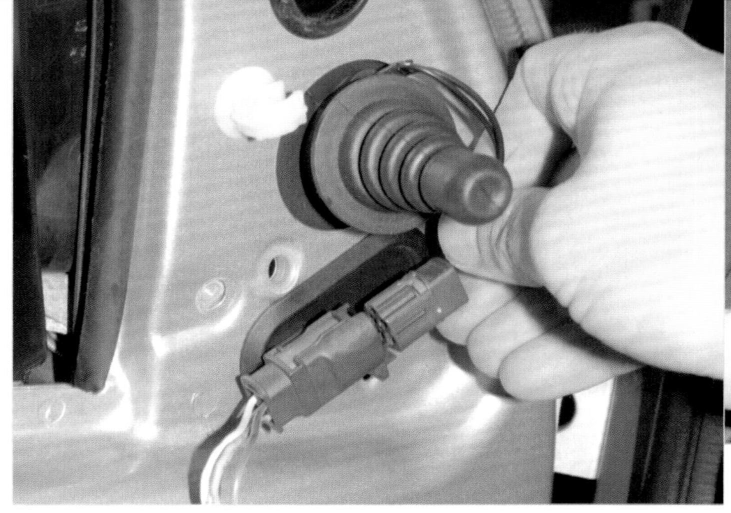

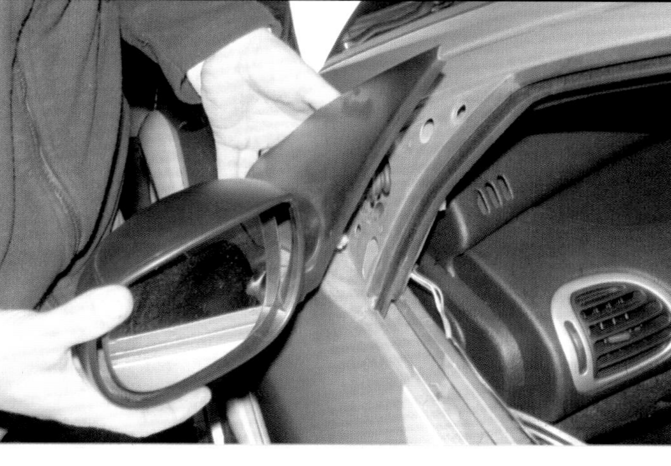

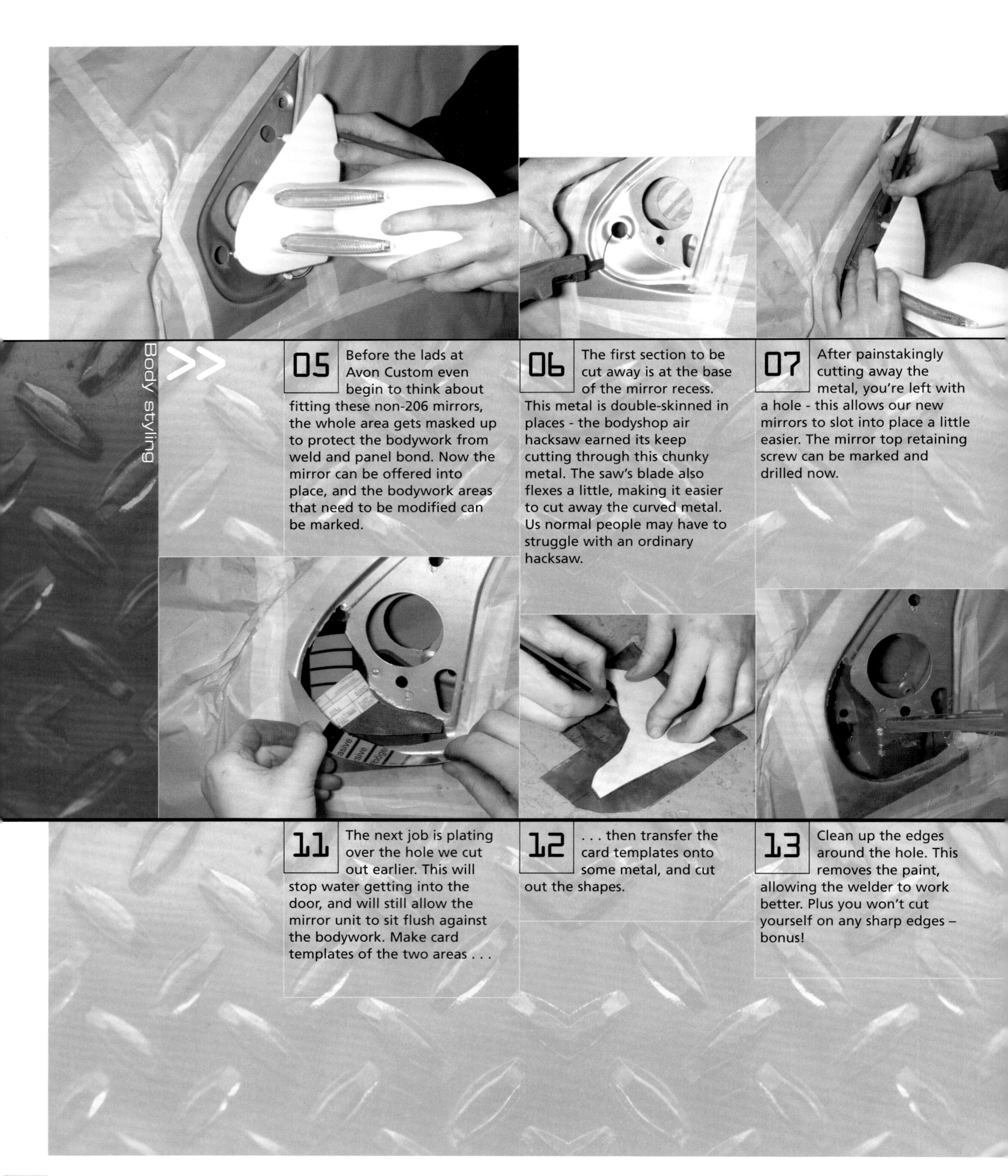

**05** Before the lads at Avon Custom even begin to think about fitting these non-206 mirrors, the whole area gets masked up to protect the bodywork from weld and panel bond. Now the mirror can be offered into place, and the bodywork areas that need to be modified can be marked.

**06** The first section to be cut away is at the base of the mirror recess. This metal is double-skinned in places - the bodyshop air hacksaw earned its keep cutting through this chunky metal. The saw's blade also flexes a little, making it easier to cut away the curved metal. Us normal people may have to struggle with an ordinary hacksaw.

**07** After painstakingly cutting away the metal, you're left with a hole - this allows our new mirrors to slot into place a little easier. The mirror top retaining screw can be marked and drilled now.

**11** The next job is plating over the hole we cut out earlier. This will stop water getting into the door, and will still allow the mirror unit to sit flush against the bodywork. Make card templates of the two areas . . .

**12** . . . then transfer the card templates onto some metal, and cut out the shapes.

**13** Clean up the edges around the hole. This removes the paint, allowing the welder to work better. Plus you won't cut yourself on any sharp edges – bonus!

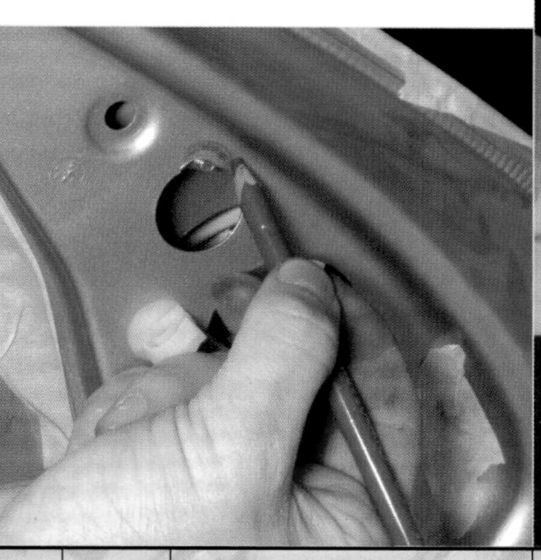

08 Once the hole has been drilled from the outside in, pop the mirror into place. Open the door and check that the screw goes through both layers of metal, and you're able to secure the mirror with a nut. We found the inner skin was stopping the screw passing through, so we had to mark the area and remove the pesky metal.

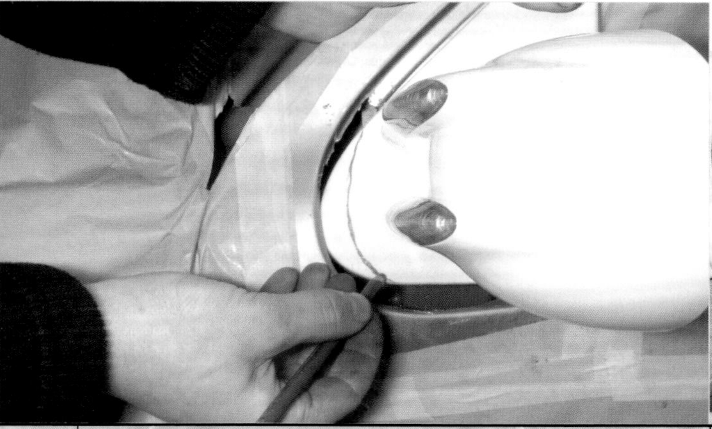

09 Now that the mirror can be slotted neatly into place, any adjustments needed to the mirror itself can be marked. In this case, the mirror plate is too large for the recess, so the excess plastic needs to be marked and trimmed away.

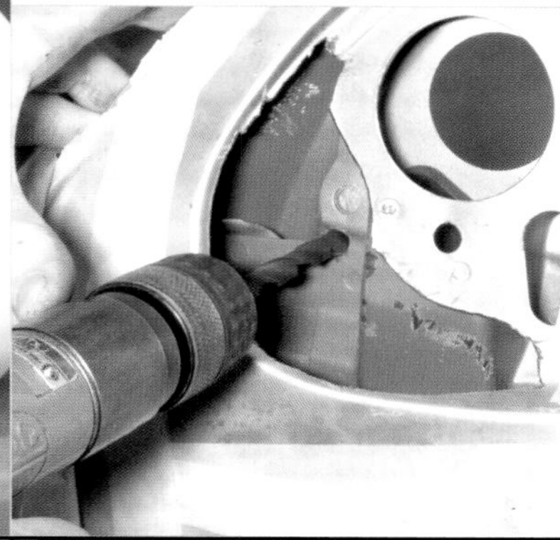

10 The remaining two retaining screw holes now need to be marked and drilled.

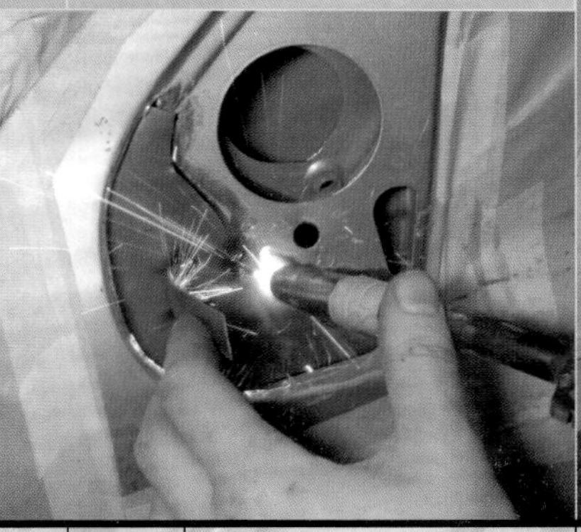

14 Now it's time to weld the plates into place. This looks a tad dangerous to us - a little more safety gear (like a welding gauntlet) would be a good idea. Still, Kevin knows what he's doing - only weld in short bursts, as too much heat from welding may distort the panel.

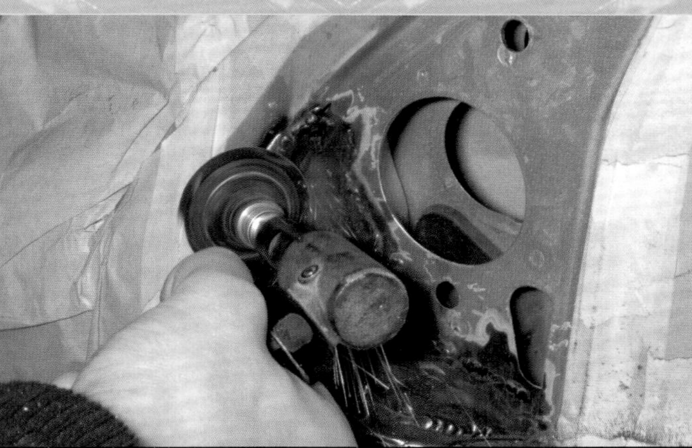

15 Welding completed, it's time to grind the weld down to create a smooth surface.

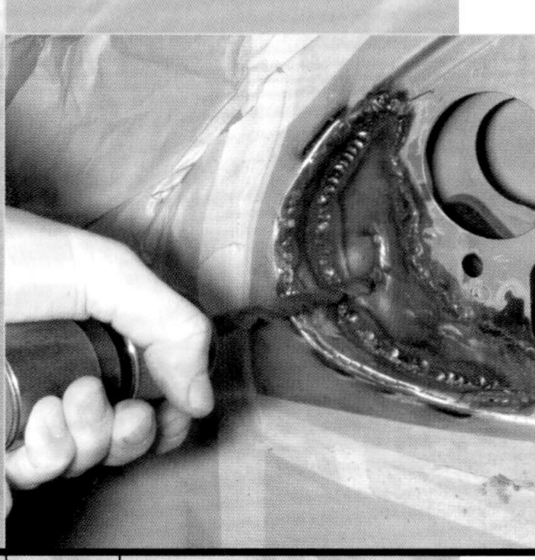

16 Line up the mirror, then mark and re-drill the lower retaining screw hole.

>>

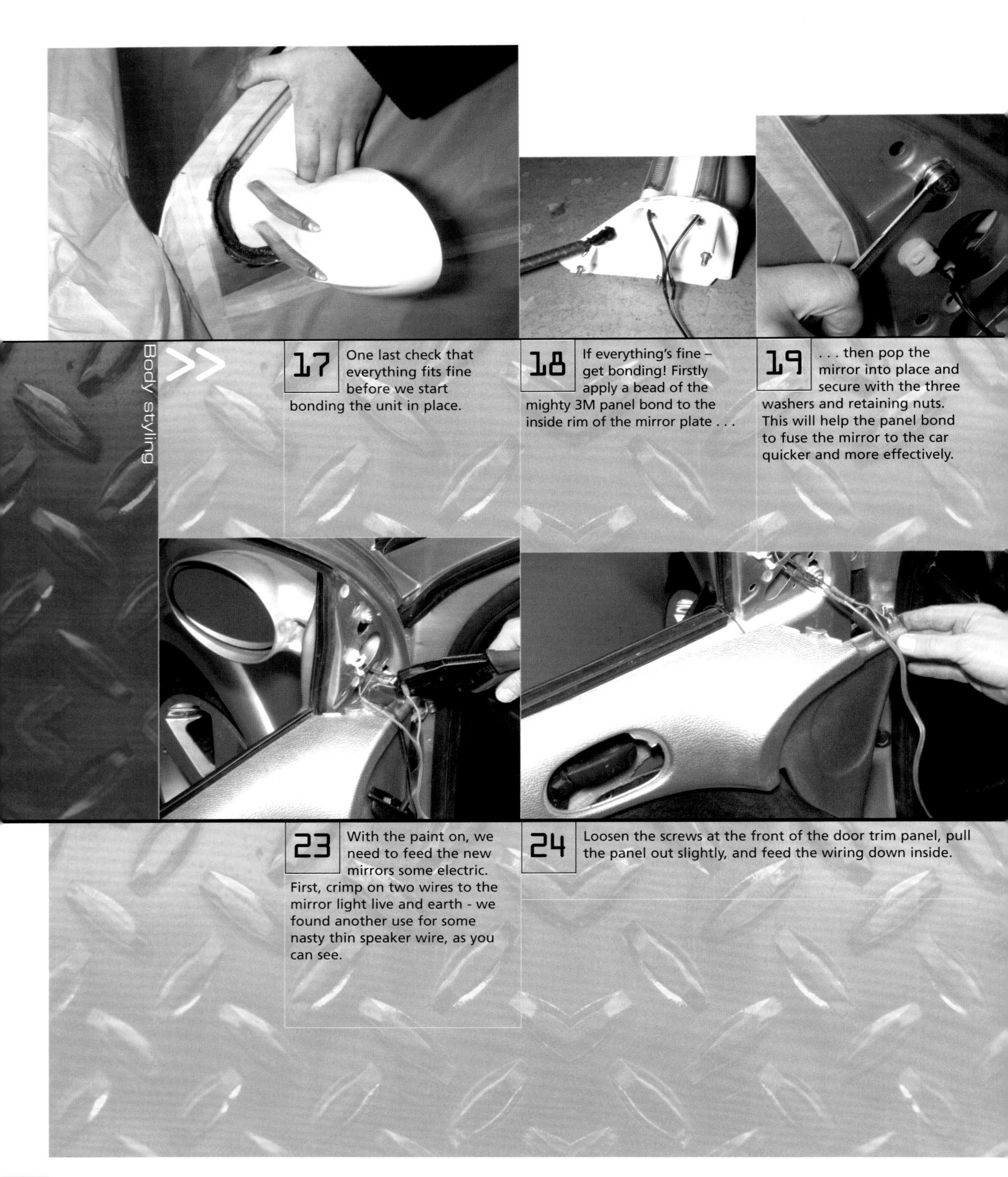

**17** One last check that everything fits fine before we start bonding the unit in place.

**18** If everything's fine – get bonding! Firstly apply a bead of the mighty 3M panel bond to the inside rim of the mirror plate . . .

**19** . . . then pop the mirror into place and secure with the three washers and retaining nuts. This will help the panel bond to fuse the mirror to the car quicker and more effectively.

**23** With the paint on, we need to feed the new mirrors some electric. First, crimp on two wires to the mirror light live and earth - we found another use for some nasty thin speaker wire, as you can see.

**24** Loosen the screws at the front of the door trim panel, pull the panel out slightly, and feed the wiring down inside.

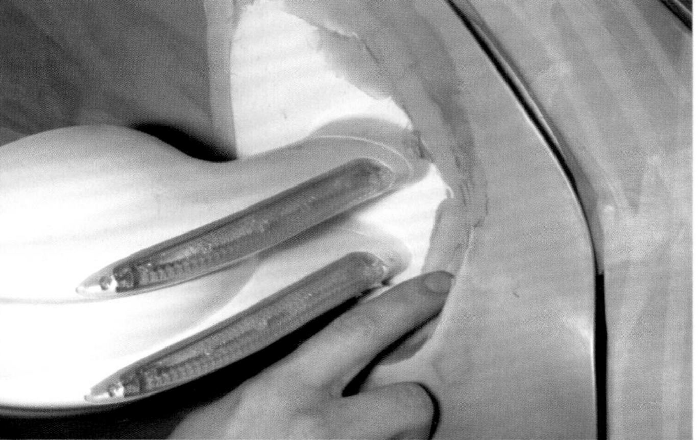

**20** Finally apply a bead of bond to the outside rim of the mirror, and smooth it into the recess between the door and mirror with a finger. It is important that you leave the bond to dry for at least 24 hours.

**21** Fibreglass was used to pad out the area between the top of the mirror and the start of the original mirror recess. This was applied, left to dry for 12 hours, then rubbed down smooth.

**22** Over the top of the fibreglass goes a skim of filler, to create a smooth area that makes the final look. Ensure that the filler covers the whole area around the mirror, including the hard-to-reach parts. Once the filler is dry, the mirrors are ready to be painted.

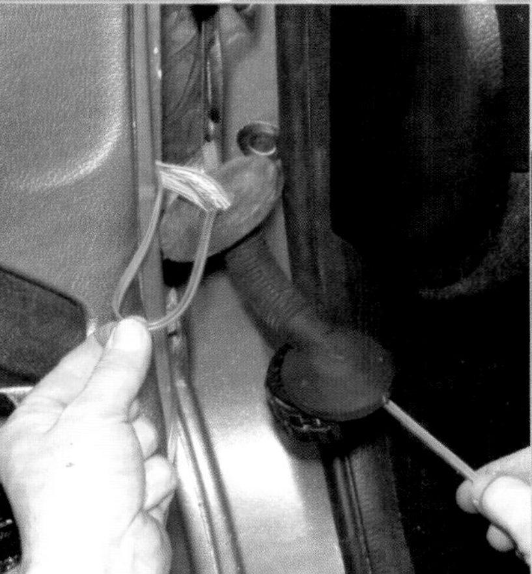

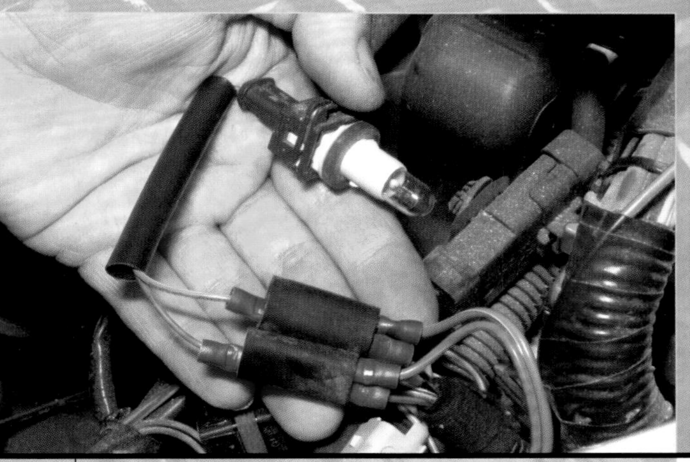

**25** To make a really neat job of the wiring, unscrew the end fitting from the door wiring rubber tube, and release the other end of the tube from the door itself. Now you can add the new wiring by poking it through inside. Doing it this way means your wire isn't getting chewed-up in the door.

**26** By making a small notch in the end of the rubber tube, and a similar notch in the plastic end fitting, the new wire can be fed out of the boot (it's going under the bonnet, not inside the car). If you make these notches so they face the front of the car, you won't even see the new wire once it's all back together.

**27** Feed the wiring into the engine bay from the inner wing, then unplug the sidelight from the back of the headlight unit. Now join the live and earth wires to the ones on the sidelight, and the mirror lights come on at night. If you want mirror indicators, tap into the indicator wiring instead. Not hard, was it?

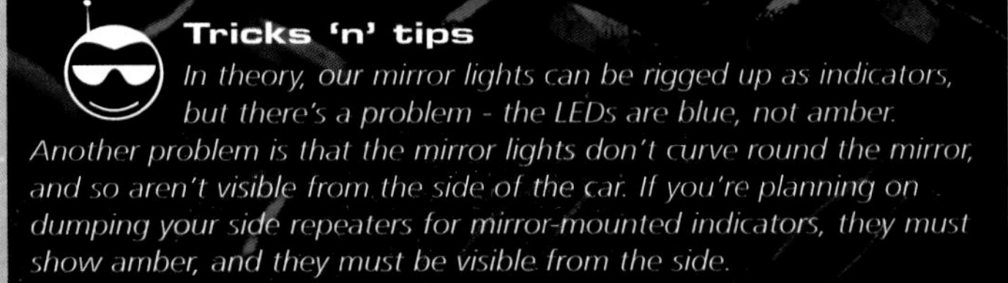

**Tricks 'n' tips**

*In theory, our mirror lights can be rigged up as indicators, but there's a problem - the LEDs are blue, not amber. Another problem is that the mirror lights don't curve round the mirror, and so aren't visible from the side of the car. If you're planning on dumping your side repeaters for mirror-mounted indicators, they must show amber, and they must be visible from the side.*

# Water features

Body styling

You've all seen them. First they started out on trucks, and we kept wondering what the heck two neon blue lights in an artic's windscreen meant. We still don't know, but they look trick on a maxed motor cruising at night, so whatever! Not only do they put a couple of LEDs on your bonnet, they also act as washer nozzles too, and the chrome finish adds a little bodywork highlight to your front end, even by day. Course, our friendly fellas in blue uniforms don't see it quite that way - showing anything other than a white light up front is illegal, and it's just another excuse to stop you. The best answer? Rig them into a well-placed switch for emergencies.

01 Before we can fit new washer jets, the old ones have to be shifted. Open the bonnet, and remove the plastic plugs which hold on the underbonnet insulation. It's a good thing if you can get a mate to help here to hold the insulation. Remove the panel and put it to one side.

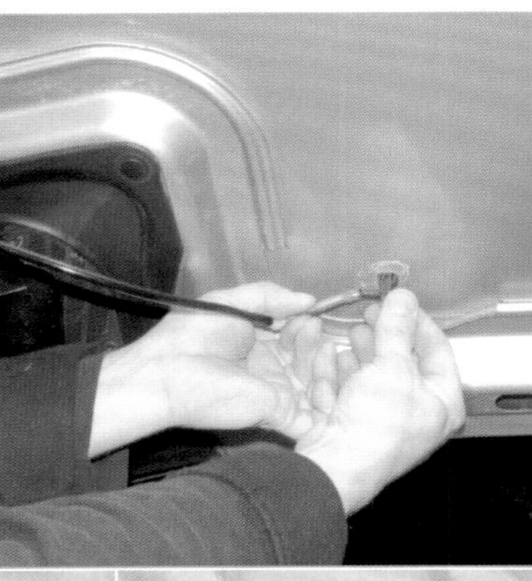

02 Disconnect the washer hose from the back of the nozzle, by carefully pulling it off. By pressing together the two small tabs, you can now push out the nozzle from the bonnet.

03 Feed the wires of the new nozzle through the bonnet. Be careful with the wire connections at the nozzle - they break easily! The new nozzle also has some clearance spacers and washers, which have to go on in the right order so as not to pinch the wires.

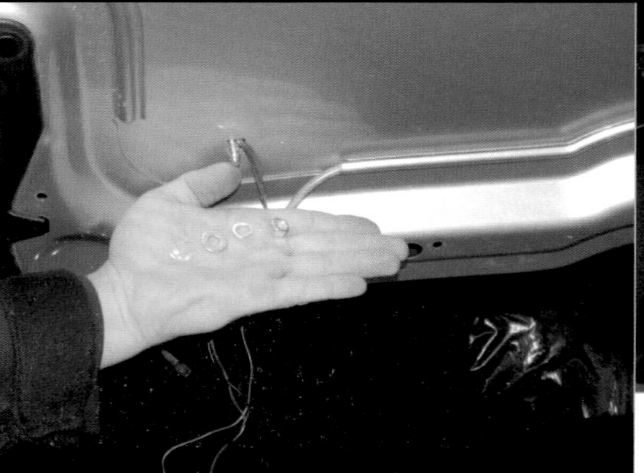

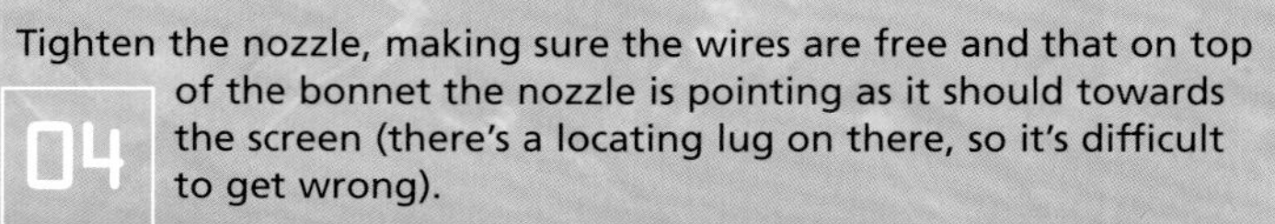

04 Tighten the nozzle, making sure the wires are free and that on top of the bonnet the nozzle is pointing as it should towards the screen (there's a locating lug on there, so it's difficult to get wrong).

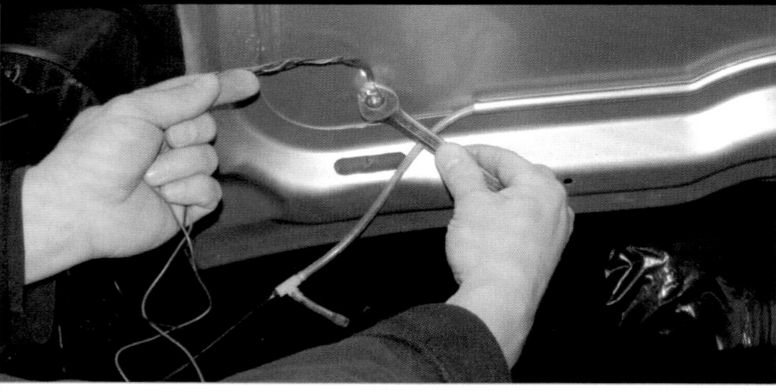

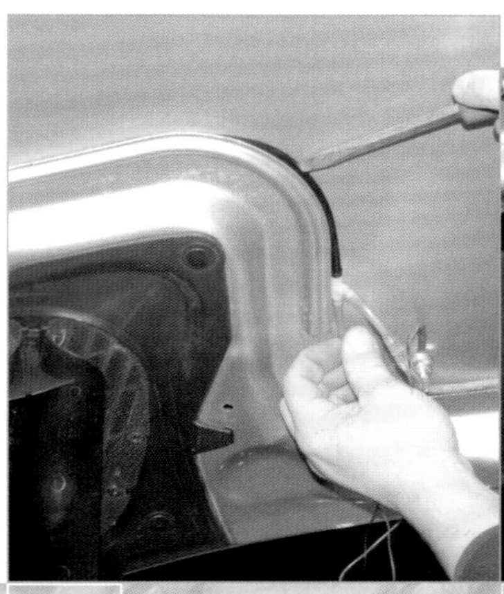

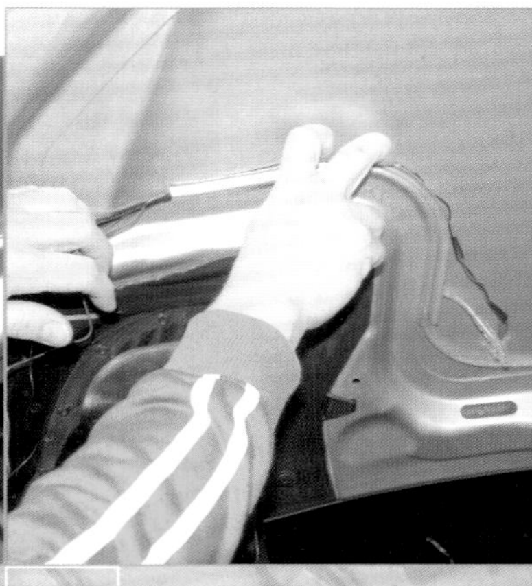

05 Connect the washer hose up to the back of the nozzle, and route the hose back into its channel on the bonnet.

06 Our washer jets gave us the option of red or blue lights (but not both, sadly). We wanted blue LEDs, so we cut the red wire off and taped it up – simple!

07 Next, tape the lead from each jet together, to make them easier to route. Run them the same way as the washer hose, so they go down into the engine bay.

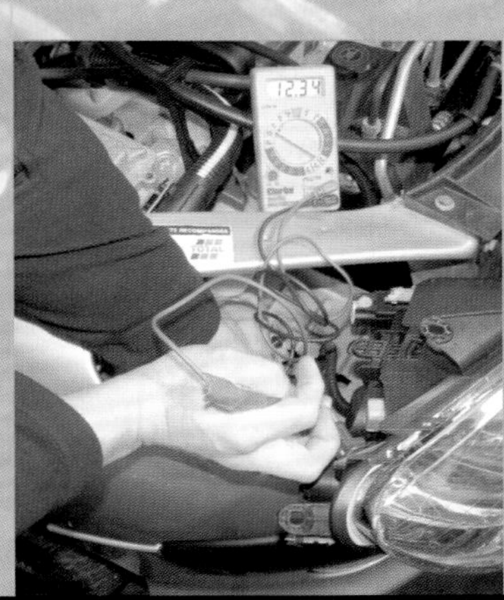

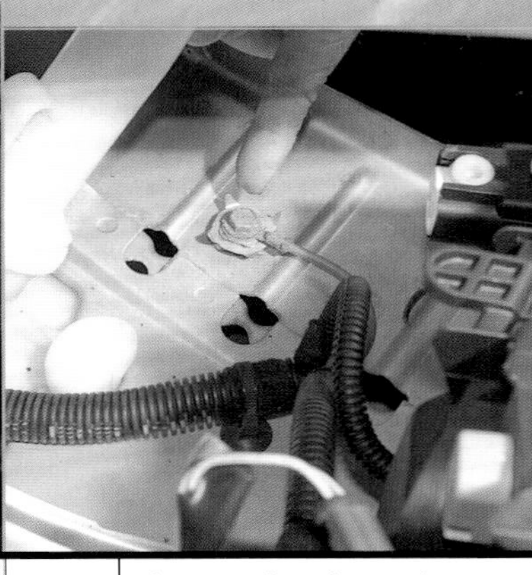

08 Remove the headlight (described in the 'lights & bulbs' section) and you'll find the sidelight connector and wiring at the upper rear corner. Just to make sure you have the right wire, turn on the sidelights and volt-check it.

09 Connect the live wire from the LED (in our case, blue) to the sidelight wire using one of the connectors provided.

10 There's a handy earth point just behind the headlight to which you can connect the earth lead from the LED. Refit the underbonnet insulation, and it's job done – your new cruising lights are ready to wash and go.

# Smoothly **does it**

Smoothing out a car's body has long been used by car modifiers to enhance shape and lines. Badges, stickers, changes in colour – all draw the eye and detract from the overall effect of a car's shape. Therefore, the more clutter you can remove from your car, the better looking its shape will be.



In the case of badges on Peugeots, removal is an easy job which takes nothing more than a few minutes heating up the badge to loosen the adhesive, but you will find on occasion badges which are fixed permanently to the body. These require bodyshop prep and paint work after removal, but nothing which should hit the wallet hard, so go ahead and de-badge for a smooth look.

## De-badging

01 Peugeot used the easiest method of fixing on their chrome i.d. badges – double-sided sticky tape. And being easy to fix on, they're pretty easy to take off too.

02 Heat the badge up using a hairdryer set on hot. Just a minute or two back and forth along the badge is enough to soften the adhesive.

03 Using either a plastic scraper, or a very blunt knife so you don't scratch the paint underneath, gently ease the badge away from the bodywork, moving from one end to the other.

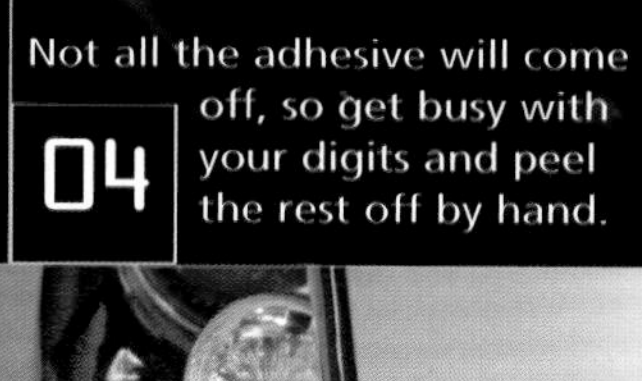

04 Not all the adhesive will come off, so get busy with your digits and peel the rest off by hand.

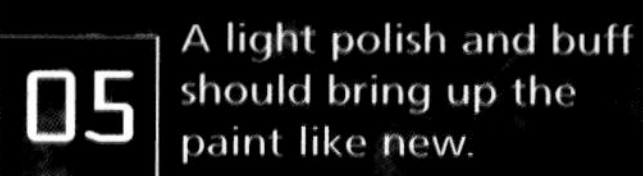

05 A light polish and buff should bring up the paint like new.

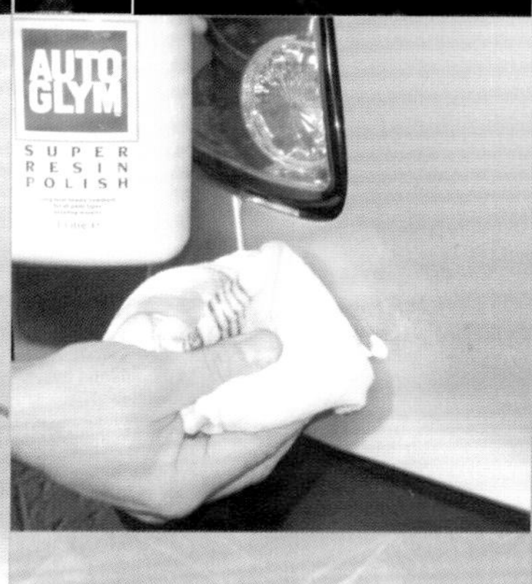

06 See how the rear looks so much smoother? With the badges gone, your eyes are drawn to the excellent rear lights instead.

## De-stripping

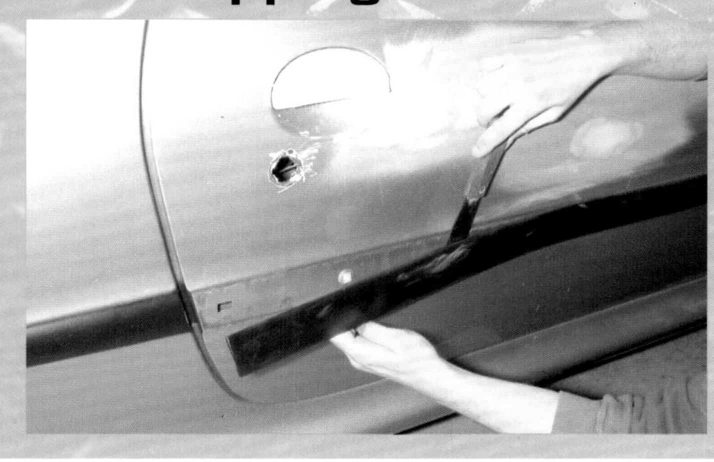

Side rubbing strips. Good - they save your paint if Mr Numpty opens his rusty Metro door into your car. Bad - they look hideous. If looks are important, removal is an option (though colour-coding's easier).

It's likely that the plastic clips holding the side rubbing strips in place will break off during removal. If the strips are going back on, either buy some more clips, or use proper bodyshop mastic/panel bond to 'glue' them on with. Those clips leave large holes in your doors, so if you're going to smooth completely, it's going to be another job for the welder (one door slam too many, and any filler will be hitting the deck).

Removing the side strips is easy and takes just a few minutes. The only tool you need is a flat-bladed prising tool, preferably with the end wrapped in masking tape, so's not to damage your paint. Slide the scraper between the door and side strip, and prise the strip outwards. As soon as you can get your fingers in the gap, pull the strips off by hand.

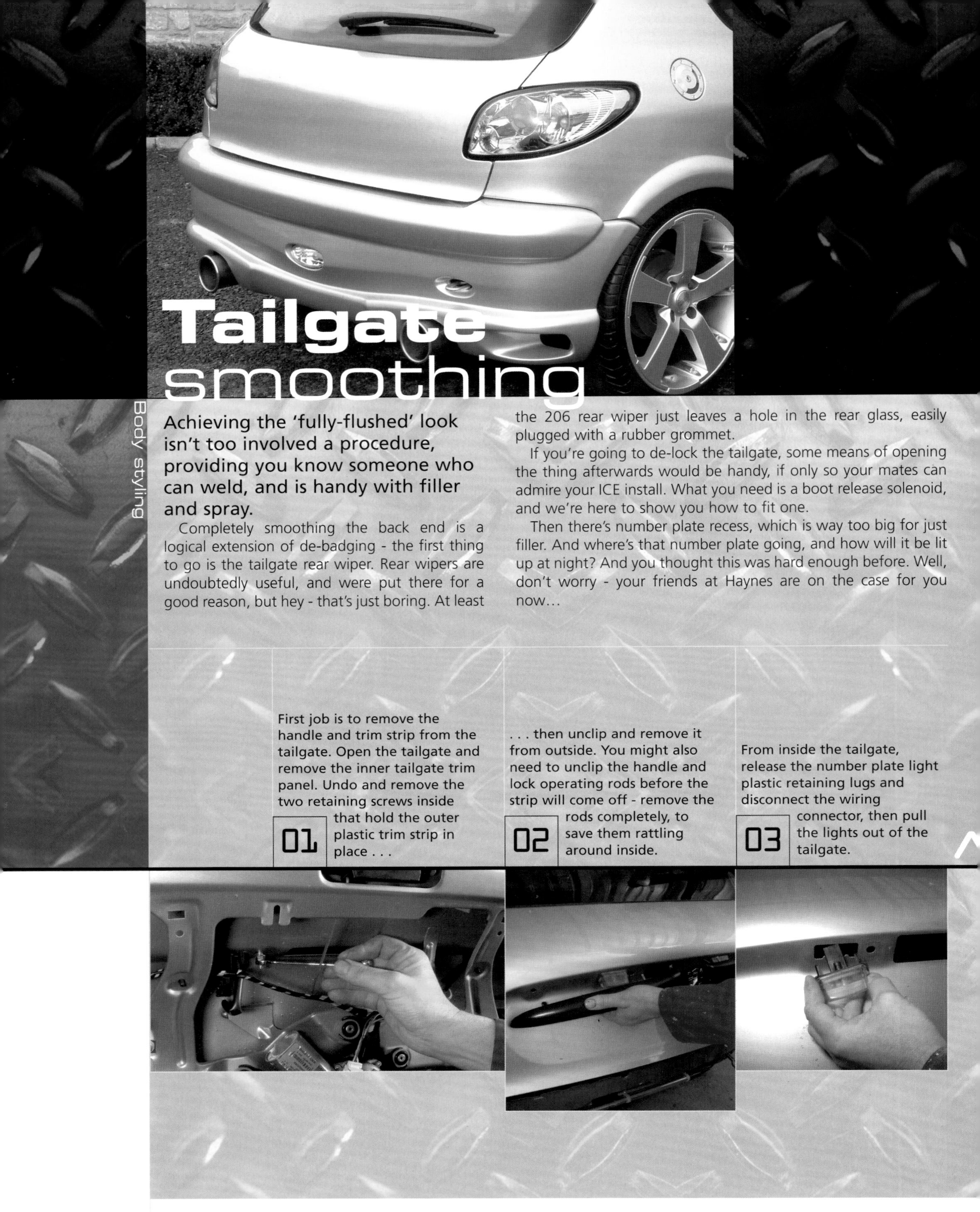

# Tailgate smoothing



**Achieving the 'fully-flushed' look isn't too involved a procedure, providing you know someone who can weld, and is handy with filler and spray.**

Completely smoothing the back end is a logical extension of de-badging - the first thing to go is the tailgate rear wiper. Rear wipers are undoubtedly useful, and were put there for a good reason, but hey - that's just boring. At least the 206 rear wiper just leaves a hole in the rear glass, easily plugged with a rubber grommet.

If you're going to de-lock the tailgate, some means of opening the thing afterwards would be handy, if only so your mates can admire your ICE install. What you need is a boot release solenoid, and we're here to show you how to fit one.

Then there's number plate recess, which is way too big for just filler. And where's that number plate going, and how will it be lit up at night? And you thought this was hard enough before. Well, don't worry - your friends at Haynes are on the case for you now...

**01** First job is to remove the handle and trim strip from the tailgate. Open the tailgate and remove the inner tailgate trim panel. Undo and remove the two retaining screws inside that hold the outer plastic trim strip in place . . .

**02** . . . then unclip and remove it from outside. You might also need to unclip the handle and lock operating rods before the strip will come off - remove the rods completely, to save them rattling around inside.

**03** From inside the tailgate, release the number plate light plastic retaining lugs and disconnect the wiring connector, then pull the lights out of the tailgate.

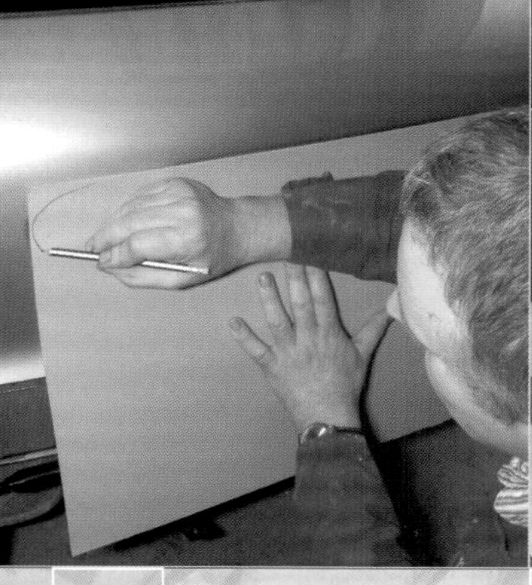

04 Now it's time for the custom bodywork to begin. The professional approach to smoothing a tailgate is to weld on a metal plate to fill the number plate recess. To get the correct-shaped metal plate, create a template of the area, using card.

05 Transfer the card template onto a sheet of metal, then cut out the plate . . .

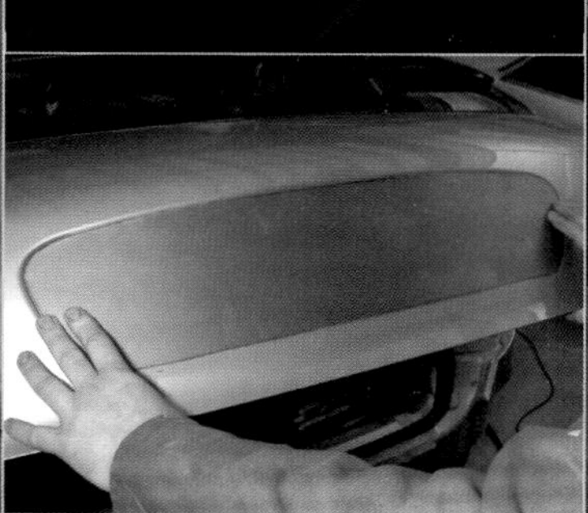

06 . . . and try it for size. After a little fine-tuning, the new plate's ready to be welded-in.

07 It's worth masking off the area above the number plate recess, to stop any grinding/welding sparks from damaging the tailgate glass. A quick touch all round the recess area with the grinder, to clean down to bare metal . . .

08 . . . and out comes the welder. Every edge must be welded up, and this is best done using short, measured blasts of the welder, so that excessive heat is not applied to the tailgate. The new plate must be well-welded all round, or it could flex, cracking any filler that sits on top of it and taking your paint with it. Luckily, the Avon Custom guys know this already.

09 Even with this many welds round the edge, the metal plate flexes and moves, so a little persuasion from the hammer's needed, to keep everything in line and pukka. More welding to do yet, then.

10 Once the welding has been completed and the metal cooled (so that it is cold to touch), run an angle grinder over the weld to smooth down any large blobs. Once this has been done, a skim of filler can be applied to the area and left at least 24 hours to dry. The longer you can leave the filler to dry, the better.

11 Before the car is wheeled into the paintshop for its full-body makeover, the filler must be rubbed down smooth (this is an artform in itself). That's it – hi-ho, it's off to paintshop we go!

# Tailgate **solenoid**

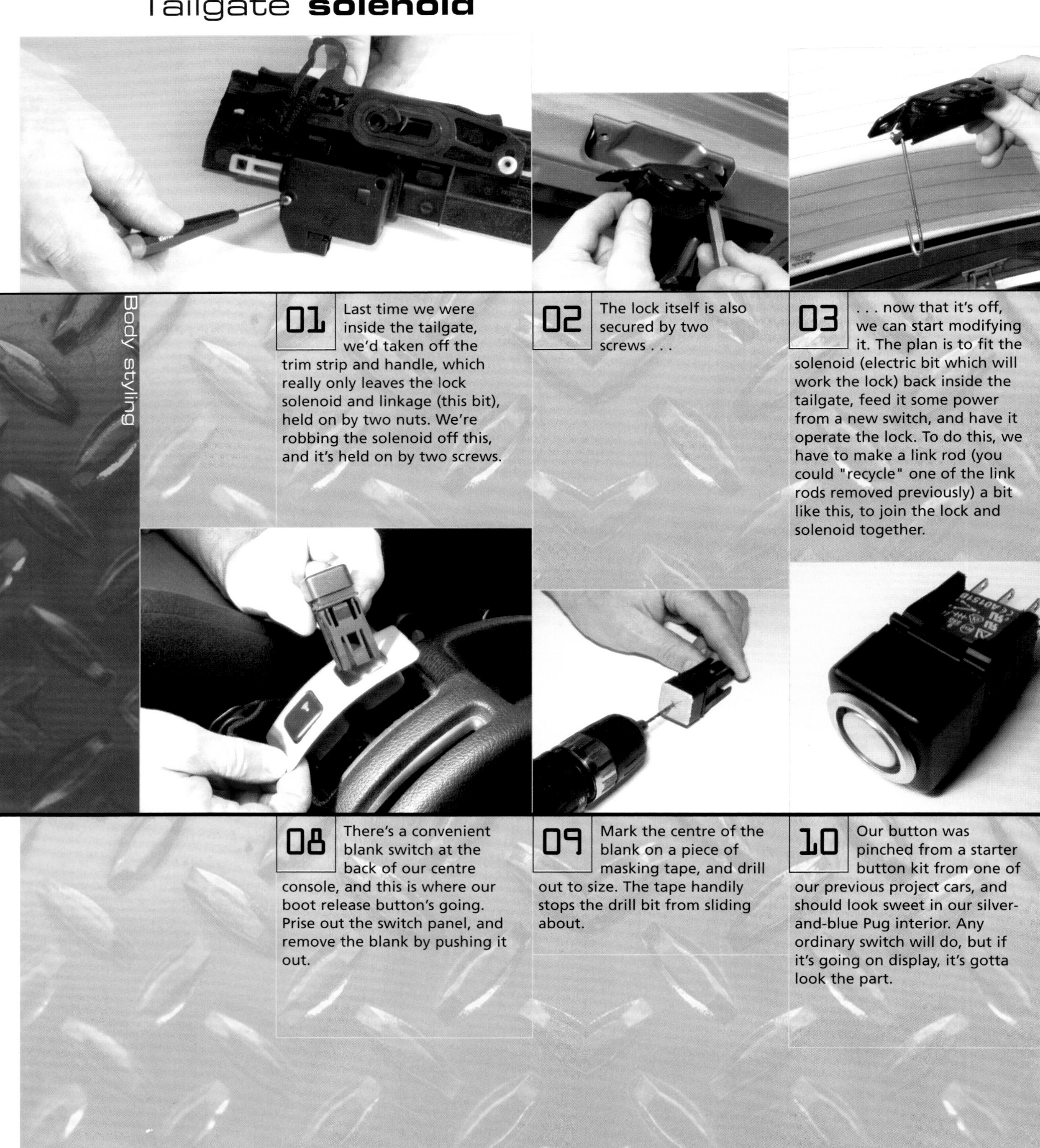



**01** Last time we were inside the tailgate, we'd taken off the trim strip and handle, which really only leaves the lock solenoid and linkage (this bit), held on by two nuts. We're robbing the solenoid off this, and it's held on by two screws.

**02** The lock itself is also secured by two screws . . .

**03** . . . now that it's off, we can start modifying it. The plan is to fit the solenoid (electric bit which will work the lock) back inside the tailgate, feed it some power from a new switch, and have it operate the lock. To do this, we have to make a link rod (you could "recycle" one of the link rods removed previously) a bit like this, to join the lock and solenoid together.

**08** There's a convenient blank switch at the back of our centre console, and this is where our boot release button's going. Prise out the switch panel, and remove the blank by pushing it out.

**09** Mark the centre of the blank on a piece of masking tape, and drill out to size. The tape handily stops the drill bit from sliding about.

**10** Our button was pinched from a starter button kit from one of our previous project cars, and should look sweet in our silver-and-blue Pug interior. Any ordinary switch will do, but if it's going on display, it's gotta look the part.

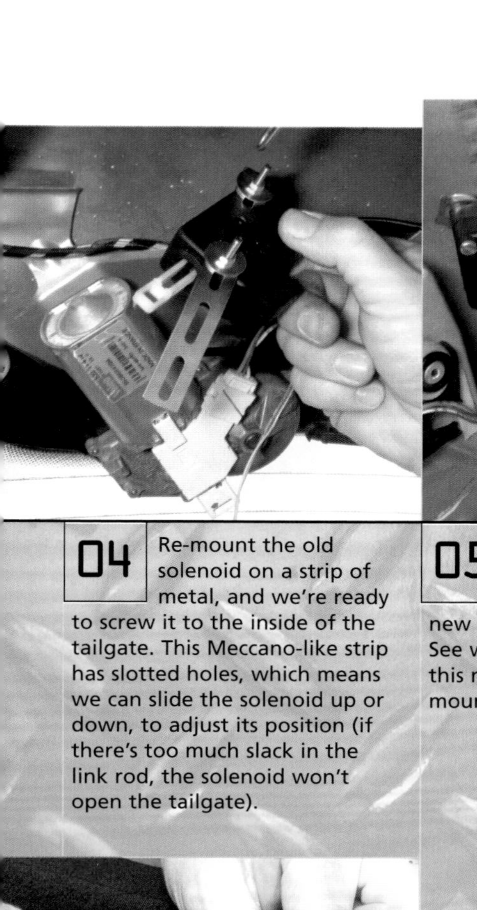

**04** Re-mount the old solenoid on a strip of metal, and we're ready to screw it to the inside of the tailgate. This Meccano-like strip has slotted holes, which means we can slide the solenoid up or down, to adjust its position (if there's too much slack in the link rod, the solenoid won't open the tailgate).

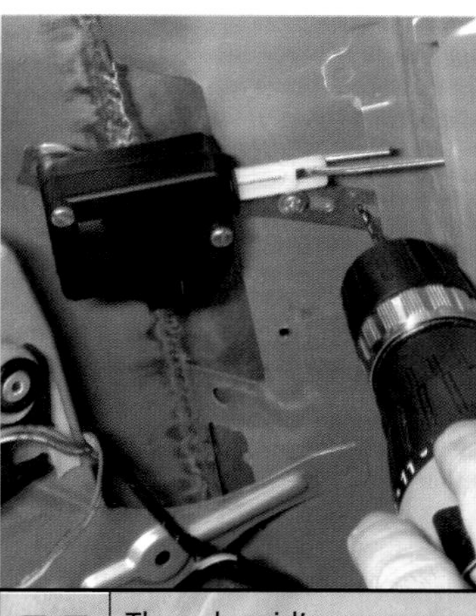

**05** The solenoid's now almost mounted, the lock's refitted, and our new link rod is, well... linked. See where we're going with this now? Just one more mounting hole to drill.

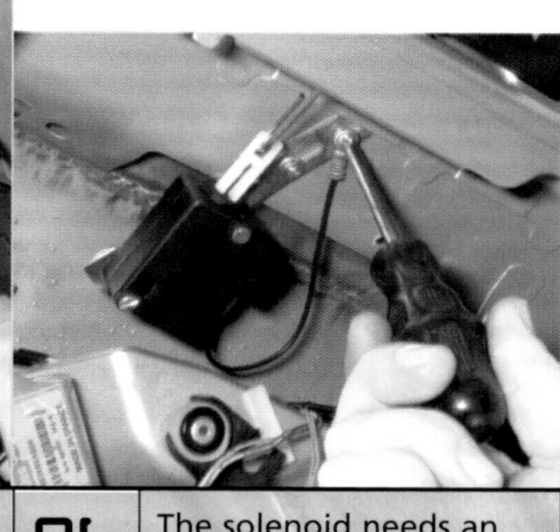

**06** The solenoid needs an earth connection, so we're using one of our new mounting screws as an earth point . . .

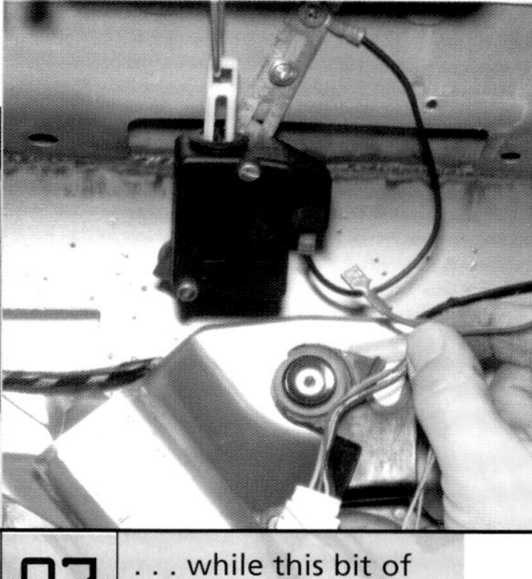

**07** . . . while this bit of blue wire will be our live feed. We ran this wire back inside the car, through the wiring tubes at the top of the tailgate. If you're dumping your rear wiper, a neat solution would be to grab a live from the existing wiper motor wiring - then you have a tailgate release working off your wiper stalk, which is pretty cool.

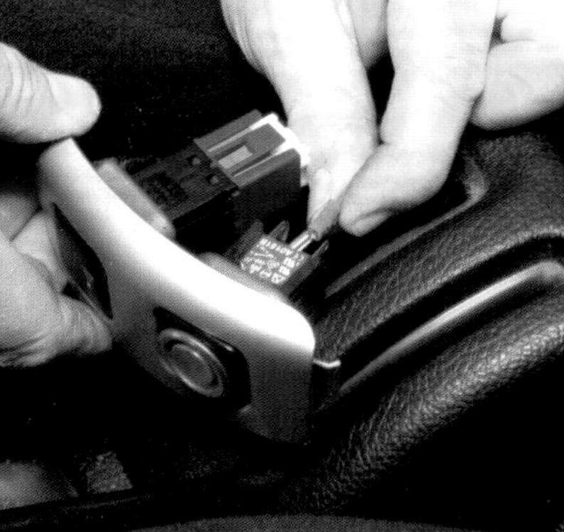

**11** Obviously, our butchered blank switch fits back perfectly in its former hole, so all we need to do now is wire up the button. On goes our blue wire, fed through all the way from the tailgate . . .

**12** . . . then we prised out the console window switches . . .

**13** . . . to tap into the fag lighter wiring for our live feed. An in-line fuse is a sensible precaution, fitted in seconds.

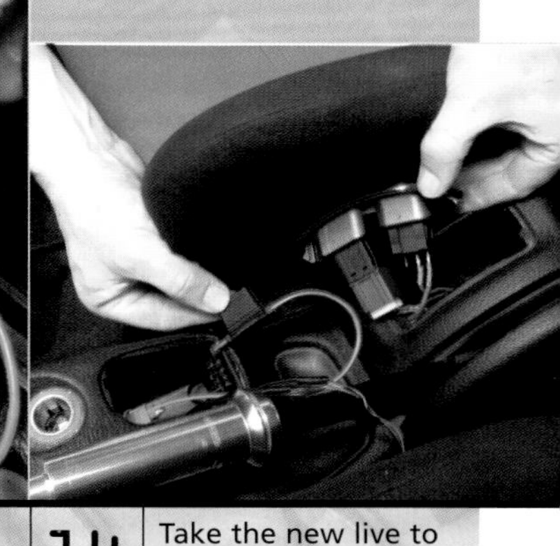

**14** Take the new live to the other side of the switch/button, and you should have a fully-functioning tailgate release (minor adjustments may be needed, so check it's working with the tailgate open, not slammed shut). Fit it all back up front, making a neat job of tidying the wiring, and that's it.

# **Number plate** mounting and lighting

Though you probably wouldn't think it, this is one of the most forgotten-about items - and it causes no end of problems. Try and think ahead when planning a boot-smooth, as an illegal number plate is a bit of a come-and-nick-me to you-know-who.

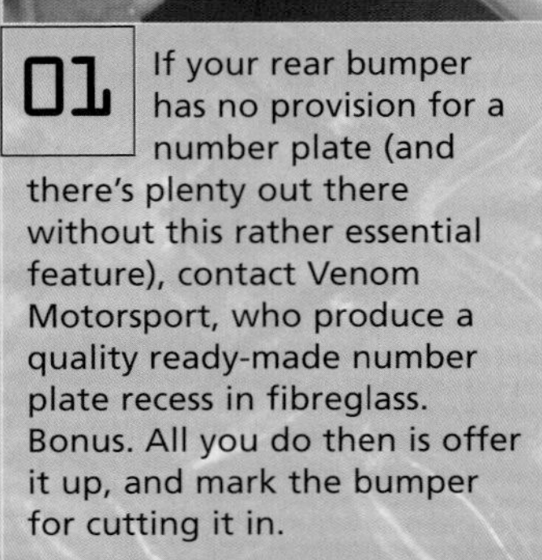

**01** If your rear bumper has no provision for a number plate (and there's plenty out there without this rather essential feature), contact Venom Motorsport, who produce a quality ready-made number plate recess in fibreglass. Bonus. All you do then is offer it up, and mark the bumper for cutting it in.

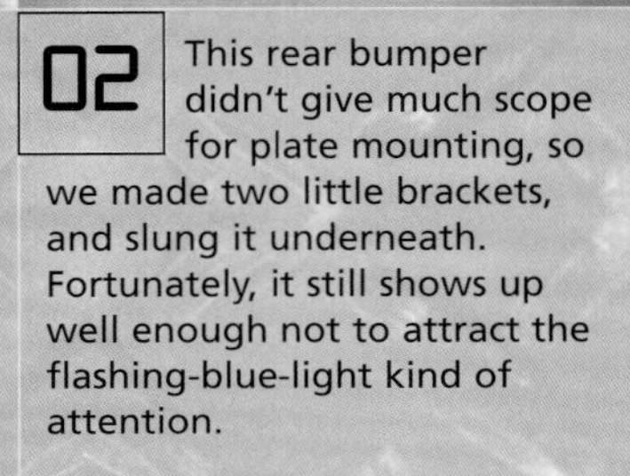

**02** This rear bumper didn't give much scope for plate mounting, so we made two little brackets, and slung it underneath. Fortunately, it still shows up well enough not to attract the flashing-blue-light kind of attention.

**03** This lighting solution might not be strictly legal, but at least we tried, and again, this might be enough of a gesture to avoid getting pulled. A row of white LEDs mounted above the plate will hopefully be bright enough to do the job. Wired, in case you wondered, from the existing number plate light circuit.

## Fill 'er up!

**Ever since motor racing modifications made it onto the street, alternative filler caps have been marketed.**

Some cars hide the caps behind a door which retains a smooth finish, but those who like to show off their racing accessories will, more likely, choose a trick way to show off where the gas goes in.

There are a number of safety features you have think about when choosing a cap, but you also have to consider ease of use. And something which replicates the way the factory cap works, as in the case of this Ecosse piece, should suit your needs, especially since it comes in a trick polished finish. By the time you've read this far, you could have fitted it.

**01** Hey, here's a tough one. You know the fuel filler cap which you shove loads of unleaded down each week?

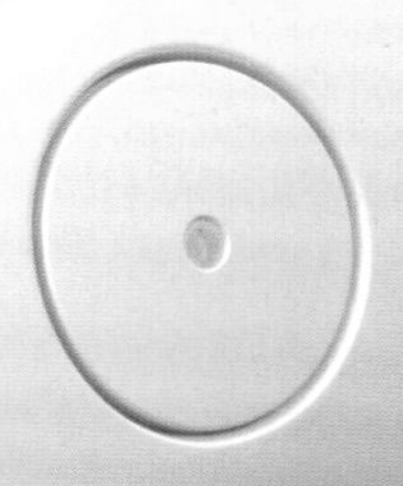

**02** Well, unlock and remove it.

**03** And here comes the tricky part – using the new cap and its key, fit it in place and lock it!

**04** Wow - after all that work, you deserve a drink.

# **Enhance** your glass

**As we've said elsewhere in this book, with uniform surfaces to look at, the eye isn't distracted from the shape of the object that it looks at. Hence, when you look at a car and see dark windows rather than the car's interior through clear glass, it immediately focuses your eye on the overall look of the car. This is why window tinting works so well on a modified car.**

Yet tinting has more benefits, especially during the summer when it can stop a lot of the harmful UV rays from the sun coming in through the windows and heating the interior. It also drastically reduces the ageing of the plastic and rubber inside your car which is caused by the same rays.

Tinting at home is not that easy, and you'll find that if you ever get the chance to watch a professional tinter at work it's a lesson in patience and careful procedure. So, take your time, make sure the window you're tinting is spotless and completely dust-free, and you should be rewarded with good results.

It's worth picking your day, and your working area, pretty carefully - on a windy day, there'll be more dust in the air, and it'll be a nightmare trying to stop the film flapping and folding onto itself while you're working. Applying window tint is best done on a warm day (or in a warm garage - if there is such a thing), because the adhesive will begin to dry sooner. For fairly obvious reasons, don't try tinting when it's starting to get dark... Having a mate along to help out is a good idea, but only if they can keep any criticism of your work to themselves!

### Legal eagle

*The law on window tinting currently is that there must be no more than a 25% reduction in light transmission through windscreens, and a limit of 30% reduction on all other glass. How the heck do you measure light reduction? Also, many cars come with tinted glass as standard - so can you fit a tinting kit on top and still be legal? Hard to know what line to take, if you're stopped by Plod - try and choose a tinting kit which is EC-approved (ask before you buy, and if you think it could be a serious issue, get a letter from the company to support the legality of the kit, to use in your defence). Some forces now take this seriously enough to have portable test equipment they can use at the roadside - if your car fails, it's an on-the-spot fine. Stick to a lightish tint, and on side glass only (limo-black on front windows is asking for a pull on safety grounds, as is a blacked-out rear screen).*

## **Tinting** windows

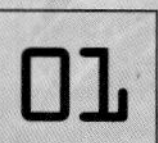

**01** The Folia Tec tinting kit is good quality and comes with a sharp knife with renewable blade, a bottle of fluid to make up the spray-on solution, plus a roll of tinting film which should cover all four side windows at least (assuming no disasters). We went with their light smoke tint, to try and keep things legal.

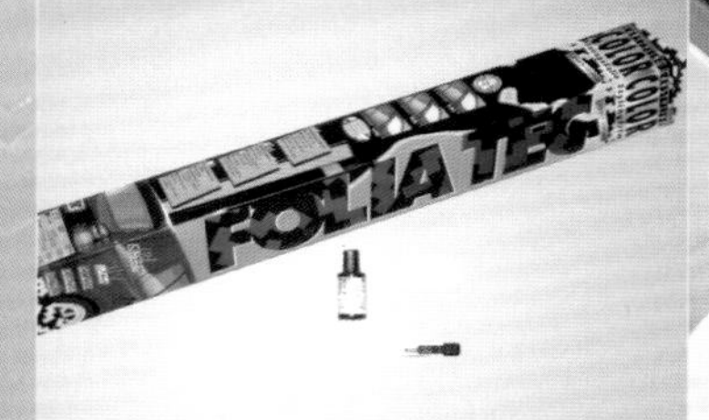

**02** Remove the outer window trim seal, by prising it up. Don't be too violent, or you'll bend it, and watch that paintwork . . .

**03** . . . then shift the inner trim the same way.

**04** Measure up the size of your window. You'll need the maximum height plus at least an inch, and the maximum width plus at least an inch. Better to cut big here, as you can easily trim back at a later stage.

**05** Unroll the tint somewhere clean, making sure you have the Folia Tec mark reading correctly and facing you, then measure out and cut the amount you need.

**06** Make up your spray solution using two capfuls of the supplied fluid to 0.5 litre of distilled water, which is available from any motor accessory shop (for topping-up batteries) and most DIY stores.

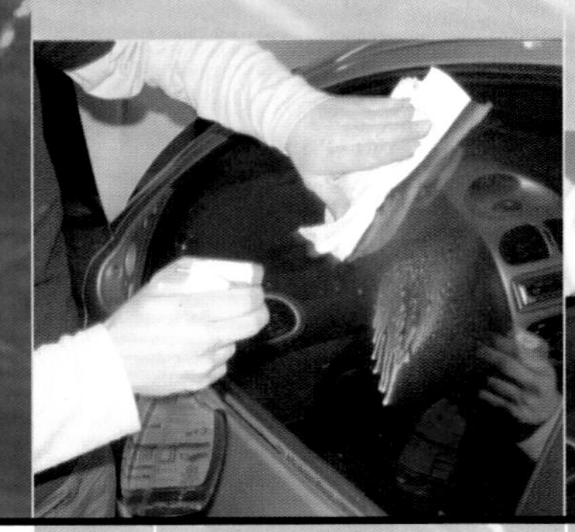

**07** Time to get clean! First remove any dealer/security stickers which might be attached on the inside of the glass, then give the glass a thorough clean both inside and out. In the case of stickers, you may need some thinners to get the sticky stuff off successfully.

**08** Pay special attention to the cleaning the window edges, and make sure you wind the window down to clean the top edge.

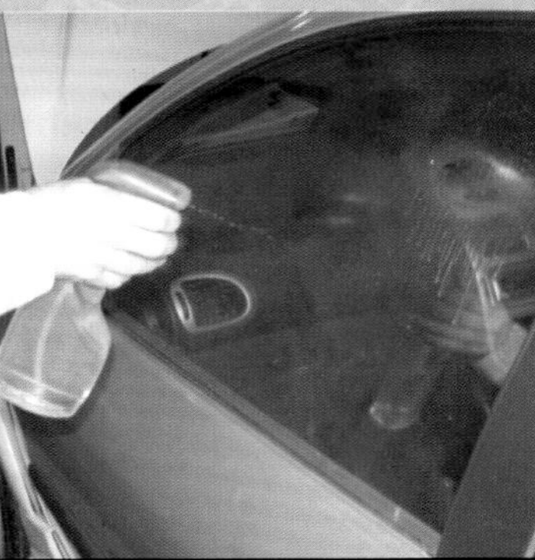

**09** Once your window is spotless, spray on the soapy solution you've mixed up onto the outside of the window, using an old spray cleaner bottle.

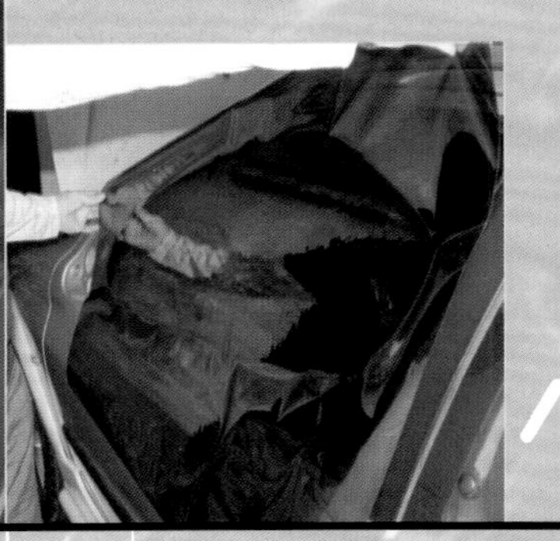

**10** Apply the film to the outside of the window.

**11** Spray the outside of the film with your solution (yes, you'll get through lots, doing the whole car).

**12** Smooth the film down with the supplied squeegee, so that it's roughly fitting the window, with the edges overhanging.

**13** Using the supplied knife, cut off the excess film at each edge. This is very sharp and should slice through the film no problem. Beware of scratching your paintwork at this point.

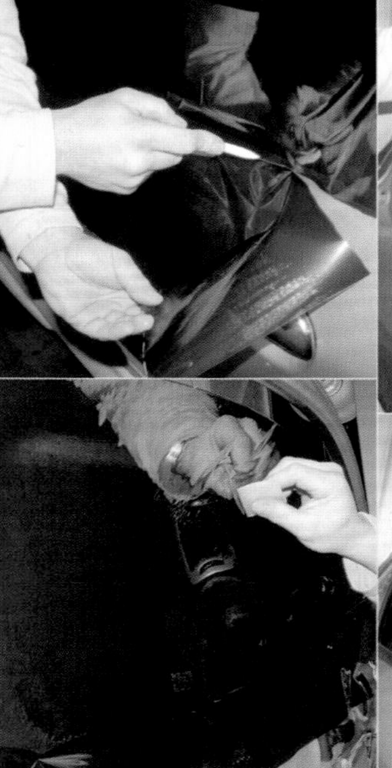

**14** Squeegee to push the film to the edges and make sure there are no overhangs left, especially on the top edge.

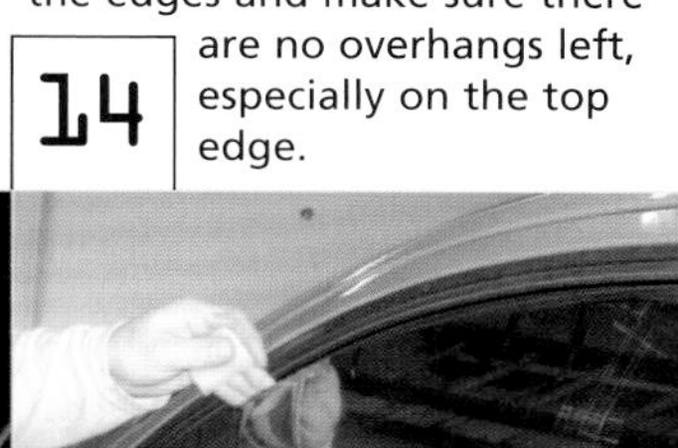

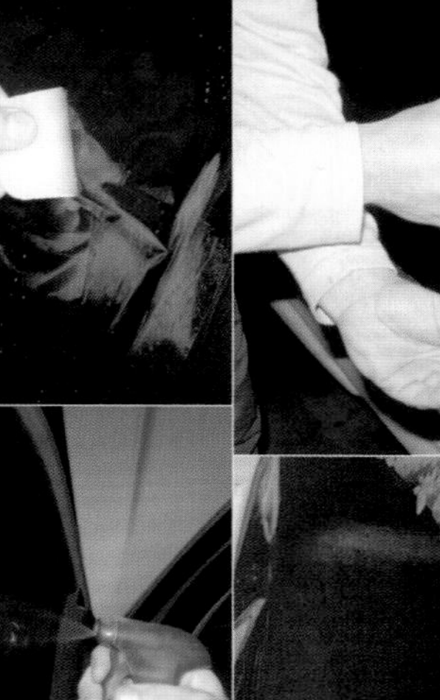

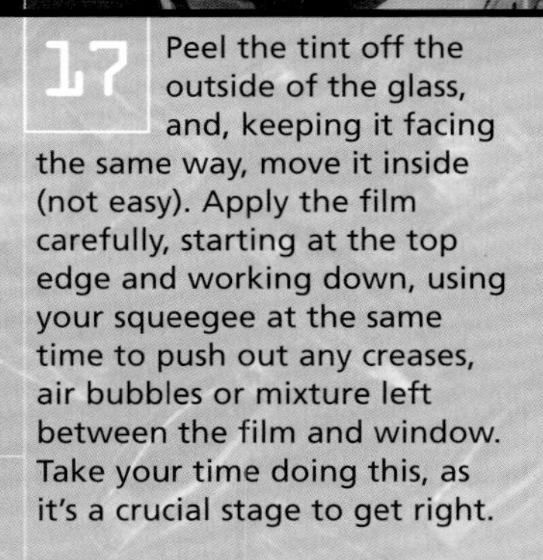

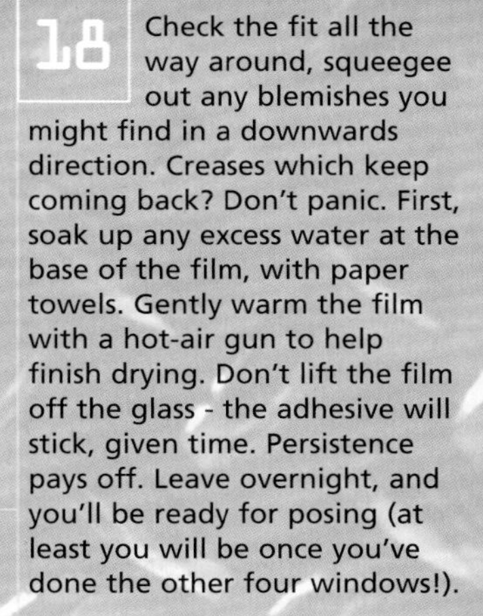

**15** Separate the film sections - the clear, outer film that peels away is the one to be discarded, while the one left on the window is the actual tint, which gets peeled off and stuck to the inside. Once the outer film's gone, try not to handle the tint too much until it's stuck on the inside.

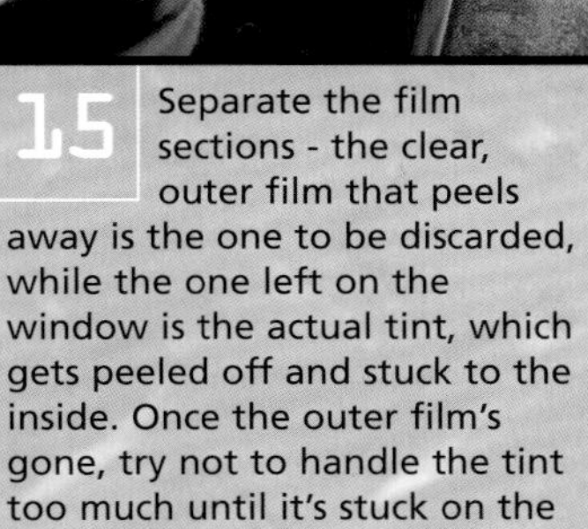

**16** Thoroughly wet the inside of the window with the solution. Your front door trim will obviously be off for this part of the job, but when you're in the back doing the rear windows, try not to soak your rear trim panels too much.

**17** Peel the tint off the outside of the glass, and, keeping it facing the same way, move it inside (not easy). Apply the film carefully, starting at the top edge and working down, using your squeegee at the same time to push out any creases, air bubbles or mixture left between the film and window. Take your time doing this, as it's a crucial stage to get right.

**18** Check the fit all the way around, squeegee out any blemishes you might find in a downwards direction. Creases which keep coming back? Don't panic. First, soak up any excess water at the base of the film, with paper towels. Gently warm the film with a hot-air gun to help finish drying. Don't lift the film off the glass - the adhesive will stick, given time. Persistence pays off. Leave overnight, and you'll be ready for posing (at least you will be once you've done the other four windows!).

# Fitting a **sunstrip**

The modern sunstrip, first seen as a lovely green shadeband on Cortinas and Capris back in the 70s, usually bearing imaginative slogans such as 'DAVE AND SHARON'. Just goes to show that some things improve with age.

There are two options to make your car look (and maybe even feel) cooler:

**a** The sunvisor, a screen tint band inside the screen, which is usually a graduated-tint strip. As this fits inside, there's a problem straight away - the interior mirror. Your 206 mirror may be bonded to the screen, and it seriously gets in the way when trying to fit a wet and sticky (nice!) strip of plastic around it. Go for a sunstrip instead.

**b** The sunstrip, which is opaque vinyl, colour-matched to the car, fits to the outside of the screen. Much more Sir.

A really wide sunstrip imitates the 'roof chop' look seen on American hot rods, and colour-coded, they can look very effective from the front - plus, of course, you can use the space to advertise your preferred brand of ICE (no, no, NO! Not a good idea!). As it's fitted to the outside of the screen, the sunstrip has a good chance of seriously interfering with your wipers (or wiper, if you've been converted). If this happens to the point where the wipers can't clean the screen, Mr MOT might have a point if he fails your car... The wiper blades may need replacing more often, and the sunstrip itself might start peeling off - still want one? Well, you've got to, really.

**Legal eagle**

*The rule for tinting or otherwise modifying the windscreen is that there must be no more than a 25% light reduction from standard. In theory, this means you can have a sunstrip which covers up to 25% of the screen area, but some MOT testers may see it differently. A sunstrip's got to come down the screen a fair way, to look any sense (otherwise, why bother?). You could argue that accurately measuring and calculating the windscreen area isn't actually that easy, if you get stopped, and anyway, a sunstrip also cuts out harmful glare! If you go so far down the screen that you can't see out, though - well, that's just stupid.*

**01** This is only stuck to the outside, so only the outside of the screen needs cleaning - excellent! Do a good job of cleaning, though - any dirt stuck under the strip will ruin the effect.

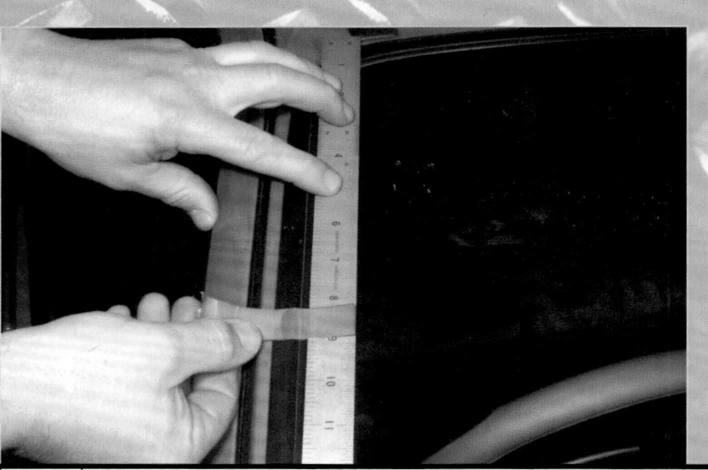

**02** With the help of an assistant (if you have one handy), lay the strip onto the car, and decide how far down the screen you're going to go. Legally-speaking, you shouldn't be lower than the wiper swept area - so how much of a 'badboy' are you? If you measure and mark the bottom of the strip with tape, you'll be sure to get it level, even if it's not legal.

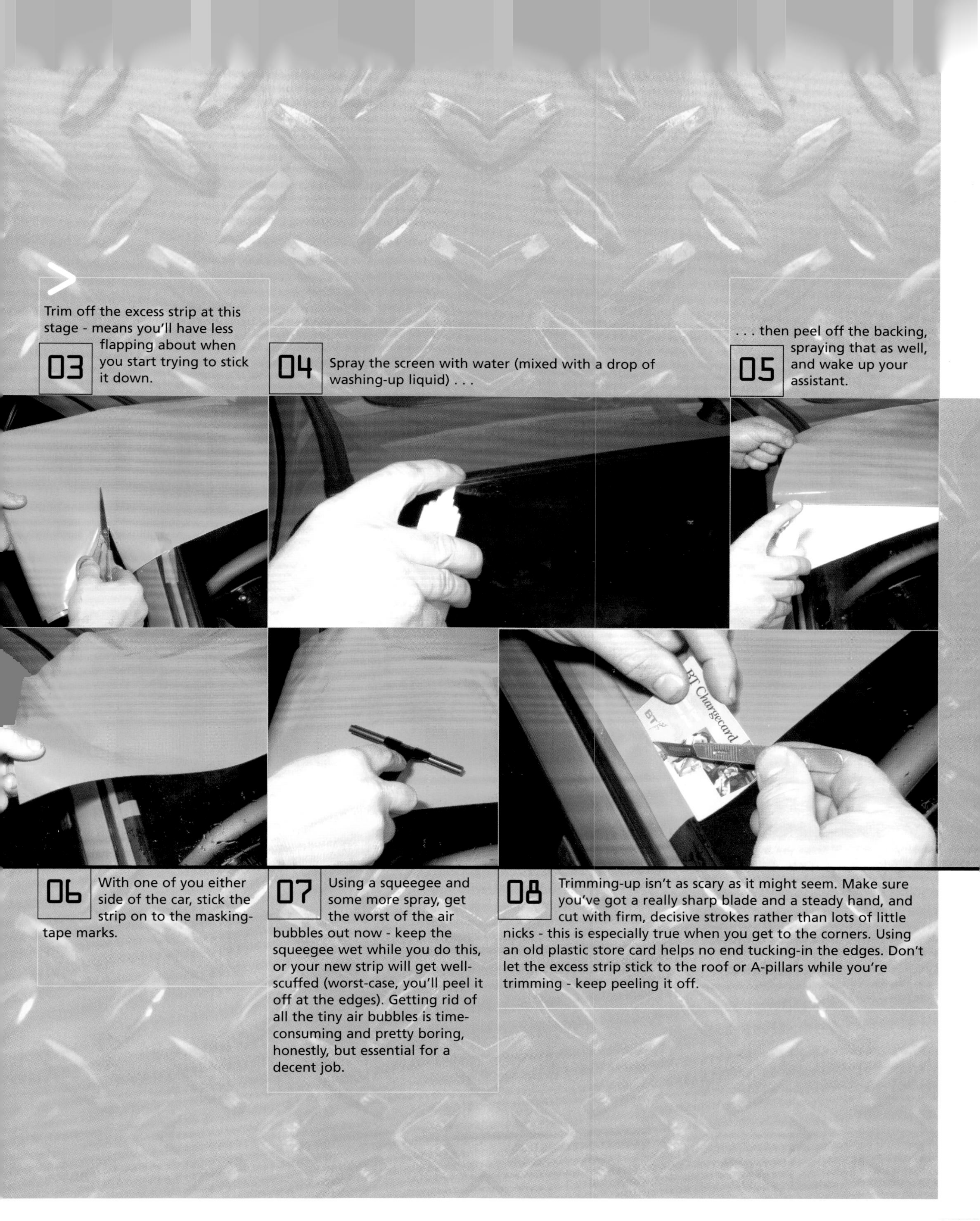


Trim off the excess strip at this stage - means you'll have less flapping about when you start trying to stick it down.

**03**

**04** Spray the screen with water (mixed with a drop of washing-up liquid) . . .

. . . then peel off the backing, spraying that as well, and wake up your assistant.

**05**

**06** With one of you either side of the car, stick the strip on to the masking-tape marks.

**07** Using a squeegee and some more spray, get the worst of the air bubbles out now - keep the squeegee wet while you do this, or your new strip will get well-scuffed (worst-case, you'll peel it off at the edges). Getting rid of all the tiny air bubbles is time-consuming and pretty boring, honestly, but essential for a decent job.

**08** Trimming-up isn't as scary as it might seem. Make sure you've got a really sharp blade and a steady hand, and cut with firm, decisive strokes rather than lots of little nicks - this is especially true when you get to the corners. Using an old plastic store card helps no end tucking-in the edges. Don't let the excess strip stick to the roof or A-pillars while you're trimming - keep peeling it off.

# Glow **for it**

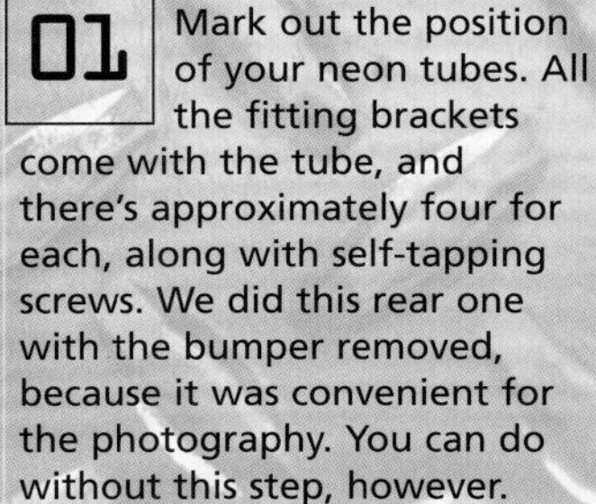

**01** Mark out the position of your neon tubes. All the fitting brackets come with the tube, and there's approximately four for each, along with self-tapping screws. We did this rear one with the bumper removed, because it was convenient for the photography. You can do without this step, however.

**Years and years ago, when 'boy racers' first appeared in the UK, jacking up a car's height was all the rage. This did nothing for the handling, but it did allow posers to show off the underside of their cars.**

Occasionally, a particular car's underside, say one with chromed suspension, would be worth showing off, and at night the owner of such a vehicle would flick a switch and this would light up his show-worthy running gear along with the road, giving a cool red foglight glow as the car cruised the streets.

That look has progressed over the years, in fact lights weren't cool for a long time, until that is someone discovered how to adapt neon lighting to car use. Then the current trend of underbody lights hit the streets - this is far more effective than the old foglight trick, because of the glow the neon tubes emit. The look of neons is out of this world – literally. You'll look like ET's mothership as you head down the street.

The kits available make it simple to add that same glow to your car. You just have to make sure you can get the car up high enough to work on, as the tubes have to fit under or behind panels so they don't directly show to the front, side or rear. This is illegal and will get you pulled faster than you can say "You're nicked son". The tubes are connected in series, ie one after the other, all the way around the car, with the transformer acting as the last connection point. The transformer is controlled by a switch housed inside the car, which needs a permanent or ignition-sourced 12 volts, plus of course an earthing point. Look on at least a day to complete the job, working solo.

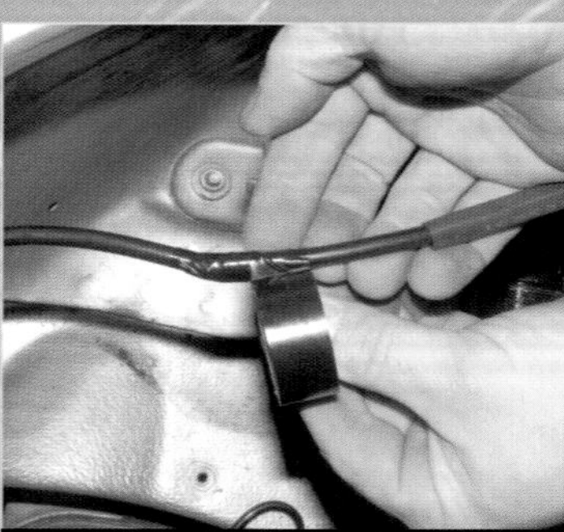

**06** . . . and wrap the joint well with insulating tape. Slide over the insulating sleeve, and tape this into place too. Can't have too much protection, y'know.

**07** Find a position for the transformer out of harm's way. We found that the vent area just at the rear of the engine bay was perfect for this, so drilled and screwed the unit in place. Connect the neon feeds and the switch wires to the transformer - check the kit instructions if necessary.

**08** Next find a space for the switch. These blank switch covers to the right of the steering column are ideal.

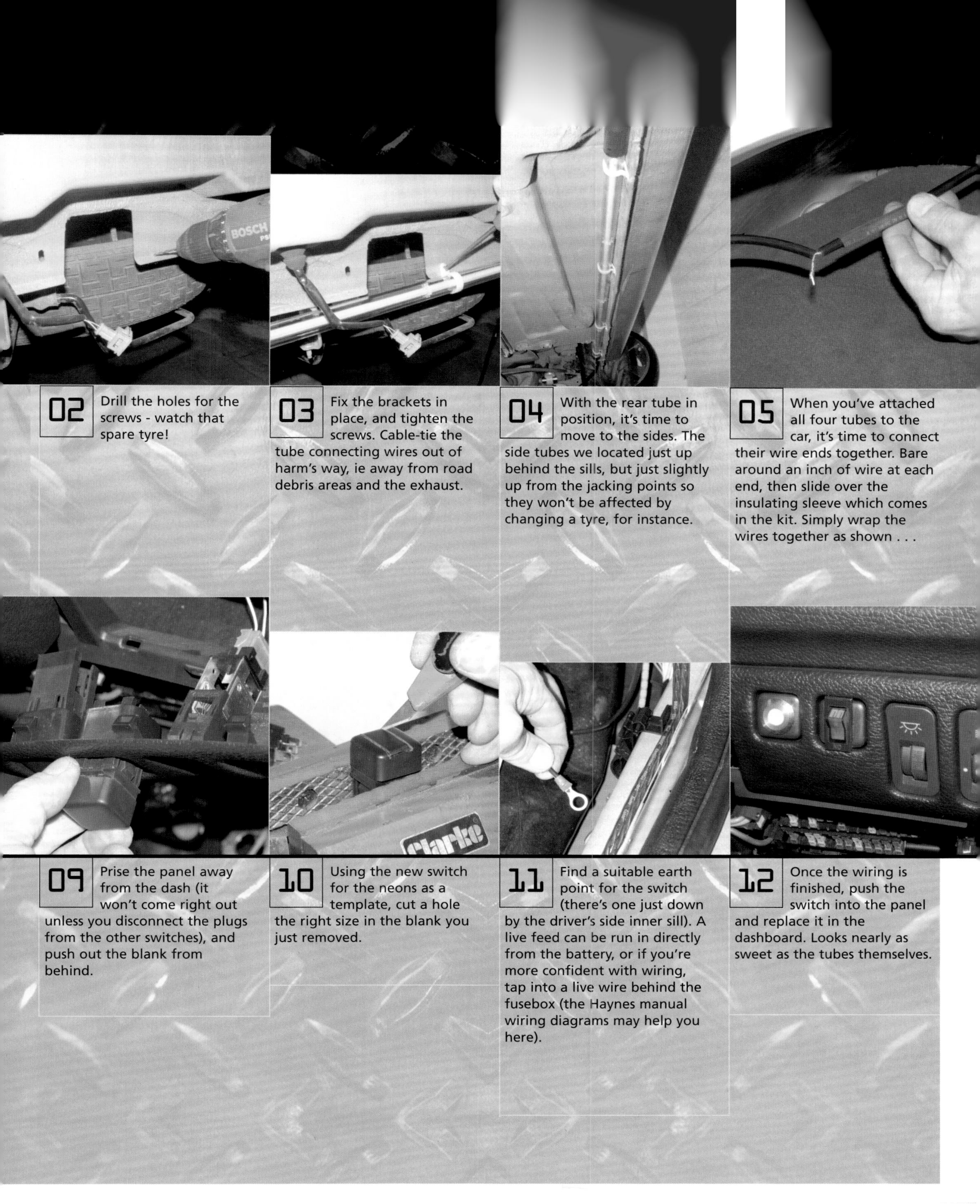


**02** Drill the holes for the screws - watch that spare tyre!

**03** Fix the brackets in place, and tighten the screws. Cable-tie the tube connecting wires out of harm's way, ie away from road debris areas and the exhaust.

**04** With the rear tube in position, it's time to move to the sides. The side tubes we located just up behind the sills, but just slightly up from the jacking points so they won't be affected by changing a tyre, for instance.

**05** When you've attached all four tubes to the car, it's time to connect their wire ends together. Bare around an inch of wire at each end, then slide over the insulating sleeve which comes in the kit. Simply wrap the wires together as shown . . .

**09** Prise the panel away from the dash (it won't come right out unless you disconnect the plugs from the other switches), and push out the blank from behind.

**10** Using the new switch for the neons as a template, cut a hole the right size in the blank you just removed.

**11** Find a suitable earth point for the switch (there's one just down by the driver's side inner sill). A live feed can be run in directly from the battery, or if you're more confident with wiring, tap into a live wire behind the fusebox (the Haynes manual wiring diagrams may help you here).

**12** Once the wiring is finished, push the switch into the panel and replace it in the dashboard. Looks nearly as sweet as the tubes themselves.

# Painting by **numbers**

This is not the section where we tell you how to respray your entire 206 in a weekend, using only spray cans, okay? Mission Impossible, we ain't. This bit's all about how to spray up your various plasticky bits before final fitting - bits such as door mirrors, light brows, spoilers, splitters - hell, even bumpers if you like. As we've no doubt said before, with anything new, fit your unpainted bits first. Make sure everything fits properly (shape and tidy up all parts as necessary), that all holes have been drilled, and all screws etc are doing their job. Then, and only when you're totally, completely happy with the fit - take them off, and get busy with the spray cans.

**01** The first job is to mask off any areas you don't want painted. Do this right at the start, or you could be sorry; on these door mirrors, we decided to mask off just at the lip before the glass, to leave a black unpainted edge - if we hadn't masked it as the very first job, we would've roughed up all the shiny black plastic next, and wrecked the edge finish.

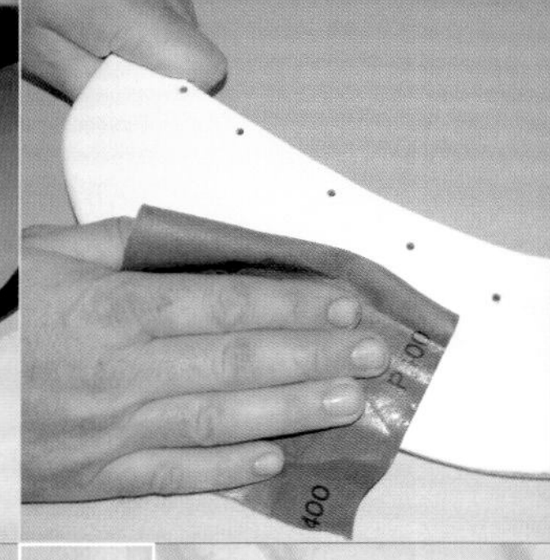

**02** Remove any unwanted 'seams' in the plastic, using fine sandpaper or wet-and-dry. Some of these seams look pretty cool, others don't - you decide. Also worth tidying up any other areas you're not happy with, fit-wise, while you're at it.

**03** Especially with 'shiny' plastic, you must rough-up the surface before spray will 'bite' to it, or - it'll flippin' flake off. Just take off the shine, no more. You can use fine wet-and-dry for this (used dry), but we prefer Scotchbrite. This stuff, which looks much like a scouring pad, is available from motor factors and bodyshops, in several grades - we used ultra-fine, which is grey. One advantage of Scotchbrite is that it's a bit easier to work into awkward corners than paper.

**04** Once the surface has been nicely 'roughened', clean up the surface using a suitable degreaser ('suitable' means a type which won't dissolve plastic!). Generally, it's ok to use methylated spirit or cellulose thinners (just don't inhale!), but test it on a not-so-visible bit first, so you don't have a disaster.

**05** Before you start spraying (if it's something smaller than a bumper) it's a good idea to try a work a screw into one of the mounting holes, to use as a 'handle', so you can turn the item to spray all sides.

**06** Another good trick is to use the screw to hang the item up on a piece of string or wire - then you can spin the item round to get the spray into awkward areas.

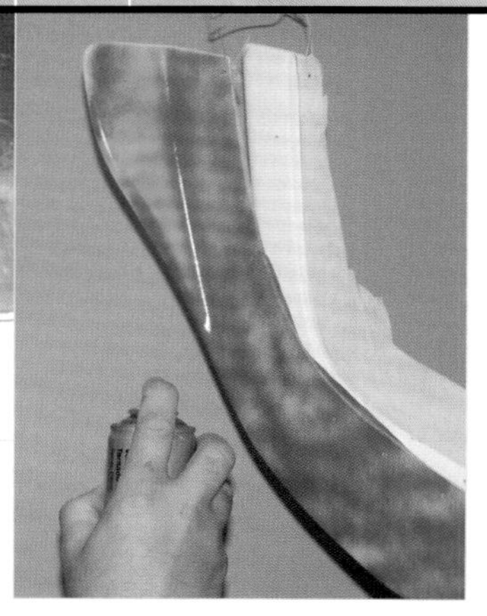

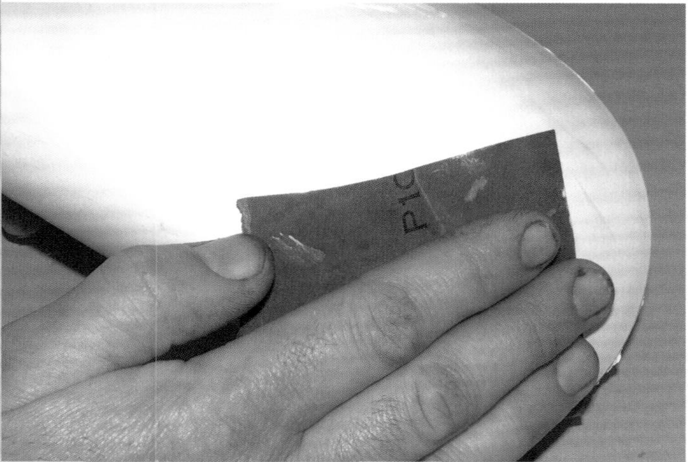

07 If you like a bit of wildlife in your paint, you can't beat the great outdoors. If it's at all windy, you'll end up with a really awful finish and overspray on everything (which can be a real pain to get off). Even indoors, if it's damp weather, you'll have real problems trying to get a shine - some kind of heater is essential if it's cold and wet (but not one with a fan - stirring up the dust is the last thing you want).

08 If you're a bit new at spraying, or if you simply don't want to balls it up, practise your technique first (steady!). Working left-right, then right-left, press the nozzle so you start spraying just before you pass the item, and follow through just past it the other side. Keep the nozzle a constant distance from the item - not in a curved arc. Don't blast the paint on too thick, or you'll have a nasty case of the runs - hold the can about 6 inches away - you're not trying to paint the whole thing in one sweep.

09 Once you've got a patchy 'mist coat' on (which might not even cover the whole thing) - stop, and let it dry (primer dries pretty quickly). Continue building up thin coats until you've got full coverage, then let it dry for half an hour or more.

10 Using 1000- or 1200-grade wet-and-dry paper (used wet), very lightly sand the whole primered surface, to take out any minor imperfections (blobs, where the nozzle was spitting) in the primer. Try not to go through the primer to the plastic, but this doesn't matter too much in small areas.

11 Rinse off thoroughly, then dry the surfaces - let it stand for a while to make sure it's *completely* dry, before starting on the top coat.

12 Make sure once again that the surfaces are clean, with no bits left behind from the drying operations. As with the primer, work up from an initial thin mist coat, allowing time for each pass to dry. As you spray, you'll soon learn how to build a nice shine without runs - any 'dry' (dull) patches are usually due to overspray landing on still-wet shiny paint. Don't worry if you can't eliminate all of these - a light cutting polish will sort it out once the paint's hardened (after several hours).

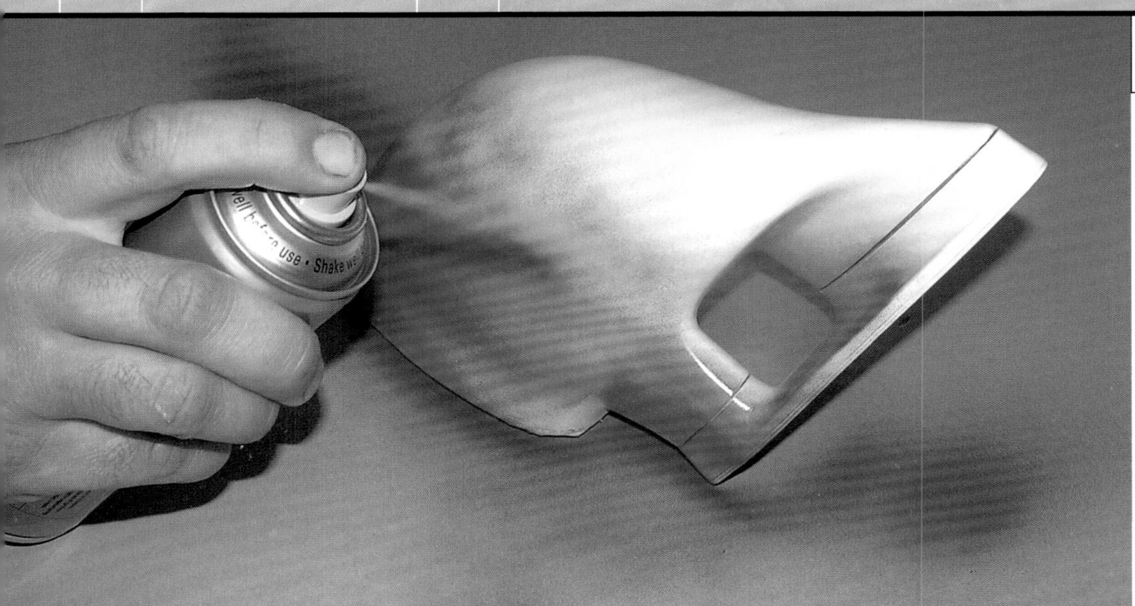

13 Especially with a colour like red (which is notorious for fading easily), it's a good idea to blow on a coat or two of clear lacquer over the top - this will also give you your shine, if you're stuck with a very 'dry' finish. It's best to apply lacquer before the final top coat is fully hardened. The spraying technique is identical, although pro sprayers say that lacquer should be applied pretty thick - just watch those runs! Lacquer also takes a good long while to dry - pick up your item too soon, for that unique fingerprint effect!

One way to tidy up the 206 lines is to do away with the door locks, and even the door handles - but be careful.

# There's no way in

Flushing the rear door handles (on 5-door models) is okay, legally/MOT-speaking, but removing the front door handles will land you in trouble, come MOT time.

Construction & Use regs require your car to have an independent mechanical means of door opening from outside (so fire-fighters can get you out, if you stick your all-action 206 on its roof, or in a ditch...) If you must lose the front handles, find some trick mirrors which have door catches built-in, underneath.

At least every 206 (apart from the billy-basic L and Style) has remote central locking as standard, meaning you're not stuck once you've ditched the lock barrels in your front doors - nice one, Peugeot.

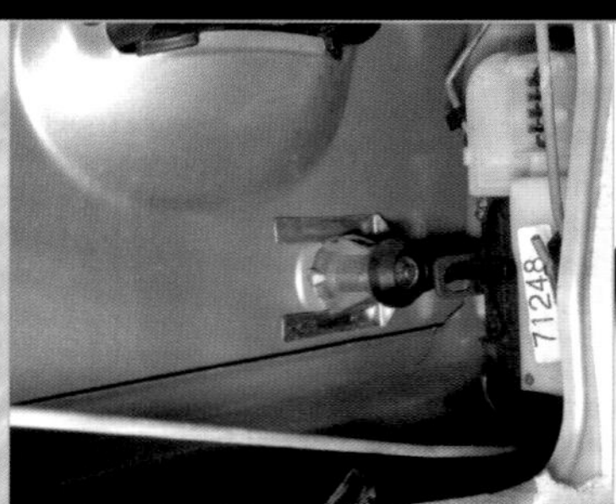


**01** First job is to remove the door card, as described in 'interiors'. With the door trim off, remove the alignment pegs from the top of the foam membrane, and carefully peel/cut back membrane to reveal the door lock barrel. Fully raise the window glass.

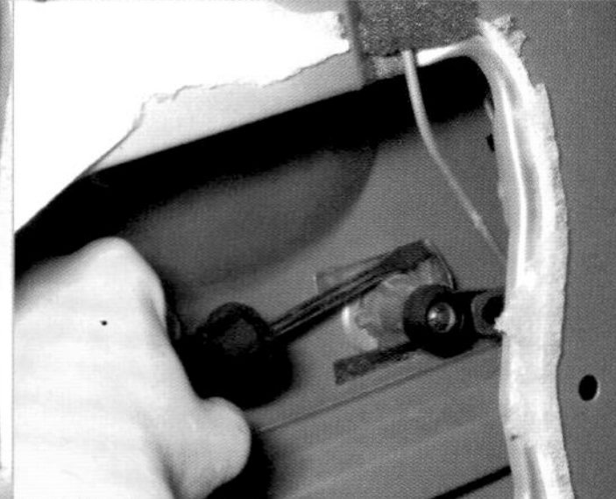

**02** Now the lock barrel needs to be removed. Take a flat-bladed screwdriver, and use it to slide off the large retaining clip from the lock cylinder. Push the tip of screwdriver against the raised part of the retaining clip until it slides out of place. Easy.

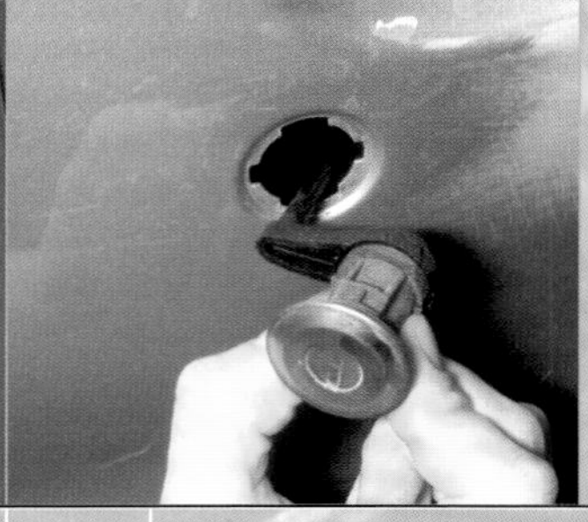

**03** Once the clip has slid out of place, just remove it from the car and store in a safe place. The lock barrel is linked to the door handle by a metal rod, which is held on by little metal clips - unclip and remove the rod completely. The lock barrel just pushes out through the door.

**04** Now it's time to strip the paint off the lock area in readiness for welding a plate over the hole. The plate actually goes in from behind, followed by a skim of filler over the top.

**05** The bodywork specialist we use for our cars (Kevin, from Avon Custom) has already cut out a piece of metal, just a bit bigger than the lock barrel hole. With one hand he holds the metal in place from inside the car, whilst with the other hand, he tack-welds the metal in place.

**06** With the metal tacked in place, the whole area gets welded up, using short, measured bursts to reduce the risk of the panel warping from excessive heat.

**07** After the welding has been completed, and an angle grinder has flattened the blobs of weld nicely, a skim of filler is applied to the area. Once the filler has been left to dry (at least 24 hours), it can be rubbed down smooth, ready for painting.

**Tricks 'n' tips**

***If your battery goes flat, you'll be locked out. We ran two thin wires from the battery terminals (with a 10-amp fuse in the live, and the ends insulated), and tucked them away for access from below in an emergency. By connecting a slave battery to these wires (do not try jump-starting), you'll put enough juice into the system to operate the locks, saving you a red face. Think it over.***

## Remote locking

If your 206 doesn't have central locking as standard, don't despair. There's several kits out there to help you towards your goal, such as the Microscan kits which we've fitted to some of our project cars. All come with good instructions, and a helpline number if you get stuck - armed with the Haynes manual wiring diagrams, your 206 could have lazyboy locks inside a day.

# Improve your handle-bling

Elsewhere in this book we mention about badge and trim removal, and its benefit in making your car look smoother overall. Well, there are other ways you can lift the appearance of your 206, by highlighting its good points. Manufacturers do this by chrome-plating certain areas in order to draw your eye to the design points.

Plenty of aftermarket extras in chrome are out there, but it's choosing ones which don't look like an add-on that'll make your car stand out. We used these chrome handle covers along with chromed light surrounds to make our Peugeot distinctive, and they worked really well, just lifting the neat design enough to enhance the overall look of the car. The quality of the parts was such that they look liked manufacturer's optional extras. They also work well with clear headlights and taillights, because of the matching chrome inside the light lenses.

This is easy stuff to do, in fact you could probably put the kettle on, and be back before it boils.

**01** The stock door handle stands out because it's black on a silver background, so the shape either needs painting to make it blend in, or enhancing to make it a highlight. The MHW Car Dynamics handles (from ABC Design) are decent pieces which should last the life of the car if fitted with care.

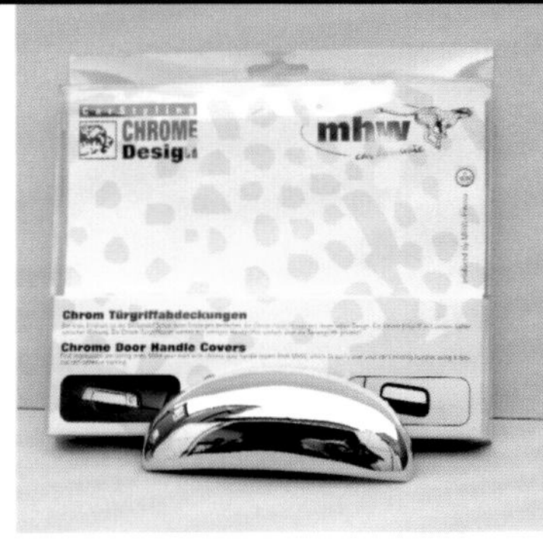


**02** The success of many jobs is down to good preparation, and this is no exception. To make sure the adhesive sticks, clean the handle thoroughly, and give it time to dry.

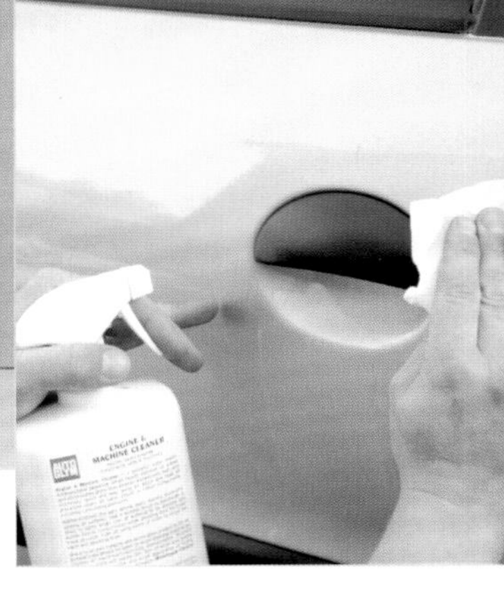

**03** It's worth doing a trial fitting of your handle covers before you peel off the backing, just to check the alignment. When you're totally happy it's all going to work, peel the backing off the sticky tape on the rear of the new handle cover.

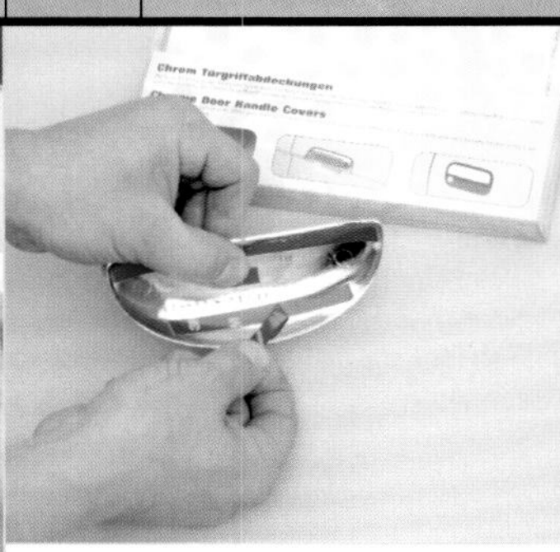

**04** Carefully position then press on the handle, making sure it's stuck in all areas. Now stand back and admire your five-minute mod.

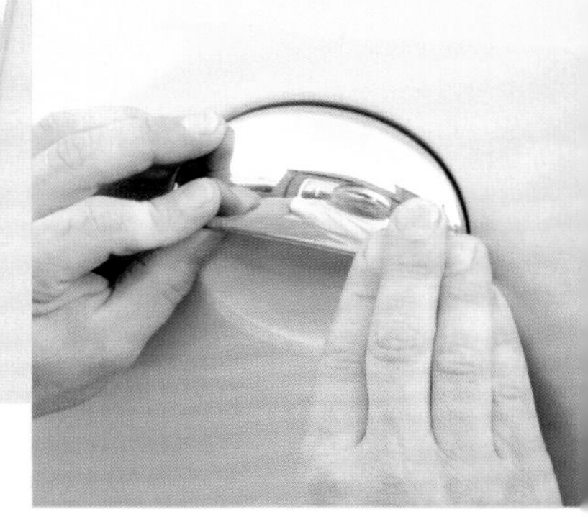

# Don't mesh with me, boy

A meshed grille or bumper is just one way to demonstrate who's the daddy of the cruise, and it does a great job of dicing any small insects or rodents foolish enough to wander into the path of your motor. So if you're sick of scrubbing off insect entrails from your paint, and fancy getting even, read on...

Which style of mesh to choose? Classic diamond-shape, or round-hole? In our humble opinion, the round-hole mesh works best on modern roundy-shaped cars (like say, a Corsa) - for everything else, we'll settle for the original and best. But wait - the choice doesn't end with what shape you want. Mesh can now be had in various anodised colours too, to match or contrast with the rest of your chosen paint scheme.

01 Anyone can mesh a hole. Ab-so-lutely anyone - it's dead easy. First, measure your hole, then cut out a roughly-sized piece of mesh, and place it over the hole. Mark the shape of the hole on the mesh for cutting, leaving some over the sides to bend around the edges of your hole.

02 Of course, holes usually have corners - and some of the sides you'll encounter aren't exactly straight. Make small cuts in the edge of the mesh at strategic points, and bending over the edges will be much easier. The main mesh panel will also stay flatter, and you'll be less stressed, too.

03 There's loads of ways to secure your mesh. One of the most permanent is to use small self-tapping screws, but this won't always be possible. You can use mastic (quick-setting, exterior-use type), builder's 'no-nails' adhesive, or Isopon P40. Mastic can be cut once it's set, meaning the mesh can be removed when the panel's being sprayed.

04 Now for the really meshy part. Press the mesh into place, and smooth your chosen adhesive on by hand, to 'squidge' it over the mesh. Keep the adhesive off parts of the mesh which you'll see from outside.

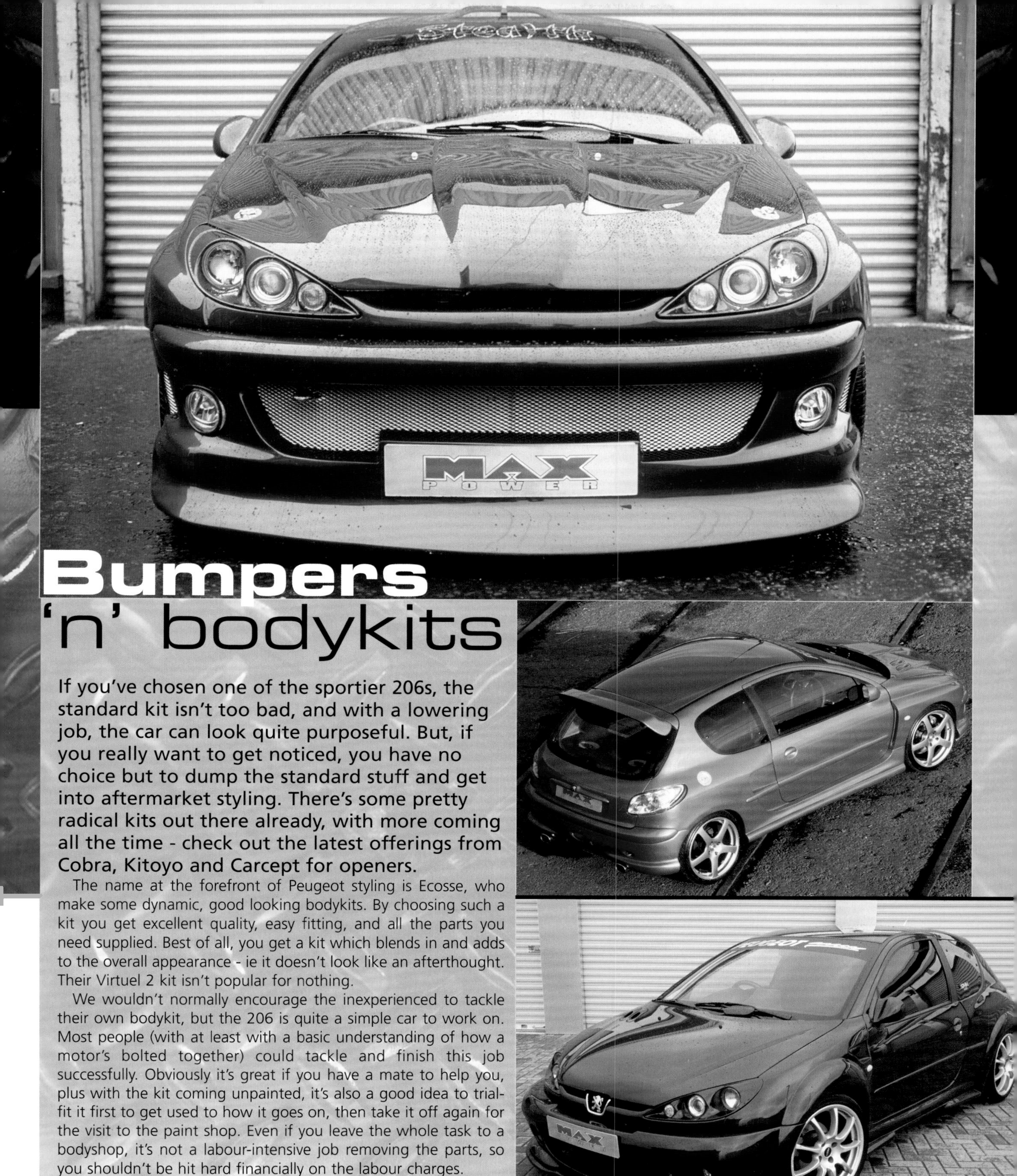


# Bumpers 'n' bodykits

**If you've chosen one of the sportier 206s, the standard kit isn't too bad, and with a lowering job, the car can look quite purposeful. But, if you really want to get noticed, you have no choice but to dump the standard stuff and get into aftermarket styling. There's some pretty radical kits out there already, with more coming all the time - check out the latest offerings from Cobra, Kitoyo and Carcept for openers.**

The name at the forefront of Peugeot styling is Ecosse, who make some dynamic, good looking bodykits. By choosing such a kit you get excellent quality, easy fitting, and all the parts you need supplied. Best of all, you get a kit which blends in and adds to the overall appearance - ie it doesn't look like an afterthought. Their Virtuel 2 kit isn't popular for nothing.

We wouldn't normally encourage the inexperienced to tackle their own bodykit, but the 206 is quite a simple car to work on. Most people (with at least with a basic understanding of how a motor's bolted together) could tackle and finish this job successfully. Obviously it's great if you have a mate to help you, plus with the kit coming unpainted, it's also a good idea to trial-fit it first to get used to how it goes on, then take it off again for the visit to the paint shop. Even if you leave the whole task to a bodyshop, it's not a labour-intensive job removing the parts, so you shouldn't be hit hard financially on the labour charges.

# Front bumper

**01** To get to the front bumper bolts you first have to remove the grille (described later in this section). Unscrew the three Torx screws on top of the bumper.

**02** The headlights also need to come out, to reach the bolts which connect the bumper to the front wing (see our 'lights & bulbs' section for headlight removal).

**03** Next, undo and remove the bolts underneath the bumper.

**04** It's a good idea at this stage to remove the front arch liner, so take out the plastic plugs locating it . . .

**05** . . . then you can undo the screws which connect the arch liner to the bumper at the front edge.

**06** Remove the arch liner, and put it to one side. There's new glassfibre arches to go in eventually, but you may want to do the arch extensions first.

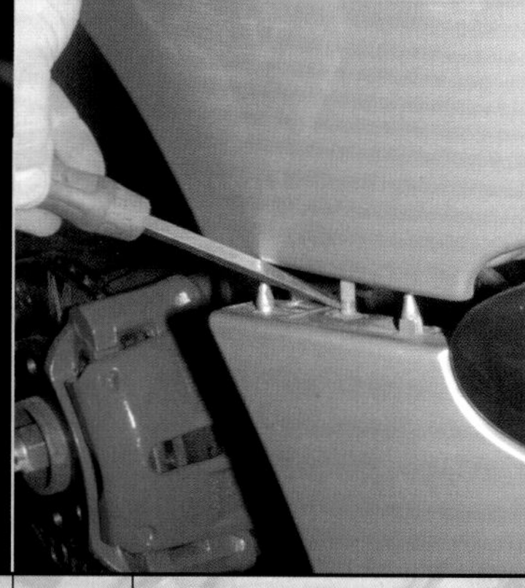

**07** With all the bolts out, you can lever the bumper off the wing, to separate the locating lug.

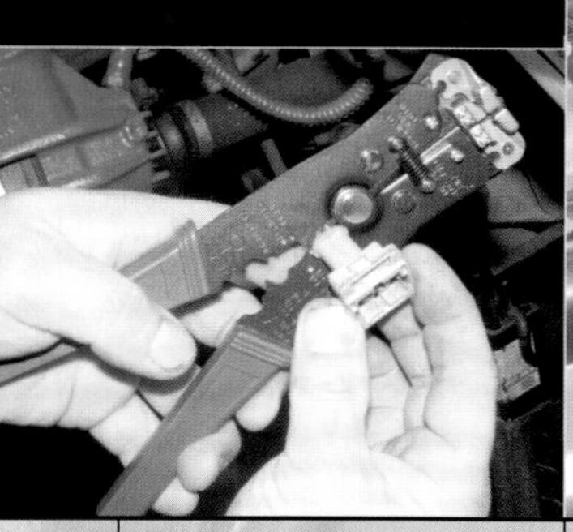

**08** For those of you with factory front fogs, disconnect the foglight wiring plugs. As you'll be replacing the standard foglights with aftermarket items from the Ecosse kit, cut off the factory connector. This will be re-wired later when the spotlights go in.

**09** The front bumper should now pull off its mountings. It's not heavy, so you should be okay by yourself.

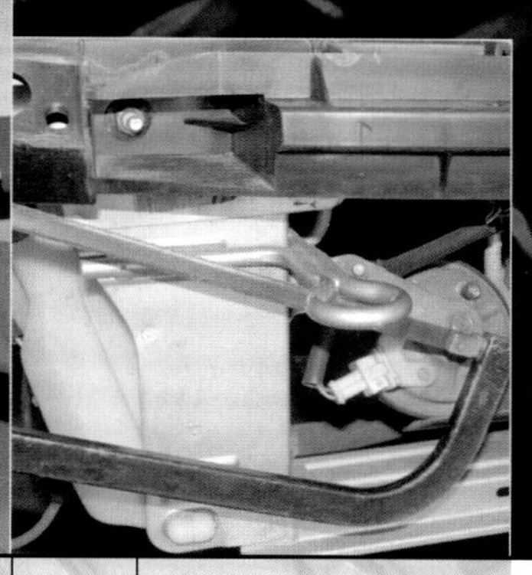

**10** As the front towing eye can no longer be used, it should be hacksawed off, to prevent any clearance issues behind the new bumper.

**11** Trial-fit the bumper first, to make sure it goes on and all the bolt holes line up without a problem.

**12** Bolt the new bumper into place, using as many of the original fixing points as possible.

**13** Underneath, the bumper has a new bracket, for which we have to mark and drill a new mounting hole. As this is directly beneath the radiator, don't drill too far; just break through the sheet metal.

**14** With the new bumper in place, your 206 should look like this – tough and purposeful. With the new spots wired-in (see 'lights & bulbs'), you'll be able to flood the roads with light, come the dark hours.

**Tricks 'n' tips**

*Always do a basic trial fitting of your new bumpers, preferably as soon as they arrive, and definitely before you start drilling any holes in them. You won't get your money back if you've tried to mod them yourself. Expect a little 'adjustment' to be needed to make them fit, but bear in mind you might have been sent the wrong ones, before you go too far.*

# Rear bumper

As part of the Ecosse Virtuel 2 package for the 206, the rear bumper extends the bodywork downwards and gives a pair of great openings for dual exhaust tailpipes (which we cover elsewhere in this book). The same hole is left for the foglight, which we filled with a crystal unit to match the overall theme on our 206.

01 To remove the bumper you first have to take our the arch liners, which means pulling out their plastic plugs, then removing the screw at the back, holding the liner to the bumper.

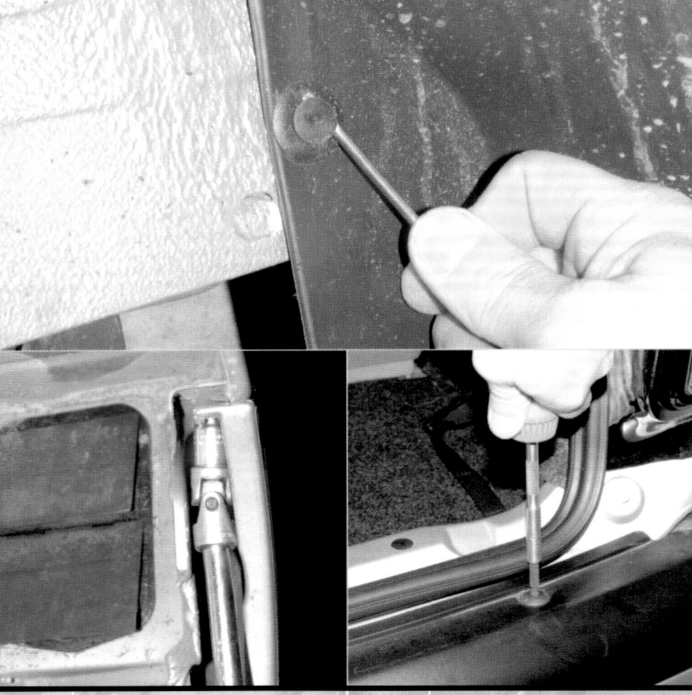

02 The arch liner should then come out. There are replacement sections which come with the package, which use the standard arch mounting points.

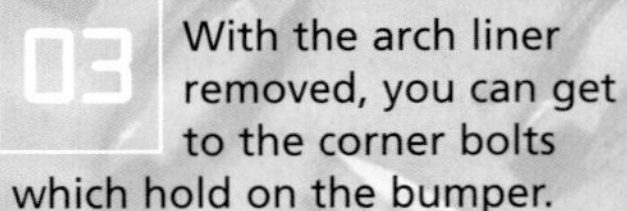

03 With the arch liner removed, you can get to the corner bolts which hold on the bumper.

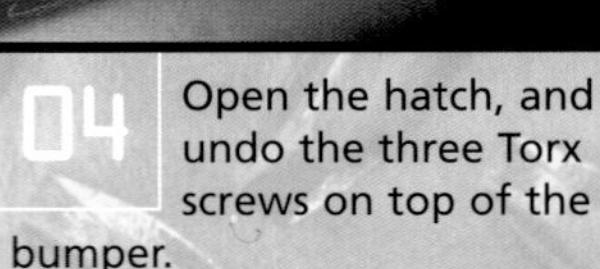

04 Open the hatch, and undo the three Torx screws on top of the bumper.

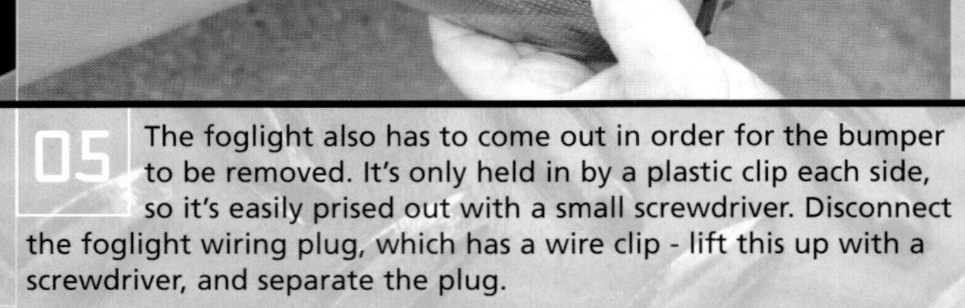

05 The foglight also has to come out in order for the bumper to be removed. It's only held in by a plastic clip each side, so it's easily prised out with a small screwdriver. Disconnect the foglight wiring plug, which has a wire clip - lift this up with a screwdriver, and separate the plug.

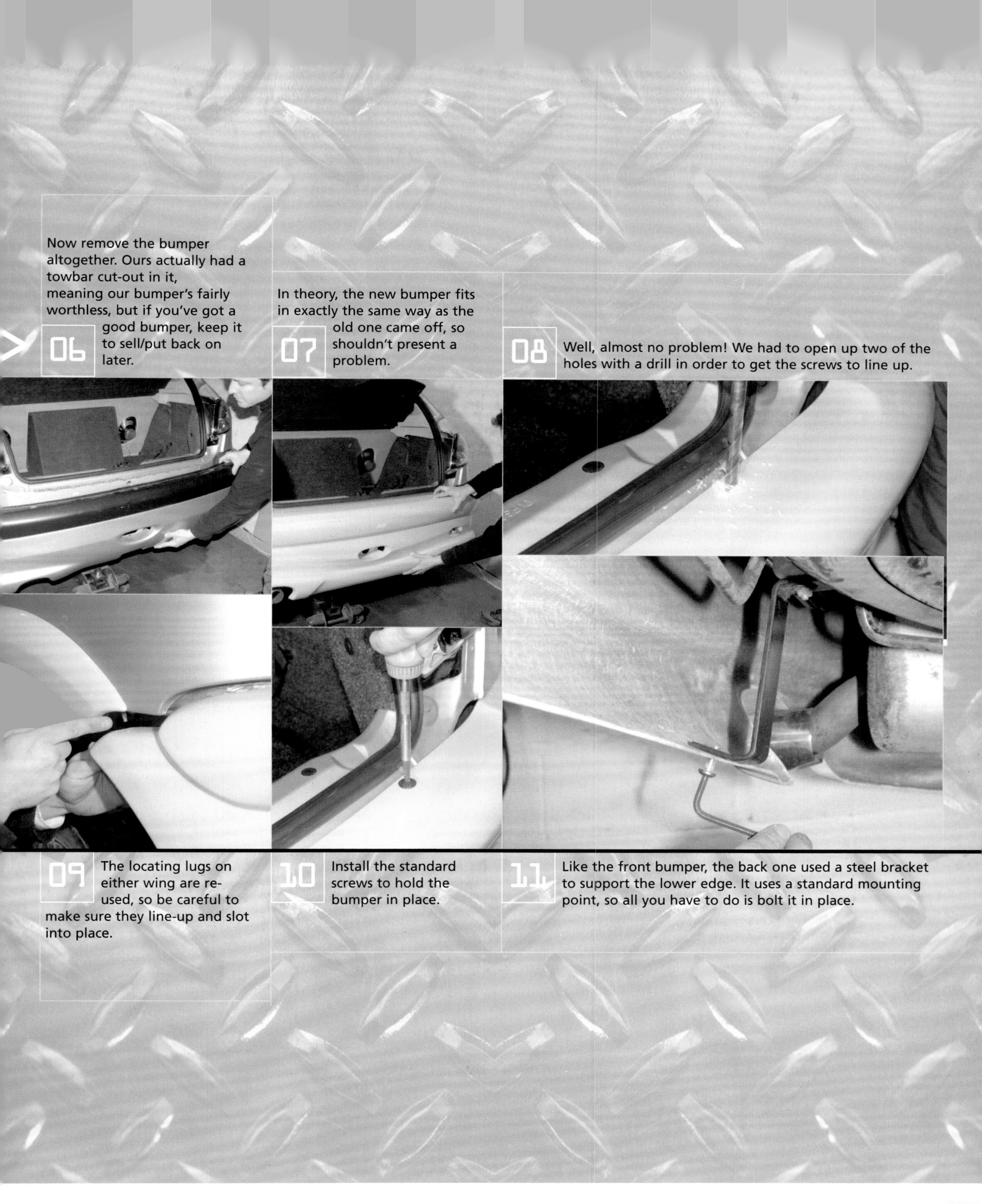

Now remove the bumper altogether. Ours actually had a towbar cut-out in it, meaning our bumper's fairly worthless, but if you've got a good bumper, keep it to sell/put back on later.

06

In theory, the new bumper fits in exactly the same way as the old one came off, so shouldn't present a problem.

07

08

Well, almost no problem! We had to open up two of the holes with a drill in order to get the screws to line up.

09

The locating lugs on either wing are re-used, so be careful to make sure they line-up and slot into place.

10

Install the standard screws to hold the bumper in place.

11

Like the front bumper, the back one used a steel bracket to support the lower edge. It uses a standard mounting point, so all you have to do is bolt it in place.

# Side **skirts and** arches

**Obviously, it's no good having front and rear bumpers which add to the ground effect of your 206, then not putting on the skirts to hold the look down each side. Likewise for the arch extensions, which bolt on to each corner and give extra wheel coverage, as well as widening the body to make it look more aggressive.**

Both these items really help finish off the dramatic improvement on the standard wedge-like 206 body. And both are easy to install, but need all the plastic arch liners removing to allow access to the bolts which will fix the arch extensions to the wings.

**01** Unscrew the arch liner inside the arch, and at this rear position under the sill. Remove the arch liner and lob it – it'll be replaced with a new glassfibre piece anyway.

**02** Using the templates supplied in the Ecosse kit (which hug the 206 body, to make them very accurate), mark the arch extension holes on each wing front and rear.

**03** Drill the holes, first with a 3mm drill as a pilot hole, then out to 8mm. Take it slowly here, because a big drill can easily grab the thin bodywork and twist it.

**04** Fit the arch into position, feeding the studs through the drilled holes. Finger-tighten the nuts on the back of their threads to hold it in place.

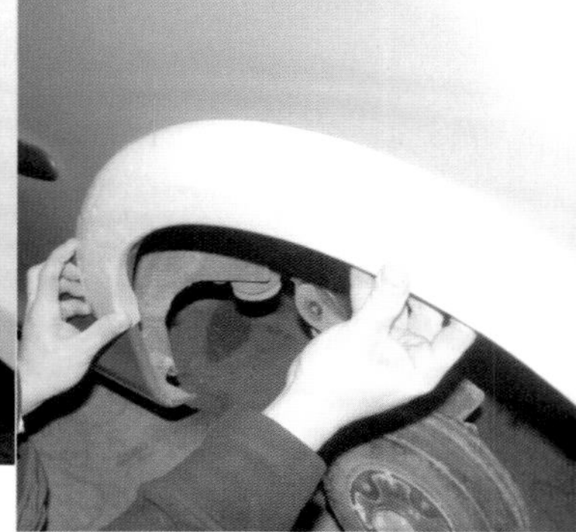

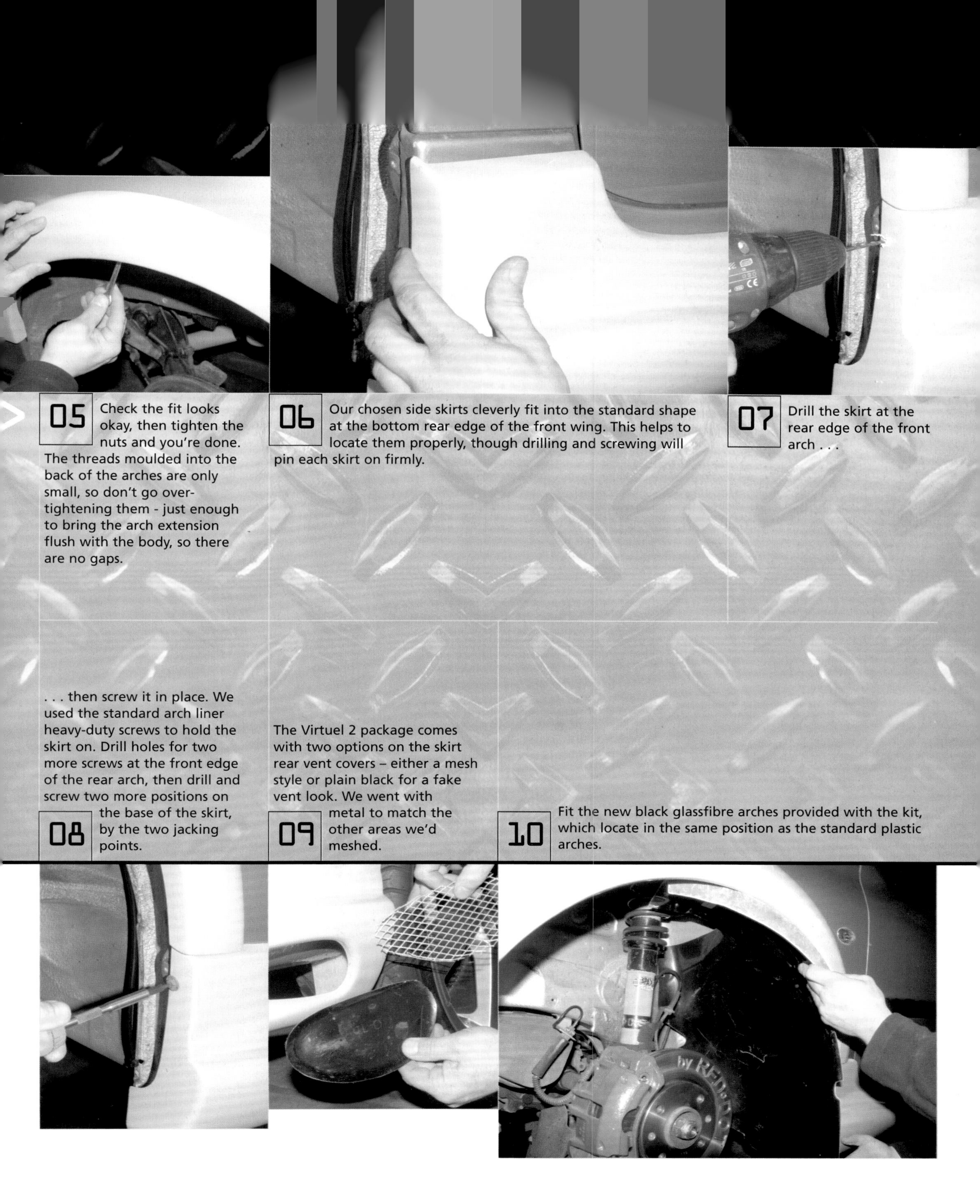

05 Check the fit looks okay, then tighten the nuts and you're done. The threads moulded into the back of the arches are only small, so don't go over-tightening them - just enough to bring the arch extension flush with the body, so there are no gaps.

06 Our chosen side skirts cleverly fit into the standard shape at the bottom rear edge of the front wing. This helps to locate them properly, though drilling and screwing will pin each skirt on firmly.

07 Drill the skirt at the rear edge of the front arch . . .

08 . . . then screw it in place. We used the standard arch liner heavy-duty screws to hold the skirt on. Drill holes for two more screws at the front edge of the rear arch, then drill and screw two more positions on the base of the skirt, by the two jacking points.

09 The Virtuel 2 package comes with two options on the skirt rear vent covers – either a mesh style or plain black for a fake vent look. We went with metal to match the other areas we'd meshed.

10 Fit the new black glassfibre arches provided with the kit, which locate in the same position as the standard plastic arches.

# How to spoil your 206

Although the sportier 206s have a standard rear spoiler, it's just too subtle. To help enhance the rear end, the Virtuel 2 package from Ecosse provides a well-shaped, high spoiler much like the WRC Peugeots, only these versions have an extra trick in the form of a pair of LED indicators, mounted either side. The trickiest part of this job is marking out the spoiler mounting holes - effectively, you're doing it blind. The method we used was to first make sure we were happy with how the spoiler was going to mount, then dab some paint around the edge of each spoiler hole, therefore when it went on to the tail hatch, it left marks. Simple when you know how. Fitting a spoiler is one time you'll be glad of a mate to help.

**01** To mount our spoiler, this plastic trim piece at the top corner of the tailgate has to come off. Push through the two plastic centre pins to release the mounting plugs holding the trim piece to the hatch. Check your spoiler's instructions - removing this item may not be necessary in every case.

**02** To mark the spoiler mounting holes, simply dab some paint around the holes on the spoiler itself, then try the spoiler in place before it dries.

**07** Thread the indicator wires from both sides down through the sleeve. This is very fiddly, and may take some time. Attaching the indicator wiring to a piece of stiffer (but still thin) wire may help to push it through.

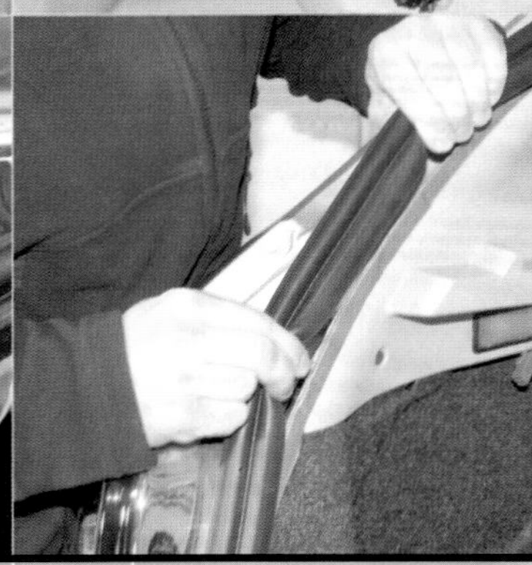

**08** Carefully pull off the tailgate rubber sealing strip, just above the rear light cluster . . .

**03** Line up the spoiler and press into place, which will mark the tailgate with mounting point holes. Remove the spoiler, and check that the marks are an equal distance from the edge of the tailgate each side - this means the spoiler should be central.

**04** Drill through the tailgate, and you'll find the holes come out roughly where the plastic trim piece you removed earlier was positioned.

**05** Our LED indicators fit in either side of the spoiler, into the oval recesses. They're equipped with retaining clips and a rubber seal, both of which are fitted to the light unit before offering it in place. Of course, there's also the associated wiring, which you feed into the spoiler, and out the back.

**06** Now another hole has to be drilled in the tailgate, for the wiring. Before pushing the wires inside the tailgate, add a rubber grommet to the new hole, to stop the wire chafing through on the sharp metal edge. With the tailgate open again, unclip the wiring sleeve at the top to get access to the inner metalwork.

**09** . . . and unscrew the inner panel to get access to the rear light wiring.

**10** Undo the rear light cluster nuts, and pull out the light to get to the indicator wiring. According to the Haynes manual wiring diagrams, the left indicator live is a white wire, with the right one a beige wire. In both cases, the earth is green/yellow. Join up the appropriate wires . . .

**11** . . . and check for the correct result. Don't often see lights up there - nice touch.

**12** Lastly, mount the spoiler in place, and do up the mounting bolts good 'n' tight. If you're worried about water leaks into the boot, apply a good blob of silicone sealant around the various holes before final fitting (that's after you've had it sprayed).

**Achtung!**

*Wire colours may vary. The Haynes manual wiring diagram also gives you wire ID code numbers, which are more reliable. Or you can use a voltmeter or test light*

# Front **grille**

In the case of Ecosse's 206 grille, fitting can be done separately from the rest of the bodykit. The Esquiss badgeless grille is separate to the front bumper, and uses all the standard mounting points, so is simple to install. As it removes the Peugeot lion badge in the centre, it leaves a slight recess in the bonnet lip, which you may want to address at a later date in the bodyshop, but otherwise it makes the nose of the car look a whole lot meaner.

**01** The standard grille uses a whopping great badge, and extends right across below the headlights. Getting rid is essential, whether doing the rest of the bodykit or not. With the bonnet open, remove the two top Torx screws either end of the grille opening.

**02** There's one more screw which isn't as easy to get to, just in front of the bonnet catch.

**03** The grille's also held on with plastic push-in plugs, which have to be levered out.

**04** All that's holding the grille on now are two clips either end, below the headlights. These simply click into place as the grille goes on in the factory, so as the grille's being removed, you have to ease these out with a long screwdriver. Be careful here – the clips break easily, as we found out...

**05** The new grille comes complete with a pair of mesh panels, which you can either fit now (see the section on meshing), or wait 'til after the grille panel's been sprayed. Either way, we don't need to stress the importance of mesh to the final look, do we? When it's finished, the new grille clips back on just like the old one came off. That's quality for you.

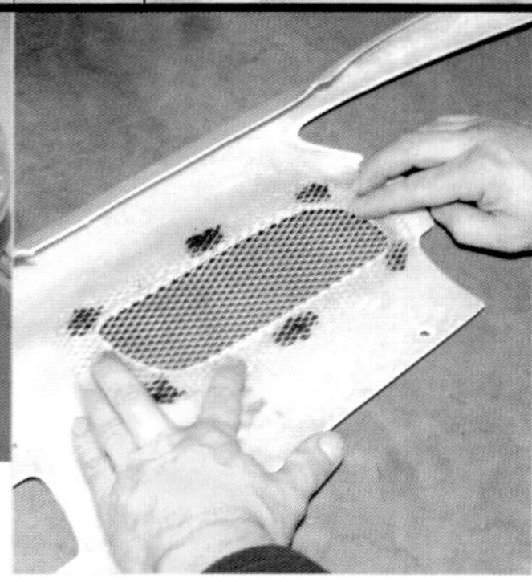

# Wheelarch mods

**The law states that your wide rubber shouldn't be so wide that it sticks out from your arches, and the MOT crew will not be impressed if your new rubber's rubbing, either.**

This presents something of a problem, if you're determined to get 19s or 20s on, especially if the car's also having a radical drop job (like our 206, on coilovers). If you've got rubbing problems on 17s or 18s, something's very wrong. Check that your wheels are the right offset (see *'Wheels & tyres'*), or chat to your wheel supplier about spacers. 206 arches are quite roomy, so you should only hit major problems above 18-inch rims.

Sometimes, all you need to stop those nasty grinding noises is a small amount of violence. Any non-vital protrusions into the under-arch area can be trimmed off or flattened with a hammer. Also, try removing those (oh-so-practical) wheelarch liners.

Serious wheelarch mods are best done at a bodyshop. Having the arches professionally rolled, using the proper tool, should only cost about £50 per arch (assuming they haven't also got rust or filler to deal with as well). Less satisfactory would be having the arch edges cut or ground off - this leaves a bare-metal edge, and encourages rust (as well as weakening the wings).

The best answer to arches which just aren't roomy enough is, of course, a wide-arch bodykit. And bank loans are so cheap these days.

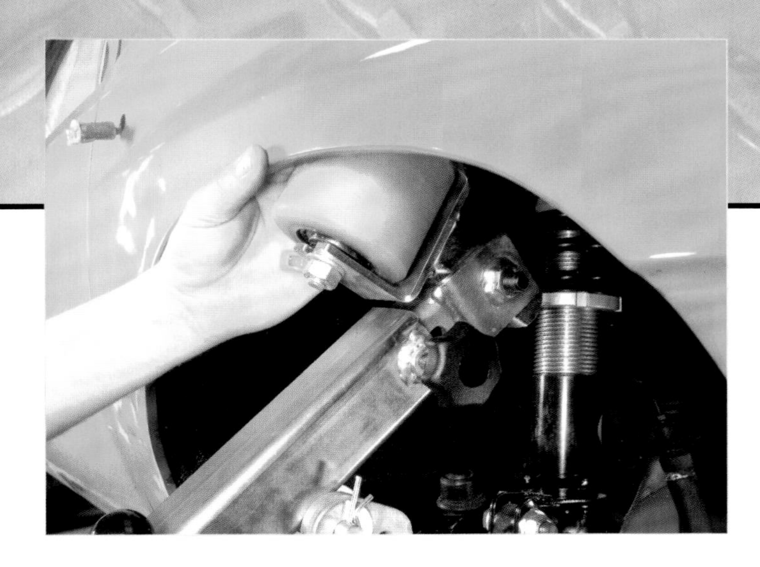

# Bonnets and **vents**

**Once you've got your bodykit on, it's only natural you'll want a bonnet vent, isn't it? Respect. But this is one scary job to tackle yourself, unless you're really that good, or that brave. Plenty of options - you can get little louvres stamped in as well, to complement your Evo, Impreza, Integrale or F50 main vent.**

For maximum respect in the bonnet department, you can't beat carbon fibre. If you can find a ready-made, pre-vented carbon bonnet, it's not even hard to fit (just hard to pay for??).

Back in the real world, the 206 has a bonnet vent straight from the factory. Unfortunately, it isn't used to direct air into the engine, but instead into the car. This doesn't mean you can't make it look trick though, and thankfully Ecosse have a neat twin nostril 'Cristal' vent to replace the naff factory piece. Fitting's très simple, but once finished, it'll set your car apart from others and give your 206's styling a lift.

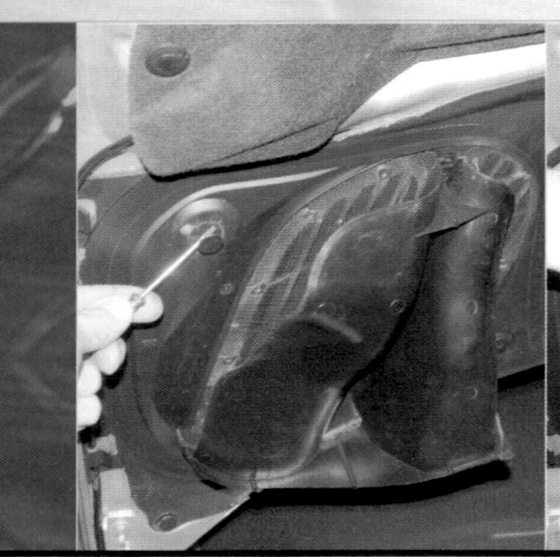

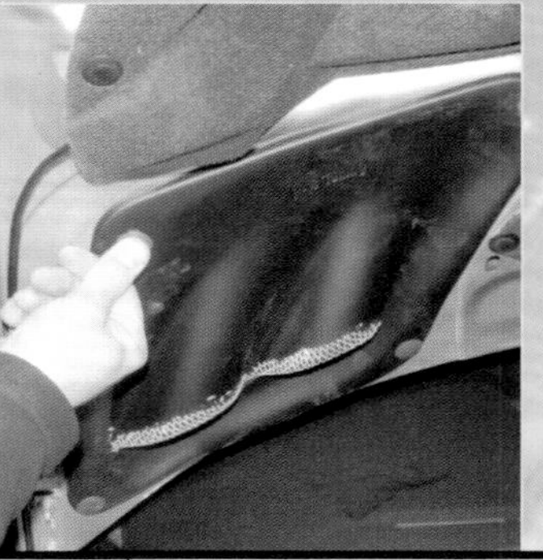

**01** The standard vent does nothing more than allow air into the car. When the car's moving, a high-pressure area forms at the back of the bonnet, so the vent gets force-fed air. Pity it's not going into the engine! To remove the standard vent, prop the bonnet open. Lever out the four plugs at each corner of the vent - these plugs are used all over the car to hold on plastic parts, so you've probably seen them before.

**02** Remove the standard vent and 'round-file' it. Or keep it, if you're thinking of turning the car back to standard at a later date.

**03** The new vent looks much more purposeful, and keeping it black makes it more menacing still. It can easily be sprayed if you want, and would take very little preparation for spraying as it has a smooth finish. Naturally, it's also equipped with meshed holes.

**04** Hold the new vent in position, and, using the four plugs supplied in the kit, fix it into place. The finished vent sits almost flush with the bodywork, but looks heaps better with those twin nostrils.

Not happy with your 206's 'pensioner blue' paint? Time to call in the pros. There's no such thing as a simple DIY respray (not one that'll look good afterwards, at any rate). We just thought you'd like to see some of the stages involved.

**01** A respray involves massive amounts of rubbing-down - and not just between the various coats, either. Even perfectly-sound original paint has to have a touch of the rough stuff, to take the shine off, and give the new primer something to "bite" to. Edges are favourite areas for paint to start lifting and peeling, so nothing can be missed.

**02** Doing a full respray means getting all those door shuts and other areas of painted metal inside, but not the dash, seats, and carpets (unless you're going to completely gut the entire dash and interior afterwards). You can never do too much masking, and the lads at Avon Custom know this better than anyone.

**03** Hang on, are you sure that's still our 206 under there? For a full respray, it's often better to remove fixed glass completely, rather than spend time masking it all up. That means windscreen, tailgate, and all the side glass. Still fancy having a go yourself?

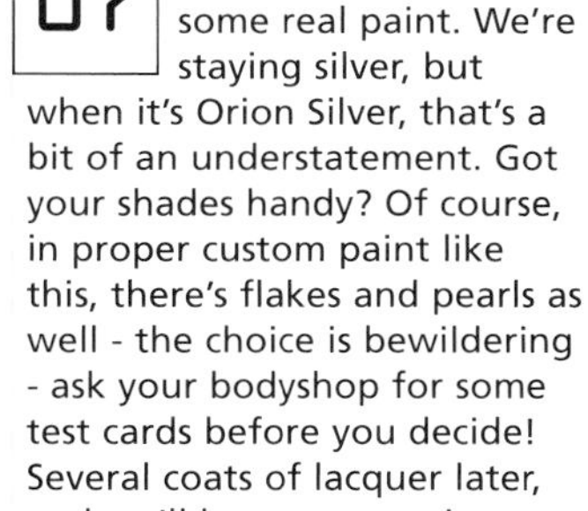

**04** Mixing the paint is an important, but often overlooked, stage in any spraying process - even ambient temperatures have a bearing on the final paint mix. Topcoats and lacquer especially have complex mixing ratios for the thinners, hardener, activator, and any 'flex' additives for bumpers and such - get it wrong, and even top-notch paint like this won't work.

**05** Making sure the paint surface is clean between steps is another often-overlooked essential item. Our bodywork experts use a water-based wash, as solvent-based products can lift the paint (or react with the next coat). The final stage is cleaning using tack-rags (net-like material, impregnated with resin - very sticky, picks up any bits).

**06** What's this? Spraying primer - that's pretty boring, isn't it? Well, no - this green stuff's an epoxy primer, used to ensure good paint adhesion on any bodywork that's had "extreme" work done. The main primer for our chosen colour is actually metallic itself, which enhances the finished shine. Metallic primers (base coats) are unique to House of Kolor, apparently. Still think it's boring?

**07** Now we're ready for some real paint. We're staying silver, but when it's Orion Silver, that's a bit of an understatement. Got your shades handy? Of course, in proper custom paint like this, there's flakes and pearls as well - the choice is bewildering - ask your bodyshop for some test cards before you decide! Several coats of lacquer later, and we'll have an amazing shine.

# Lights & bulbs



## Being scene

Lights - one of the easiest and coolest ways to trick up your 206. Several options here, so we'll start at the front, and work back.

# Headlights

## Almost nothing influences the look of your 206 more than the front end, so the headlights play a crucial role.

### What's available?

The popular cheap option is stick-on headlight 'brows', available in all sorts of styles. Brows are best sprayed to match the car, before fitting - most are fitted using stick-on Velcro pads. Street-cred on the cheap (as long as you choose wisely).

Another cheap option is again stick-on - this time, it's stick-on covers which give the twin-headlight look. This is basically a sheet of vinyl/plastic (shaped to the headlights, and colour-matched to your car) with two holes cut in it. Dead easy to fit, but dare we say, a bit tacky? Just our opinion. A cheap and simple way to get close to the twin-light look.

If you want tinted headlights, you could try spray-tinting them, but go easy on the spray. Turning your headlights from clear glass to non-see-through is plain daft, even if it's done in the name of style. A light tint is quite effective, and gives you the chance to colour-match to your 206.

**Pub trivia**

*The popular twin-headlight look was derived from a cunning tweak first employed in the Touring Cars, years ago. Some teams homologated a twin-headlight unit, but for racing, turned one pair of the 'headlights' into air inlets, to direct air from the front of the car to brake ducts or into the engine air intakes, as required. Think about it - why else would the touring cars bother with headlight mods? Until recently, there were no night races!*

A very popular look on the 206 is the all-round crystal lights, and yes, you can also get headlights this style. Make sure they're UK-legal (which means avoiding the cheap rubbish), and they should plug straight in - no awkward roadside conversations with the dibble, then.

Finally, the most popular choice in headlight upgrades - Morette twin headlights. Pricey, but so worth it - and you don't even start a 206 project unless you've got cash to splash. Maximum attitude, so no-one's gonna accuse you of owning a 'girly' Peugeot ever again!

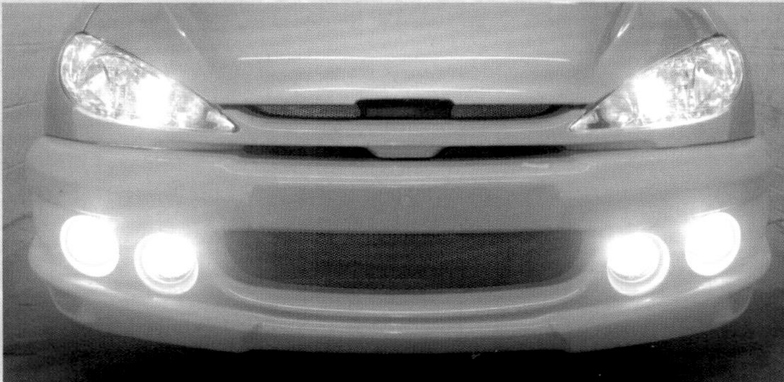

# Headlight brows

This is the cheap n' cheerful approach, and it really doesn't get much simpler than this. Is there any benefit with fitting headlight covers? Er, no, except that is that it'll make your car look different from all the other 206s. But they don't affect the light you'll see at night. This is even a mod you can 'undo' easily, if your MOT geezer objects. So what do you usually get? Two bits of plastic, and two strips of Velcro - but this time, our kit was a little different.

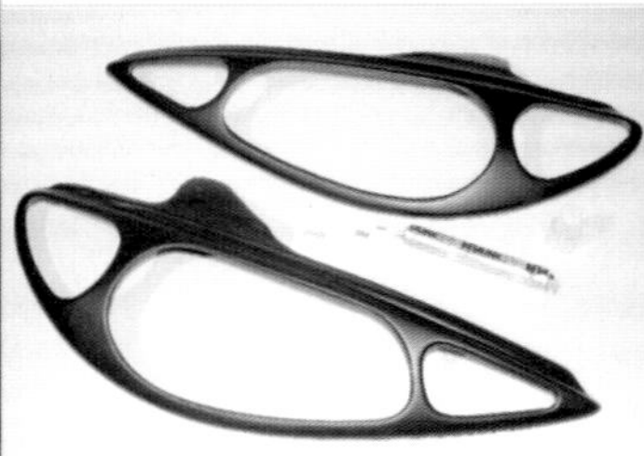

**01** These RGM light masks come complete with strong adhesive and a cleaner-impregnated tissue to thoroughly clean the headlight glass. The headlight function isn't badly affected by fitting these - they just 'divide up' the three main parts of the light.

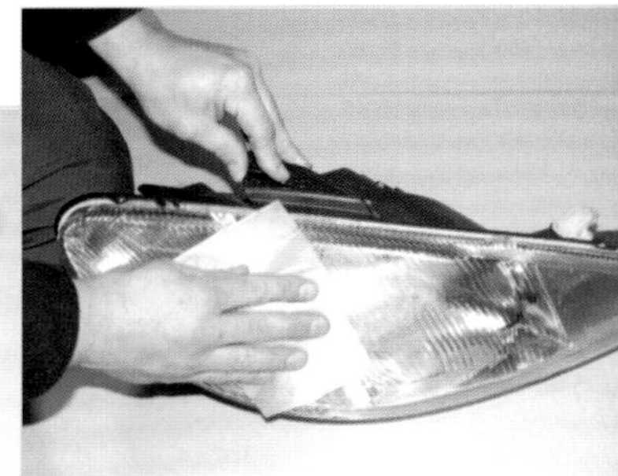

**02** To make a decent job of fitting these masks, it's best to remove the headlight completely, as described later in this Chapter. With the headlight out, clean it thoroughly using the supplied tissue. Actually, it's best to wash the lights first to get any major dirt and bugs off, then once dry go over it with the tissue.

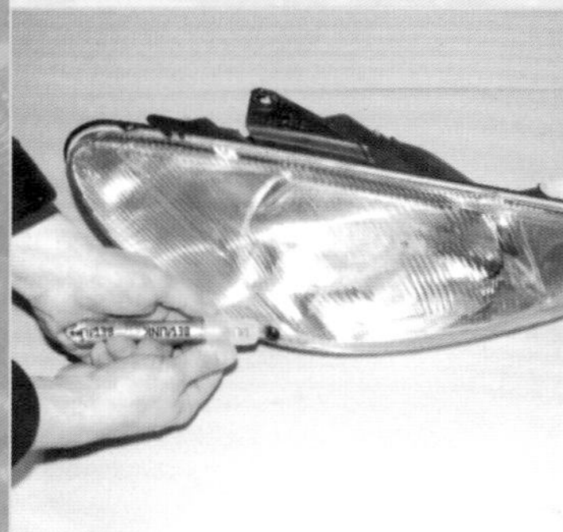

**03** Check the fit of the covers on the light, and fix the adhesive in small dabs to all areas behind the mask. Don't go mad here, because too much adhesive will just squeeze out once the mask goes on anyway.

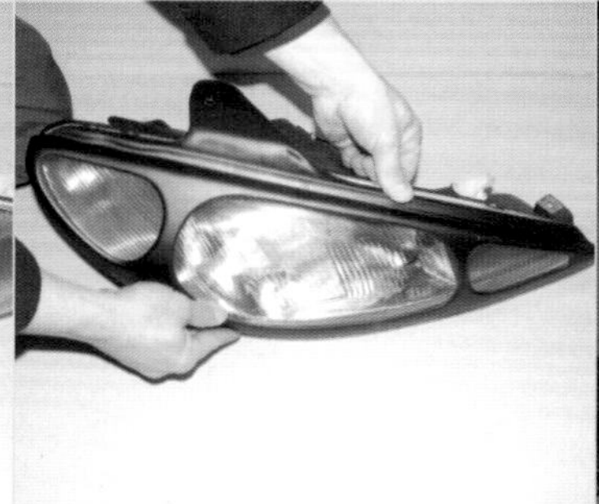

**04** Push the mask into place, and wipe any excess adhesive off before it's dry.

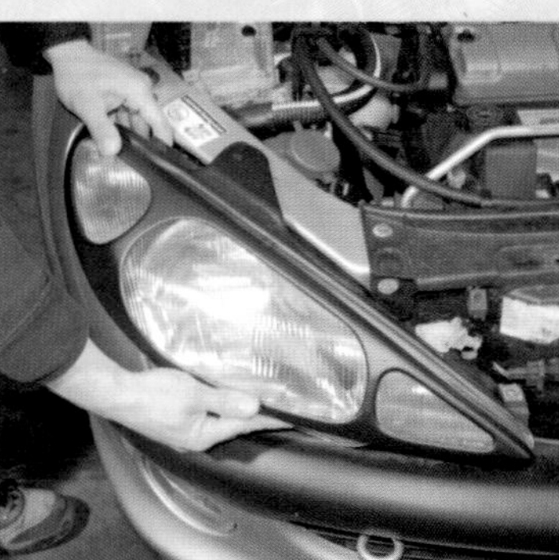

**05** Offer the headlight back into place . . .

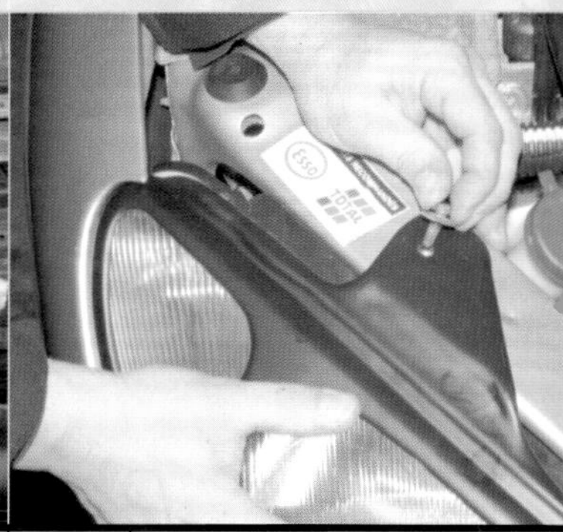

**06** . . . and you may need to make a hole in the mask for one of the headlight mounting bolts. All done? Most people colour-code the masks before fitting, but we think it goes well with the other black parts such as the bumper. Might not look so good when the bodykit goes on, though.

# A touch of chrome

Chrome bits on cars. Last seen in vast amounts on cars from the 70s, and now making a comeback. It'll be starting-handles next. As an alternative way of blinging up your 206 lights, try some chrome rings. These should fit our 206, as they're made by French company ALD Tuning (supplied by Planet Line).

You won't be surprised to learn there's not much to fitting these things. Make sure the light in question's clean, then peel off the backing . . .

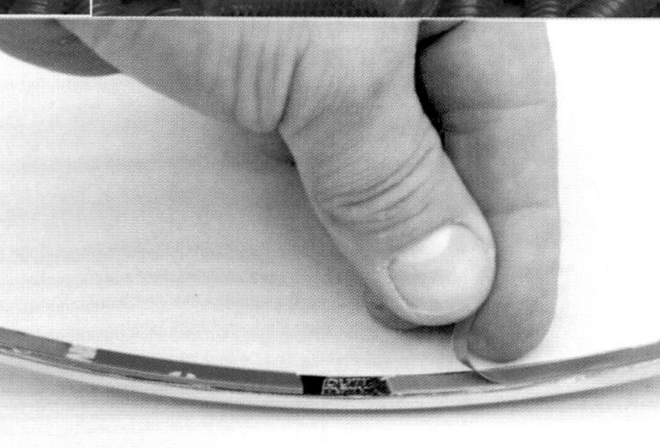

. . . line it up, and stick it on.

Nice way to trick up a set of stock lights - how cool would it look on some crystals?

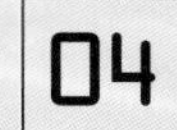


The same company also do chrome trims for the 206 headlights. Could be a unique look for your machine, to get you noticed.

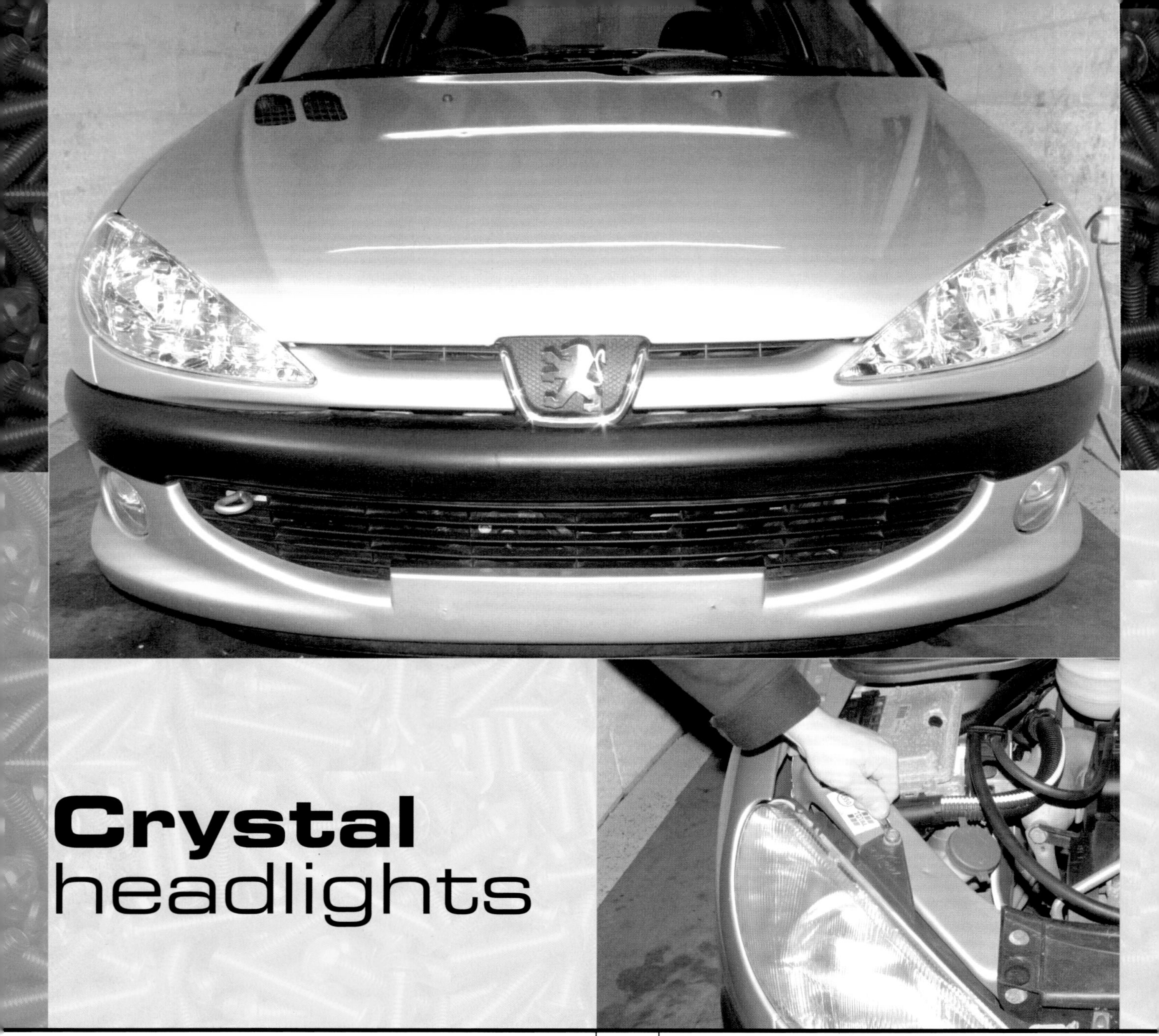

# **Crystal** headlights

Making the front end of your car look different is easily achieved with a set of new headlights. Clear-lens lights have come into style on new cars in the past few years, hence they can update the look of your 206 too. Better still, these new units usually contain far superior projector-style lights, so at night they'll be a lot more effective.

Ecosse supplied these crystal lights, which plug straight in as per the standard unit, and even keep the headlight adjuster (if fitted to your model of 206). Don't bin the old headlights - even if they're never going back on your car, they're worth a few beer tokens to someone.

**01** Time to shift those old headlights, then. Lift the bonnet and undo the bolt on the slam panel.

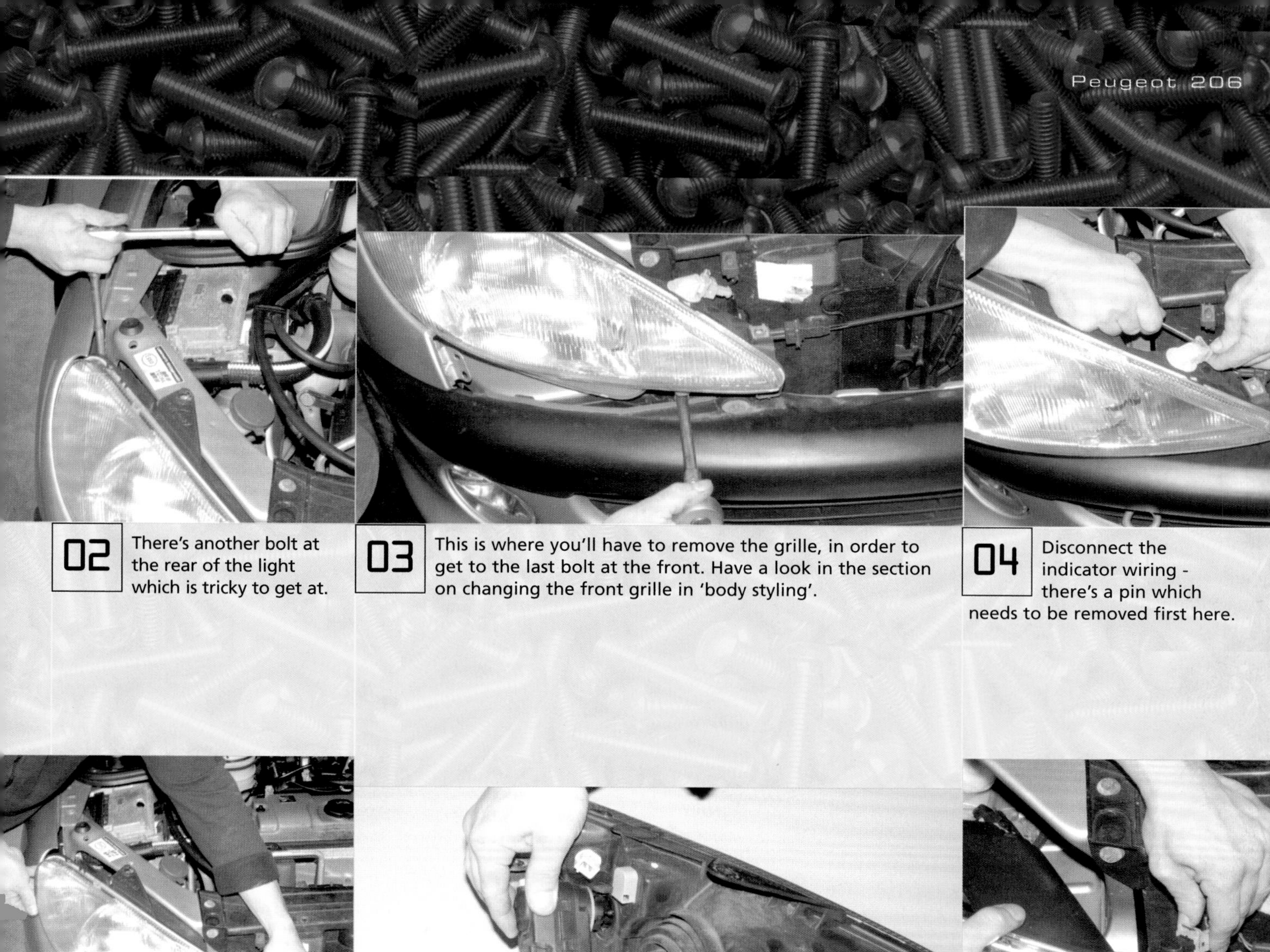

**02** There's another bolt at the rear of the light which is tricky to get at.

**03** This is where you'll have to remove the grille, in order to get to the last bolt at the front. Have a look in the section on changing the front grille in 'body styling'.

**04** Disconnect the indicator wiring - there's a pin which needs to be removed first here.

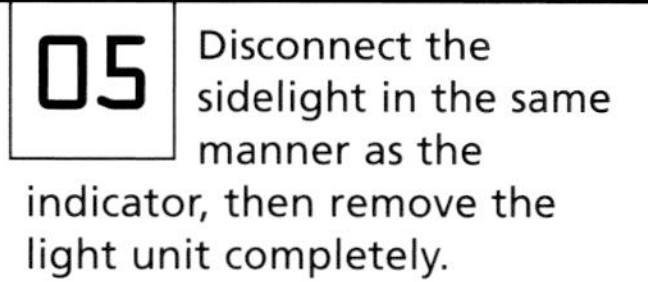

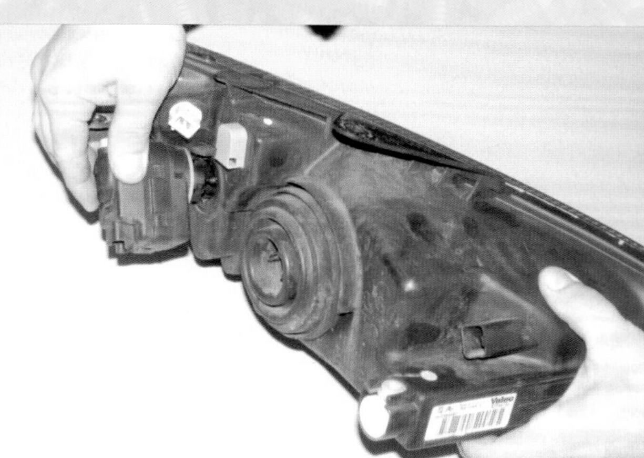

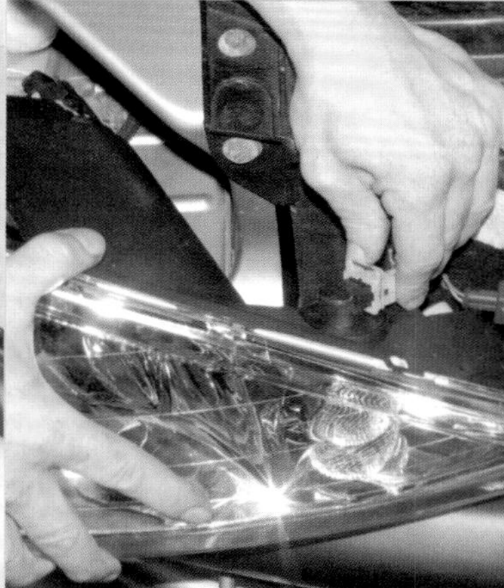

**05** Disconnect the sidelight in the same manner as the indicator, then remove the light unit completely.

**06** Twist and pull the headlight adjuster unit, which can be a little tricky. Take care with this, as the adjustment ball-and-socket arrangement is thin and can break easily. Fit this unit into the new headlight.

**07** Reconnect the light bulbholders, and bolt in the new unit. Repeat for the other side and you're finished. Now you've just got to wait for it to get dark, for a proper pose - er, we mean test.

# Headlight **bulbs**

Make your 206 look like an Audi or a Beemer, the easy way. Bad-weather and 'blue' headlight bulbs are an excellent way to boost headlight performance, and are perfect with other blue LED accessories like washer jets and number plate screws. The blue bulbs you buy in most accessory shops will be legal, 60W/55 bulbs, and are no problem. Don't be tempted to buy the mega-powerful bulbs you can get from rallying suppliers (any over 60W/55 are in fact illegal for use in this country) - as with all other non-standard lights, the boys in blue will love pulling you over for a word about this, so ask before you buy.

Even if you're not bothered about the legality of over-powerful bulbs (and you might well argue that being more powerful is the whole point of fitting), there's other problems with monster bulbs. First, they give off masses of heat, and loads of people have melted their headlights before they found this out. Don't believe us? Try fitting some 100W/90s and put your hand in front of the light, close to the glass. Hot, isn't it? The excess heat these bulbs generate will damage the headlights eventually, either by warping the lens, burning off the reflective coating, or melting the bulbholders. Maybe all three.

The increased current required to work big bulbs has also been known to melt wiring (this could lead to a fire) and will almost certainly burn out your light switch. There's no headlight relay fitted as standard, so the wiring and switch were designed to cope only with the current drawn by standard-wattage bulbs; if you're going for high power, a relay must be fitted (much as you'd have to, to fit foglights or spots).

# Side repeaters

**One of the smallest lights on your car can have a big effect on how it looks. The side repeaters are right in amongst the largest expanse of bodywork, so the more they can blend in, the more free of clutter your side bodywork will look. In standard form Peugeot have at least got it right in making the repeaters white, which on a silver car don't look too bad. But if you're going for clear lenses all over the car, the side repeaters will have to be included, particularly as they're a cheap mod anyway.**

Side repeaters must still show an orange light, and must be sufficiently bright (not easy to judge, and no two coppers have the same eyesight!). If your stock bulbs are clear, make sure you get orange bulbs too. You can actually get orange bulbs that look clear, to avoid the 'fried egg' effect. Alternatively, get LED side repeaters, like we did on our Fiesta project car.

Besides the various colour effects, side repeaters are available in many different shapes (triangular Focus-style side reps, for instance). But the standard 206 ovals are recessed into the wings, so making other shapes fit properly may need a bit of bodywork.

Or how about ditching the repeaters altogether, and get some tasty Merc-style mirrors, with side reps built-in? You could smooth your front wings, then...

01 In theory you can remove the side repeater by simply prising it out. In practice it's a lot easier if you can get at the back of it by removing the arch liner. Unbolt it at the rear . . .

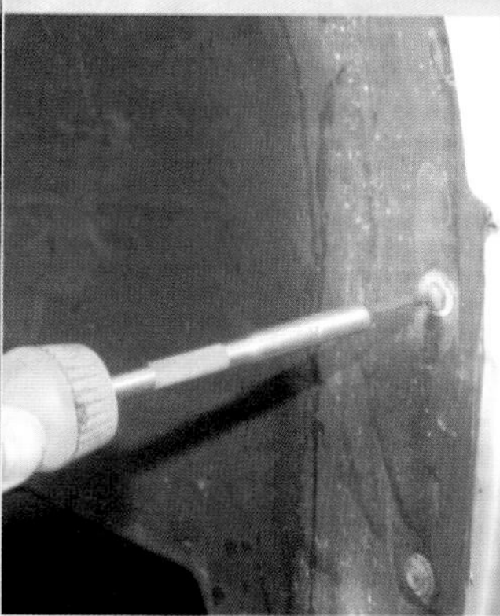

02 . . . then two screws must be removed from the arch lip.

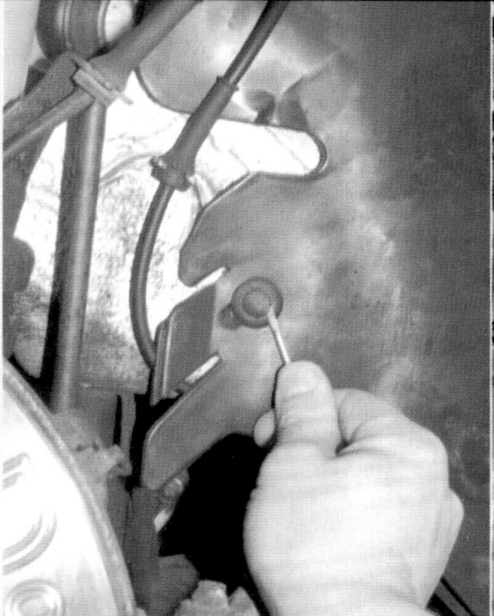

03 This type of clip has a central plug which you prise out (push it back in to re-secure it later) . . .

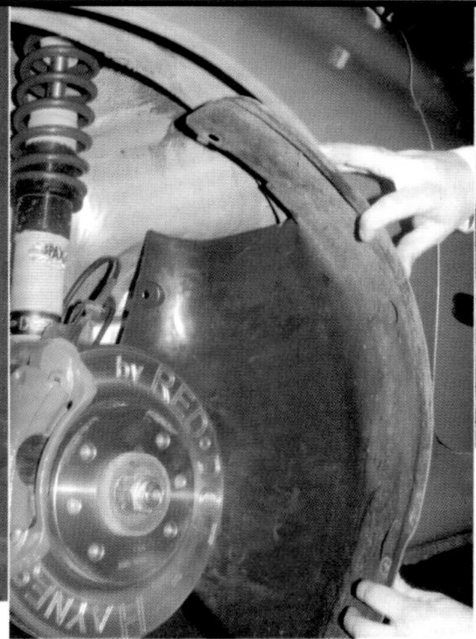

04 . . . then the arch liner can be removed completely.

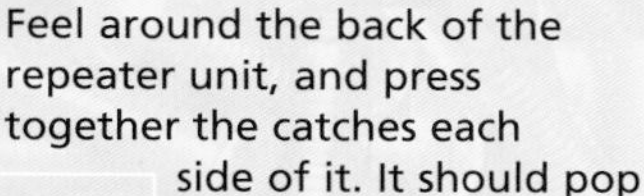

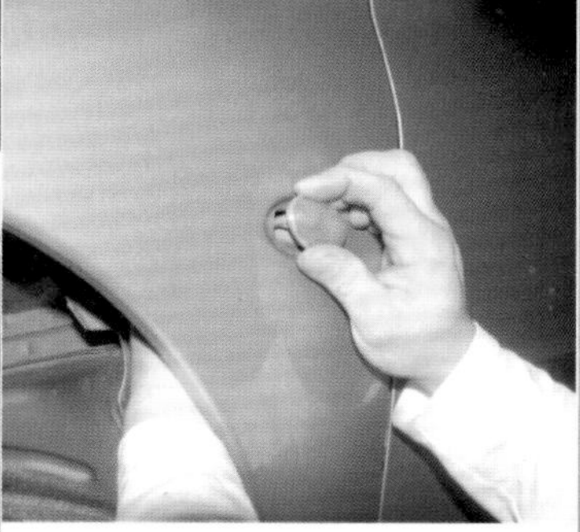

05 Feel around the back of the repeater unit, and press together the catches each side of it. It should pop out with a bit of pressure.

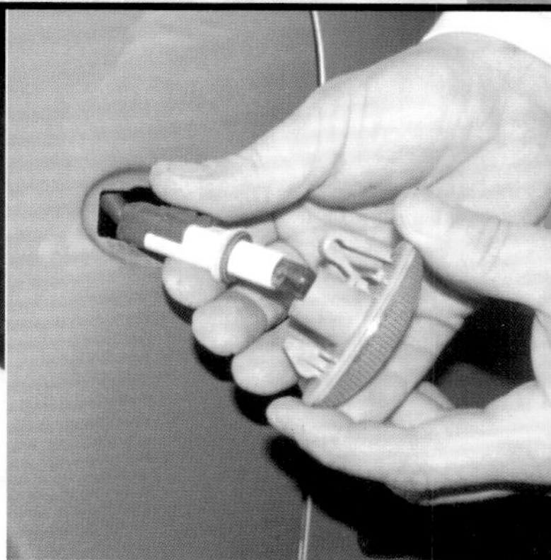

06 Twist and disconnect the bulb holder from the housing. MHW's clear side repeaters (supplied by ABC Design) come with an orange bulb, but if you already have the white lenses from Peugeot like us, you won't need these, so just keep them as spares. Twist and connect the clear housing, then refit it to the wing. Install the arch liner and it's job done.

# Front fog/spotlights

**This is a job which ideally is done at the same time as fitting the bodykit's front bumper - our fog and spotlights came with our Ecosse Virtuel 2 kit, fitted in 'body styling'. There again, you might be fitting a discarded GTI front bumper to your more-humble 206, and fancy wiring-in the extra lights. Remember, if you fit extra lights, they have to work or it's an MoT fail.**

Extra lights are useful for adding features to the 206's rather bland front end, even if they are a bit harder to fit than mesh. Most front bumpers have the facility for one or more pairs of lights, so it's gotta be done, really.

If you're fitting fogs, they must be wired in to work on dipped-beam only, so they must go off on main beam. The opposite is true for spotlights (they should only work on main beam). For foglights, pop out the main light switch and check for a wire which is live ONLY when the dipped beams are on. The Haynes wiring diagrams will help here - on our 206, it was a white wire we needed, with the lights fed by fuse numbers 31 and 32 (pull the fuses to check you've got the right wire).

Once you've traced your wire, this is used as the live (+ve) feed for your foglight relay. Did we mention you'll need a relay? You'll need a relay. A four-pin one will do nicely. Splice a new wire onto the feed you've found, and feed it through to the engine (use one of the bulkhead grommets). Decide where you'll mount the relay (next to the battery seems obvious) and connect the new wire onto terminal 86.

For your other relay connections, you'll need an earth to terminal 85 (plenty of good earth spots around the battery). You also need a fused live supply (buy a single fuseholder, and a 15 or 20-amp fuse should be enough) and take a new feed straight off the battery positive connection - this goes to terminal 30 on your relay.

Terminal 87 on your relay is the live output to the fogs - split this into two wires, and feed it out to where the lights will go. Each foglight will also need an earth - either pick a point on the body next to each light, or run a pair of wires back to the earth point you used earlier for your relay. Simple, innit?

With the wiring sorted, now you'd best fit the lights. Over to you. Most decent foglights come with some form of mounting brackets - you must be able to adjust the aim, even if only slightly. To look their best, hopefully your new lights can slot into pre-cut holes in your new front bumper/bodykit.

To connect the wiring to the lights, you'll probably need to splice on your wires from terminal 87 to the new wiring plugs which came with the lights - not too difficult. Plug it all together, and test - you should now have some rather funky fogs!

# Rear lights

**Lexus started it all off with their clear rear lights, which at the time looked ultra-trick on a regular saloon car. People soon caught on, adapting the lights to various other models, before the aftermarket started pushing out clear-lens versions of rear lights for every popular model on the street.**

It's important to check out the various types of clear rear lights available, because they vary in both quality and appearance, with some looking more aggressive and purposeful. The ABC Design units we went with suit our 206's theme perfectly, looking cool and menacing. They're even fully street-legal - they'd be a great addition to any 206 we reckon.

## Light legality

Lots of 206 rear clusters there may be, but - often, they're not UK-legal (even lights which are E-marked sometimes have no reflectors). Mr. Plod is well-informed on this point, and those sexy rear lights are way too big a come-on for him to ignore.

You can buy stick-on reflectors, but these are about as sexy as NHS specs, so there's no easy answer on this. You'd have to be pretty unlucky to get pulled just for having no rear reflectors, but don't say we didn't warn you. And what happens if your car gets crunched, parked at night with no reflectors fitted? Will your insurance try and refuse to pay out? You betcha.

Any questions on light legality? Why not check out the ABC Design website tech tips page, at www.abcdesignltd.com - if you've any questions after that, you can e-mail them. We're so good to you...

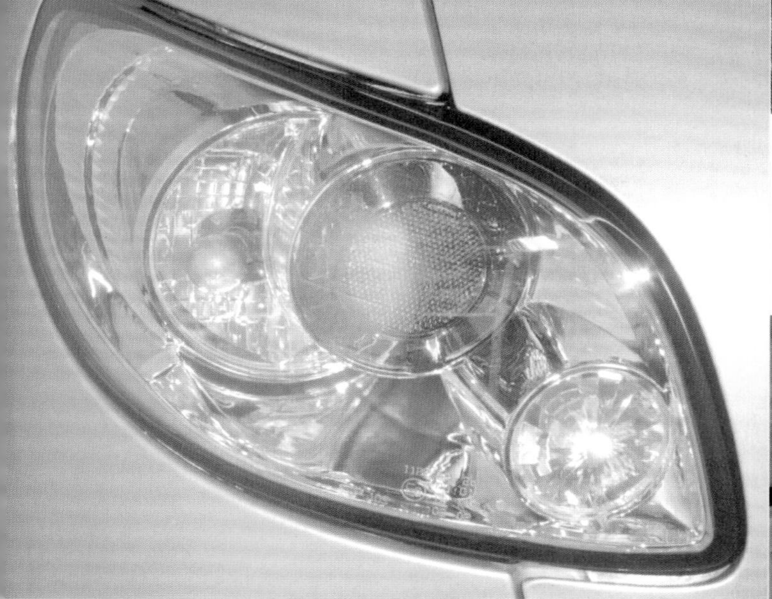

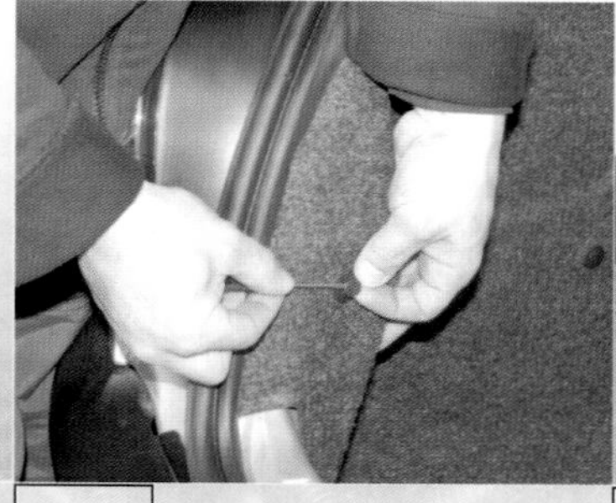

# Rear **clusters**

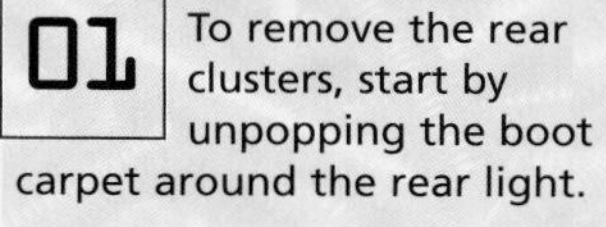

**01** To remove the rear clusters, start by unpopping the boot carpet around the rear light.

**02** At the rear of the light there's just one plastic nut to undo - it's designed to be done by hand, at least. Keep one hand on the outside of the light, or it could fall out.

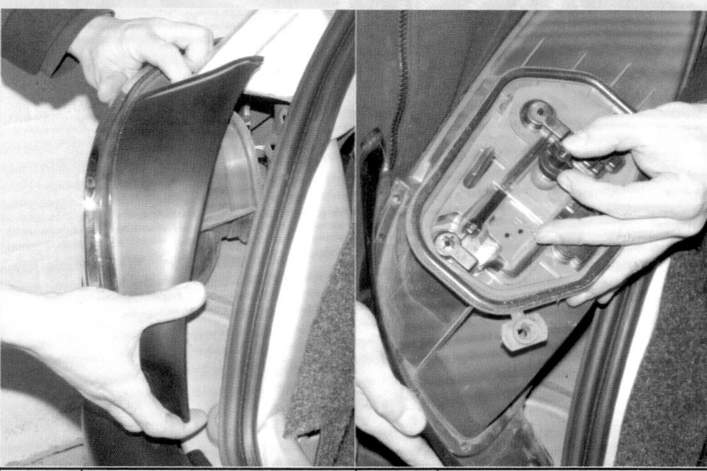

**03** If it hasn't fallen out already, remove the light cluster, disconnecting the wiring plug from it as you go.

**04** Once the light's out, the location of the plastic nut is more obvious. Take it off to re-use on the new light.

**05** Really clear clusters like ours will need a new, orange indicator bulb - fit the new bulb into its socket, and twist the bulbholder into place in the back of the new light.

**06** Connect up the new light to the old wiring plug, then fit it, taking care not to trap any of the wiring. Tighten the mounting nut, refit the boot carpet, and you're done (well, there's the other one still to do, but you know what we mean). Check everything's working before venturing out into the land of Plod.

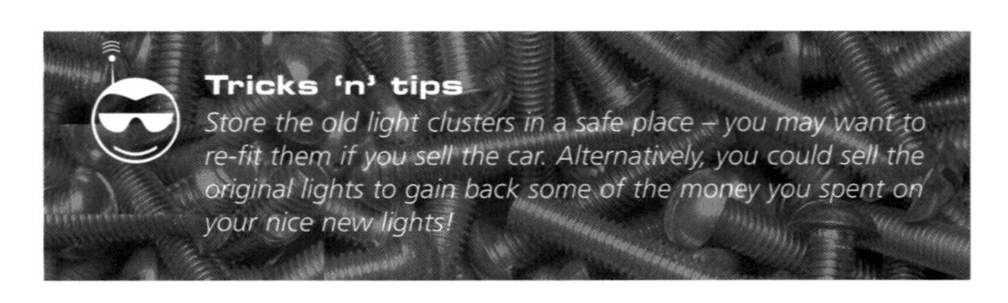

# High-level **brake light**



**There are some really smart clear-lensed lights on the market today, giving scope for great mods on your 206.**

They work with almost any colour, providing a contrast on dark shades, or adding a chrome-type highlight on colours such as silver. Thing is, you really need to add clear lenses all the way around your car for the look to work to maximum effect. Which means forking out for even the smallest lights, like the high-level brake light. We chose the In Pro Design stoplight, distributed in the UK by Ecosse. The clear unit is a quality piece, and a direct replacement for the standard Peugeot item; because it has LEDs fitted in place of the standard bulbs, the new light responds quicker than the old one, which even means it's safer.

**01** The standard brake light fits flush into the standard rear spoiler, with two fixing bolts poking through inside the tailgate. Undo the nuts holding on the brake light.

**02** It's a tight fit, so the light will want some gentle prising with a small screwdriver to release it.

**03** Once the light's been removed from its recess, cut off the standard wires. Cut fairly close to the old light, to leave as much wire as poss for connecting on the new unit.

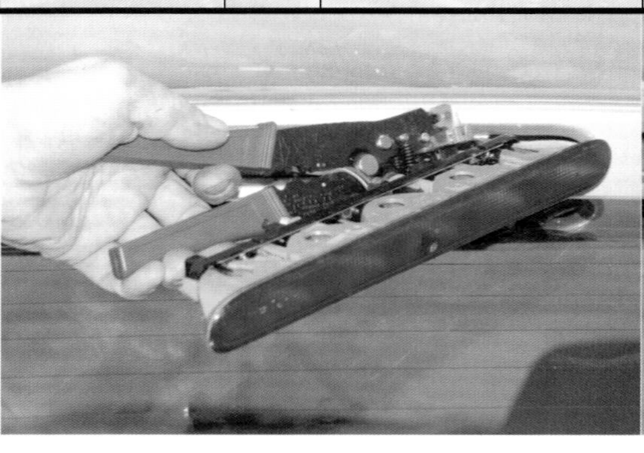

**04** Disconnect the washer hose and remove the nozzle completely from the light.

**05** Join the new wires using the supplied connectors - check your unit's instructions for details. Check the light works before bolting it in. Refit the washer nozzle and hose, then fit the new light and tighten its mounting nuts. If the new light isn't quite as good a fit as the old one, it might let water into the car from the tailgate - seal it with silicone if necessary.

As the 206's standard red foglight is smack-bang in the centre of the rear bumper, it stands out a lot. Peugeot has designed some decent shape into it at least, but it still needs a modifier's touch. This is especially true if you've gone for clear rear clusters, when a clear foglight becomes essential. This is another item we chose from Ecosse's Ultra Clear range - it comes with its own bulb, but otherwise fits exactly like the standard piece.

At least having a cool foglight available gives you less reason to ditch it altogether, which you might be tempted to do when the bodykit goes on. Three words of advice on this - don't do it. That's the foglight, not the bodykit. Having no rear fog means your car's illegal on the road, giving Officer Dibble all the excuse he needs to flash you over.

**01** Remove the standard light by levering out one side first (don't damage the bumper paint), which should release the side clips.

**02** Using a small screwdriver, lift the wire clip which secures the foglight wiring plug, then disconnect the plug.

# Rear foglight

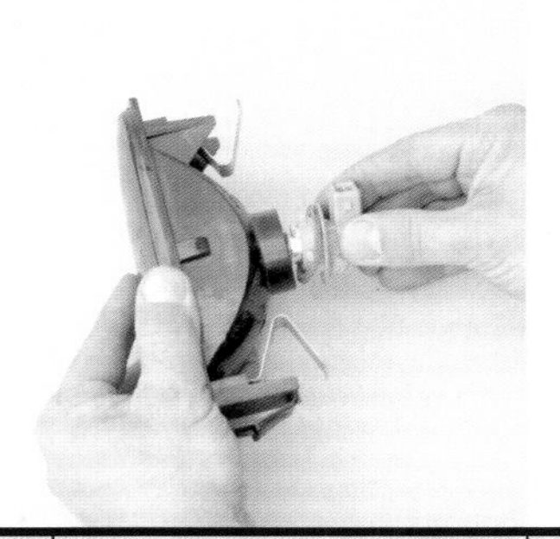

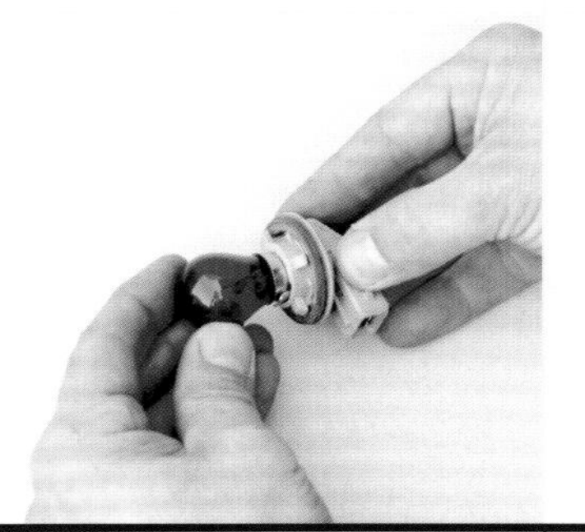

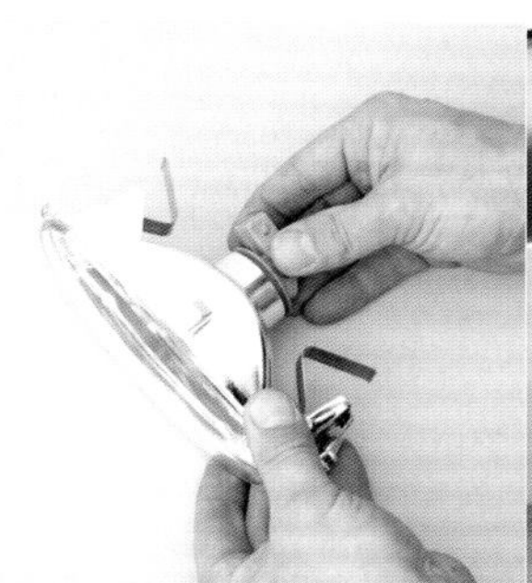

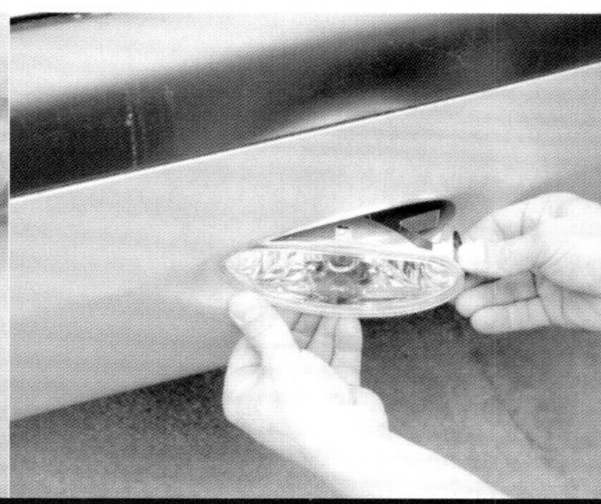

**03** Twist off the foglight bulbholder . . .

**04** . . . fit the (supplied) new red bulb . . .

**05** . . . then fit the holder and new bulb to the new light, twisting it into place.

**06** Reconnect the old wiring plug to the new light, then push the new unit into place, until you hear both side clips click. That's miles better - on a silver car, you hardly notice the light (except when it's on, of course).

07

Wheels & tyres

# Wheels & tyres

## Your most **important decision** ever?

You don't need us to tell you just how important wheels and tyres are on your motor. They're a hefty investment, so are well worth taking your time over. Get the right style and your car can turn from average to amazing in a matter of minutes. Get the selection wrong and not only will it affect the looks of car, it can seriously hurt your finances.

1

For a change, some standard 206 alloys are quite tidy (GTI 180s especially), but anything Peugeot is really a bit too common, and should be ditched when funds allow it. Advice on which particular wheels to buy would be a waste of space, since the choice is so huge, and everyone will have their own favourites. For what it's worth, though, it's gotta be something with a curvy kinda vibe on a 206, to look right, with plenty of people choosing Mille Miglia (Evo 5, Action), OZ Vela or Oxigin 1. This year's look is chrome (looks sweet on a 206 with the full set of crystal lights) and the US-based sites have plenty to see (Motorsport International, for starters, and DM Tech America). Even Wolfrace have recently jumped on the chrome bandwagon - or try Cam chromes for a value choice.

One point not to overlook when choosing wheels is the wheel offset. Most normal cars fall somewhere in the mid-30s to early 40s, and fortunately, the 206 is no oddball, at 34. Going for a lower than 34 offset makes the wheel 'stick out' more - for really big rims, your arches won't just have to be 'trimmed' - they'll be butchered! Any higher on the offset, and the wheels could be hitting the suspension on the inside. Fitting wheels with the wrong offset may also do unpleasant things to the handling.

## Lead us not into temptation

Before we go any further into which wheels are right for you, a word about insurance and security. Fitting tasty alloys to your 206 is one of the first and best ways to make it look cool. It follows, therefore, that someone with dubious morals might very well want to unbolt them from your car while you're not around, and make their own car look cool instead (or simply sell them, to buy spot cream and drugs).

Since fitting a set of top alloys is one of the easiest bolt-on ways to trick up any car, it's no surprise that the market in stolen alloys is as alive and kicking as it currently is - your wheels will also look very nice on any number of other cars, and the owners of those cars would love to own them at a fraction of the price you paid... It's not unknown for a set of wheels to go missing just for the tyres - if you've just splashed out on a set of fat Yokohamas, your wheels look even more tempting, especially if you've got a common-size tyre.

Tell your insurance company what you're fitting. What will probably happen is that they'll ask for the exact details, and possibly a photo of the car with the wheels on. Provided you're happy to then accept that they won't cover the extra cost of the wheels if they get nicked (or if the whole car goes), you may find you're not charged a penny more, especially if you've responsibly fitted some locking wheel bolts. Not all companies are the same, though - some charge an admin fee, and yes, some will start loading your premium. If you want the rims covered, it's best to talk to a company specialising in modified cars, or you could be asked to pay out the wheel cost again in premiums. The lamest thing you can do is say nothing, and hope they don't find out - we don't want to go on about this, but there are plenty of documented cases where insurance companies have refused to pay out altogether, purely on the basis of undeclared alloy wheels.

# How **cheap** are you?

**Hopefully, you'll be deciding which wheels to go for based on how they look, not how much they cost, but inevitably (for most ordinary people at least), price does become a factor. Surely buying a cheaper wheel must have its pitfalls? Well, yes - and some of them may not be so obvious.**

Inevitably, cheaper wheels = lower quality, but how does this manifest itself? Cheap wheels are often made from alloys which are more 'porous' (a bit like a sponge, they contain microscopic holes and pockets of air). Being porous has two main disadvantages for a wheel, the main one being that it won't be able to retain air in the tyres. The days of tyres with inner tubes are long gone (and it's illegal to fit tubes to low-profile tyres), so the only thing keeping the air in are the three 'walls' of the tyre, with the fourth 'wall' being the inside of the wheel itself. If you like keeping fit by pumping up your tyres every morning, go ahead - the rest of us will rightly regard this as a pain, and potentially dangerous (running tyres at low pressure will also scrub them out very effectively - what was that about saving money?).

Porous wheels also have difficulty in retaining their paint, lacquer, or chrome finish, with flaking a known problem, sometimes after only a few months. This problem is made worse by the fact that porous wheels are much harder to clean (brake dust gets ingrained into the wheels more easily) - and the more you scrub, the more the lacquer comes off.

The final nail in the coffin for cheap wheels is that they tend to corrode (or 'fizz') more. This not only ruins the looks if visible from outside, but if you get corrosion between the wheel and the hub, you won't even be able to take the things off! Yes seriously, grown men with all the specialist tools in the world at their disposal will be scratching their heads when faced with wheels which simply **will not** come off.

**Tricks 'n' tips**

*Whenever you have your wheels off, clean off any hub corrosion with wet-and-dry paper, then coat the hub mating surfaces with copper (brake) grease. There's no way you'll suffer stuck-on wheels again. 'Proper' alloys come with a plastic collar which fits inside the wheel - an essential item, it centres the wheel properly and reduces wheel-to-hub corrosion. Do not chuck out.*

Buying an established, popular make of wheel has another hidden benefit, too. Choosing a popular wheel will mean more suppliers will stock it, and the manufacturers themselves will make plenty of them. And if you're unlucky enough to have an accident (maybe a slide on a frosty road) which results in non-repairable damage to one wheel, you're going to need a replacement. If you've chosen the rarest wheels on the planet, you could be faced with having to replace a complete set of four, to get them all matching... A popular wheel, even if it's a few years old, might be easier to source, even second-hand.

## The Sunday morning ritual

**It's a small point maybe, but you'll obviously want your wheels to look as smart as possible, as often as possible - so how easy are they going to be to clean?**

The real multi-spokers and BBS-style 'wires' are hell to clean - a fiddly toothbrush job - do you really want that much aggro every week? The simpler the design, the easier time you'll have. For those who like nothing better than counting their spokes, though, there are several really good products out there to make your life less of a cleaning nightmare.

**Tricks 'n' tips**

*It's worth applying a bit of car polish to the wheels - provided it's good stuff, and you can be sure of getting the residue out of the corners and edges, a polished wheel will always be easier to clean off than an unpolished one. You can also buy waxes which are tailor-made for the job.*

## Bolt from the blues

**Don't forget about locking wheel bolts (see *"Hold on to your wheels"* further on) - bargain these into a wheel/tyre package if you're buying new.**

A word of warning about re-using your existing wheel bolts, should you be upgrading from steel wheels. Most steel-wheel bolts are not suitable for use with alloy wheels (and vice-versa, incidentally). Make sure you ask about this when buying new wheels, and if necessary, bargain a set of bolts into the price. Most bolts for use with alloys will have a washer fitted, for two very good reasons - 1) the bolt will pull through the wheel hole without it, and 2) to protect the wheel finish.

Another point to watch for is that the new wheel bolts are the correct length for your fitment, taking into account whether you've fitted spacers or not. Bolts that are too short are obviously dangerous, and ones that are too long can foul on drum brakes, and generally get in the way of any turning activities. If in doubt ask the retailer for advice. Always check that the wheels turn freely once they've been put on, and investigate any strange noises before you go off for a pose.

## Other options

**If you're on a really tight budget, and perhaps own a real 'basic' model 206, don't overlook the possibility of fitting a discarded set of standard alloys (a set of 206 GTI rims would do).**

If you get offered a set of rims from another Peugeot entirely, the bolt pattern (PCD) will be right, but the offset probably won't - many earlier Pugs have an offset in the range 16 to 20, which means they'll stick out hugely when bolted on. Unless your 206 has a wide-arch kit, old Peugeot alloys won't work - it's definitely try before you buy.

If the Peugeot range of wheels is too limiting, don't be too quick buying (for instance) alloys from other car makes altogether. For instance, some Ford alloys have the same bolt pattern (4x108), so they'll go on alright, but the offset's usually a wee bit higher on Ford rims (around 41), which could pull the wheel in too far. In the case of some alloys (VW, Vauxhall, or Renault, for example), the bolt pattern may be only fractionally different (4x100), but if you put these on, the strain on the wheel bolts is too great, and they can fracture...

**Tricks 'n' tips**

*If you're keeping a steel wheel as your spare (or even if you're keeping an original alloy), keep a set of your original wheel bolts in a bag inside the spare wheel. Locking bolts especially might be too long when fitted to a thin steel wheel, and might jam up your brakes!*

## Size **matters**

For us Brits, biggest is best - there are 206s out there with 19s and up. And yes, the mags all say you can't be seen with anything less than 17-inchers. In Europe, meanwhile, they're mad for the small-wheel look, still with seriously dropped suspension of course.

While the 206 will take 18 or 19-inch rims without sorting the arches, remember that anything bigger than 17s won't do wonders for the ride or handling. If you're bothered about how your 206 takes the bends, stick to 17s instead. Providing the rest of the car's up together, get the car low (60 mm drop) and you'll still get respect. A comment we saw on one chat room was "get 19s for the look, 17s if you still wanna drive it".

**Tricks 'n' tips**

*When you have your new wheels balanced, make sure the fast-fit centre knows to use stick-on weights, inside the wheel (not on the rim edge) - old-type knock-on lead weights look lame on the outer wheel edges, and on the inner edges may foul the suspension. Stick-on weights are, however, notorious for falling off easily, even when applied to pristine new alloys.*

# We like a challenge

## To be honest, successfully fitting big wheels in combination with lowered suspension is one of life's major challenges.

As much as anything, tyre width is what ultimately leads to problems, not so much the increased wheel diameter.

If the tyres are simply too wide (or with wheels the wrong offset), they will first of all rub on the suspension strut (ie on the inside edge of the tyre). Also, the inside edges may rub on the arches on full steering lock - check left and right. Rubbing on the inside edges can be cured by fitting offsets or spacers between the wheel and hub, which effectively pull the wheel outwards, 'spacing' it away from its normal position (this also has the effect of widening the car's track, which may improve the on-limit handling - or not). Fitting large offsets must be done using special longer wheel bolts, as the standard ones may only engage by a few threads, which is highly dangerous.

Rubbing on the outside edges is a simple case of wheelarch lip fouling, which must be cured by rolling up (or trimming off) the wheelarch return edge, and other mods. If you've gone for REALLY wide tyres, or have already had to fit offsets, the outer edge of the tyre will probably be visible outside the wheelarch, and this is a no-no (it's illegal, and you must cover it up!). On GTIs with arch extensions, you may need to remove the extensions, trim off the mounting lugs which poke through inside the arch, then bond the plastic bits back on with mastic.

The other trick with fitting big alloys is of course to avoid the '206 4x4 off-road' look, which you will achieve remarkably easily just by popping on a set of 17s with standard suspension. The massive increase in ground clearance is fine for Farmer Palmer, but your 'fistable' arches won't win much admiration at cruises. Overcoming this problem by lowering can be a matter almost of inspired guesswork, as much as anything (see *'Suspension'*).

# Speedo error? Or not?

## One side-effect of fitting large wheels is that your car will go slower.

Yes, really - or at least - it will appear to go slower, due to the effects of the mechanical speedometer drive. As the wheel diameter increases, so does its circumference (distance around the outside) - this means that, to travel say one mile, a large wheel will turn less than a smaller wheel. Because the speedometer is driven from the gearbox final drive, the apparent vehicle speed is actually based on the number of complete revolutions of the wheel. Therefore, for a given *actual* speed, since a larger-diameter wheel will be turning at a slower rate than a smaller wheel, and the method for measuring speed is the rate of wheel rotation, a car with larger wheels will produce a lower *speedo reading* than one with smaller wheels - but it's NOT actually going any slower in reality. So don't worry if you think you've reduced your 206's performance somehow with the monster rims, 'cos you 'aven't.

With the ever-increasing number of those lovely grey/yellow roadside boxes with a nasty surprise inside, spare a thought to what this speedo error could mean in the real world. If (like most people) you tend to drive a wee bit over the posted 30s and 40s, your real speed on 17s could be a bit more than the bit more you thought you were doing already, and you could get an unexpected flash to ruin your day. What we're saying is, don't drive any faster, to compensate for the lower speedo reading. Actually, the speedo error effect on 17s really is tiny at around-town speeds, and only becomes a factor over 70. But then, Officer, you couldn't possibly have been going over 70, could you? Officer?

### Jargon explained

*Rolling Radius - You may have come across the term 'rolling radius', which is the distance from the wheel centre to the outer edge of the tyre, or effectively, half the overall diameter. The rolling radius obviously increases with wheel size, but up to a point, the effects are masked by fitting low-profile tyres, with 'shorter' sidewalls. Above 16-inch rims, however, even low-profiles can't compensate, and the rolling radius keeps going up.*

*PCD - this isn't a banned substance, it's your Pitch Circle Diameter, which relates to the spacing of your wheel holes, or 'bolt pattern'. It is expressed by the diameter of a notional circle which passes through the centre of your wheel bolts, and the number of bolts. Unlike the offset, the PCD often isn't stamped onto the wheels, so assessing it is really a matter of eyeing-up and trying the bolts - the wheel should go on easily, without binding, if the pattern is correct. On a 206, the PCD is 108 mm with four bolts, which is given as 108/4, or 4 x 108.*

*Offset - this is determined by the distance from the wheel mounting face in relation to its centre-line. The offset figure is denoted by ET (no, I mustn't), which stands for einpress tiefe in German, or pressed-in depth (now I KNOW you're asleep). The lower the offset, the more the wheels will stick out. Fitting wheels with the wrong offset might bring the wheel into too-close contact with the brake and suspension bits, or with the arches. Very specialised area - seek advice from the wheel manufacturers if you're going for a very radical size (or even if you're not). The correct offset for 206s of all sizes is ET 34.*

# Hold on to your wheels

The minute you bang on your wicked alloys, your car becomes a target. People see the big wheels, and automatically assume you've also got a major stereo, seats and other goodies - all very tempting, but that involves breaking in, and you could have an alarm. Pinching the wheels themselves, now that's a doddle - a few tools, some bricks or a couple of well-built mates to lift the car, and it's easy money

The trouble with fitting big wheels is that they're only screwed on, and are just as easily screwed off, if you don't make life difficult for 'em. If you're unlucky enough to have to park outside at night (ie no garage), you could wake up one morning to a car that's *literally* been slammed on the deck! Add to this the fact that your car isn't going anywhere without wheels, plus the damage which will be done to exhaust, fuel and brake pipes from dropping on its belly, and it's suddenly a lot worse than losing a grand's worth of wheels and tyres...

The market and demand for stolen alloys is huge, but since most people don't bother having them security-marked in any way, once a set of wheels disappears, they're almost impossible to trace. Thieves avoid security-marked (or 'tattooed') wheels (or at least it's a pretty good deterrent) - and it needn't look hideous!

When choosing that car alarm, try and get one with an 'anti-jacking' feature, because thieves hate it. This is sometimes now called 'anti-tilt', to avoid confusion with anti-hijacking. Imagine a metal saucer, with a metal ball sitting on a small magnet in the centre. If the saucer tilts in any direction, the ball rolls off the magnet, and sets off the alarm. Highly sensitive, and death to anyone trying to lift your car up to remove the wheels - as we said, the crims are not fond of this feature at all. An alarm with anti-shock is not enough, because a careful villain might be able to avoid creating a strong enough vibration to trigger it - mind you, it's a whole lot better than nothing, especially if set to maximum sensitivity.

# Locking nuts/bolts

## Locking wheel bolts will be effective as a deterrent to the inexpert thief (kids, in other words), but will probably only slow down the pro.

Thieves want to work quickly, and will use large amounts of cunning and violence to deprive you of your stuff. If you fit a cheap set of locking bolts, they'll use a hammer and thin chisel to crack off the locking heads. Some bolts can easily be defeated by hammering a socket onto them, while some of the key-operated bolts are so pathetic they can be beaten using a small screwdriver. So - choose the best bolts you can, but don't assume they'll prevent your wheels from disappearing. Insurance companies seem to like 'em - perhaps it shows a responsible attitude, or something...

There's some debate whether it's okay to fit more than one set of locking bolts to a car - some people we know value their wheels so highly they've fitted four sets of lockers - completely replacing all the standards! Replacement locking bolts may not be made to the same standard as factory originals, and while one set is good for security, fitting more than that may be less good for safety (bolt could fail, wheel falls off, car in ditch, owner in hospital...).

Obviously, you must carry the special key or tool which came with your bolts with you at all times, in case of a puncture, or if you're having any other work done, such as new brakes or tyres. The best thing to do is rig this onto your keyring, so that it's with you, not left in the car. The number of people who fit locking bolts and then leave the tool to undo them cunningly 'hidden' in the glovebox or the boot... You don't leave a spare set of car keys in your glovebox as well, do you?

# How to change a set of wheels

## You might think you know all about this, but do you really?

Okay, so you know you need a jack and wheelbrace (or socket and ratchet), but where are the jacking points? If you want to take more than one wheel off at a time, have you got any axle stands, and where do they go? If you've only ever had wheels and tyres fitted by a garage, chances are you're actually a beginner at this. It's surprising just how much damage you can do to your car, and to yourself, if you don't know what you're doing - and the worst thing here is to think you know, when you don't...

### What to use

If you don't already have one, invest in a decent hydraulic (trolley) jack. This is way more use than the standard car jack, which is really only for emergencies, and which isn't really stable enough to rely on. Lifting and lowering the car is much easier with a trolley jack, and you'll even look professional. Trolley jacks have a valve, usually at the rear, which must be fully tightened (using the end of the jack handle) before raising the jack, and which is carefully loosened to lower the car down - if it's opened fully, the car will not so much sink as plummet!

Axle stands are placed under the car, once it's been lifted using the jack. Stands are an important accessory to a trolley jack, because once they're in place, there's no way the car can come down on you - remember that even a brand new trolley jack could creep down (if you haven't tightened the valve), or could even fail completely under load (if it's a cheap one, or knackered, or both).

Under NO circumstances use bricks, wooden blocks or anything else which you have to pile up, to support the car - this is just plain stupid. A 206 may be a 'small' car, but it weighs quite enough to damage you convincingly if it lands on top of you - if you don't believe us, try crawling under it when it's resting on a few poxy bricks. The only place bricks can be used is in front of, and behind, any tyres which are staying on the ground (helps stop the car rolling away).

### Where to do it

Only ever jack the car up on a solid, level surface (ideally, a concrete or tarmac driveway, or quiet car park). If there's even a slight slope, the car's likely to move (maybe even roll away) as the wheels are lifted off the ground. Jacking up on a rough or gravelled surface is not recommended, as the jack could slip at an awkward moment - such as when you've just got underneath...

### How to do it - jacking up the front

Before jacking up the front of the car, pull the handbrake on firmly (you can also chock the rear wheels, if you don't trust your handbrake).

If you're taking the wheels off, loosen the wheel bolts BEFORE you start jacking up the car. It's easily forgotten, but you'll look pretty silly trying to undo the wheel bolts with the front wheels spinning in mid-air.

We'll assume you've got a trolley jack. The next question is - where to stick it? Up front, there's a chunky-looking subframe behind the engine, with the front suspension wishbones attached - as long as you don't jack under the wishbones (or the anti-roll bar at the back of the subframe), this should be fine, but put a flat offcut of wood on your jack head first, to spread the load. There's also a chunky box-section on the floorpan, running back from the subframe, which can be used for jacking, again with some wood on the jack head. You can jack on the sill jacking points (between the two indents in the sill bottom edges - there may be a plastic cover to remove first), but it's better to leave those for your axle stands.

Once you've got the car up, pop an axle stand or two under the front sill jacking points - this is the only part of the sill it's safe to jack under or rest the car on. With the stands in place, you can lower the jack so the car's weight rests on the stands. For maximum safety, spread the car's weight between the stands and the jack - don't lower the jack completely unless it's needed elsewhere.

I'm sure we don't need to tell you this, but don't jack up the car, or stick stands under the car, anywhere other than kosher jacking and support points. This means - not the floorpan or the sump (you'll cave it in), not the moveable suspension bits (not stable), and not under the brake/fuel pipes (ohmigawd).

### How to do it - jacking up the rear

When jacking up the rear of the car, place wooden chocks in front of the front wheels to stop it rolling forwards, and engage first gear.

If you're taking the wheels off, you don't have to loosen the wheel bolts before lifting the car, but you'll be relying on your handbrake to hold the wheels while you wrestle with the bolts. Much cooler (and safer) to loosen the rear wheel bolts on the ground too.

Jacking and supporting the 206 back-end is a little trickier. Have a good look under there before making your choice. The crossmember between the rear wheels is out, and there's a full-width fuel tank in front of that. Throw in handbrake cables, fuel and brake pipes, and it's a bit of a minefield. The best places are the box-sections which run back from the rear shock absorber top mountings, though the exhaust back box is a bit close on one side. You can also use the shock absorber mounting points on the suspension arms, but this is a very small target area - take your time aligning the jack.

For axle stands, it's the rear sill jacking point, again between the indents on the sill edge. Not so much need for a block of wood here, but still not a bad idea to use one if you can - saves your paint, spreads the load into the car.

Remember not to put your axle stands under any pipes, the spare wheel, or the fuel tank, and you should live to see another Christmas.

### Finally...

As far as possible, don't leave the car unattended once it has been lifted, particularly if kids are playing nearby - football goes under your car, they go under to get it, knock the jack, car falls... it would almost certainly be your fault.

# Changing wheels

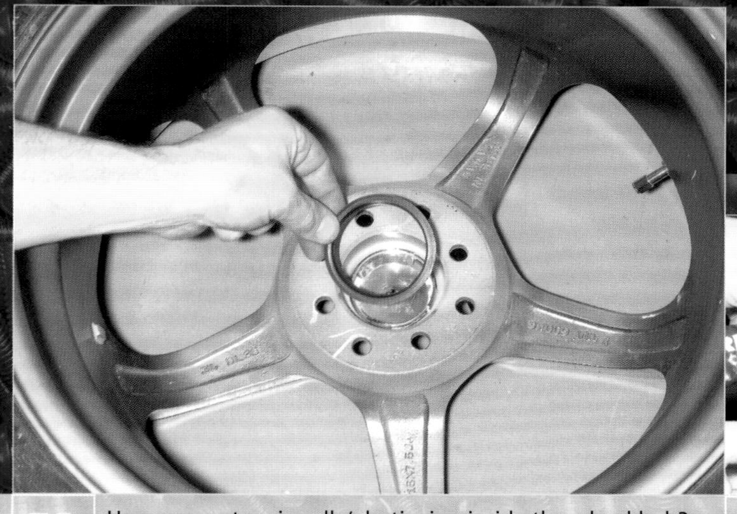

01 Have you got a nice ally/plastic ring inside the wheel hub? Make sure it's there, as it acts to centre the wheel properly, and may help to stop the wheel rusting on. Ever had a rusted-on wheel? Your local fast-fit centre will have, and they'll tell you it ain't funny.

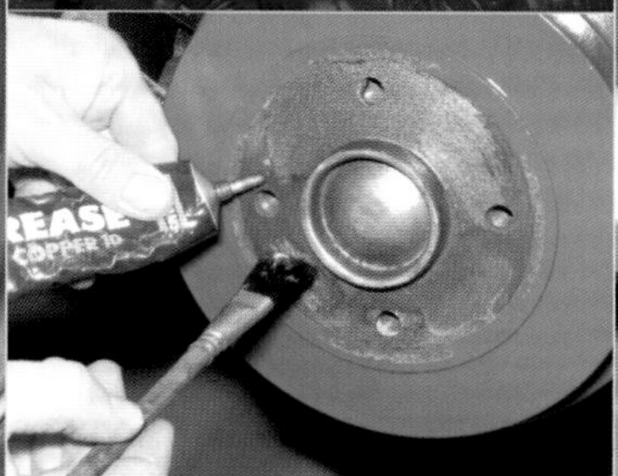


02 Even with the plastic ring of confidence, the metal bits can still corrode on. Equip yourself with some copper brake grease, and smear some on the hub. The pros 'paint' it on with a brush - the rest of us get messy. It's not a bad idea if some of that grease finds its way onto the wheel bolts, too.

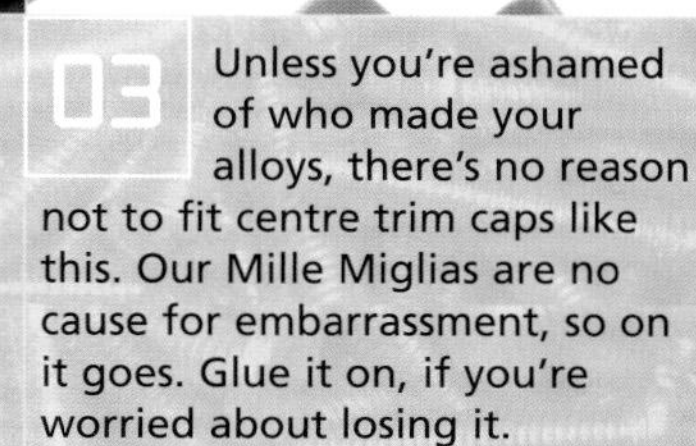

03 Unless you're ashamed of who made your alloys, there's no reason not to fit centre trim caps like this. Our Mille Miglias are no cause for embarrassment, so on it goes. Glue it on, if you're worried about losing it.

04 Pop the wheel onto the hub, then on with the nicely-greased bolts, and tighten up as far as possible by hand. You have got some locking bolts, haven't you? Keep your locking tool somewhere safe, but not obvious. The glovebox is convenient, but way too obvious!

05 With the wheel on the ground, tighten the wheel bolts securely (ideally, to the correct torque - 85 Nm). Don't over-tighten, or you'll never get them if you have a flat! If you've really blown some serious cash on your new rims, why not treat them to a special protected socket for tightening the bolts? Companies like Draper do a set of special sockets with plastic protector sleeves fitted, to stop the metal scratching your fine alloys. Makes sense to us.

Always nice to see a good brand of tyre on a decent alloy. How cool do cheap tyres look?

# Tyres

**To some people, tyres are just round and black - oh, and they're nearly all expensive, and don't last long enough. When you're buying a new set of wheels, most centres will quote prices with different tyres - buying a tyred-up set of rims is convenient, and usually good value, too.**

Some people try and save money by fitting 'remould' or 're-manufactured' tyres. These aren't always the bargain they appear to be - experience says there's no such thing as a good cheap tyre, with wheel balancing problems a well-known downside, for starters.

Choosing a known brand of tyre will prove to be one of your better decisions. Tyres are the only thing keeping you on the road, as in steering, braking and helping you round corners - what's the point of trying to improve the handling by sorting the suspension if you're going to throw the gains away by fitting naff tyres? Why beef up the brakes if the tyres won't bite? The combination of stiff suspension and cheap tyres is inherently dangerous - because the front end dives less with reduced suspension travel, the front tyres are far more likely to lock and skid under heavy braking.

Cheap tyres also equals more wheelspin - might be fun to disappear in a cloud of tyre smoke, but wouldn't you rather be disappearing up the road? Another problem with really wide tyres is aquaplaning - hit a big puddle at speed, and the tyre skates over the water without gripping - it's seriously scary when your car starts

**Tricks 'n' tips**

*When buying tyres, look out for ones which feature a rubbing strip on the sidewall - these extend over the edge of the wheel rims, and the idea is that they protect the rim edges from damage by 'kerbing'. Any decent tyre has them - discreet and very practical, and much better than a chewed-up rim.*

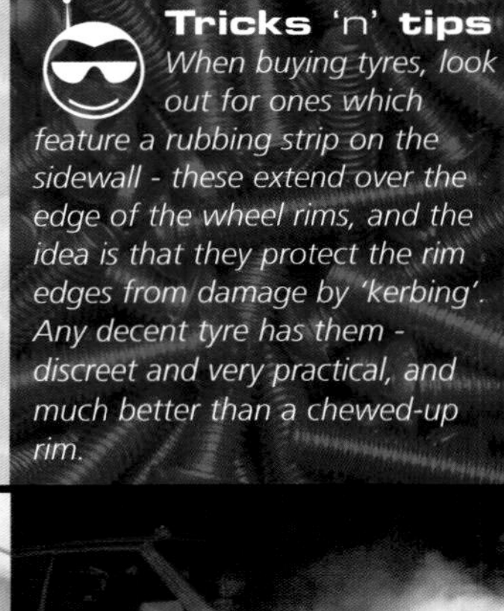

The size markings are obviously the most important, but take note of the directional marks too, if swapping wheels round. Most of the other markings are for anoraks only.

steering for you. Fitting good tyres won't prevent it, but it might increase your chances of staying in control. The sexiest modern low-profile tyres have a V-tread pattern, designed specifically to aid water dispersal, which is exactly what you need to prevent aquaplaning - try some, and feel the difference!

Finally, cheap tyres ruin the look - a no-name brand in big letters on your tyre sidewalls says you're a pikey loud and clear. If you're spending big dosh on wheels, you've gotta kit 'em out with some tasty V-tread tyres, or lose major points for style. Listen to friends and fellow modifiers - real-world opinions count for a lot when choosing tyres (how well do they grip, wet or dry? How many miles can you get out of them?) Just make sure, before you splash your cash on decent tyres, that you've cured any rubbing and scrubbing issues, as nothing will rip your new tyres out faster.

## Marks on your sidewalls

Tyre sizes are expressed in a strange mixture of metric and imperial specs - we'll take a typical tyre size as an example:

**205/40 R 17 V**
for a 7-inch wide 17-inch rim

**205** width of tyre in millimetres

**40** this is the "aspect ratio" (or "profile") of the tyre, or the sidewall height in relation to tyre width, expressed as a percentage, in this case 40%. So - 40% of 205 mm = 82 mm, or the height of the tyre sidewall from the edge of the locating bead to the top of the tread.

**R** Radial.

**17** Wheel diameter in inches.

**V** Speed rating (in this case, suitable for use up to 150 mph).

## Pressure situation

Don't forget, when you're having your new tyres fitted, to ask what the recommended pressures should be, front and rear - it's unlikely that the Peugeot specs for this will be relevant to your new low-low profiles, but it's somewhere to start from. If the grease-monkey fitting your tyres is no help on this point, contact the tyre manufacturer - the big ones might even have a half-useful website. If you're really stuck, try 30 psi all round as a rough guide. Running the tyres at the wrong pressures is particularly stupid (you'll wear them out much faster) and can be very dangerous (too soft - heavy steering, tyre rolls off the rim; too hard - tyre slides, no grip).

## Speed ratings

Besides the tyre size, tyres are marked with a maximum speed rating, expressed as a letter code:

**T** up to 190 km/h (118 mph)

**U** up to 200 km/h (124 mph)

**H** up to 210 km/h (130 mph)

**V** inside tyre size markings (225/50 VR 16) over 210 km/h (130 mph)

**V** outside tyre size markings (185/55 R 15 V) up to 240 km/h (150 mph)

**Z** inside tyre size markings (255/40 ZR 17) over 240 km/h (150 mph)

If you've got marks on your sidewalls like this, you're in trouble - this has almost certainly been caused by "kerbing".

# 08 Suspension



**If your 206 is still sitting on standard suspension, it's probably safe to say it doesn't cut it - yet. If you've decided you couldn't wait to fit your big alloys, the chances are your 206 is now doing a passable impression of a tractor. An essential fitment, then - so how low do you go, and what nasty side-effects will lowering have?**

The main reason for lowering is of course, to make your car look cool. Standard suspension is always set too soft and too high - a nicely lowered motor really stands out instantly. Lowering your car should also improve the handling. Dropping the car on its suspension brings the car's centre of gravity closer to its roll and pitch centres, which helps to pin it to the road in corners and under braking - combined with stiffer springs and shocks, this reduces body roll and increases the tyre contact patch on the road. But - if improving the handling is really important to you, choose your new suspension carefully. If you go the cheap route, or want extreme lowering, then you could end up with a car which don't handle at all...

## How low to go?

Assuming you want to slam your suspension so that your arches just clear the tops of your wicked new rims, there's another small problem - it takes some inspired guesswork (or hours of careful measuring and head-scratching) to assess the required drop accurately, and avoid any nasty rubbing sounds and the smell of burning rubber.
Lowering springs and suspension kits will

As for what to buy, there are basically three main options when it comes to lowering, arranged in order of ascending cost below:

1. *Pair of front lowering springs.*
2. *Matched pair of front lowering springs and shock absorbers, and a pair of rear shocks.*
3. *Pair of front 'coilovers' (and rear shocks)*

only produce a fixed amount of drop - this can range from 20 mm to a more extreme drop of anything up to 80 mm. Take as many measurements as possible, and ask around your mates - suppliers and manufacturers may be your best source of help in special cases. Coilovers have a range of adjustment possible, which is far more satisfactory - at a price.

The 206 does have scope for extreme lowering. One 206 GTI we know of has a coilover front end, which the owner reckons could go lower than the 75 mm drop it's already running; a torsoin bar three-spline drop at the rear has the 17-inch rims inside the arches already, with more possible. Start with either a 40 or 60 mm drop on the front, then go one spline at a time on the back, until you're happy.

## Bar-brawls - best avoided

Sorry to start on a negative note, but lowering the rear-end of your 206 properly really is a job for a professional. The reason for this is the manufacturer's choice of rear suspension - the 206 is fitted with a torsion bar rear axle (a favourite choice amongst the French manufacturers).

The torsion bar rear suspension doesn't use coil springs, but instead uses hefty steel bars. The steel bars are splined at each end, and link each trailing arm to the opposite end of the axle crossmember; one is positioned in front of the crossmember and the other behind it. These steel bars twist as the suspension moves up and down throughout its travel, and it's the bars' resistance to this twisting (or torsional force) which provides the rear suspension springing. Another steel bar passes through the centre of the rear axle crossmember and links both trailing arms - this is the anti-roll bar, which is stiffer than the other two, but otherwise functions on the same principle.

Resetting the rear ride height is an involved procedure - not especially difficult or dangerous, but fiddly (and you could be playing for a long time before giving up and taking it to a garage). On an older car, you could also be facing the possibility of rusted-in bits, and a slide-hammer is the only answer if you get into that. The positive side though, is that you can lower the rear ride height without purchasing any new springs - the only cost involved is the labour.

## Lowering springs

The cheapest option by far, but with the most pitfalls and some unpleasant side-effects. Lowering springs are, effectively, shorter versions of the standard items fitted to your 206 at the factory. However, not only are they shorter (lower), they are also uprated (stiffer) - if lowering springs were simply shorter than standard and the same stiffness (the same 'rate'), you'd be hitting the bump-stops over every set of catseyes. With lowering springs, you just fit the new springs and keep the original shock absorbers ('dampers') - even if the originals aren't completely knackered, you're creating a problem caused by mis-matched components. The original dampers were carefully chosen to work in harmony with the original-rate springs - by increasing the spring rate without changing the dampers, you end up with a situation where the dampers will not be in full and effective control of the spring motion. What this usually does before long is wreck the dampers, because they simply can't cope with the new springs, so you really don't save any money in the end.

The mis-matched springs and dampers will have other entertaining side-effects, too. How would you like a 206 which rides like a brick, and which falls over itself at the first sign of a corner taken above walking pace? A very choppy ride and strange-feeling steering (much lighter, or much heavier, depending on your luck) are well-documented problems associated with taking the cheap option, and it doesn't even take much less time to fit, compared to a proper solution. Even if you're a hard man, who doesn't object to a hard ride if his car looks cool, think on this - how many corners do you know that are completely flat (ie without any bumps)? On dodgy lowering springs, you hit a mid-corner bump at speed, and it's anyone's guess where you'll end up.

If cost is a major consideration, and lowering springs the only option for now, at least try to buy branded items of decent quality - some cheap sets of springs will eat their way through several sets of dampers before you realise the springs themselves have lost the plot. Needless to say, if riding around on mis-matched springs and shocks is a bit iffy anyway, it's downright dangerous when they've worn out (some inside 18 months!).

Springs are generally only available in a very few sizes, expressed by the amount of drop they'll produce - most people go for 60 mm or so, but there's usually 35 to 40 mm springs too if you're less brave (or if you've simply got massive rims). Take as many measurements as possible, and ask around your mates - suppliers and manufacturers may be your best source of help in special cases. On 17s, a 60 mm drop is no problem for a 206 on the front, and will make the car look sweet.

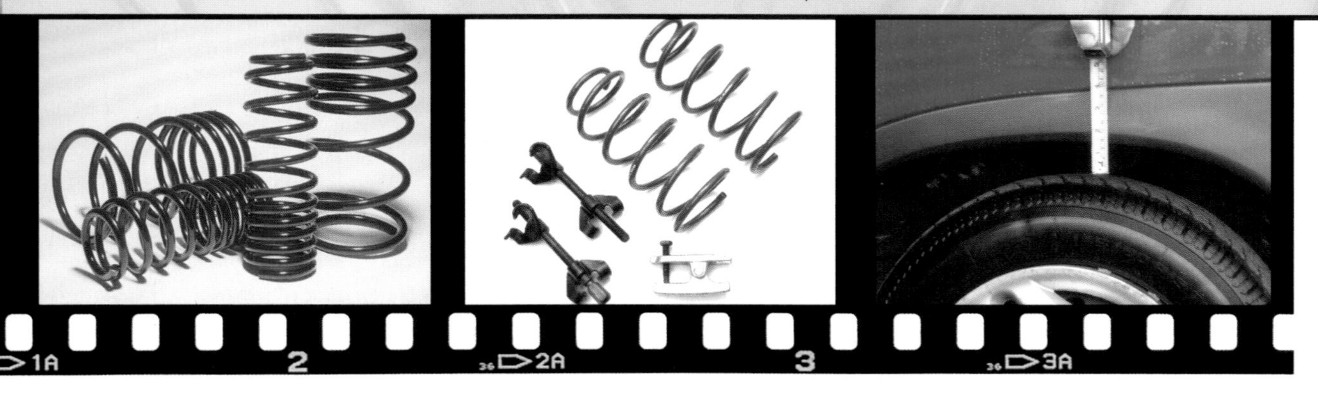

# Suspension kit

A far better choice, Sir - matched springs and dampers are a genuine 'upgrade', and respect is due. There are several branded kits available, and Peugeot specialists may do their own. With a properly-sorted conversion, your 206 will handle even better, and you'll still be able to negotiate a set of roadworks without the risk of dental work afterwards. Actually, you may be amazed how well the 206 will still ride, even though the springs are clearly lower and stiffer - the secret is in the damping.

Some of the kits are billed as 'adjustable', but this only applies to the damper rates, which can often be set to your own taste by a few minutes' work (don't mistake them for cheap coilovers). This Playstation feature can be quite a good fun thing to play around with, even if it is slightly less relevant to road use than for hillclimbs and sprints - but be careful you don't get carried away and set it too stiff, or you'll end up with an evil-handling car and a CD player that skips over every white line on the road!

Unfortunately, although you will undoubtedly end up with a fine-handling car at the end, there are problems with suspension kits, too. They too are guilty of causing changes to steering geometry (have it reset) and once again, you're into guesswork territory when it comes to assessing your required drop for big wheels. Generally, most suspension kits are only available with a fairly modest drop (typically, 35 to 60 mm).

## Coilovers

If you've chosen coilovers, well done again. This is the most expensive option, and it offers one vital feature that the other two can't - true adjustability of ride height, meaning that you can make the finest of tweaks to hunker down on your new rims (coilovers are an almost-essential choice if you're trying for 18s). Coilovers give you more scope to fit those big rims now, lower it down as far as poss, then wait 'til next month before you have the arches rolled/trimmed, and drop it down to the deck. Coilovers are a variation on the suspension kit theme, in that they are a set of matched variable-rate springs (some have separate 'helper' springs too) and shocks, but they achieve their adjustability in a way which might not guarantee as good a ride/handling mix as a normal kit.

A coilover set replaces each spring and shock with a combined unit where the coil spring fits over the shocker (hence 'coil' 'over') - nothing too unusual in this, because so far, it's similar to a normal front strut. The difference lies in the adjustable spring lower seat, which can lower the spring to any desired height (within limits).

Unfortunately, making a car go super-low is not going to be good for the ride or the handling. Coilover systems necessarily have very short, stiff springs, and this can lead to similar problems to those found with cheap lowering springs alone. If you go too far with coilovers, you can end up with a choppy ride, heavy steering and generally unpleasant handling. Combine a coilover-slammed car with big alloys, and while the visual effect may be stunning, the driving experience might well be very disappointing. At least a proper coilover kit will come with shock absorbers (dampers) which are matched to the springs, unlike a 'conversion' kit.

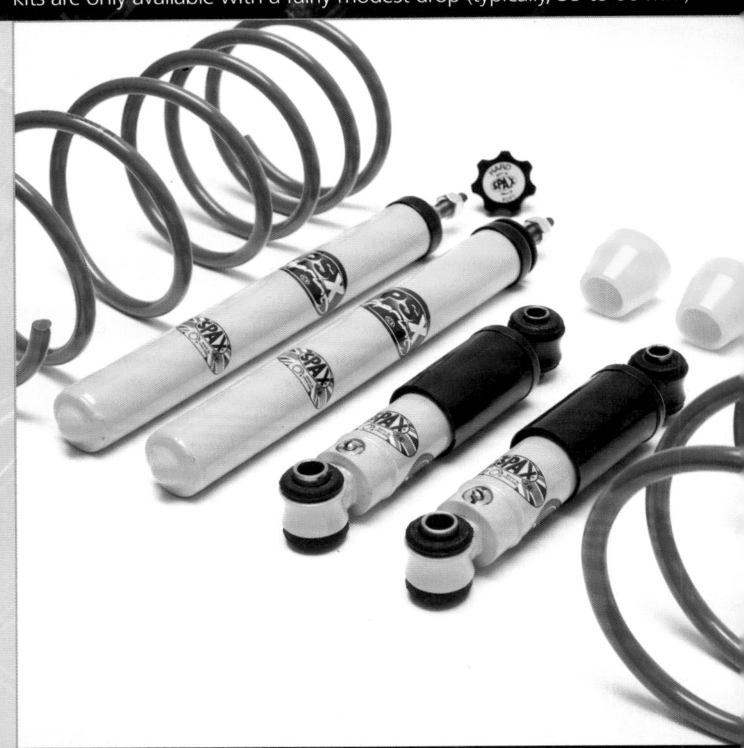


### Coilover conversion

A better-value option is the 'coilover conversion'. If you really must have the lowest, baddest machine out there, and don't care what the ride will be like, these could be the answer. Offering as much potential for lowering as genuine coilovers (and at far less cost), these items could be described as a cross between coilovers and lowering springs, because the standard dampers are retained (this is one reason why the ride suffers). What you get is a new spring assembly, with adjustable top and bottom mounts - the whole thing slips over your standard damper. Two problems with this solution (how important these are is up to you):

**1** Your standard dampers will not be able to cope with the uprated springs, so the car will almost certainly ride (and possibly handle) like a pig if you go for a really serious drop - and okay, why else would you be doing it?

**2** The standard dampers are effectively being compressed, the lower you go. There is a limit to how far they will compress before being completely solid (and this could be the limit for your lowering activities). Needless to say, even a partly-compressed damper won't be able to do much actual damping - the results of this could be... interesting...

# Nasty side-effects

## Camber angle and tracking

With any lowering 'solution', it's likely that your suspension and steering geometry will be severely affected - this will be more of a problem the lower you go. This will manifest itself in steering which either becomes lighter or (more usually) heavier, and in tyres which scrub out their inner or outer edges in very short order - not funny, if you're running expensive low-profiles! Sometimes, even the rear tyres can be affected in this way, but that's usually only after some serious slammage. Whenever you've fitted a set of springs (and this applies to all types), have the geometry checked ASAP afterwards.

If you've dropped the car by 60 mm or more, chances are your camber angle will need adjusting. This is one reason why you might find the edges of your fat low-profiles wearing faster than you'd like (the other is your tracking being out). The camber angle is the angle the tyre makes with the road, seen from directly in front. Race cars have the front wheels tilted in at the top, out at the bottom - this is extreme negative camber, and it helps to give more grip and stability in extreme cornering (but if your car was set this hard-core, you'd kill the front tyres very quickly!). Virtually all road cars have a touch of negative camber on the front, and it's important when lowering to keep as near to the factory setting as possible, to preserve the proper tyre contact patch on the road. Trouble is, there's not usually much scope for camber adjustment on standard suspension, which is why (for some cars) you can buy camber-adjustable top plates which fit to the strut tops. Setting the camber accurately is a job for a garage with experience of modified cars - so probably not your local fast-fit centre, then.

## Rear brake pressure regulator

Peugeot 206s without ABS have a rear brake pressure-limiting valve fitted, which is linked to the rear suspension. The idea is that, when the car's lightly loaded over the rear wheels, the braking effort to the rear is limited, to prevent the wheels locking up. With the boot full of luggage, the back end sinks down, and the valve lets full braking pressure through to the rear. When you slam the suspension down, the valve is fooled into thinking the car's loaded up, and you might find the rear brakes locking up unexpectedly - could be a nasty surprise on a wet roundabout! The 206's valve is not easy to adjust - the best idea would be to crawl underneath and see how it looks when unloaded (on standard suspension), and try to re-create the same condition once the car's been dropped.

On the 206, the brake pressure regulator is under the car, on the right-hand side, in front of the spare wheel (it's tucked right into the rear suspension, above the right-hand shock absorber). Chances are, if your 206 has been dropped by much more than 35 to 40 mm, mods will be necessary to make the pressure regulator work properly. The valve attaches to the suspension using a spring - if a slightly longer spring is fitted, when the car's lowered, the valve won't be triggered as soon, so it's one possible answer (though this is a very hit-and-miss approach). If you get major problems with your lowered 206 locking up at the rear under braking, another solution is to disconnect the valve's spring completely - this will limit your rear brakes to the pre-lowered level, but won't compensate for when the car's loaded at the rear (so you might have your front brakes locking under heavy braking).

Modifying anything relating to brakes is a very dodgy business - check the results of what you've done very carefully before doing any fast driving. One way to do this is to take the car to an MoT test centre, and have the brakes tested on the rollers. It's no guarantee of faultless brakes under all conditions, but it's better than nothing.

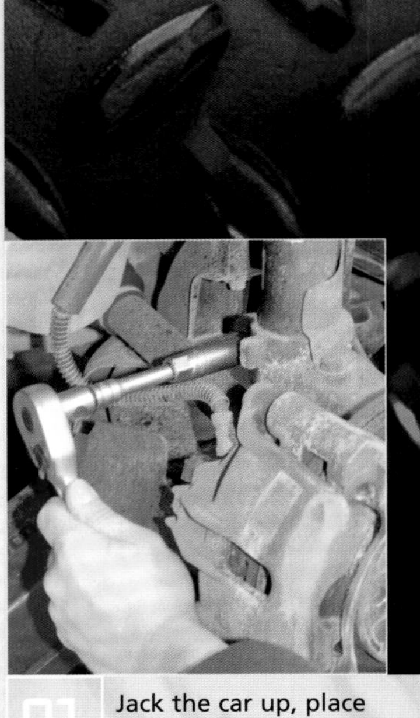

01 Jack the car up, place on axle stands and remove the front wheel. Refer to 'wheels & tyres' for more information on jacking and support - make sure the car's solid, with a good jack (something other than the Peugeot one) and an axle stand holding it up. Undo the clamp bolt at the strut's lower end . . .

**Tricks 'n' tips**
*Don't start this job without coil spring compressors, or you'll be sorry! A torque wrench is also pretty important.*

# Front Suspension

02 . . . then remove the bolt from the other side (note which way round it fits) and keep it for later.

03 Using a Torx key and spanner, undo the anti-roll bar drop link connection . . .

04 . . . then pull the drop link out of the way, clear of the strut.

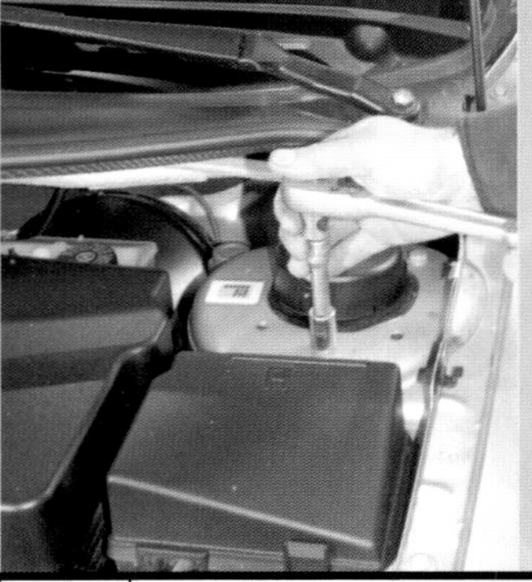

05 Loosen the three strut-top mounting bolts in the engine bay, but don't undo them completely just yet.

**Respect**

*For the next bit, you MUST use coil spring compressors ('spring clamps'). Medical attention will be required if you don't. Do we have to draw you a diagram? The spring's under tension on the strut, even off the car - what do you think's gonna happen if you just undo it? The spring-embedded-in-the-forehead look is really OVER, too.*

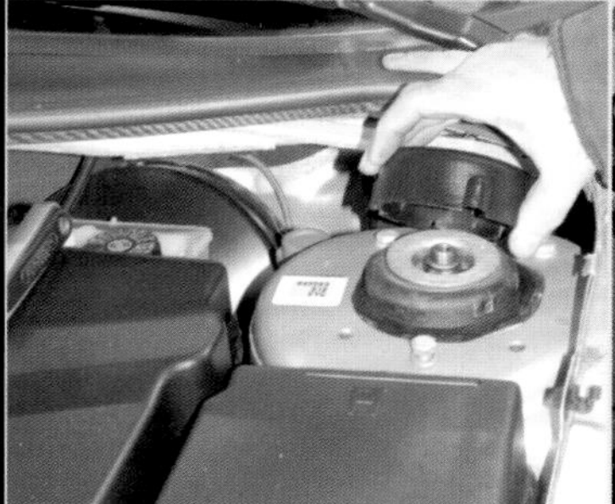

**06** Remove the plastic cover on top of the strut too, but don't touch the nut hidden below it yet.

**07** The base of the suspension strut sits in a clamp on the wheel hub, and it may be tight in there (even though you undid the clamp bolt earlier on). Beating the hub downwards off the strut may be the only way to free it. Just take care you don't hit anything which looks fragile or expensive. Once it's freed off, you may need to press the hub down to unhook the strut.

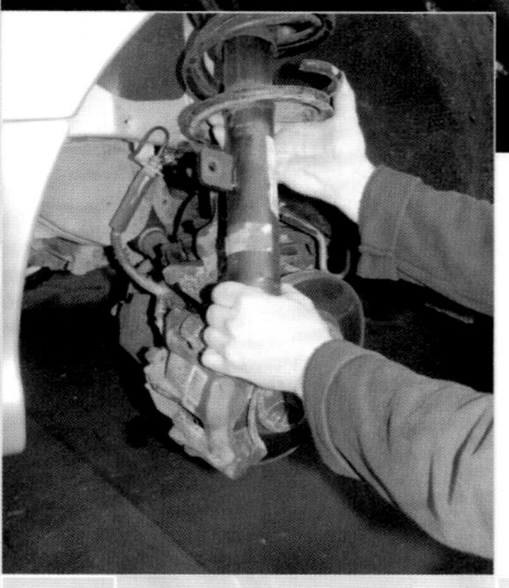

**08** Remove the three top bolts (again, leave the centre nut alone) and take out the strut altogether. Support the wheel hub while the strut is removed.

**09** Spring compressors have two clamps, each with two hooks, which sit over one of the spring coils. You won't get the hooks over the top and bottom coils, but try the next nearest. Fit the two clamps opposite each other, then tighten the big bolt up the middle of each to compress one side of the spring - this must be done evenly, one side after the other, or the un-clamped side might fly off. Respect is due here - this is scary stuff if you muck about.

**10** With the spring compressed enough to be loose on the strut, it's time to undo the centre nut which we've told you not to touch so far. This is the one holding the whole strut together, so it's tight, and awkward to undo. You'll need a cranked ring spanner, and an Allen key the right size, to stop the strut piston turning while you wrestle with the nut.

**11** Now the centre nut's gone, the strut can be dismantled. Most of the old bits won't be needed, but one that will be is the top bearing . . .

**12** . . . while this is the spring upper seat, which can be ditched . . .

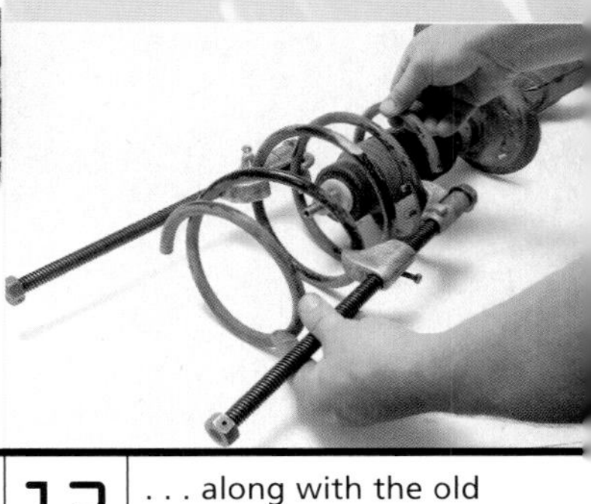

**13** . . . along with the old spring. Won't need that soggy old thing again - but take care slackening off the spring clamps (like, each one a bit at a time) if you don't fancy finding out just how springy it actually is!

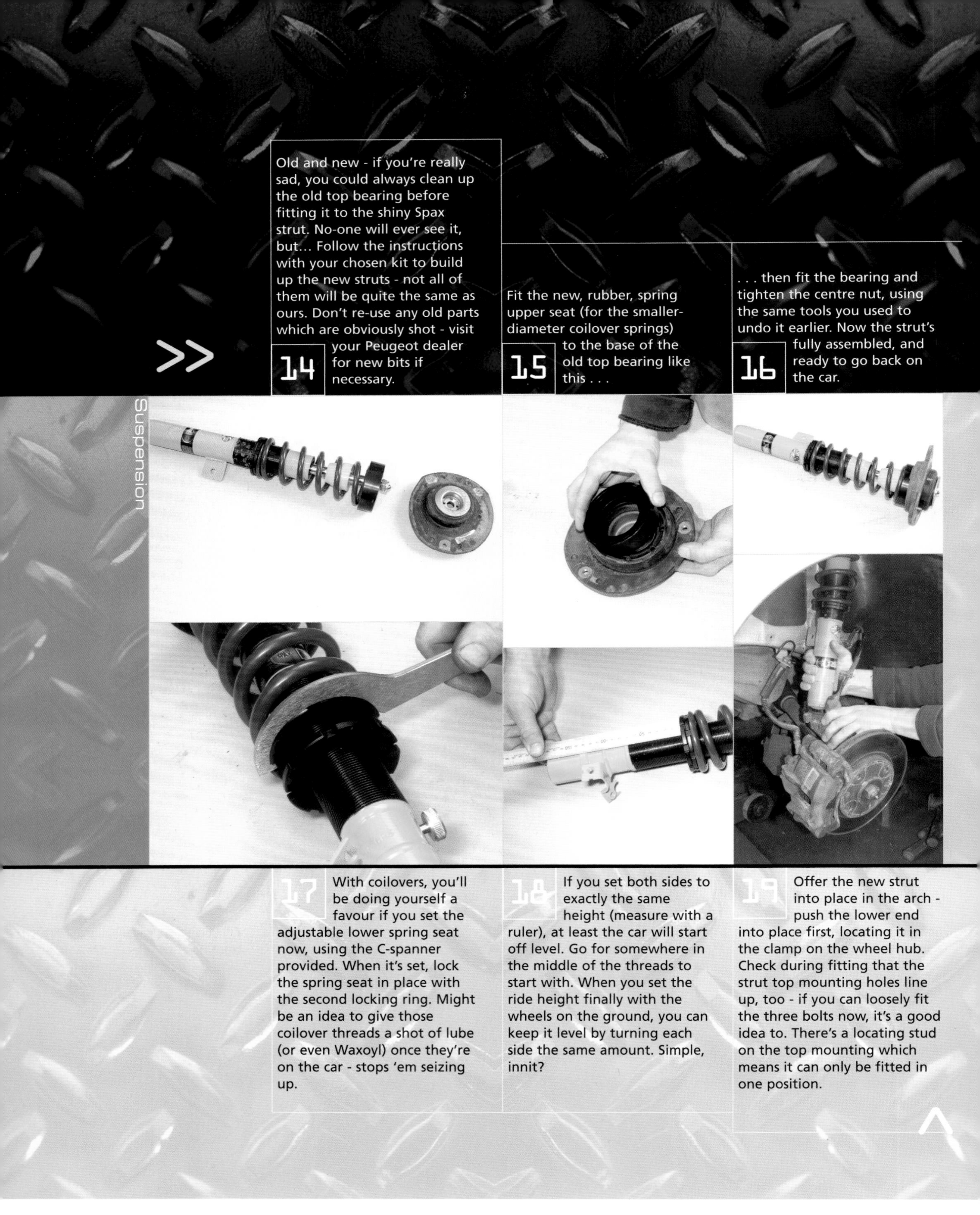

Old and new - if you're really sad, you could always clean up the old top bearing before fitting it to the shiny Spax strut. No-one will ever see it, but... Follow the instructions with your chosen kit to build up the new struts - not all of them will be quite the same as ours. Don't re-use any old parts which are obviously shot - visit your Peugeot dealer for new bits if necessary.

14

Fit the new, rubber, spring upper seat (for the smaller-diameter coilover springs) to the base of the old top bearing like this . . .

15

. . . then fit the bearing and tighten the centre nut, using the same tools you used to undo it earlier. Now the strut's fully assembled, and ready to go back on the car.

16

Suspension

17

With coilovers, you'll be doing yourself a favour if you set the adjustable lower spring seat now, using the C-spanner provided. When it's set, lock the spring seat in place with the second locking ring. Might be an idea to give those coilover threads a shot of lube (or even Waxoyl) once they're on the car - stops 'em seizing up.

18

If you set both sides to exactly the same height (measure with a ruler), at least the car will start off level. Go for somewhere in the middle of the threads to start with. When you set the ride height finally with the wheels on the ground, you can keep it level by turning each side the same amount. Simple, innit?

19

Offer the new strut into place in the arch - push the lower end into place first, locating it in the clamp on the wheel hub. Check during fitting that the strut top mounting holes line up, too - if you can loosely fit the three bolts now, it's a good idea to. There's a locating stud on the top mounting which means it can only be fitted in one position.

**20** If, like us, find that the new strut's a tight fit, treat it to some lube first (keep it away from the brakes, though). With a jack under the lower arm to lift it, the strut should soon locate properly. Note that some struts have a web on the strut body, which must fit into the slot on the inside of the clamp.

**21** When the strut is properly located, refit the clamp bolt you took out right at the start, and tighten it fully (proper torque is 54 Nm).

**22** Fit and tighten the three strut-top mounting bolts to 20 Nm . . .

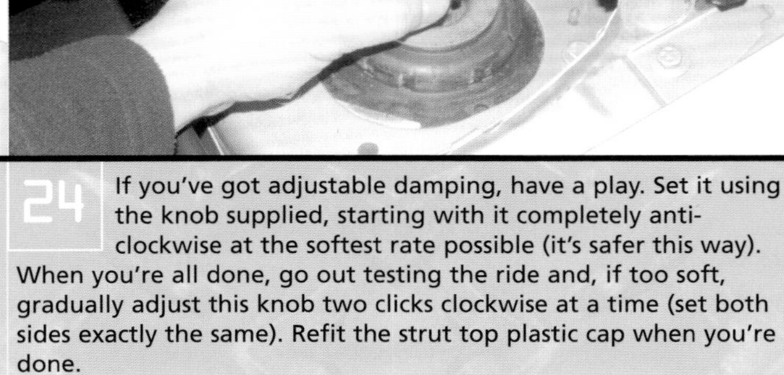

**23** . . . then check that the strut centre nut's fully tight, using the spanner and Allen key you used before. Reconnect the anti-roll bar drop link.

**24** If you've got adjustable damping, have a play. Set it using the knob supplied, starting with it completely anti-clockwise at the softest rate possible (it's safer this way). When you're all done, go out testing the ride and, if too soft, gradually adjust this knob two clicks clockwise at a time (set both sides exactly the same). Refit the strut top plastic cap when you're done.

**25** It's best to let the suspension settle before playing with the ride height too much - take it for a drive first (unless it's so low, it's scraping already). Using the supplied C-spanners, wind the spring seat up or down (the same number of turns each side, to keep it level), then tighten the lock ring up below the spring seat to hold it.

## Remember the middle pedal?

**It's the one next to the throttle - some people don't use it much. Uprating the brakes is actually a very easy bolt-on upgrade, but there are some points to consider.**

One of the strangest, given that improving the brakes should in theory also improve your chances of avoiding an accident, is that insurance companies do not like performance brakes. You should still tell them, but be prepared for bad news. To them, it seems that fitting sporty brakes must automatically make you drive like Jenson Button - the clear implication is that if you need better brakes, you've either also uprated the engine (and not told them?), or you simply drive on the limit everywhere. Shame. We just like to know our cars will stop quickly. That, actually, might be another reason why they don't like better brakes - you stop better, but does the old dodderer behind you? Crunch.

Uprating the brakes will be a complete waste of time if you're a cheapskate on tyres. Cheap, no-name tyres (or ones with no tread left) won't always be able to translate extra braking power into actual vehicle-stopping power - they'll give up their grip on the tarmac and skid everywhere. Something like 90% of braking is done by the front wheels - ie the ones you steer with. If you consider that locked-up wheels also don't tend to steer very well, you'll begin to see why top brakes and lame tyres are a well-dodgy mixture.

# Groovy discs

**Besides the various brands of performance brake pads that go with them, the main brake upgrade is to fit performance front brake discs and pads. Discs are available in two main types - grooved and cross-drilled (and combinations of both).**

When pushed hard, standard discs and pads will quickly build up heat. Too much heat, and the pads get 'glazed', as a result of the resins used in the pad material liquefying, and spreading over the pad surface. Grooved discs can help, by cleaning the glaze off the pads as the brakes are used, restoring the 'bite' - the grooves also provide a 'channel' to help the heat escape. What really helps in fast road use is a set of new pads, with better composite material.

Cross-drilled discs offer another route to heat dissipation, but one which can present some problems. Owners report that cross-drilled discs really eat brake pads, more so than the grooved types, but more serious is the fact that some of these discs can crack around the drilled holes, after heavy use. The trouble is that the heat 'migrates' to the drilled holes (as was intended), but the heat build-up can be extreme, and the constant heating/cooling cycle can stress the metal to the point where it will crack. Discs which have been damaged in this way are extremely dangerous to drive on, as they could break up completely at any time. Only fit discs of this type from established manufacturers offering a useful guarantee of quality, and check the discs regularly.

Performance discs also have a reputation for warping (nasty vibrations felt through the pedal). Justified, or not? Well, the harder you use your brakes (and we're into abuse territory now), the greater the heat you'll generate. Okay, so these wicked discs are meant to be able to cope with this heat, but you can't expect miracles. Cheap discs, or ones which have had a hard time over mega-thousands of miles, will warp. So buy quality, and don't get over-heroic on the brakes.

Performance pads can be fitted to any brake discs, including the standard ones, but are of course designed to work best with heat-dissipating discs. Unless your 206 has something seriously meaty under the bonnet, don't be tempted to go much further than 'fast road' pads - anything more competition-orientated may take too long to come up to temperature on the road. Remember what pushbike brakes were like in the wet? Cold competition pads feel the same, and old dears always step off the pavement when your brakes are cold!

Lastly, fitting all the performance brake bits in the world is no use if your calipers have seized up. If, when you strip out your old pads, you find that one pad's worn more than the other, or that both pads have worn more on the left wheel than the right, your caliper pistons are sticking. Sometimes you can free them off by pushing them back into the caliper, but this could be a garage job to fix. If you drive around with sticking calipers, you'll eat pads and discs. You choose.

# **Brake** discs and pads

Fitting huge multi-spoke wheels makes your factory-fit discs look pretty puny, so many people's idea of impressive brakes is to go large. We can understand that. But it costs, and you might have quite a search to find a company doing the bits, to start with. Then it's got to be decent quality, and fitted properly - play around with brakes, and the only mag feature you'll get is Crash of the Month.

**Remember!**

*It's a good idea to have your brake mods MOT-tested once you've fitted new discs and pads, and you might even be able to 'blag' a free brake check at your local fast-fit centre if you're crafty! Brakes are a serious safety issue, and unless you're 100% confident that all is well, demo-ing your car's awesome new-found stopping ability could find you in the ditch...*

**Remember 2!**

*New pads of any sort need careful bedding-in (gentle use over the first 100 miles) before they'll work properly - when first fitted, the pad surface won't have worn exactly to the contours of the disc, so it won't actually be touching it, over its full area. This will possibly result in very under-whelming brakes for the first few trips, so watch it - misplaced over-confidence in new brakes is a fast track to hospital...*

**Achtung!**

*Brake dust from old pads or shoes may contain asbestos. Wear a mask to avoid inhaling it.*

**01** Loosen the wheel bolts, jack up the corner of the car you're working on, and take off the wheel. Put an axle stand under a solid part of the car, just in case the jack gives out (see "wheels & tyres" for more info on jacking up). Undo the two bolts on the rear of the caliper - these will be very tight, so watch your knuckles.

**02** Ease the caliper off the disc, and be ready with a cable-tie, length of wire, string, or a bungee hook . . .

**07** We've heard of personalised registrations, but brake discs? Red Dot did the biz for us - give them a call for your own custom discs. With ordinary grooved discs, the grooves must be positioned in a certain way - check your paperwork, as you might have picked up the wrong disc from the box.

**08** Refit the two disc retaining screws, and nip them up tight – they don't need excessive force. The disc is clamped in place by the wheel and its four bolts.

. . . to save the caliper hanging on the brake hose, which could damage it. Hang the caliper up towards the rear of the arch - **03** this will keep it out of the way while you're working.

Using a screwdriver through the one of the disc holes to stop it **04** turning, undo the two Torx screws holding the disc in place.

With a soft mallet, tap the disc **05** gently all the way round, to unseat it from the hub.

Time to clean the rust and muck from the hub face using a wire brush or emery cloth. This is actually more vital than you might think - any muck in there will stop the new disc from sitting on square, and if that happens, your brakes won't work too well, and **06** you'll eat through brake pads. So do a good job.

**09** Remove the caliper from its hanging point and, using a pair of grips ('water pump' or 'slip-joint' pliers are ideal), slowly squeeze the inner brake pad back into the caliper. The new brake pads are thicker than the old ones, so you need to make room for them, like this.

**10** Remove the old pads, which just unclip (they have spring clips on the back). The new pads, to no-one's great surprise, fit exactly the same way. Which is nice. Make sure you get the right ones out of the box, and keep the pads clean by keeping your hands clean (unless you like extra-long braking distances).

**11** Slide the caliper and pads over the new disc, making sure the pads aren't dislodged in the process. Tighten the caliper bolts like you mean it (the correct torque for these is 105 Nm, which is very tight), and you're almost finished.

**12** It's wise to clean the disc after installation so there's no contamination on its surface which can get on the pads. No, do not adjust your medication - the calipers really have suddenly turned blue. If you were thinking of painting yours, doing it while the brakes are apart is a very good plan.

**Achtung!**

*Pushing the brake pads back into the calipers might damage the fluid seals, from the reverse-flow of brake fluid. It's a very slight risk, but... The safest way to do the job is to connect a brake bleeder kit to the caliper bleed screw, and open the screw slightly with a spanner, before squeezing the piston in. Tighten the bleed screw and top-up the brake fluid afterwards.*

# Cool coloured **stoppers**

This is a modification which has been done for years, and that's because it looks so effective. Reason is, most of the time we see nothing but grimy and black calipers on road cars, so when a rim is backed by a shiny disc and bright caliper, it stands out. Also, because the majority of aftermarket expensive caliper packages are painted in bright motorsport colours, this work makes your car look more purposeful than any standard 206.

Painting the calipers requires that they're clean - really clean. Accessory stores sell aerosol brake cleaner, which (apart from having a distinctive high-octane perfume) is just great for removing brake dust, and lots more besides! Some kits come complete with cleaner spray. Many of the kits advertise themselves on the strength of no dismantling being required, but we don't agree. Also, having always successfully brush-painted our calipers, we wouldn't advise using any kind of spray paint.

We know you won't want to hear this, but the best way to paint the calipers is to do some dismantling first. The kits say you don't have to, but trust me - you'll get a much better result from a few minutes' extra work. The best time to paint would be while you're fitting new discs, but nobody thinks that far ahead.

## **Painting** drums

**01** At least there's no dismantling with drums - get the rear end jacked up, wheels off (see *'Wheels & tyres'* if you need jacking info) and just get stuck in with the wire brush . . .

**Achtung!**

*Brake dust from old pads or shoes may contain asbestos. Wear a mask to avoid inhaling it.*

**02** . . . then sandpaper (to smooth the surface), spray on the brake cleaner, and wipe thoroughly. Wiping is important - don't rely on the spray alone, as you won't get the surfaces clean.

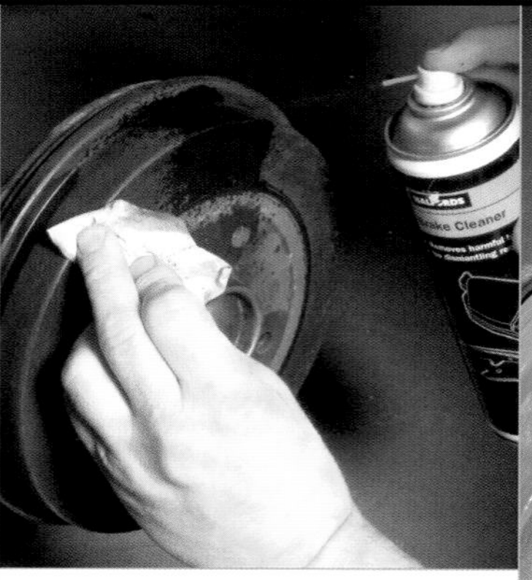


**03** Painting the drums is much easier than the fiddly calipers, but use a decent brush with soft bristles. For a max-shine finish, you need to be generous with the paint, and smooth with your stroke (oh, baby). Try not to get any paint on the brake backplate (the fixed part).

**04** You definitely don't want any paint down the wheel bolt holes - in fact, you don't really want it where the wheels will touch the drum (you can't see this bit, once the wheel's on). Masking-up shouldn't be necessary if your hand is steady. Let off the handbrake and turn the drum half a turn every so often until the paint's dry. Nobody likes the runs, after all.

# Painting **calipers**

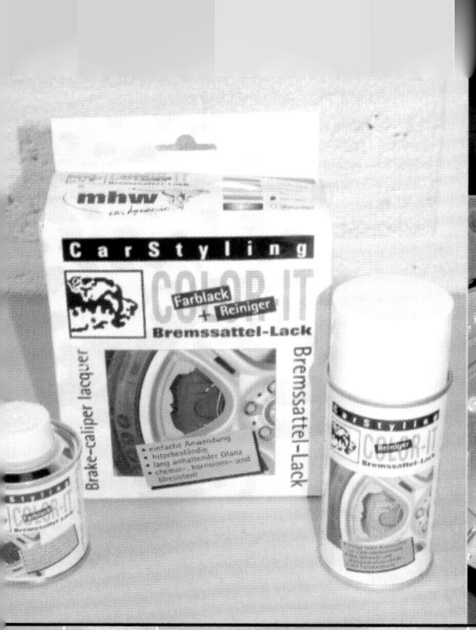

**01** Caliper paint has to be the right stuff, otherwise it won't last. We chose MHW's special caliper paint, which comes in a two-part pack, giving you a spray can of cleaner and a tin of paint.

**02** Through preparation will ensure the best paint job on your caliper, so give it a good wire-brush to loosen any dust and rust.

**03** Use the aerosol brake cleaner to wash the worst of the stuff out, particularly in any corners the wire brush couldn't reach.

**04** Finally, degrease the caliper with a cloth, which should get the last of the debris off, to give you a smooth surface (don't rely on the spray alone). Leave it to dry for five minutes.

**05** Get painting, using a small brush, as it helps for all the difficult-to-reach areas. Don't paint it on too thick, or it'll run.

**06** The new caliper looks much more trick, especially behind aftermarket 18-inch rims.

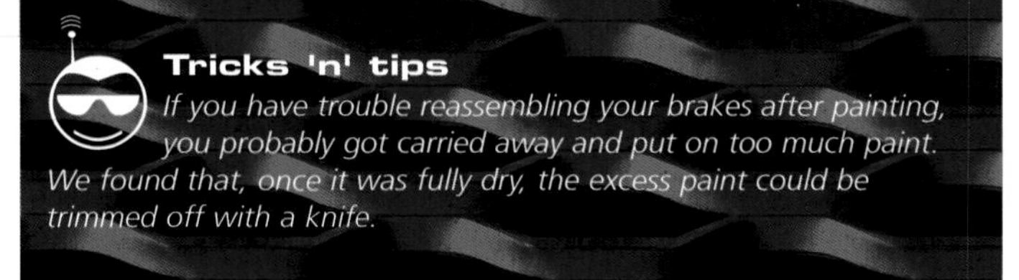

**Tricks 'n' tips**

*If you have trouble reassembling your brakes after painting, you probably got carried away and put on too much paint. We found that, once it was fully dry, the excess paint could be trimmed off with a knife.*

# Interiors

What do we think of the standard 206 dash? Well, it doesn't feel like it's about to fall apart (something you can't say about all French cars). But what about those grained plastics - inspired by the back ends of large grey animals with tusks, seen roaming about in Africa. Not pleasant. Also not very easy on the eye are some of the seat fabrics - this is where words like 'bright' and 'cheerful' actually mean 'gross'. But nothing was ever built that can't be improved, and the interior really is one area where the goodies are easy to fit. Choose one 'theme' and stick to it, and the end result won't look like anything from a production line.

As with exterior styling, fashions can change very quickly - so don't be afraid to experiment with a look you really like, because chances are, it'll be the next big thing anyway. Just don't do wood, ok? We've a feeling it's never coming in, never mind coming back...

## Removing stuff

### Take it easy and break less

Many of the procedures we're going to show involve removing interior trim panels (either for colouring or to fit other stuff), and this can be tricky. It's far too easy to break plastic trim, especially once it's had a chance to go a bit brittle with age. Another 'problem' with the 206 is that the interior trim is pretty well-attached (and the designers have been very clever at hiding several vital screws), meaning that it can be a pig to get off. We'll try and avoid the immortal words 'simply unclip the panel', and instead show you how properly, but inevitably at some stage, a piece of trim won't 'simply' anything.

The important lesson here is not to lose your temper, as this has a highly-destructive effect on plastic components, and may result in a panel which no amount of carbon film or colour spray can put right, or make fit again. Superglue may help, but not every time. So - take it steady, prise carefully, and think logically about how and where a plastic panel would have to be attached, to stay on. You'll encounter all sorts of trim clips (some more fragile than others) in your travels - when these break, as they usually do, many of them can be bought in packs from accessory shops, and rarer ones will be available from a Peugeot dealer, probably off the shelf. Even fully-trained Peugeot mechanics aren't immune to breaking a few trim clips!

# Door trim panels

You'll find plenty of excuses for removing your door trim panels - fitting speakers, re-trimming the panel, de-locking, even window tinting, so we'd better tell you how ...

**01** Removing the door card is really easy, and takes just a few minutes. First, undo the screw at the front of the door, just above the door pocket. As you can see, access is a little tricky.

**02** Remove the screw in the door pull. Didn't even know there was one in there, eh? Take out the door pull panel, or it'll only fall out later. Removing it also makes it easier to line up the hole when refitting.

**03** Prise off the small panel towards where the mirror control comes through (you may have a tweeter in there - if so, disconnect its wiring) . . .

**04** . . . and the last door screw to remove is behind the panel.

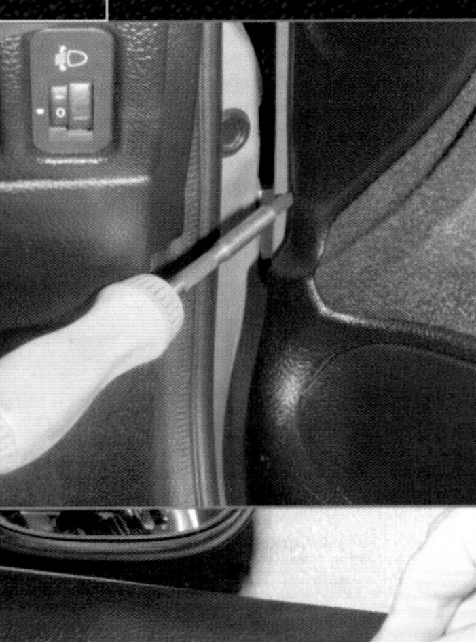

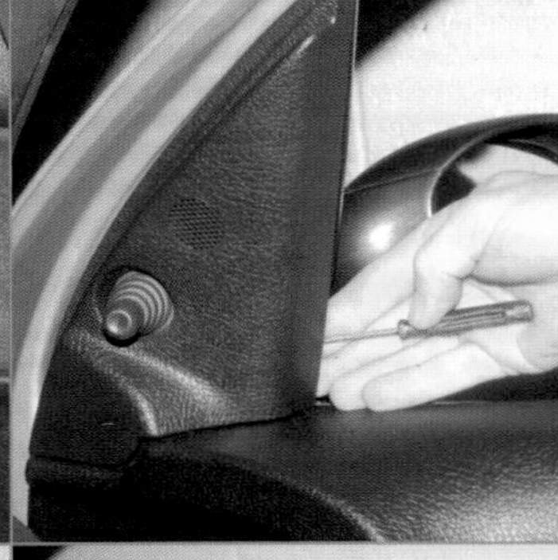

**05** Remove the door handle surround, prising it off carefully with a small screwdriver.

**06** Lever the door panel off carefully, starting at the lower rear corner, until your hear the retaining plugs pop.

**07** Remove the door panel and put to one side in a safe place.

**Tricks 'n' tips**

*Find something like an old ice-cream or margarine tub to keep all the little screws and bits in, as you take them off. This approach is far superior to the chuck-them-all-on-the-floor method most people use, until they lose something vital.*

# Anything but black?

The interior trim on the 206 at least hides its age well, and doesn't rattle much. And that's about it - for a lover of elephant-hide and art nouveau seat fabric, it's heaven. For normal people, it's something else. Fortunately, there's plenty you can do to personalise it, and there are three main routes to take:

*1) Spray paint - available in any colour you like, as long as it's... not black. This Folia Tec stuff actually dyes softer plastics and leather, and comes in a multi-stage treatment, to suit all plastic types. Don't try to save money just buying the top coat, because it won't work! Special harder-wearing spray is required for use on steering wheels. Ordinary spray paint for bodywork might damage some plastics, and won't be elastic - good primer is essential. Make sure you also buy lots of masking tape.*

*2) Adhesive or shrink-fit film - available in various wild colours, carbon, ally, and, er... walnut (would YOU?). Probably best used on flatter surfaces, or at least those without complex curves, or you'll have to cut and join - spray is arguably better here. Some companies will sell you sheets of genuine carbon-fibre, with peel-off backing - looks and feels the part (nice if you have touchy-feely passengers).*

*3) Replacement panels - the easiest option, as the panels are supplied pre-cut, ready to fit. Of course, you're limited then to styling just the panels supplied.*

If you fancy something more posh, how about trimming your interior bits in leather? Very saucy. Available in various colours, and hardly any dearer than film, you also get that slight 'ruffled' effect on tighter curves.

# Get the cans out



Any painting process is a *multi-stage* application. With the Folia Tec system (thanks to Eurostyling for supplying ours), many of you apparently think you can get away just buying the top coat, which then looks like a cheap option compared to film - WRONG! Even the proper interior spray top coat won't stay on for long without the matching primer, and the finish won't be wear-resistant without the finishing sealer spray. You don't necessarily need the special foaming cleaner - you could get by with a general-purpose degreaser, such as meths. Just watch the grey/black plastic doesn't suddenly turn white - if it does, you're damaging the finish! This might not be too important to you, as it's being sprayed over anyway, but if you take out the grey too far on a part that's not being sprayed all over, you'll have to live with a cacky-looking white-grey finish to any non-painted surface...

Providing you're a dab hand with the masking tape, paint gives you the flexibility to be more creative. For instance, you could try colour-matching the exterior of the car - but will ordinary car body paint work on interior plastics? Course it will, as long as you prep the panels properly.

Choice of paint's one thing, but what to paint? Well, not everything - for instance, you might want to avoid high-wear areas like door handles. Just makes for an easier life. The glovebox lid and instrument panel surround are obvious first choices, as are the dash centre section and side vents. The centre console's not lighting anyone's fire in standard Peugeot grey, so hit it with some spray too. Any panels which just pop out are targets, in fact (lots less masking needed) - just make sure whatever you're dismantling was meant to come apart, or it'll be out with the superglue instead of the cans.

Don't be afraid to experiment with a combination of styles - as long as you're confident you can blend it all together, anything goes! Mix the painted bits with some tasteful carbon-fibre sheet or brushed-aluminium film, if you like - neutral colours like this, or chrome, can be used to give a lift to dash bits which are too tricky to spray.

# Painting **trim**

Years ago, when painting plastic parts you had to use regular body paint and hope that you didn't flex the part when you put it on.

But the great thing about car styling is the sheer amount of new products it has made accessible, and Folia Tec's complete paint range makes it possible to revamp your interior in a completely different colour, giving it a brand new look.

We chose to pick out shapely parts on the car for respraying, creating highlights on the interior's strong points. We kept preparation in mind because the better you do it, the better the paint finish will be and the longer it will last.

**01** The range comprises cleaner, primer, spray and finally sealer. Good as they are, these paints will not cover surface imperfections (such as the heavily-grained finish on the 206 dash) . . .

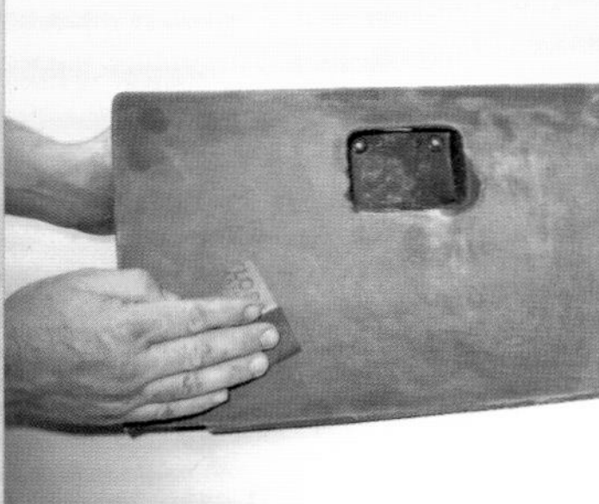

**02** . . . for a real professional look, plastics should be sanded smooth . . .

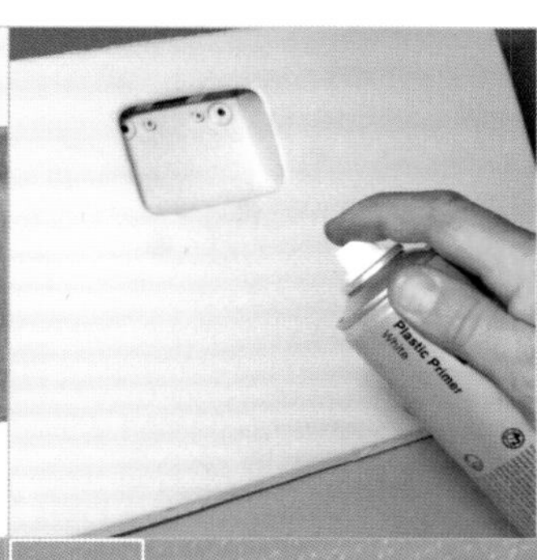


**03** . . . then treated to several coats of high-build plastic primer.

**04** Start by removing the parts you want to spray. The vents come out easy once you've levered up the edge. Disconnect the vent pipe from the heating system and the vent will come off completely.

**05** The dash centre levers up and will prise free. Try levering at various points all the way down rather than just one point, otherwise you could crack it. Disconnect the wiring on the rear.

**06** Lay out the parts you want to colour, leaving plenty of room in between them to make sure they're completely sprayed. Clean the parts with the foam cleaner, which will need to wiped off afterwards with kitchen towel or similar. Once dried, spray the parts with the primer. Two thin coats, 10 minutes apart, will suffice.

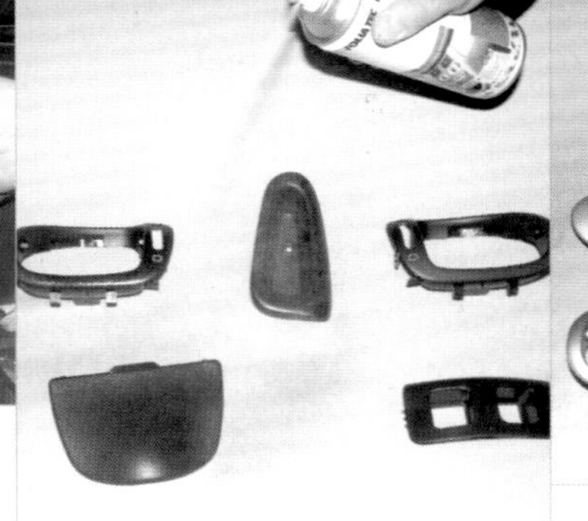

**07** Spray the colour next, with three thin coats and again at least 10 minutes between each. You may find some colour sprays have less pigment, and you'll need more coats. The manufacturer also recommends a coat of their clear sealer, which protects the painted finish from damage. Makes sense to us. Re-assemble your dash and admire your new interior.

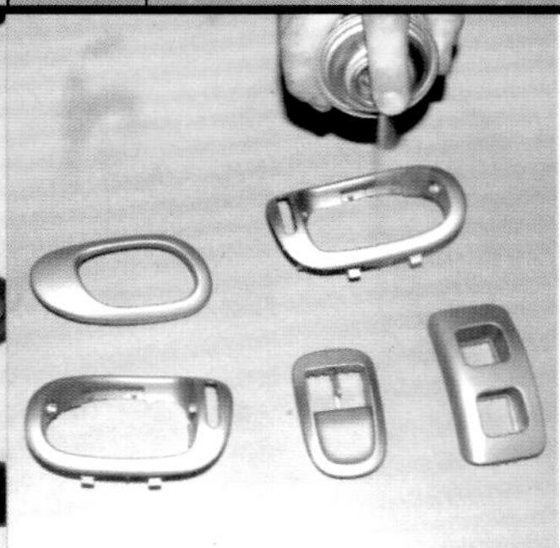

# Dash dynamics

**Dressing up your dashboard is a must to lift it from the all-too-common black expanse of plastic. There's a wealth of aftermarket parts out there to help you, so mostly it's down to what style of finish you want. Aluminium? Carbon-fibre? Please, not wood.**

The Dash Dynamics kit covers the centre dash panel and the air vents either side. What we recommend when fitting this kit is getting the interior of the car nice and warm, along with the product itself and the dashboard. This helps to mould the plastic-based aluminium-look trim, avoiding creases, or edges which won't stick.

**01** The styling kit covers the centre dash panel, heater control, ashtray, radio and each fresh air vent on the dash outer edges.

**02** First, you need to thoroughly clean the dashboard parts the trim is going on, especially since most interior cleaners (which you've probably used) have silicone in them. The trim backing will not stick if this isn't cleaned off, so go over the dash twice with the cleaning solution provided in the kit.

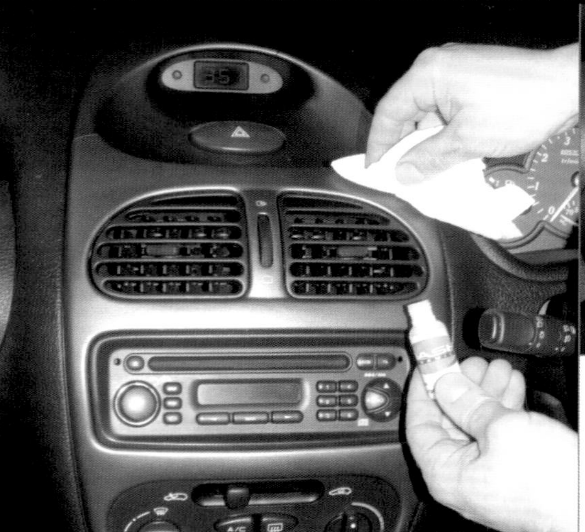

**03** Warm up the dashboard with a hairdryer . . .

**04** . . . and give the styling kit the same treatment. Providing you don't actually melt it, this makes the sections as mouldable as possible, which will help get the best finish. Line each section up carefully, and press firmly into place - it's that simple.

# Filming your 206

If you fancy creating a look that's a bit more special than plain paint colours, film is the answer - but be warned - it's not the easiest stuff in the world to use, and so isn't everyone's favourite. If you must have the brushed-aluminium look, or fancy giving your 206 the carbon-fibre treatment, there really is no alternative (apart from the lazy-man option of new panels, of course).

**01** Cut the film roughly to size, remembering to leave plenty of excess for trimming - it's also a good idea to have plenty to fold around the edges, because thin film has a nasty habit of peeling off, otherwise.

**02** Next, we gently warmed up both the panel, and the film itself. Just following the instructions provided, and who are we to argue?

**03** Peel off the backing, being careful that the film stays as flat as possible. Also take care, when you pick the film up, that it doesn't stick to itself (our stuff seemed very keen to do this!).

**04** Stick the film on straight - very important with any patterned finish. Start at one edge or corner, and work across, to keep the air bubbles and creases to a minimum. If you get a really bad crease, it's best to unpeel a bit and try again - the adhesive's very tacky, and there's no slide-age available.

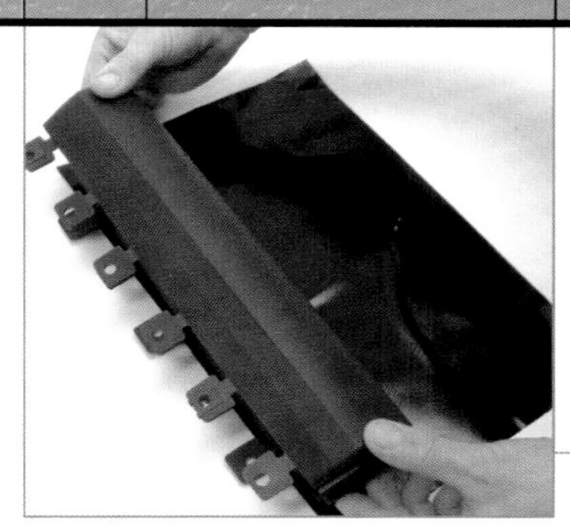

**05** Work out the worst of the air bubbles with a soft cloth - get the stuff to stick as best you can before trimming, or it'll all go horribly wrong. To be sure it's stuck (especially important on a grained surface), go over it firmly with the edge of your least-important piece of 'plastic' - ie not a credit card.

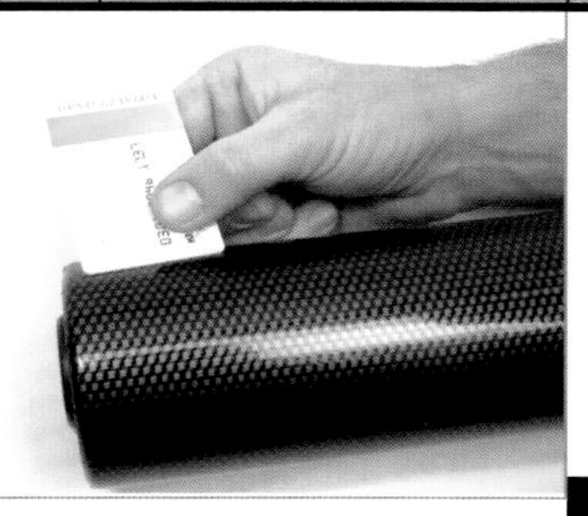

**06** Once the film's laid on, it's time for trimming - which (you guessed it) is the tricky bit. We found it's much easier to trim the tricky bits once the film's been warmed up using a hairdryer or heat gun, but don't overdo it! Make sure you've also got a VERY sharp knife - a blunt one will ripple the film, and may tear it (one good thing about film is that blood wipes off it easily!).

**07** To get the film to wrap neatly round a curved edge, make several slits almost up to the edge, then wrap each sliver of film around, and stick on firmly. If the film's heated as you do this, it wraps round and keeps its shape - meaning it shouldn't try and spring back, ruining all your hard work.

**Bum notes**

*There are limitations to using film, and the quality of the film itself has a lot to do with that. We had major problems doing any kind of job with one particular make of brushed-aluminium-look film - it was a nightmare to work with, and the edges had peeled the next day. Buying quality film will give you a long-lasting result to be proud of, with much less skill requirement and LOTS less swearing. But it still pays not to be too ambitious with it.*

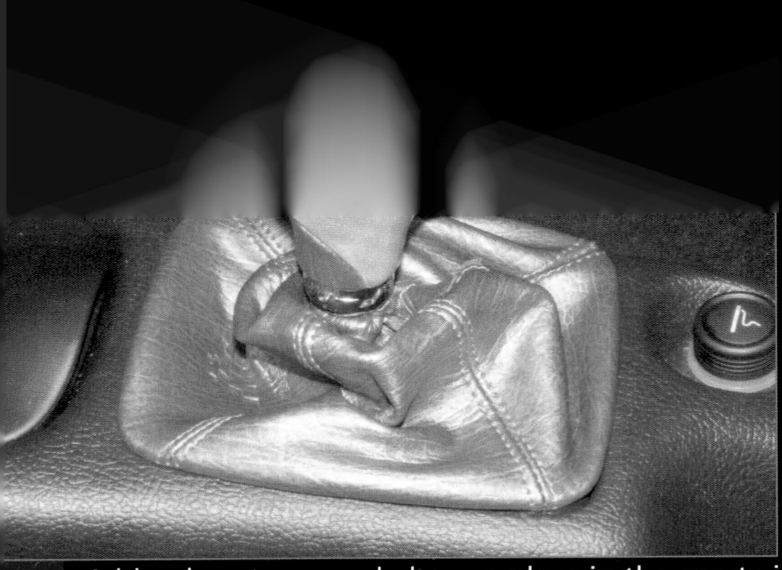

# Gear knob jobs

If you're doing a complete job on your knob, it ought to be both the knob and gaiter which get swapped together. If so, pull the knob off, straight upwards. It is tight, but will come eventually - if yours proves stubborn, try warming it

**01** with a hairdryer or heat gun, and twisting slightly to loosen it.

**A bland centre console has no place in the sporty interior of a 206, and our Peugeot's was plain-as.**

Black shifter, black gaiter, black centre console, black handbrake, black ashtray, black cigarette lighter… get the picture? It might be cheap for Peugeot to produce it like this, but the look is naff. On a positive note, the dark *noir-avec-noir* look means that even the slightest colour or material change on the centre console will stand out. Hence, a shifter gaiter in electric blue with chrome surround should make a huge difference.

It would be senseless to go through the huge range of gear knobs out there, which you can use to update or re-style your 206. It really depends on what look you're going for, but for something wild, how about our Simoni Racing Graffio? Otherwise it's going to be an aluminium or carbon fibre finish - anything's better than standard, no matter how sweet 'n' subtle. Whatever you choose, test it first for 'feel' - metal gear knobs are damn cold in winter, and roasting in summer!

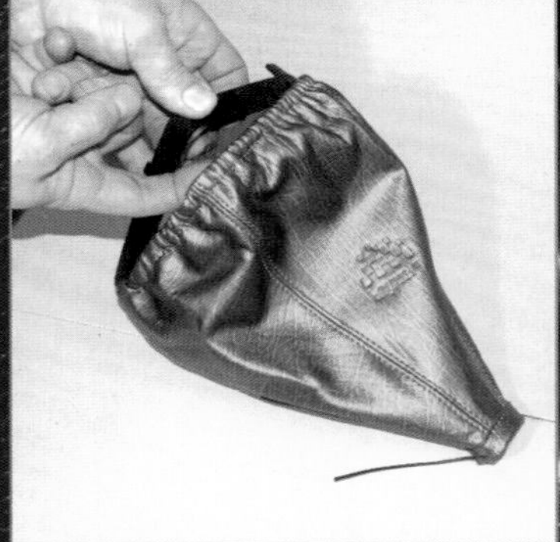

**06** As the new gaiter is elasticated at the base, it can simply slip over the frame without being clipped into place.

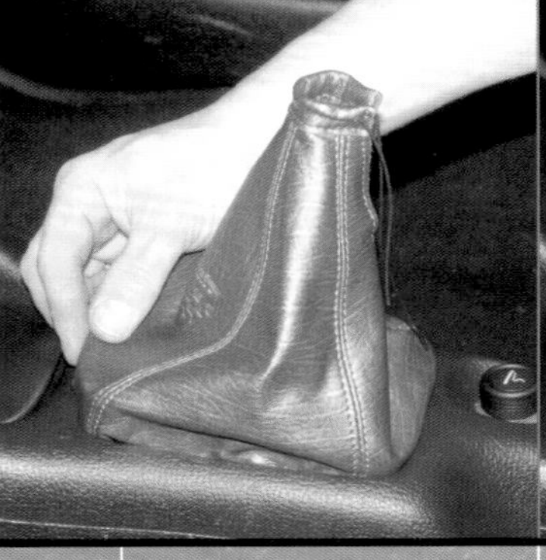

**07** Push the frame and new gaiter into place, rear in first then the front. If the new gaiter's too baggy, just pull it over the housing some more. You can then tighten the pull string at the top of the gaiter to hold it in place.

**08** Our gear knob is a 'universal-fit' item (a term which normally makes us cringe, as it means 'hard to fit'). But this is a well-thought-out product, which comes with grub screws in varying lengths, plus different-sized rubber sleeves to make the knob secure. Fit the appropriate rubber sleeve depending on the size of the gear lever shaft. It should be a snug fit on the end.

**09** Most gear knobs come with a chrome lower ring, which screws up to the base of the main knob. Ours is no different - fit the collar now.

02 Removing the gaiter is much easier - it's mounted on a plastic frame, which is clipped into the centre console. Prise it out, front first.

03 If that gear knob isn't getting the treatment today, turn the gaiter inside-out and cut the cable-tie just under the knob.

04 The gaiter plastic frame uses clips to secure the material, so lever these off carefully with a small screwdriver. Take care - we're planning on re-using that frame for our new gaiter.

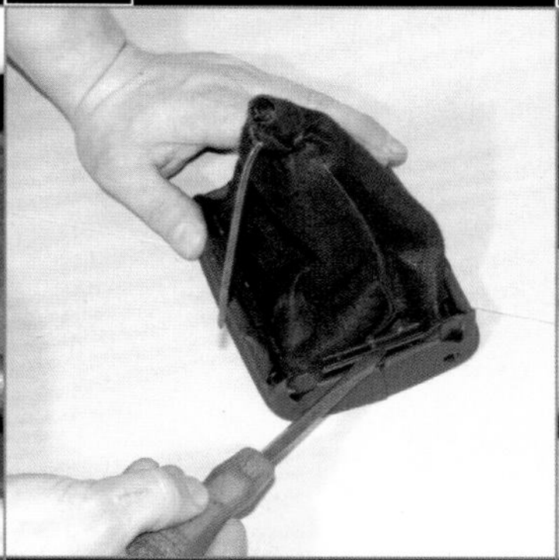

05 Peel the old material off the frame. That's the last time we need to look at the nasty stock item - anyone think of a possible use for a second-hand gear gaiter?

10 Fit the knob itself - the rubber sleeve shouldn't move as you slide it on.

11 Install and tighten the grub screws to hold the knob in place, using the Allen screws and key in the kit.

12 Screw the collar up to the base of the knob. Tie the gaiter up to the base of the new knob, and the job's a winner.

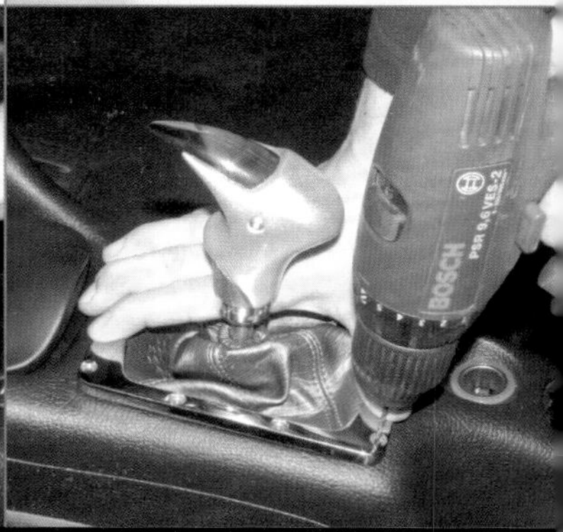

13 The manufacturers also make this universal chrome surround, which is the perfect finishing touch. Simply hold the surround in place and drill each hole, then put the screws in to hold it down. Sweet.

# Handbrake knob

**It's the little touches will make the difference on your car, and make other people notice it. So small, tasteful modifications here and there can go a long way.**

Aluminium has always looked tasteful, and such accessories can really brighten up a car's dull and bleak interior. Richbrook make some neat ally components to help your task. Their handbrake handle is a solid, quality aluminium piece, with anodised finish so it should last and remain good looking. It fits with minimum hassle, and will get rid of the nasty rubber handbrake cover Peugeot throw in there as standard.

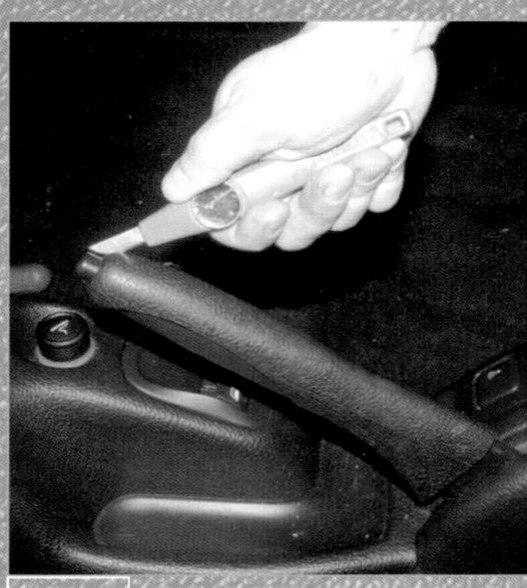

01 Start the job by taking a knife to the standard rubber cover. It's a bit brutal, but it's gotta be done.

02 Remove the unpleasant rubber cover and chuck it. As you can see, there's not much scope for fitting a handbrake gaiter on a 206, but we can still make things look a whole lot better.

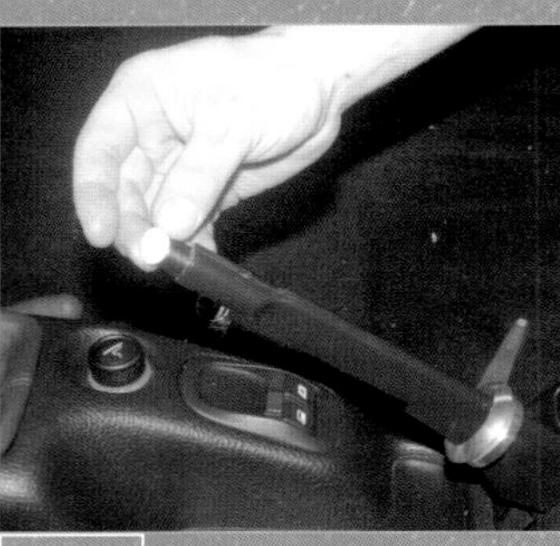

03 Install the small, circular white soft pad on the front of the standard handbrake button.

04 Wrap the supplied black circular sponge pad around the handle and cut it to size so its edges butt together.

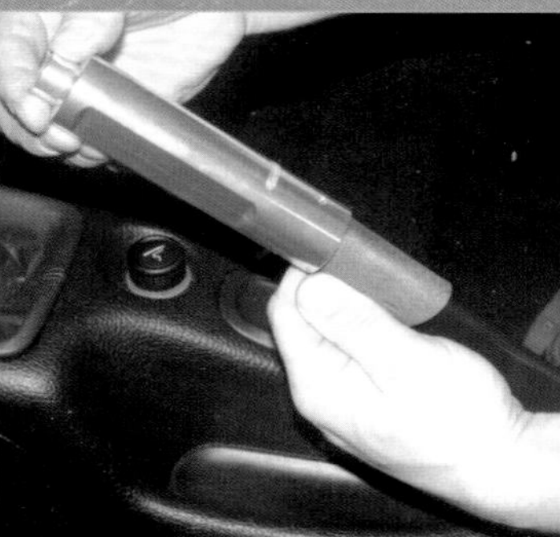

05 Holding the black pad tight, slide the new aluminium cover over the top, making sure the aluminium button is at the front of the cover.

06 There are three short grub screws and three long, which can be used in various combinations to centralise the universal cover on your handbrake lever. We found that one long one at the top and two shorter ones below worked best.

07 Assemble the collar on to the base of the new cover, using the grub screws to tighten it. Your 206 is now a little less dull inside - don't stop here, though.

# Door sill **trim plates**

**Anything to dress up the sill area of your 206 will make a difference every time you get in or out, so having a pair of stainless steel plates is a worthy addition.**

Having them illuminated so they show up at night is a real pose. The Isotta kit we used for the 206 comes with a pair of laser-cut stainless steel sill covers, and all the necessary wiring.

**01** Pull up the door rubber seal, along the full length of the door opening to get at the sill properly.

**02** Clean the sill thoroughly to get rid of any dust, grease or anything else that will hinder adhesion of the sill plate's sticky pads.

**03** Measure up to find the middle of the sill, so you can centralise the plate. Offer the plate in position, so you can check it fits properly, without risking getting it permanently stuck in the wrong place. Once you've got it central (or however else you'd like it), make a pencil mark on the sill at each end, so you can line the plate back up again when you're finally sticking it down.

**04** Peel off the backing from the sticky pad, take a deep breath . . .

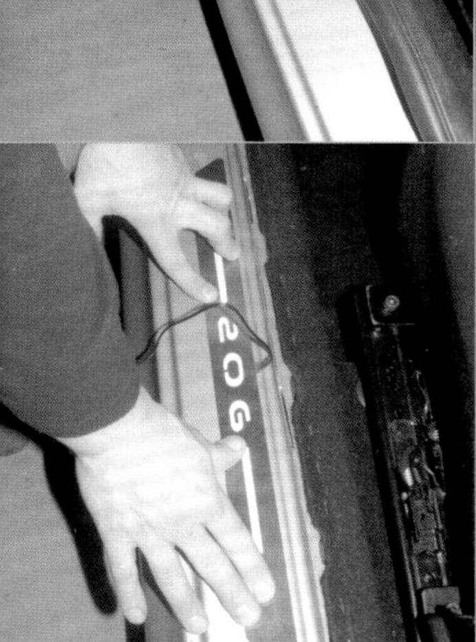

**05** . . . and stick down the plate, making sure the writing is the right way up (duh!) and the wiring directed towards the inside of the car.

**06** The wiring will have to be carefully moulded over the metal lip onto which the rubber seal sits, or drill a small hole in the lip, and feed the wires through. Either way, make sure the wires are protected from sharp metal edges, or your new plates won't light up for long.

**07** Inside the car, run the wiring down the inner sill, and connect it up to the transformer. The black wire can go to any good chassis earth. The red wire should go to an ignition-switched live (use a permanent one, off the battery, and your sill plates are on all the time). For max cool, tap into the interior light live, at the back of fuse 8 (in-car fusebox). Then your plates come on when the doors open.

# A 206 that really shifts

Changing the gearshift mechanism on your 206 for something with a shorter throw is one of the biggest bangs for the buck you can get, at least as far as the driving experience is concerned. It'll make your gearshifting much tighter and quicker, so you'll no longer have to feel that sloppiness of the standard gearstick.

B&M have for years made shifters in the States, and just a few years ago launched into Europe with a huge range of short-throw shifters for the Euro market. The construction and completeness of their kits is unsurpassed, so you know that once you've fitted one, it's going to last for many years and not pull out in your hand at the first sign of a rapid gearchange. With the gearstick being 'remote', ie not directly acting inside the gearbox, you've to get to the actuating shaft under the car, which is only accessed through taking off the front section of exhaust and its heat shield. Changing the shifter is no five-minute job, but it's not too tricky either, as long as you have a decent jack and axle stands.

01 Start by removing the gear gaiter and gear knob, as described in the gear knob section (funnily enough). You can now undo the four nuts which hold the gear lever on.

02 Push the gear lever down, so the four mounting bolt threads disappear down through the holes, releasing the lever mountings from the floor. Now would be a good time to get the car in the air, supported securely on some axle stands - you'll be working underneath a fair bit. See 'wheels & tyres' for jacking and supporting info.

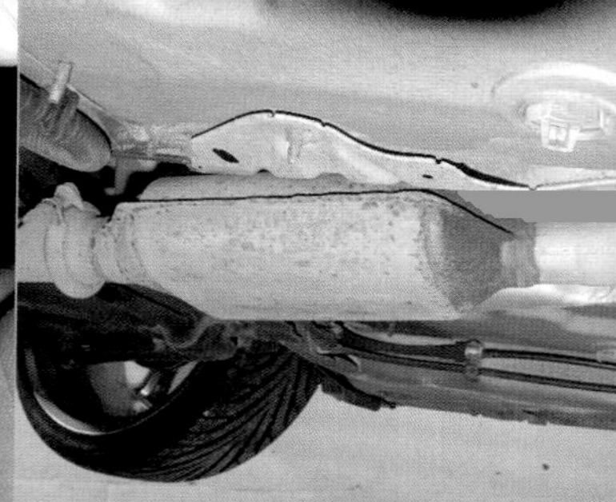

03 The centre section of the exhaust (where the cat is) needs to come off at this point. Trace the wiring up from the oxygen sensor (screwed into the cat body), and disconnect its wiring plug. Now there's just a clamp to undo each end, and the centre section can be separated and removed. Don't let it fall on the floor - the cat is a bit delicate (and a bit expensive).

08 Prise out the bushes in the bottom of the lever with a screwdriver.

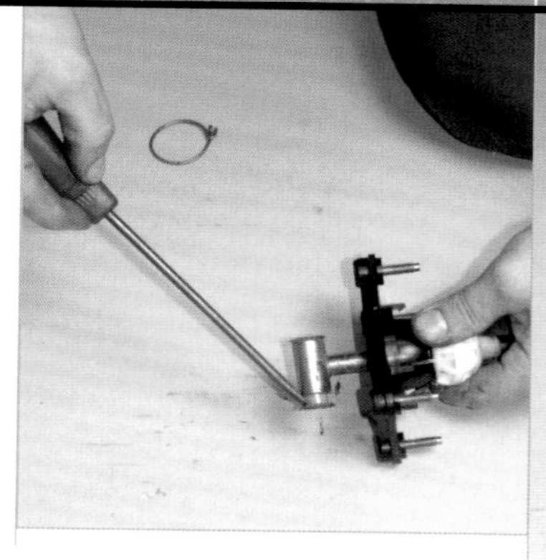

09 Lever off the retaining ring from the ball-and-socket connection . . .

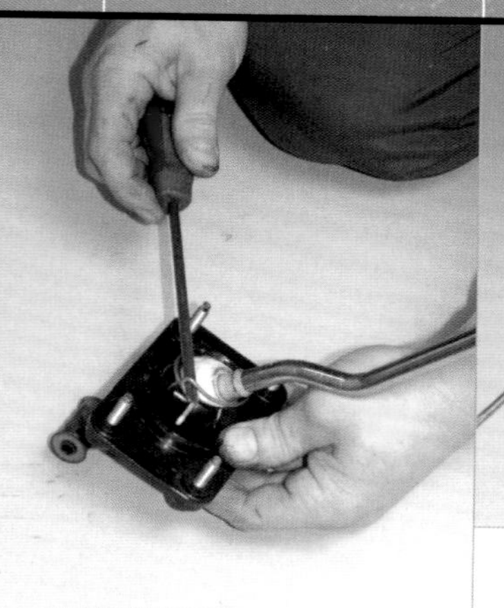

10 . . . then push the mounting plate downwards off the gear lever, and remove it - we'll be recycling this later, so don't bin it.

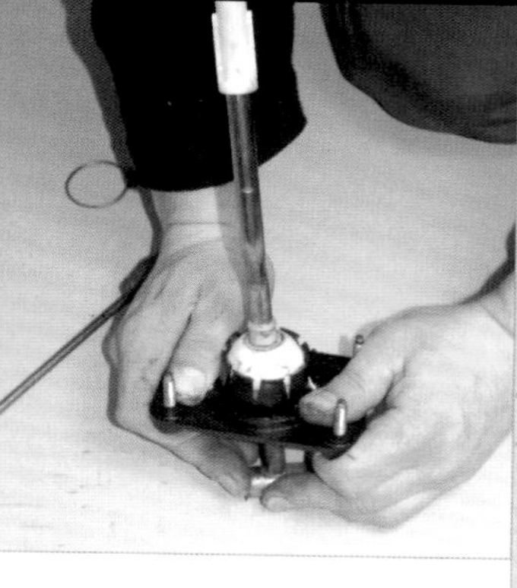

11 Old stick, new stick. In case you were wondering, the new one's on the right. Compare them, and you can see where the extra leverage comes from (if you can't, you'll have to take our word for it).

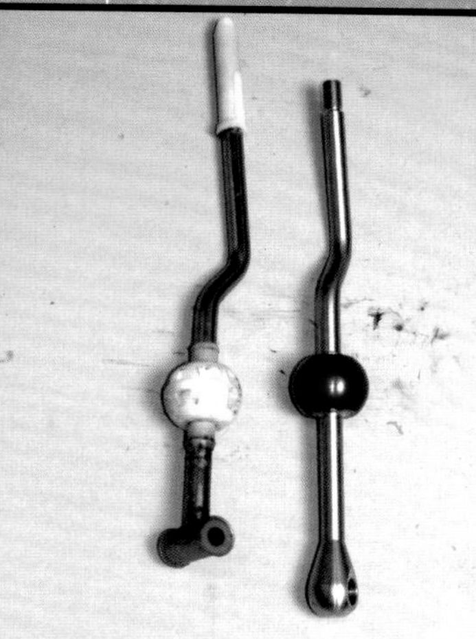

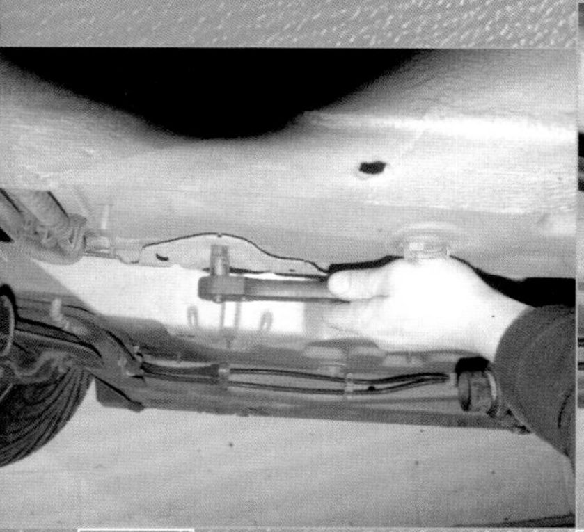

**04** Undo the six bolts and remove the shiny exhaust heat shield - this lets you get to the gear lever, from below.

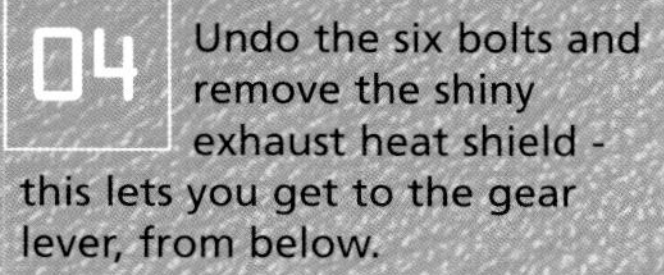

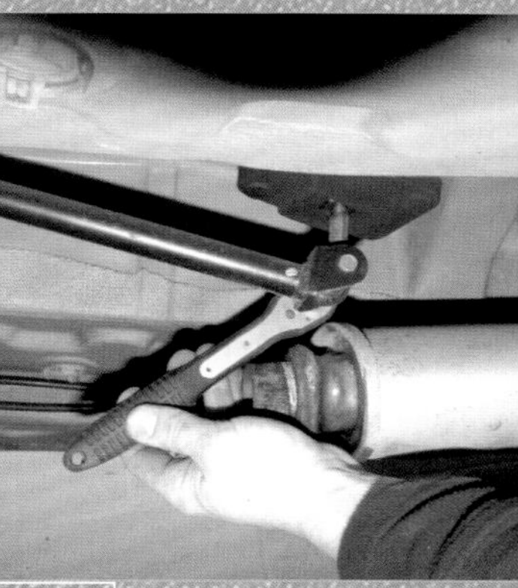

**05** You should be able to see the gear lever hanging down now, so undo the horizontal bolt which connects it the gearbox link rod. Lower the gear lever out from under the car, and take it to the bench for surgery.

**06** Pull the lower rubber seal away from the gear lever . . .

**07** . . . and the upper seal can come off, too.

**12** Grease up the new ball using the supplied lubricant. Clip the mounting plate into position on the ball, with the mounting threads facing upwards - secure it with the retaining ring you levered off in step 9. Now the upper and lower rubber seals can be refitted too.

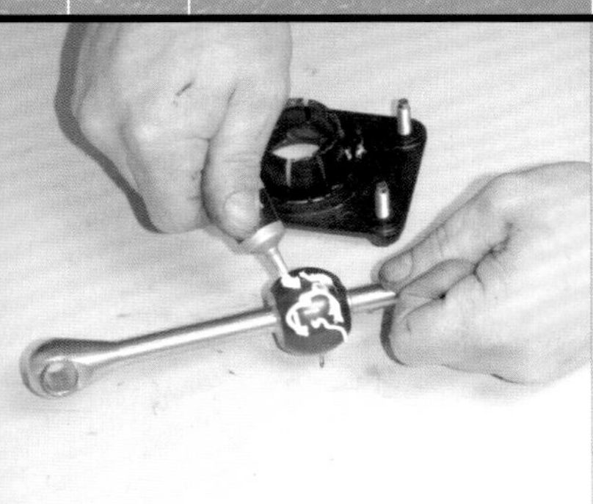

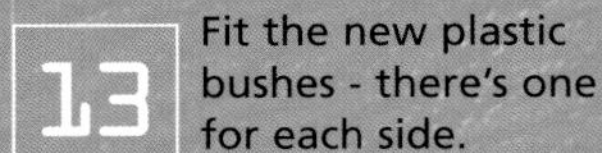

**13** Fit the new plastic bushes - there's one for each side.

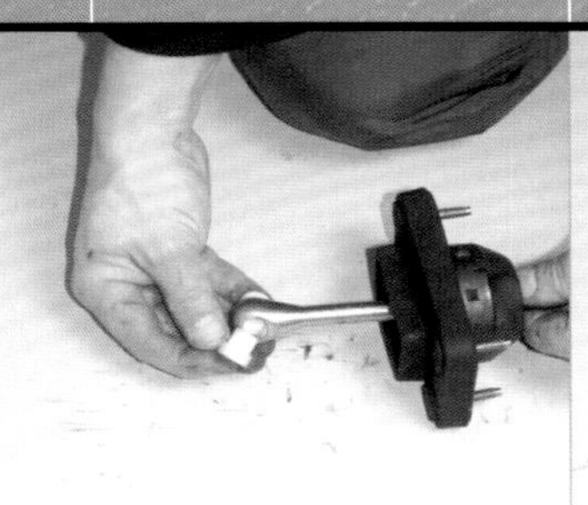

**14** The reassembled shifter is now ready to be refitted from underneath the car. Connect it to the gearbox link rod first, then push it upwards so the mounting threads fit up into the four holes in the floor. If you can get a mate to lean inside the car and tighten the four mounting nuts at this point, things will be a lot easier.

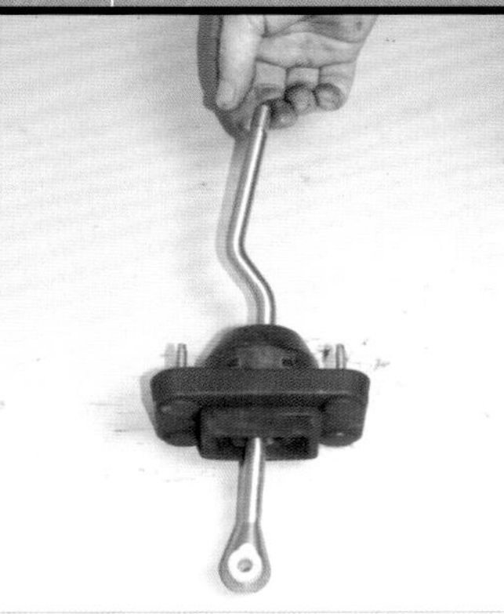

**15** When we offered up the heat shield, we could see it was going to catch on our new linkage. We decided it needed a hole cutting at the time, but afterwards realised we could probably have got away with a bit of careful massaging of the shield, with a hammer. Once that and the exhaust centre section are back on, it's play-time.

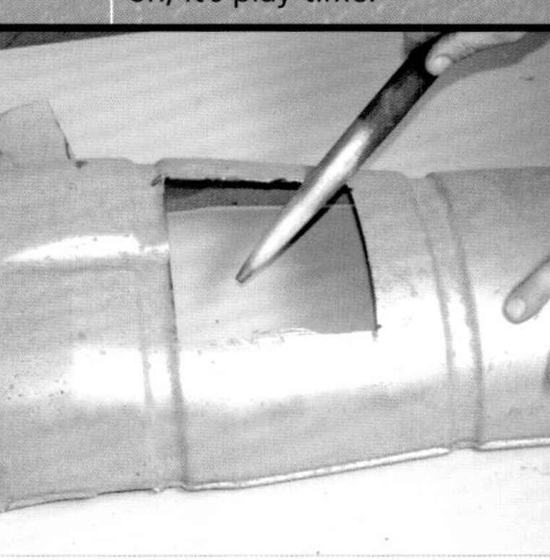

# Racing starts



Race-style ignition buttons are so cool, and have made the transition from circuit to modified street cars so well, manufacturers have even started putting them on their base models. They look trick, are a good pose and using them is heaps more satisfying than twisting a key.

While fitting this Richbrook Pro Start kit is almost all wiring work, you shouldn't be too intimidated because with a Haynes workshop manual as your guide, it shouldn't present a problem. Unless, that is, you have a voltage phobia, in which case call an auto-electrician. Just remember to disconnect the battery earth lead before you start work.

01 The hardest part of fitting this kit is deciding where to mount the button - yep, that's about as hard as it gets. We decided to mount ours on the dash to the right of the steering wheel, so the first job is to take this bit of the dash off. Remove the side panel by levering it out with a small screwdriver.

02 You can disconnect all the wiring plugs at this point, or simply remove the switch blank you're choosing to use and leave the panel hanging.

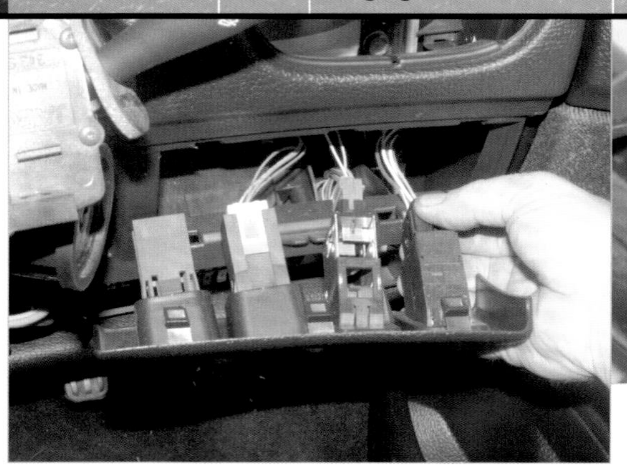

03 With the switch blank removed and mounted in a vice for drilling, we can see the button surround was just a little bit too large for our needs. As this is really just an optional dress-up ring, we elected to not use it. Drill a hole large enough to take the threaded section of the button, then fix the button in place with the nut provided, from behind.

**Achtung!**

*This is one job where you'll be messing with big wires, carrying serious current - more than any other electrical job, don't rush it, and don't skimp on the insulating tape. Do it properly, as we're about to show you, and there's no worries. Otherwise, at best, you'll be stranded - at worst, it could be a fire.*

**04** The relay for the unit should ideally be mounted on the bulkhead (though it could stay inside the car, under the dash). We located a spare bolt at the rear of the engine bay, so all we needed was a nut to fit it. Sorted - saves drilling another hole in an awkward space.

**05** Connect the two black wires from the new starter button to the relay.

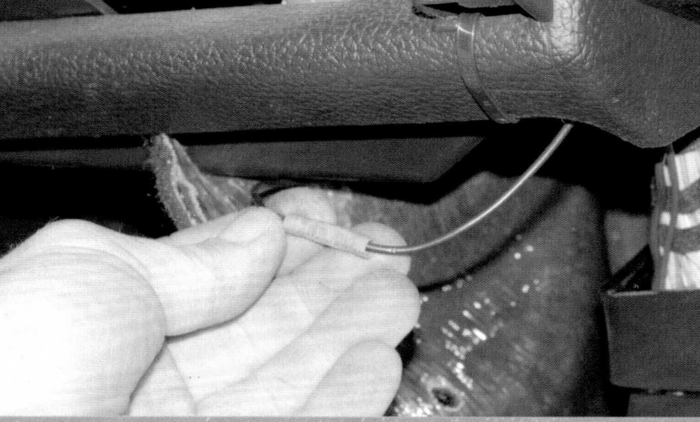

**06** At the rear of the engine on the starter motor solenoid there's a white wire - connect the blue wire from the relay to it.

**07** Unscrew and remove the steering shroud's lower half, for access to the back of the ignition switch.

**08** Now you need to tap into the starter motor command wire at the back of the ignition switch. Wiring diagram says it's yellow, on our car it's orange - it should have an ID label '100'. Shave the insulation off it and wrap the white wire from the relay to it. Make the connection permanent with solder, then surround this connection well with insulation tape - leaving the wire just twisted up is asking for a fire (or a non-starting car). Tuck the wire back in, and replace the steering shroud.

**09** Pop the starter button back into the panel you removed earlier, and it's sat there, close to the ignition switch, looking neat and purposeful.

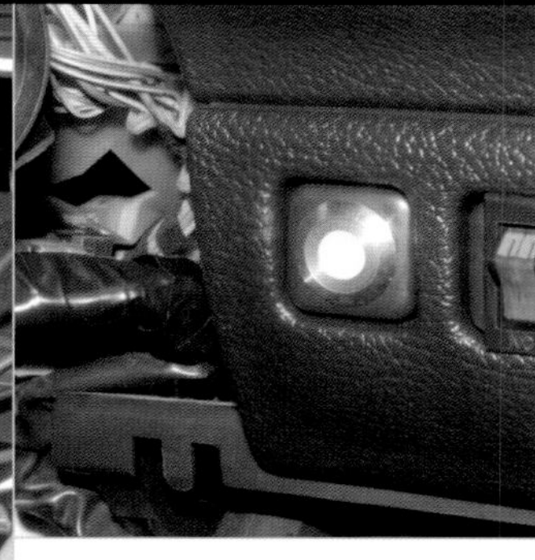

# All white, dials?

## The whole point of having your dash enclosed in a cowl is so it can be seen, so why then do manufacturers go and make the gauges in black?

You want to see your dials, so they've gotta stand out. The remedy is a dash dial kit, and another area down to personal choice as to what style/colour is used. We opted for blue because it goes with a blue and silver theme, but faces also come in white, green, yellow, silver, red and carbon-fibre effect. We chose to go with Lockwood's kit which has full and very clear instructions on how to do the swap, including detailed pictures and even plastic strips to help you get the dial housing apart. And you can do all this without having to remove the needles.

Dial kits aren't that difficult to fit, but you will need some skill and patience not to damage the delicate bits inside your instrument panel - the risk is definitely worth it. Just make sure you get the right kit for your car, and don't start stripping anything until you're SURE it's the right one - look carefully. Most dial kit makers, for instance, want to know exactly what markings you have on your speedo and rev counter. If they don't ask, be worried - the kit they send could well be wrong for your car, and might not even fit.

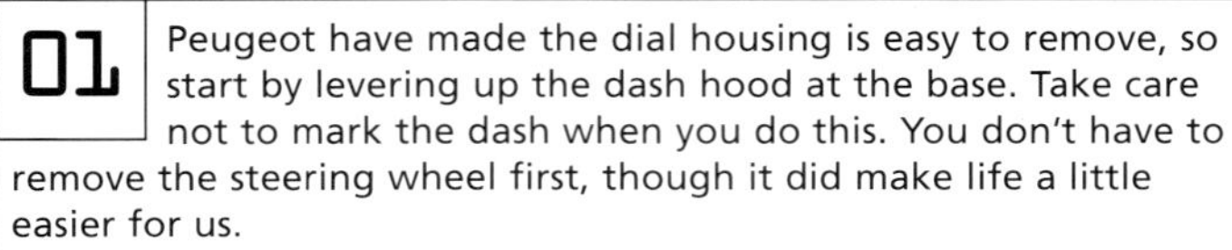

**01** Peugeot have made the dial housing is easy to remove, so start by levering up the dash hood at the base. Take care not to mark the dash when you do this. You don't have to remove the steering wheel first, though it did make life a little easier for us.

**02** One Torx screw holds the housing in place, so undo this and the housing should come forward.

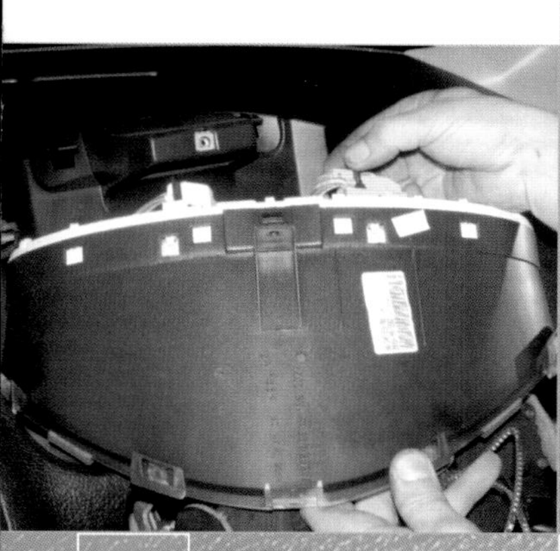

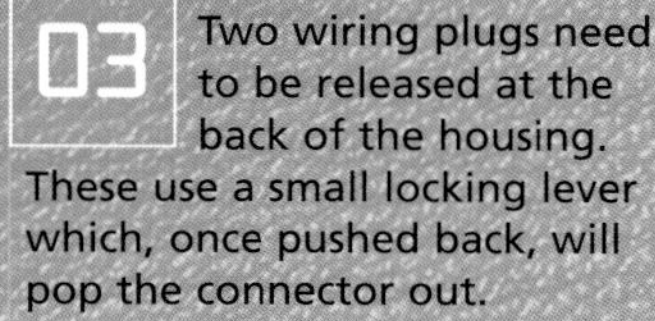

**03** Two wiring plugs need to be released at the back of the housing. These use a small locking lever which, once pushed back, will pop the connector out.

**04** You can now remove the housing and take it somewhere easier to work on.

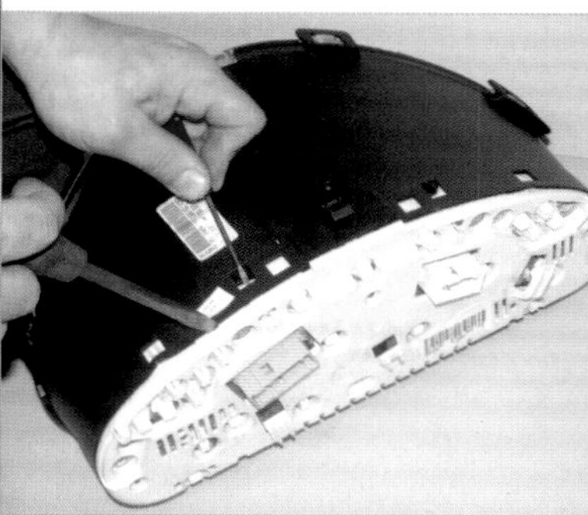

**05** While tools are provided to help slide off the instruments from the housing, a similar job can be done with a pair of small screwdrivers to release the clips round the edge. Separate the instruments from the housing, and put the housing to one side. While it's off, why not give it a coat of paint to liven it up?

**06** Look closely under most of the needles, and you'll see a little plastic peg sticking out of the panel. These are the needle stops - bet you didn't even know you had any. Before we can slice off the old dials and fit the new ones, these pegs have to be pulled out. Equip yourself with a cup or tray to store little bits like this in, or you'll lose them.

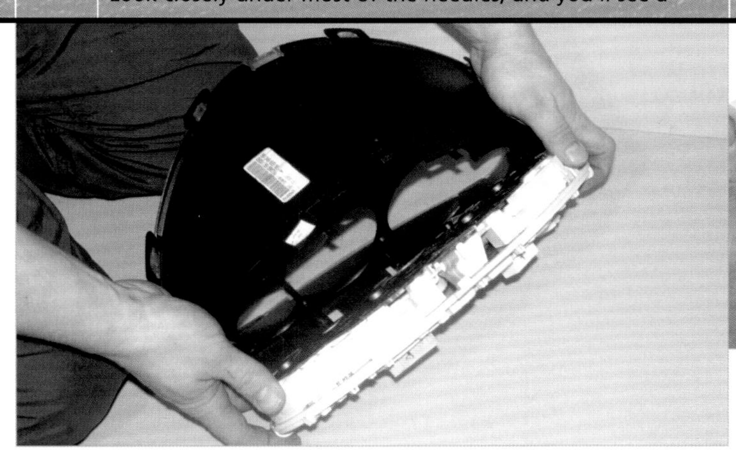

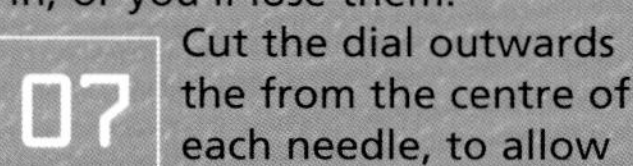

**07** Cut the dial outwards the from the centre of each needle, to allow the old face to be moved. Make as many cuts as you like, but don't bend the needle (it's delicate). Remove all sections of the old, dull face and shove it in the bin.

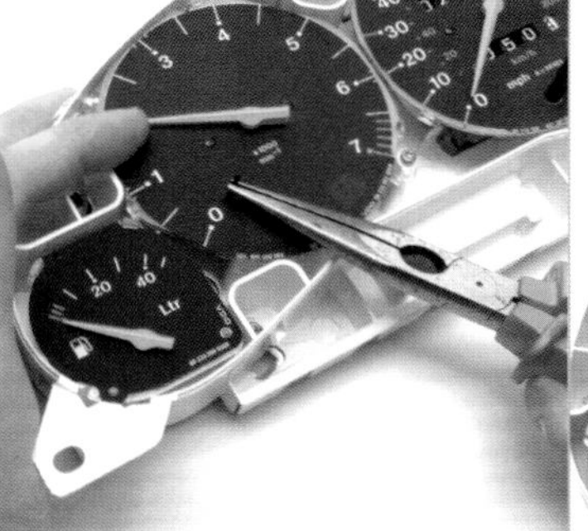

**08** The makers of our kit supply a packet of what they charmingly

>>

**Tricks 'n' tips**

*Before peeling off the backing, and sticking the dials in place, have a trial run at it. Fitting the dials over the needles isn't easy when you first try - with practice, it ain't so bad!*

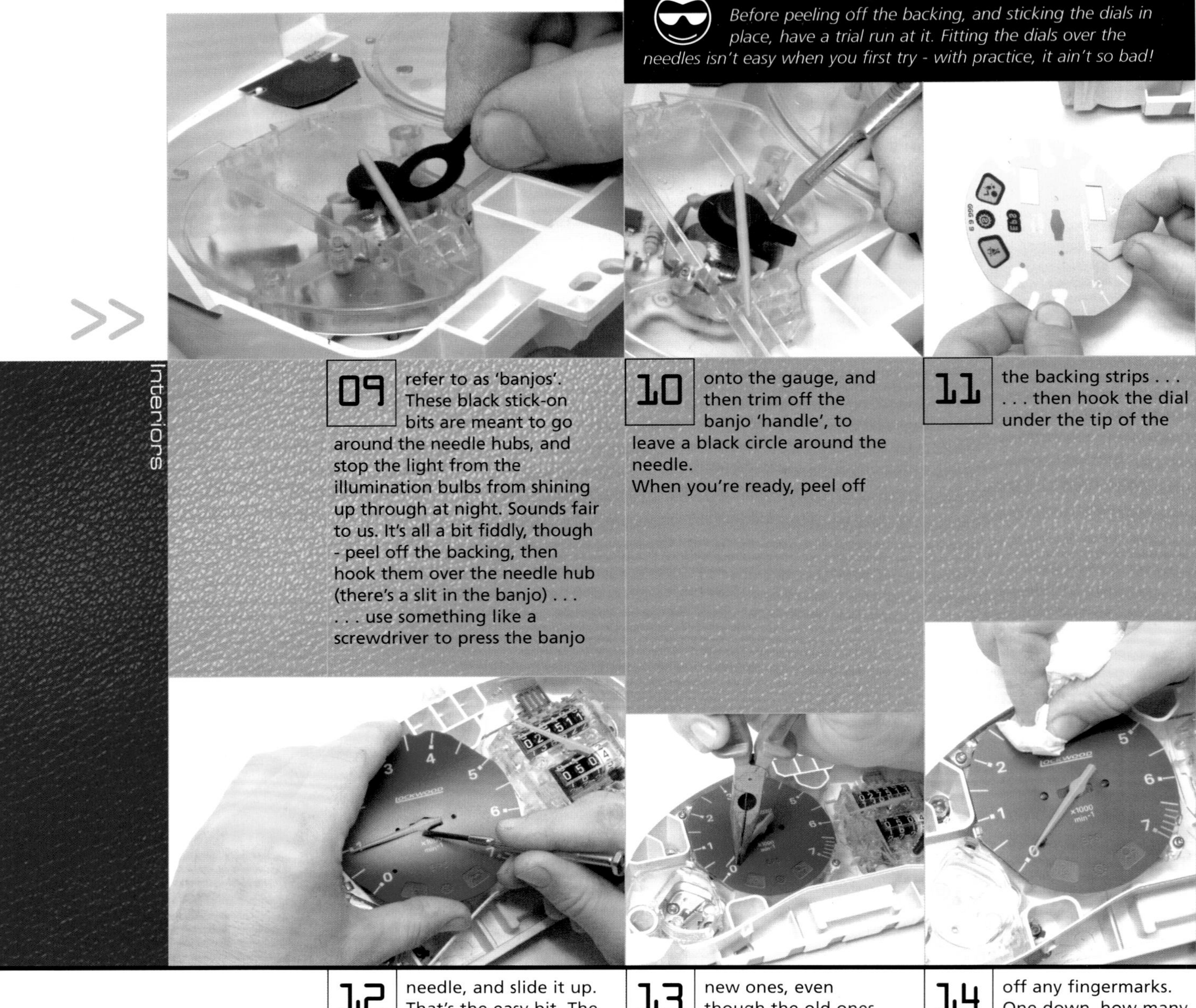

**09** refer to as 'banjos'. These black stick-on bits are meant to go around the needle hubs, and stop the light from the illumination bulbs from shining up through at night. Sounds fair to us. It's all a bit fiddly, though - peel off the backing, then hook them over the needle hub (there's a slit in the banjo) . . .
. . . use something like a screwdriver to press the banjo

**10** onto the gauge, and then trim off the banjo 'handle', to leave a black circle around the needle.
When you're ready, peel off

**11** the backing strips . . .
. . . then hook the dial under the tip of the

**12** needle, and slide it up. That's the easy bit. The tricky bit is, there could be three different needles involved. Keep the dial curved between your fingers, to stop the stickies from sticking. This is the point where you're in greatest danger of bending the needles, so keep your cool. Do not be tempted to remove the needles - you're on your own if you do.
Press in the stop-pegs, where fitted - our kit supplied us with

**13** new ones, even though the old ones hadn't rolled off onto the floor. They're so thoughtful.
Press the dial down, and clean

**14** off any fingermarks. One down, how many to go? When you're done, clip the instruments back onto the housing (check that the housing lens is clean first), then refit the housing to the main dash, and admire your handiwork. You'll enjoy maxing out the revs even more now.

# Under neon light

Neon lighting works well with stereo installs, helping to show off the hard work you've done. It works well by adding a glow to brightly-lit products, so just one or two here or there in the cabin of your car can give it a club feel, without being overpoweringly bright.

There's not a great deal to this, really - decide where you want 'em, where you're going to get a live and an earth (and a switch, if necessary), then fit 'em. For this project car, we wanted our neons up under the dash, to light up the footwells. The first thing to do is offer one in place - remember, it would be sort-of

**01** useful if your feet don't hit them as you work the pedals...

It's always easiest if you can choose to mount your footwell neons on easily-removable panels - if not, you might be

**02** spending some time with your head stuck under the dash.

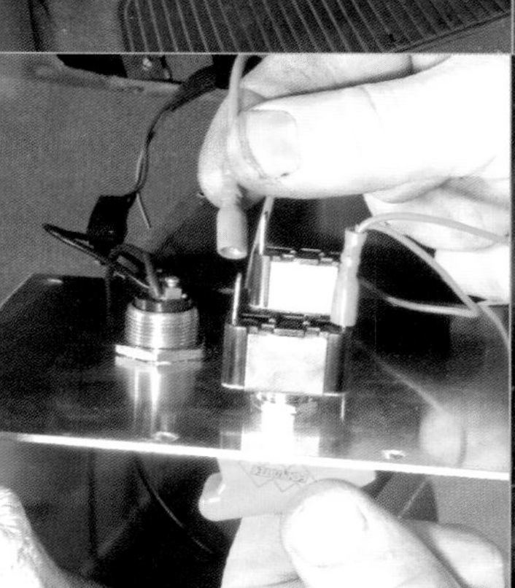

Sit the neon under your chosen panel, mark the holes

**03** either end, and drill yourself a pair of holes.

**04** To make extra-sure your neons don't fall off, try sticking them in place with double-sided tape. But use some self tappers as well, or small nuts and bolts, like us. Okay, so neons don't exactly weigh lots, but take some pride in the job.

**05** Neons usually come with a plug for the fag lighter. Too easy, and a bit naff. Join the two black wires together, using a ring terminal, and fit the ring terminal to a good earth point. This can be one you make by drilling a hole in the car's metal body, and fitting a self-tapping screw, or look for an existing earth point behind the dash, and add onto that.

**06** Join the neon red wires together into a spade terminal, and run it to one side of your new switch. Mount the switch somewhere you can get at it quickly (remember what we said earlier about the legal issues here).

**07** All we need now is a live feed, to run from the other side of the switch. This means either poking about with a test light and your Haynes wiring diagrams for an existing wire to splice into, or running one into the car from the battery. Like we found when fitting the ICE, there's a live supply point provided in the underbonnet fusebox.

**Bum notes**

*Interior neons have recently been declared illegal, and some places don't even sell them any more. Exterior neons have been illegal from day one. If you fit interior neons, make sure they're at least easily switched off, should you get pulled. Remember that driving at night with a brightly-lit interior makes it even harder to see out. Neons are best used at shows, cruises, or when you're parked up.*

# Boring **flooring?**

**Alright, so carpets have always been a dull colour because they have to not show the dirt - when was the last time you heard of a car with white carpets? What goes on the floor needn't be entirely dull, though, and can still be easy to clean, if you're worried.**

Ripping out the old carpets is actually quite a major undertaking - first, the seats have to come out (you might be fitting new ones anyway), but the carpets and underfelt fit right up under the dashboard, and under all the sill trims and centre console, etc. Carpet acts as sound-deadening, and is a useful thing to hide wiring under, too, so don't be in too great a hurry to ditch it completely. Unless, of course, your 206 is having a full-on race/rally style treatment, in which case - dump that rug!

Chequerplate flooring has an enduring appeal - it's tough but flexible, fairly easy to cut and shape to fit, has a cool mirror finish, and it matches perfectly with the racing theme so often seen in the modified world. Looks trick with interior neons, too.

**Tips 'n' tricks**

*If you're completely replacing the carpet and felt with, say, chequerplate throughout, do this at a late stage, after the ICE install and any other electrical work's been done - that way, all the wiring can be neatly hidden underneath it.*

# **Chequer** mats

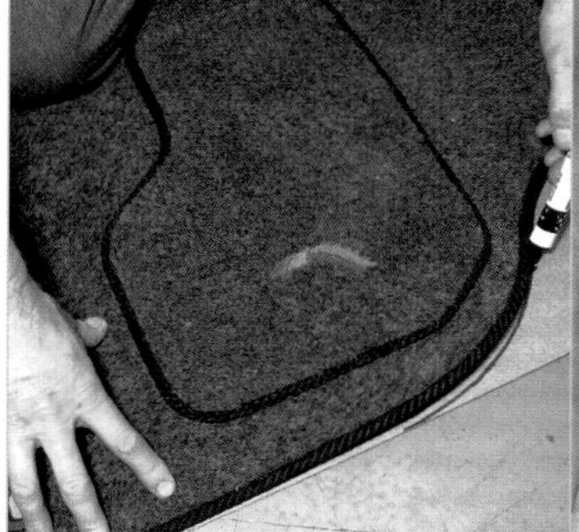

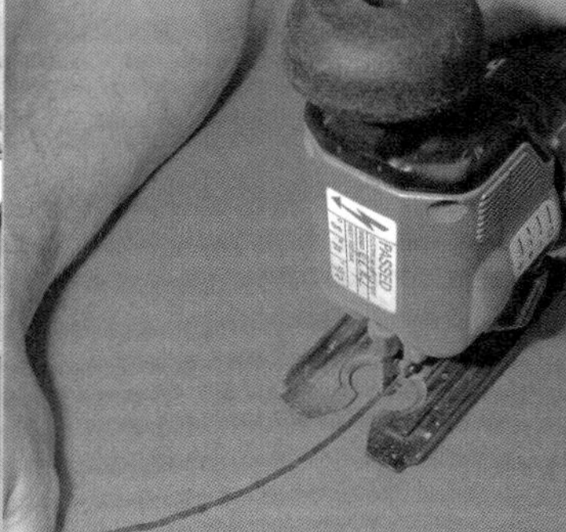

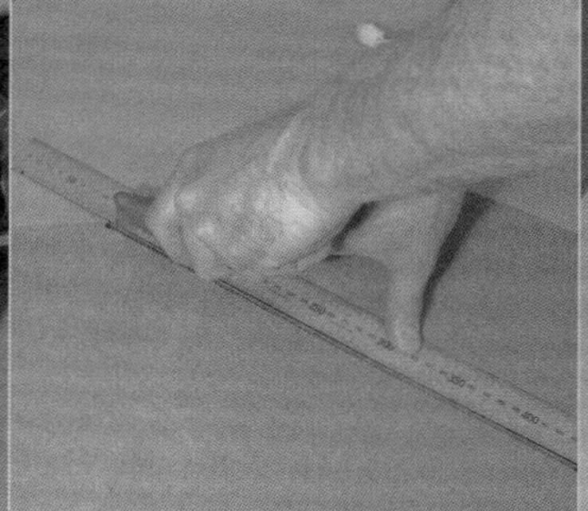

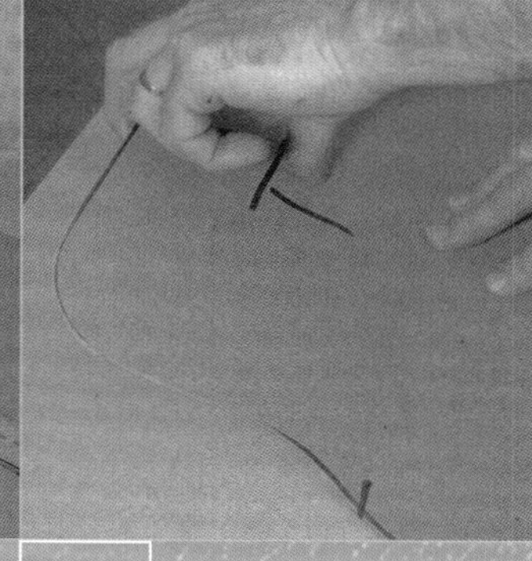

01 The halfway-house to a fully-plated interior is to make up your own tailored mats (you can buy ready-mades if you're not allowed to play with sharp knives). Unless you buy real ally chequer, what you'll get is actually plastic, and must be supported by mounting it on hardboard. Take one of the lovely 'Granny' mats your car might have come with, and use it as a template to mark the shape onto the hardboard (you could always make a template from some thin card).

02 With the shape marked out, it's time for the jigsaw - next to a cordless drill, this has to be one of the most useful tools ever invented for the modder.

03 To make the hardboard fit better into the footwells, score it at the bend where it goes up under the pedals . . .

04 . . . then carefully 'fold' the hardboard back to the required shape - trust us, this will make your new chequer mats fit superbly.

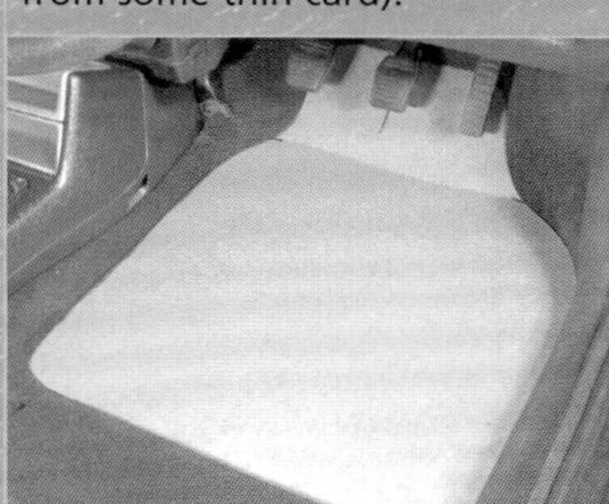

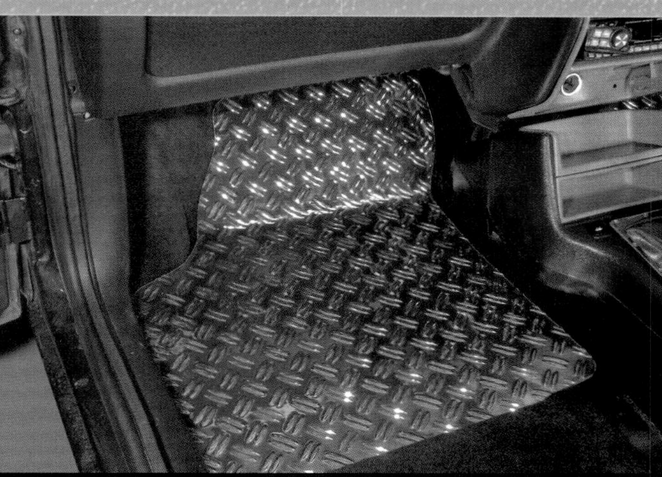

05 Not unlike this in fact. Try your hardboard mat in place, and trim the corners and edges as necessary to get it fitting as flat as poss.

06 Now you can use your hardboard as a template, for cutting out the chequer. Try to make the chequer fractionally bigger overall than the hardboard, so you don't see the wood edge (you shouldn't anyway, if your board is a tidy fit). Stick the chequer to the board, using some decent glue - spray glue's convenient, but usually not quite up to the job. You can't beat good old brush-on Evo-Stik (and no, we're not being paid to say that).

07 Do it right, and you too can have a floor like this - looks sweet, and the mats don't slip. Sorted.

**With the big plastic blob of a standard wheel in the Peugeot, you'll no doubt be raring to get something more sporty both in looks and feel into your car. There are literally hundreds of wheel options to choose from, so take your time, choose a style that will suit you and, if you get the chance, try out a few different wheels - like those in your mates' cars - to see how they feel.**

A trick feature worth investigating is the detachable wheel/boss. This feature comes in handy when you park up and would rather the car was still there when you come back (something most people find a bonus). It's all very well having a steering wheel immobiliser or steering lock, but not many thieves will be driving off in your car if the steering wheel's completely missing! Also, removing the wheel may remove the temptation to break in and pinch... your wheel!

We wanted a radical look with our 206, so chose the Simoni Racing Volante wheel which, despite its carved chunky look, is actually quite comfortable to use. You have to buy a boss (adapter) for the wheel also, which comes with all the bolts necessary, plus two horn push options depending what type of horn connectors you have on the back of the standard wheel.

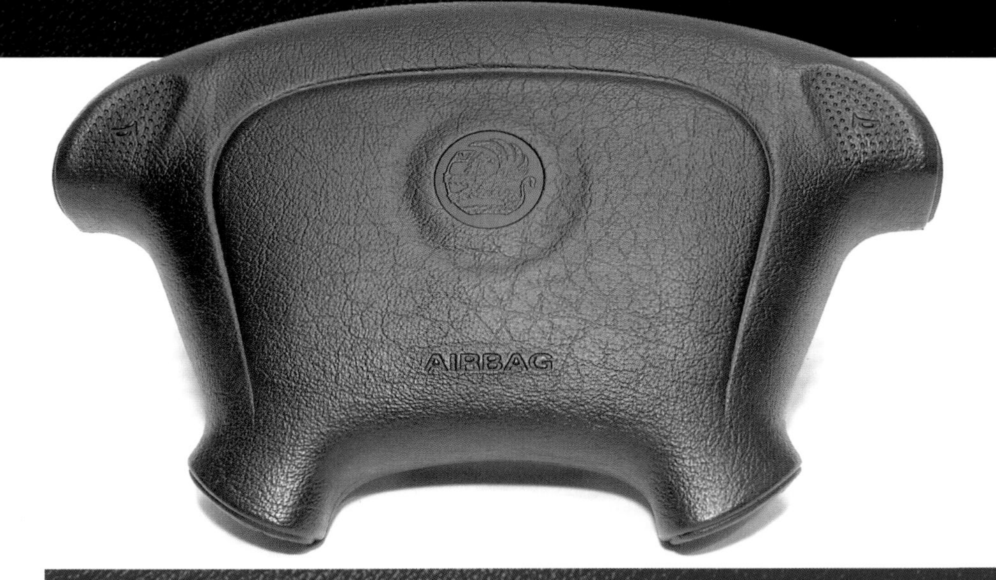


# A word about **airbags**

All 206s have at least a driver's airbag, built into the steering wheel centre pad. So far, the market for replacement wheels with airbags hasn't materialised, so fitting your tasty new wheel means losing what some (old) people think is a valuable safety feature.

So just disconnect the thing, right? Wrong. Then your airbag warning light will be on permanently - not only is this irritating, your newly-modded motor will fail the MOT (having the airbag itself isn't compulsory, but if the warning light's on, it's a fail - at least at the time this was written). Two ways round this - either take out the clocks (see the section on fitting white dials) and remove the offending warning light bulb, OR bridge the airbag connector plug pins with two lengths of wire attached to either side of a 5A fuse. Bridging the pins this way 'fools' the test circuit (which fires up every time you switch on the ignition) into thinking the airbag's still there, and the warning light will go out as it should.

Disabling the airbag is yet another issue which will interest your insurance company, so don't do it without consulting them first. We're just telling you, that's all.

***Warning: Airbags are expensive to replace (several £100s), and are classed as an explosive!!! Funny, that - for a safety item, there's any number of ways they can CAUSE injuries or damage if you're not careful - check this lot out:***

**a** Before removing the airbag, the battery MUST be disconnected (don't whinge about it wiping out your stereo pre-sets). When the battery's off, don't start taking out the airbag for another 10 minutes or so. The airbag system stores an electrical charge - if you whip it out too quick, you might set it off, even with the battery disconnected. True.

**b** When the airbag's out, it must be stored the correct way up.

**c** The airbag is sensitive to impact - dropping it from sufficient height might set it off. Even if dropping it doesn't actually set it off, it probably won't work again, anyway. By the way, once an airbag's gone off, it's scrap. You can't stuff it back inside.

**d** If you intend to keep the airbag with a view to refitting it at some stage (like when you sell the car), store it in a cool place - but bear in mind that the storage area must be suitable, so that if the airbag went off by accident, it would not cause damage to anything or anyone. Sticking it under your bed might not be such a good idea.

**e** If you're not keeping the airbag, it must be disposed of correctly (don't just put it out for the bin men!). Contact your local authority for advice.

**f** Airbags must not be subjected to temperatures in excess of 90°C (194°F) - just remember that bit about airbags being an explosive - you don't store dynamite in a furnace, now do you? Realistically in this country, the only time you'll get THAT hot is in a paint-drying oven.

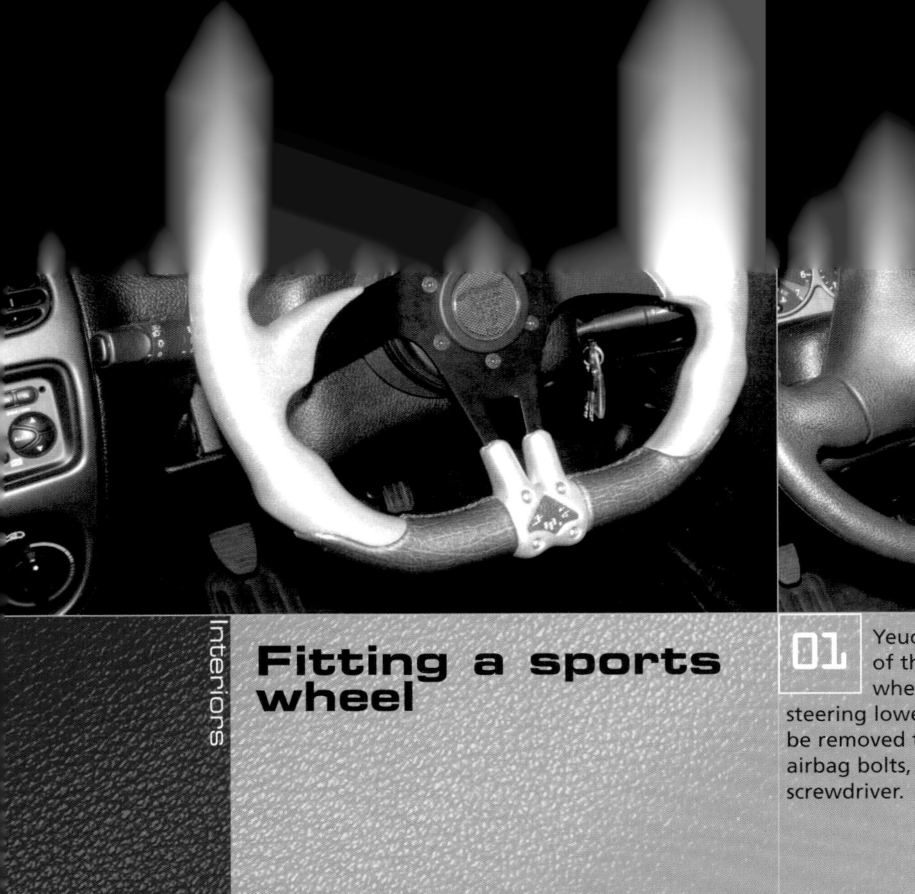

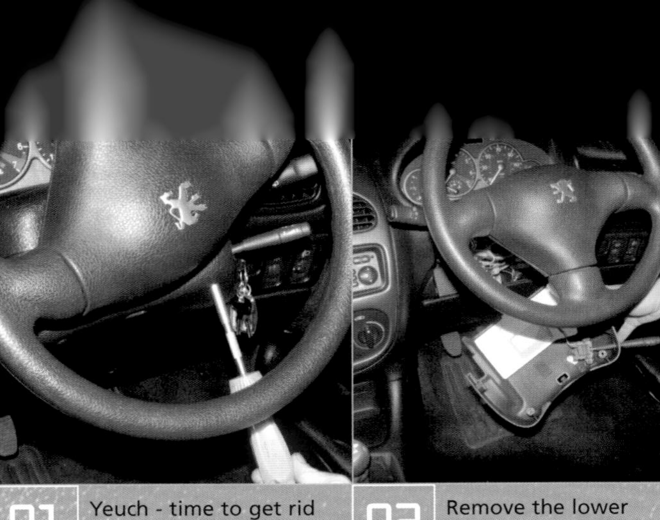



# Fitting a sports wheel

**01** Yeuch - time to get rid of that nasty rubber wheel! First, the steering lower shroud needs to be removed to access the airbag bolts, so get your screwdriver.

**02** Remove the lower shroud, and hang it under the dash for now.

**03** Now unclip the upper shroud and put it to one side. Of course, while it's off, you could always paint it. Just a thought.

**04** Disconnect the battery negative (earth) lead and wait for 10 minutes before proceeding to remove the steering wheel. If you don't disconnect the battery, or don't wait, the airbag could go off in your face. The airbag bolts are in the back of the wheel - turn the wheel a quarter-turn to reach the first one, and remove it. Turn the wheel half a turn from here, and remove the second bolt.

**05** Pull the airbag carefully towards you, to unclip it from the steering wheel. Don't pull too hard - there's still wiring attached to the back of the airbag . . .

**06** . . . which you disconnect next. Do both the airbag and the horn wiring.

**07** You can now get to the main steering wheel bolt, so undo it. You should hold the steering wheel rim with your other hand, to brace it as the bolt (which will be quite tight) is undone. Don't rely on the steering lock to hold the wheel - the force required to shift the bolt might break the lock.

**08** Before you pull the old wheel off, set it straight-ahead, and check that the front wheels are in fact pointing forwards. The wheel should now be free to come off - if not, tap it carefully from behind. Feed the horn and airbag wiring through the wheel as it comes off.

**09** You can now start fitting the new wheel, so feed the wires through the new wheel boss.

**10** Fit the new boss onto the steering column, making sure you point the arrow marked on top of the boss upwards. Fit the original steering wheel bolt, and tighten it by hand just to hold it for now.

**11** Connect the new wheel's short wiring harness (supplied) to the standard horn wires.

**12** Put the new wheel in place, line it up straight, and tighten the bolts. Before clipping the horn push into place, grab the wheel rim and tighten the centre bolt fully (proper torque is 35 Nm). And that's it – the new wheel smartens up the interior a treat.

# Pedalling your 206

**A tasty race-equipment touch to your modded machine, pedal extensions really look the part.**

The clutch and brake must have rubbers fitted - sensible (so your feet don't slip off them at an awkward moment) and also a legal requirement. Don't buy extensions without. The Simoni Racing Sport Action pedal set we chose had no worries on this point - the rubber sections are what give them the look, so safety can be cool, after all.

**01** Pedal extensions are dead easy to fit. Well, they're easy if you're prepared to squeeze under the dash and in front of the driver's seat. Due to a lack of contortionist training, we opted for the driver's seat being out. Remove the standard pedal rubbers and you'll find steel sections behind them. Except for the throttle, which uses thick plastic.

**02** Mark the pedal cover's screw hole positions with either a black marker pen (or white correction fluid for better visibility).

**03** Drill the holes as required for the screw fixings. When fitting any aftermarket pedals, you must have a minimum distance of 50mm between each one (or at least, the gaps should be equal - check out the instructions on your kit). Common sense says if the pedals are too close together, it could be curtains - you have been warned.

**04** Tighten the bolts – these come with locking nuts, so you'll need to get a spanner on the back to do the job properly.

**05** These extensions come with stickers which fit over the bolt heads. Very nice. At this point on some others we've fitted, you'd be sticking on the pedal rubbers. If you think you don't need rubber bits on your clutch and brake, try driving when the soles of your shoes are wet. Or rather, don't

**Achtung!**

*Check with your insurance before fitting pedal extensions. A while ago there was a big fuss after a couple of cars fitted with pedal extensions crashed.*

# The personal touch - re-trimming

**Okay, so you're definitely not happy with how the inside of your 206 looks, but you're not sold on any of the off-the-shelf options for tricking it up, either. You know how you want it to look, though, so get creative!**

There are any number of upholsterers in Yellow Pages, who will be able to create any look you want (we got one in our own back yard, almost - Pipers of Sparkford, Somerset, and very helpful lads they are, too). If your idea of 206 heaven is an interior swathed in black and purple leather, these guys can help. Don't assume that you'll have to go to Carisma, to get a car interior re-trimmed - they might well be the daddies at this, but any upholsterer worth the name should be able to help, even if they normally only do sofas!

Of course, if you're even slightly handy with things like glue and scissors, you might be inspired to get brave and DIY. An upholsterers will still be a useful source for materials (and maybe advice too?).

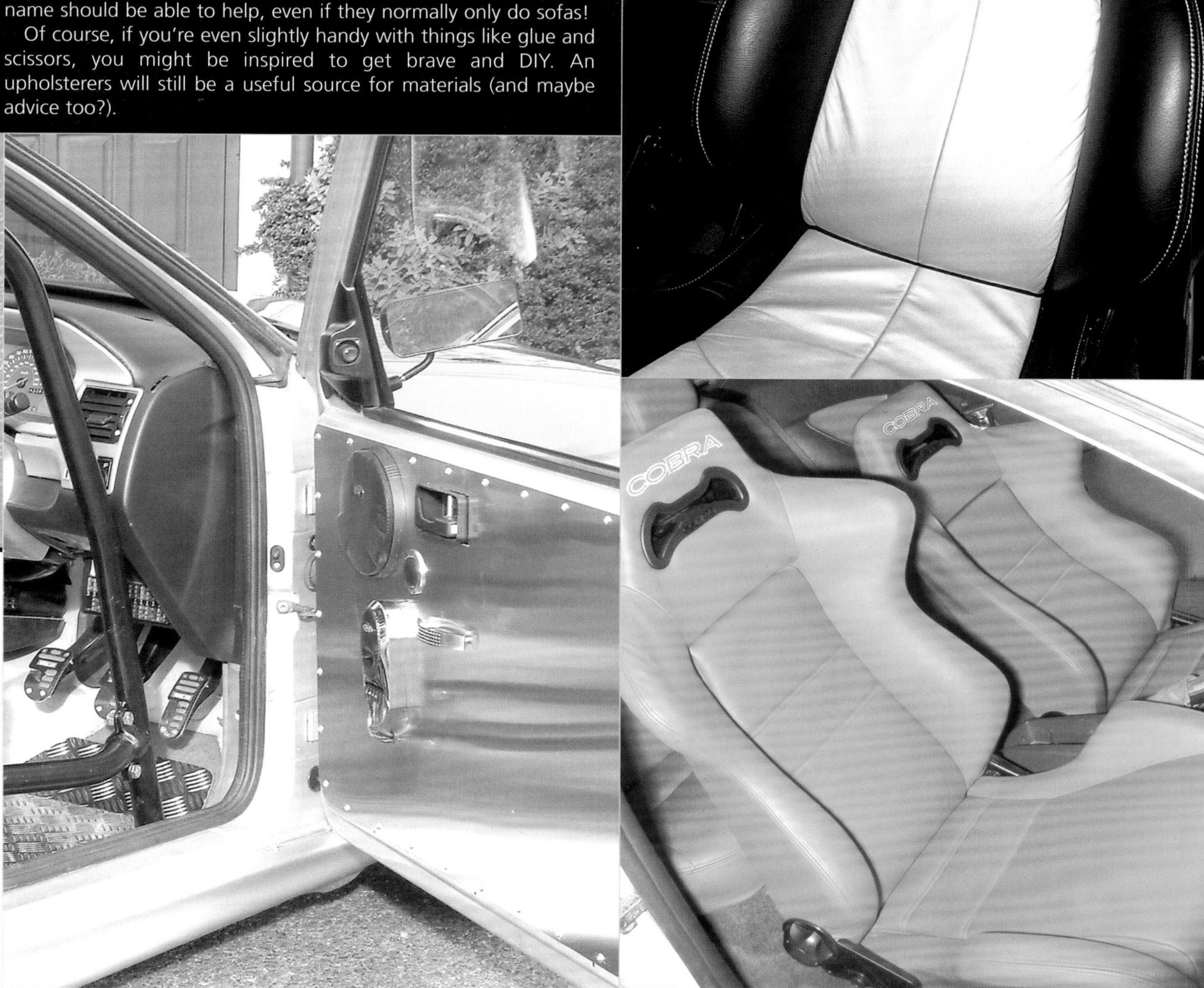

# Are you sitting stylishly?

**We could go on for a whole chapter about the benefits on aftermarket sports seats. They are so crucial for satisfying driving, they're almost the first thing you should modify on the car.**

This is particularly true on the 206 because the standard seats aren't exactly supportive. The car itself in standard form can be chucked around - last thing you want to be is chucked around inside with it.

The name Corbeau is synonymous with sports seating and a recent design of theirs, the RS2, attracted our attention as it gives fabulous leg, hip back and shoulder support. It uses reinforced bars in the lumbar supports as opposed to just stiffened sponge, which can flop over and flatten in time, from all the getting in and out of the car. The RS2s also have one long slot across the head support, making it easier to install retractable harnesses such as the ones we used. They're also recliners, which might not matter so much in a car like ours where the rear seats have been removed, but for those who still want rear seat use, it's an essential feature.

01 The standard seat has four Torx bolts, one at each corner. Slide the seats fully back, then fully forwards, to get at the bolts (which may also be hidden under flaps in the carpet). Save the bolts - we'll be re-using them for the new chairs.

02 With the bolts undone, the seat can be removed. It's awkward and weighty, so be careful of your paintwork when removing it.

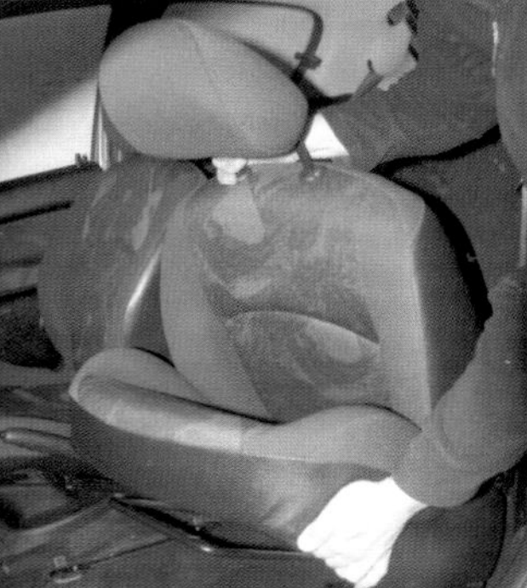

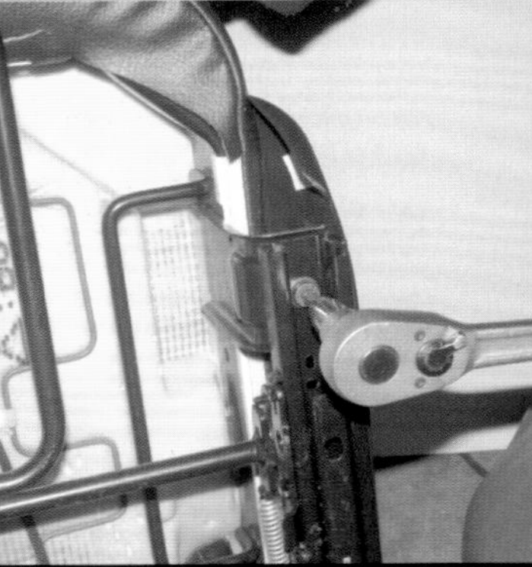

03 Flip the old seats over, then unbolt . . .

04 . . . and remove the runners. Keep them handy, as they'll be re-used on the Corbeaus.

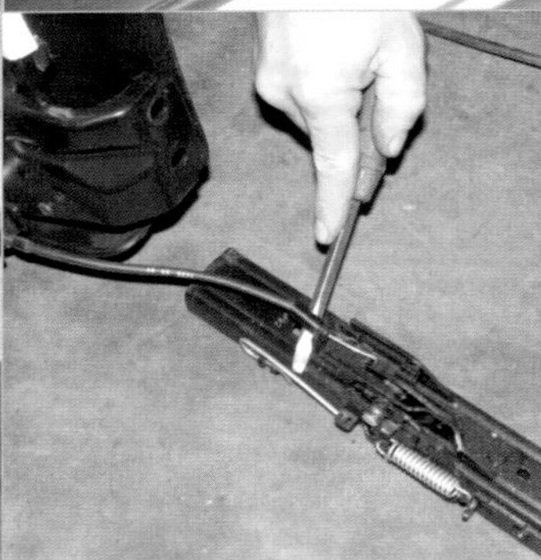

05 Release the standard seat's safety lock cable from the runner. This can't be re-used as it's attached to the seat.

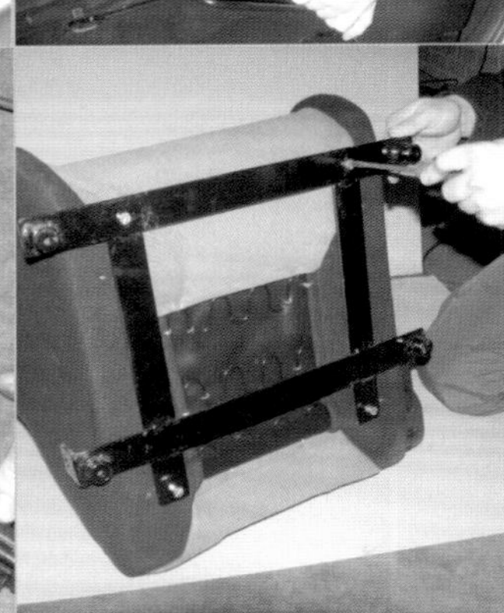

06 When you're buying seats, remember to also budget for the subframes, or you won't have anything to attach the seat to the car. Attach the subframe securely to the seat base using the screws supplied in the seat.

**07** If you're re-using the standard three-point seat belt, attach the standard buckle at this point. With harnesses, this is the one of the mounting points you'll be using later.

**08** Trial-fit the seat runner to make sure it will bolt on without any obstructions. We found the bolt holes didn't quite line up, so a bit of filing to elongate them was required.

**09** Bolt on the first runner, then offer up the second . . .

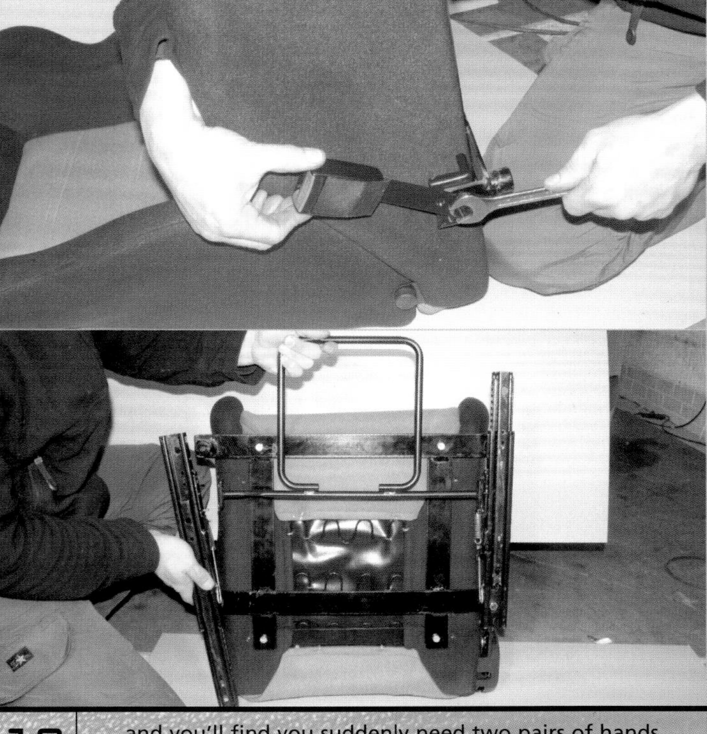

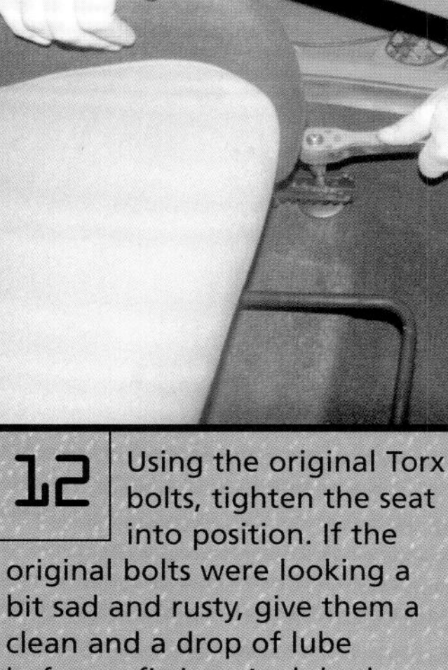

**10** . . . and you'll find you suddenly need two pairs of hands. The seat runner pull is spring-loaded, and will try and push the runners apart.

**11** Enough mucking about with subframes and runners - let's get the seats in where it counts.

**12** Using the original Torx bolts, tighten the seat into position. If the original bolts were looking a bit sad and rusty, give them a clean and a drop of lube before refitting. And do them up tight. Your new seats should give many miles of hard-core, hard-cornering pleasure.

# Race harnesses

While a new seat will help a huge amount in making your car feel more sporty, race harnesses will keep you properly in that seat and, therefore, help you drive better. Only problem is, race harnesses don't give you any room to manoeuvre once tightened, and when you need to reach and change a CD, stroke your other half's leg, or grab your shades from the glovebox, that's no help.

What we need is the practicality of an inertia reel (like the standard three-point belt), with the holding ability of a four-point harness. Safety Devices, also famous for roll cages and fire extinguishers, have just the thing - a retracting harness. Made by German company Schroth, it's a very clever set-up which, once supplied with 12V through the wiring connections provided, will allow you to move while the ignition's on, but will lock under sharp movement, whether that be in acceleration, braking or cornering. It does this by using a tilt switch, which has a ball inside that sits across two terminals. As the car creates G-force in any one direction, so the ball rolls off the contacts and disconnects the supply, thus locking the harness in place. Great pieces of kit - well worth the investment, and pretty much essential when you've fitted aftermarket seats with harness slots.

01 The complete kit, with a range of bolts to suit various applications (the kits are universal). So far, it mostly looks like a normal harness, apart from that black box (the belt reel) and the wiring.

02 Start by removing the standard seat belt and its mounting point bolts. This is the floor-mounted sliding rail, which unbolts at the front . . .

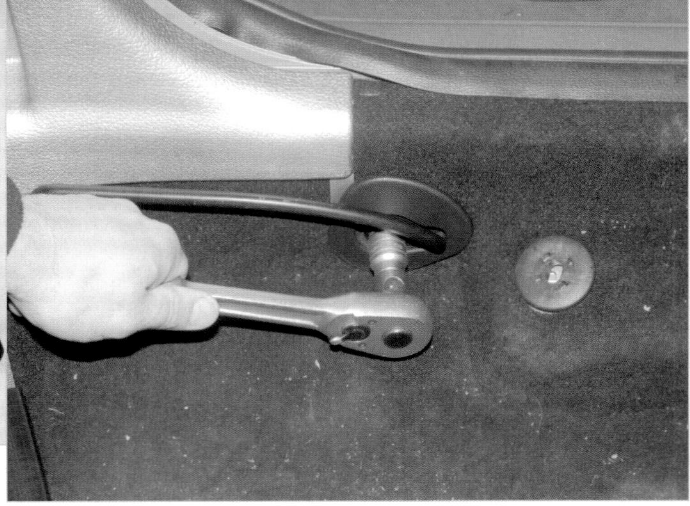

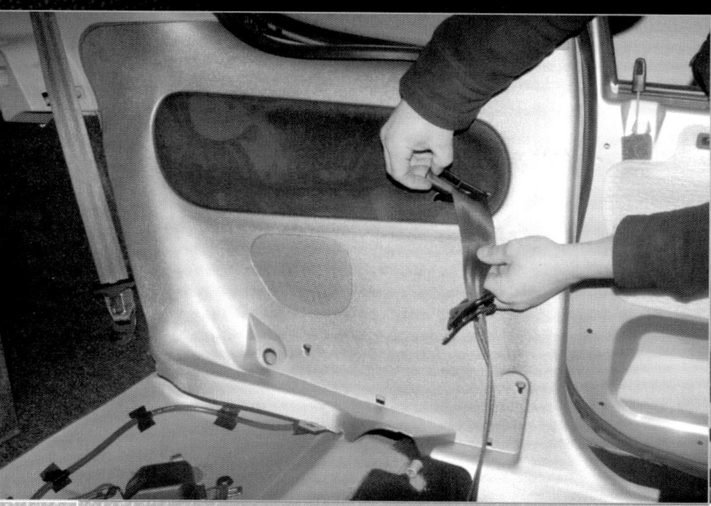

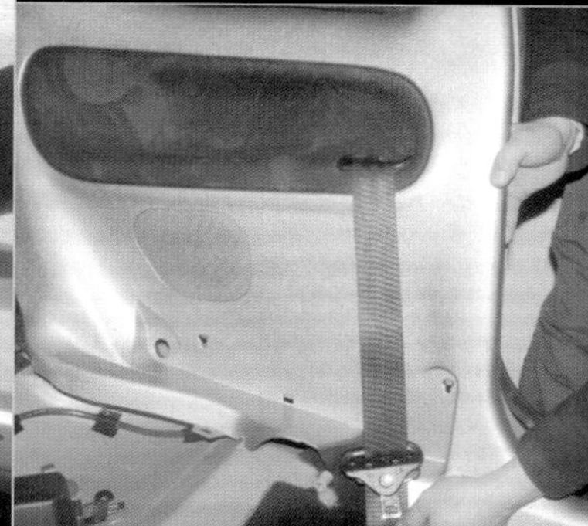

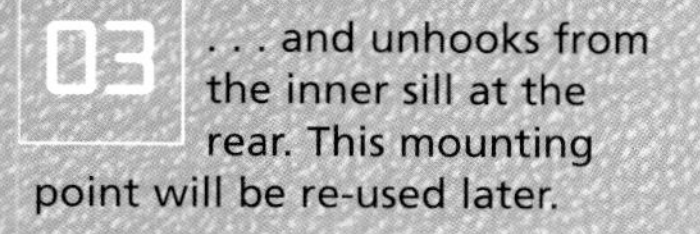

03 . . . and unhooks from the inner sill at the rear. This mounting point will be re-used later.

04 Unclip the seat belt plastic guide in the rear panel.

05 Remove the rear panel (unclip all the edges) and slide the belt through as it comes off.

**Achtung!**

*Removing any safety-related kit like the airbag or seat belt tensioners might be of interest to your insurers (and you can bet they won't like it). But if you don't tell them, and have to make a claim, you won't like it. Don't say we didn't warn you.*

06 Undo the standard inertia reel behind the interior panel.

07 Switch off the ignition, then disconnect the battery negative lead, and wait at least 10 minutes - we're about to interfere with the airbag circuit, and it may go off if you don't remove the power and wait. Disconnect the wiring plug from the seat belt pre-tensioner. This unit goes off in an accident to pin you into your seat, as the world turns into a blur. Now we're removing it.

08 Unscrew and unclip the C-pillar trim panel (with the rear belt going through it), and put it to one side.

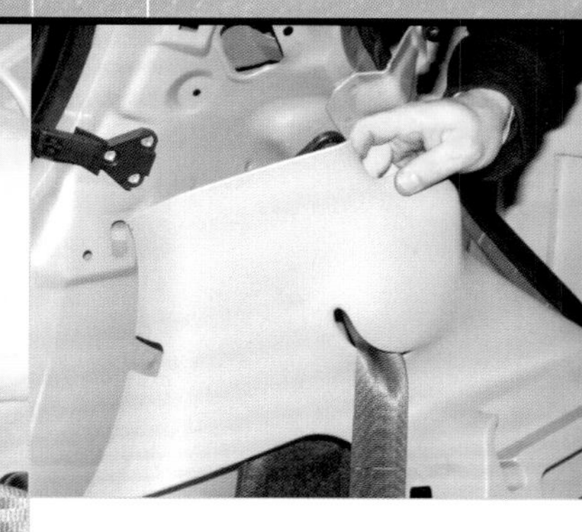

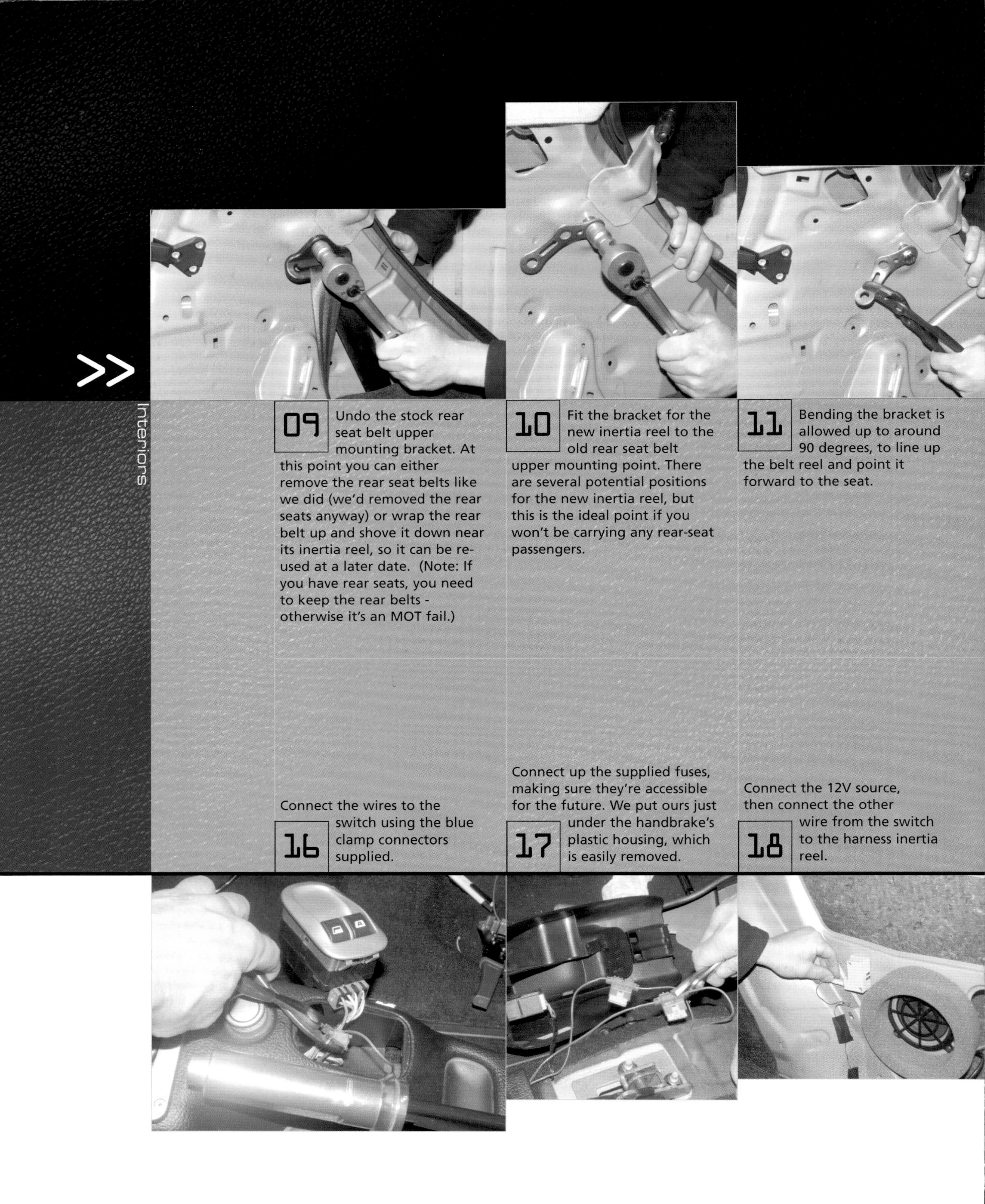



**09** Undo the stock rear seat belt upper mounting bracket. At this point you can either remove the rear seat belts like we did (we'd removed the rear seats anyway) or wrap the rear belt up and shove it down near its inertia reel, so it can be re-used at a later date. (Note: If you have rear seats, you need to keep the rear belts - otherwise it's an MOT fail.)

**10** Fit the bracket for the new inertia reel to the old rear seat belt upper mounting point. There are several potential positions for the new inertia reel, but this is the ideal point if you won't be carrying any rear-seat passengers.

**11** Bending the bracket is allowed up to around 90 degrees, to line up the belt reel and point it forward to the seat.

**16** Connect the wires to the switch using the blue clamp connectors supplied.

**17** Connect up the supplied fuses, making sure they're accessible for the future. We put ours just under the handbrake's plastic housing, which is easily removed.

**18** Connect the 12V source, then connect the other wire from the switch to the harness inertia reel.

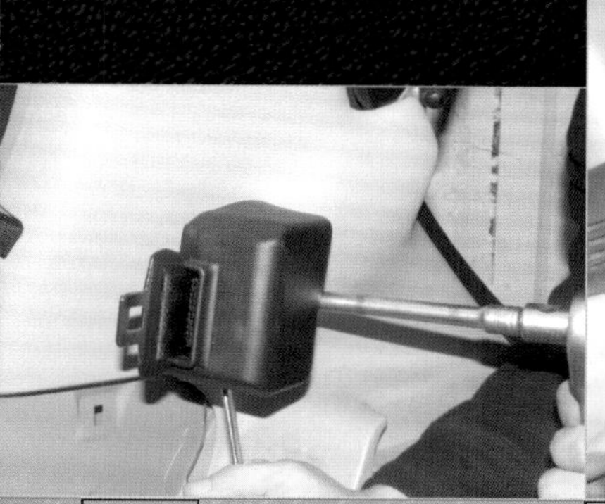

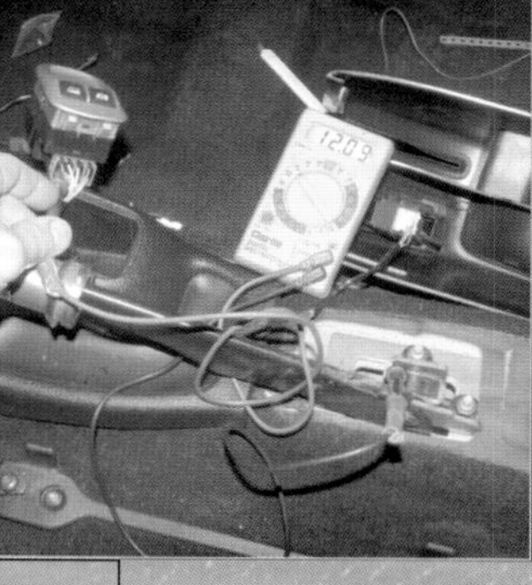

**12** Bolt on the harness inertia reel using the bolts provided in the kit.

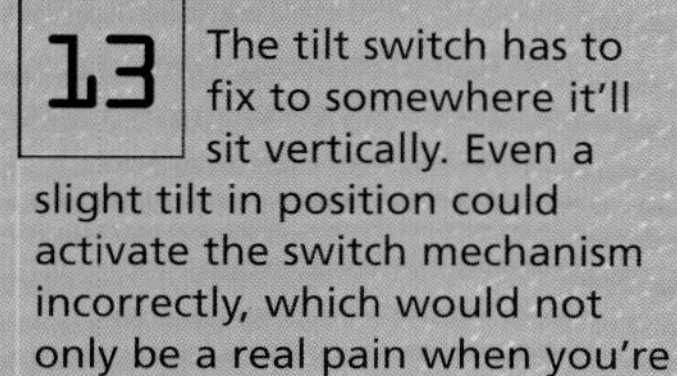

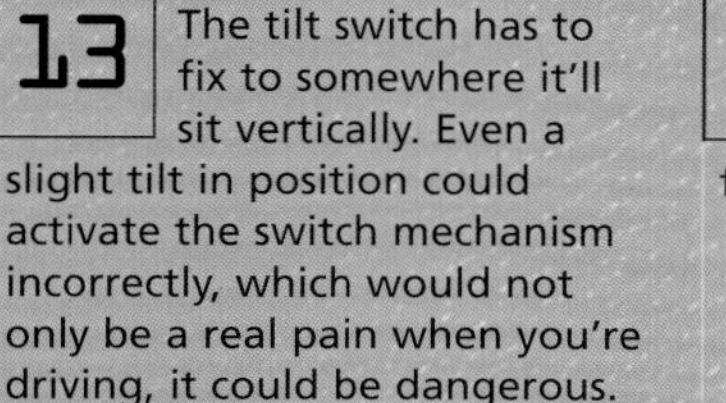

**13** The tilt switch has to fix to somewhere it'll sit vertically. Even a slight tilt in position could activate the switch mechanism incorrectly, which would not only be a real pain when you're driving, it could be dangerous. Mark and drill the position of the tilt switch . . .

**14** . . . then tighten the self-tapping screws into the sheet metal to fix the switch.

**15** Find an ignition-switched 12V source, so that as you turn the key the seat belts go into inertia mode, which will make them easier to put on. We found our 12V at the electric window switches in the centre console.

**Achtung!**

*When you're fitting harnesses, you should always re-use the existing seat belt mounting points - never try making up your own. Peugeot structural engineers spent plenty of time selecting mounting points and testing them for strength. Drilling your own holes and sticking bolts through is fine for mounting speakers and stuff, but you're heading for an interview with the Grim Reaper if you try it with seat belts. The forces in a big shunt are immense. We're not convinced either that the practice of slinging harnesses round a rear strut brace is kosher, from the safety angle - they're not strong enough.*

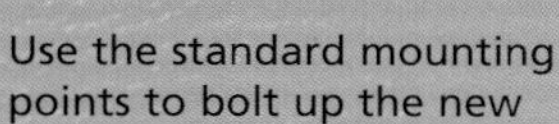

**19** Use the standard mounting points to bolt up the new harness. These bolts need to be done up very securely.

**20** Feed the harness through the seat slots . . .

**21** . . . then turn on the ignition, and pull the inertia reel out to connect to the new harness. And that's it - your new harness is ready to hold you in place when the going gets quick.

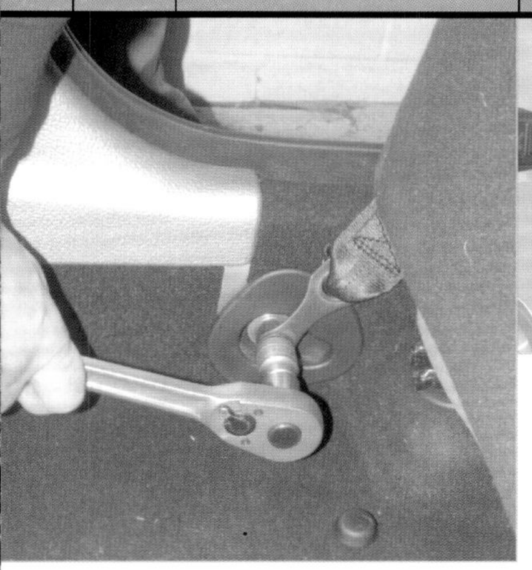

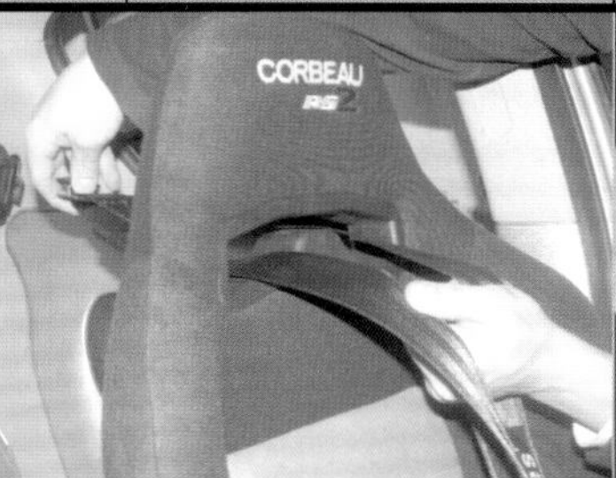


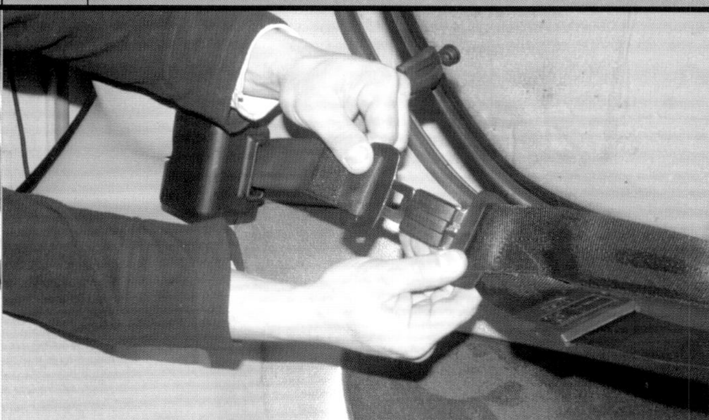

# ICE Headset

01 Carefully lever off the top centre dash section - use a small screwdriver, and take care not to mark the dash. Lever the panel at several points around its edge, or you might crack it. Once the panel's free, reach in below and disconnect the plug for the hazard warning light switch.

Remove the old head unit from the front of the dash cover. Be gentle with it - you might put it back in when you sell the car. 06

At the heart of your sound system is the head unit. It's the part you use most and look at most, so it has to both function well and look the business. Kenwood are one of the top brands out there producing quality head units and it was their KDC 4024 CD/tuner that we chose as a typical unit people would install. If you're looking to add an amp to your set-up like ours, then it's a good idea to find a head unit which has RCA pre-outs, to send a signal direct to the amp, from which your speakers or subwoofer can be powered. Also, bear in mind that you will need an ISO connector to suit your car. Fortunately, the Kenwood head unit comes with one which will connect up in most modern cars (Peugeot 206 included).

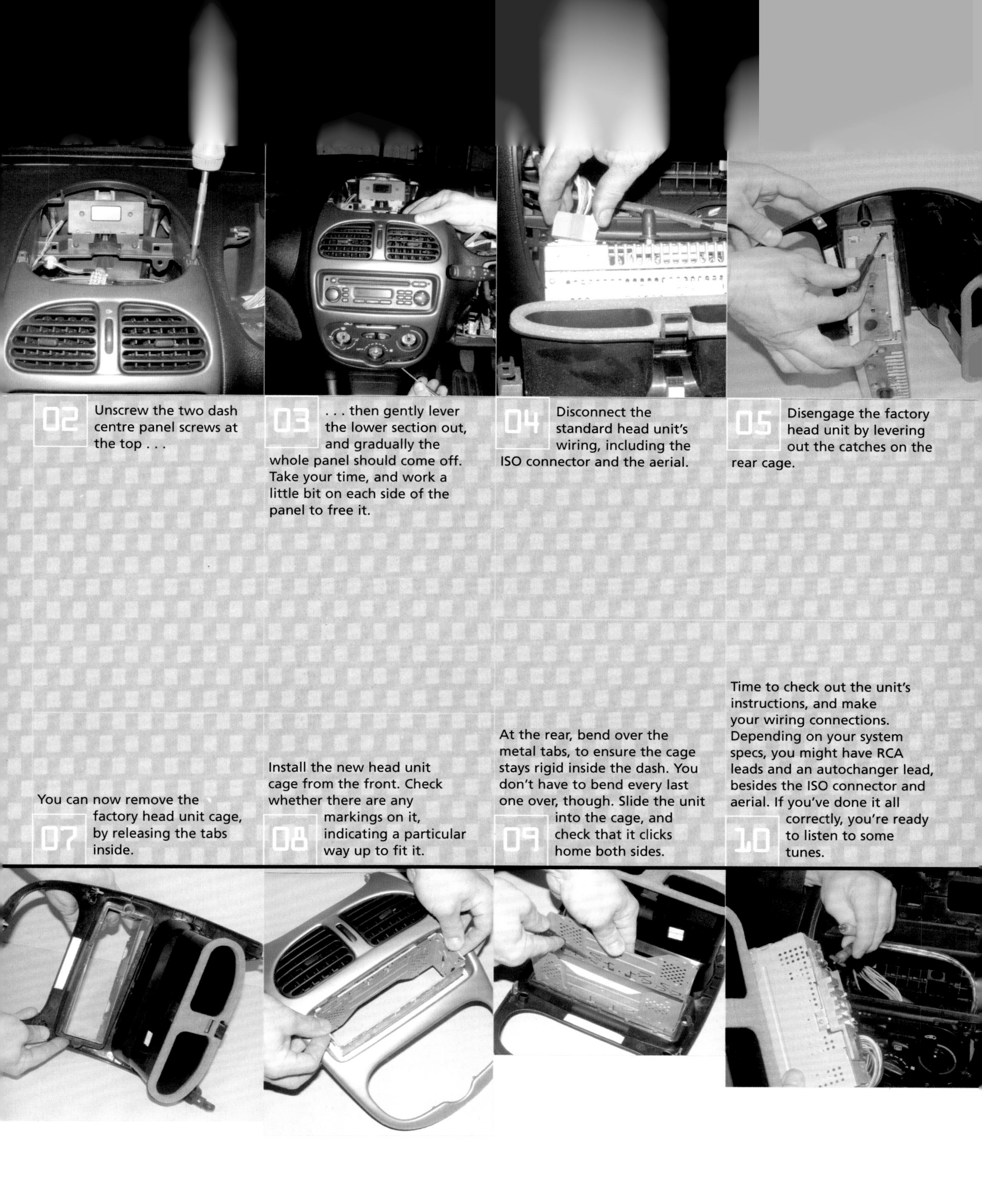

02 Unscrew the two dash centre panel screws at the top . . .

03 . . . then gently lever the lower section out, and gradually the whole panel should come off. Take your time, and work a little bit on each side of the panel to free it.

04 Disconnect the standard head unit's wiring, including the ISO connector and the aerial.

05 Disengage the factory head unit by levering out the catches on the rear cage.

07 You can now remove the factory head unit cage, by releasing the tabs inside.

08 Install the new head unit cage from the front. Check whether there are any markings on it, indicating a particular way up to fit it.

09 At the rear, bend over the metal tabs, to ensure the cage stays rigid inside the dash. You don't have to bend every last one over, though. Slide the unit into the cage, and check that it clicks home both sides.

10 Time to check out the unit's instructions, and make your wiring connections. Depending on your system specs, you might have RCA leads and an autochanger lead, besides the ISO connector and aerial. If you've done it all correctly, you're ready to listen to some tunes.

# Front speakers

**For a complete sound, you have to have a system with speakers that surround you, but equally you have to have speakers which will be well-matched around the car, ie you don't want rear speakers that overpower the fronts, and vice-versa.**

In our 206's system, we have a massive sub in the rear seat position, plus a couple of 6x9s which are simply powered off the head unit. With a four-channel amp installed, we're using two amp channels (bridged) for the sub, while the other two power the front Boss components.

**01** The Boss door speakers are a direct replacement for the standard 206 items. They'll handle up to 400W peak power – that should make the door panels resonate! Look at those crossovers - chromed, and like something out of an old episode of Star Trek. No way are we hiding those - they're going on display.

**02** Remove the door trim and unscrew the standard door speakers, which are secured by four small Torx screws.

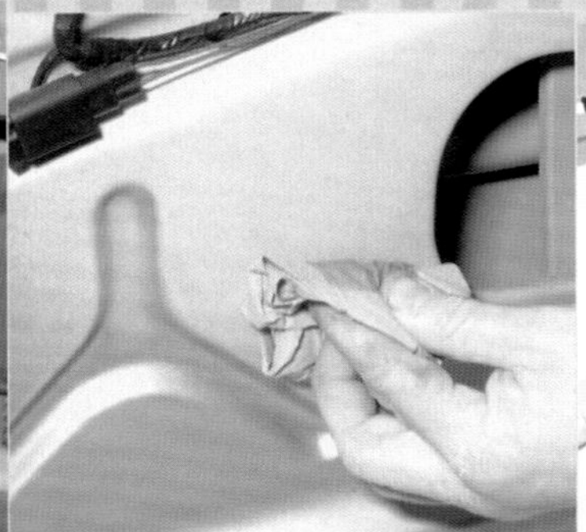

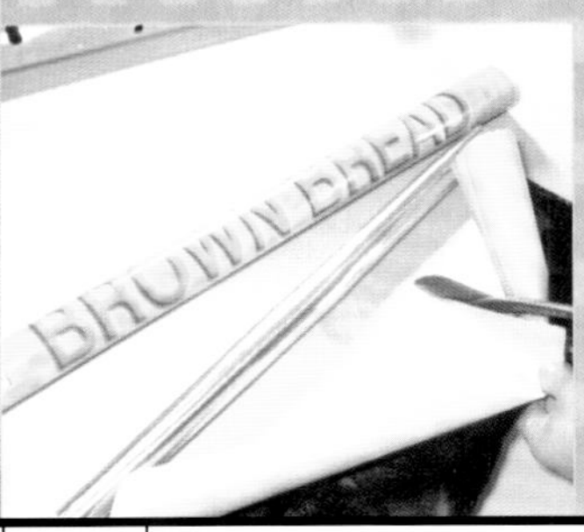


**03** Pull the speaker out of the door, disconnect the wires on the rear, and remove the speaker.

**04** Run the supplied new wiring to the new speaker. The larger speaker terminal is the positive - typically, the wire to this terminal will have writing or a stripe on it. Keep this in mind for all your speaker wiring, and you'll only hear sweet music, not nasty noises.

**05** Now it's time to think vibration. If you don't want all that kicking power to set your door panel tizzing, you need to invest in some sound-deadening. Yes, the market leader's Dynamat - but - it comes at a price. What else is out there? Brown Bread. Sounds dead. And it's cheaper. Clean up the door panel with some decent solvent . . .

**06** . . . then cut it, and get it onnn. Don't get too carried away in your quest for sonic perfection, or you might find you've covered up some useful door features - like vital screw holes, or door trim panel clips. Trim round with a sharp knife to re-liberate your holes, etc.

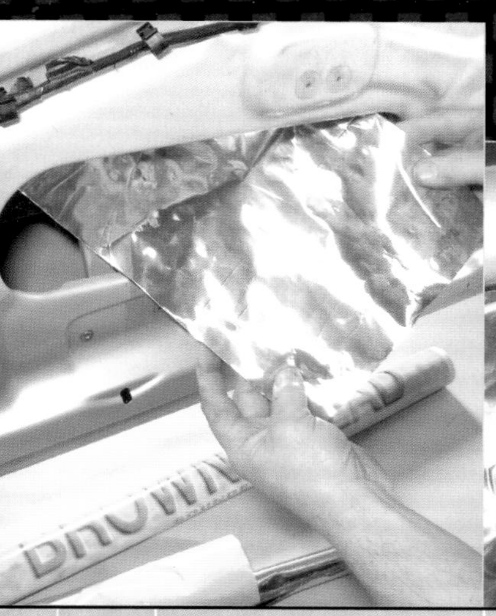

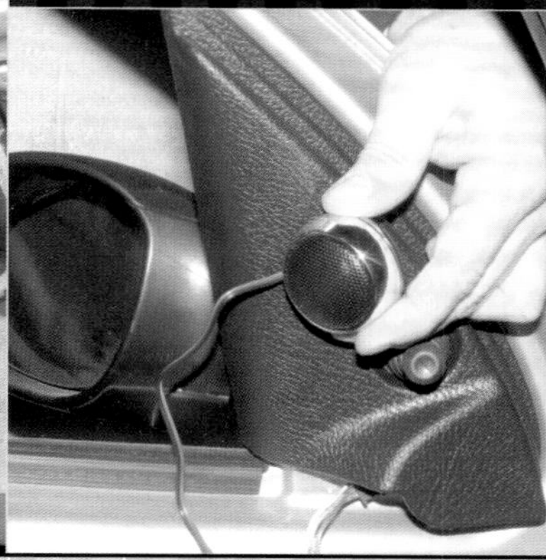

**07** Real pro's will sound-deaden the outer door panel, too - for the best results, you'll need to budget for at least a sheet of the stuff per door, if not more.

**08** You mainly want to deaden the large 'floppy' areas of the door which will vibrate, but some deadening round the speaker holes will help too. Either cut the speaker hole out completely, or slice across like a pizza and fold it in. Two things about this stuff - use it warm (warm it up with a heat gun, on a cold day), and watch your fingers (the metal foil edges are sharp!).

**09** Screw the new speaker in place, using the standard holes (and even the standard screws).

**10** Find a place where you want to put the tweeters. The ideal place we found was the mirror trim panel, which is the position used by Peugeot themselves on top-of-the-range models. The mounting cup allows you to aim the tweeter straight at you, for maximum listening pleasure (helps to show off the chrome tweeter housing, too).

**11** Mark the tweeter position on the panel, then screw the tweeter housing in place using the screws provided. You'll need to drill a small hole in the trim panel, too, for the tweeter wire.

**12** Find a suitable place for the crossover unit. On a 206, the door pocket is ideal, with plenty of room. This means drilling a fairly large (10 mm) hole on the rear of the door trim panel, into the door pocket, to allow the speaker wires to go through to the crossover.

**13** Feed the speaker wires through and connect them all to the crossover unit - time to check your instructions. On our units, the amp supply is connected on the left set of terminals, then gets split to the main speaker at the middle set, and to the new tweeter from the right set.

**14** Screw the crossover into place in the panel, and it'll get noticed whilst not reducing storage space for your CDs, phone, etc.

# **Rear** speakers

If we're talking about a set of 6x9s, rear shelf-mounting is the simplest option. If you don't want to butcher your standard shelf (always a flimsy item), either make a new one from MDF (using your stock shelf as a template), or buy a ready-made acoustic 'stealth' shelf. Either way, make hiding your new speakers a priority - tasty speakers on display in the back window could soon mean no rear window, and no speakers...

A good pair of rear speakers combined with a subwoofer with give you a rich quality with plenty of oomph. Well, that's what we found anyway, when we chose a pair of Alpine 6x9 two-ways to sit either side of our 12-inch sub. These 6x9s are being powered straight off the head unit, otherwise we'd have had a sound system with too much rear bias. With less power going to them, the rear speakers now provide a nice amount of rear 'fill' to the sound.

**01** These 6x9s can handle heaps of watts, and come in our favourite colour – blue (er, this is the theme on our 206, along with silver).

**02** Cut out the perforated section on the back of the speaker box, which also gives you full instructions on how to fit your new purchase.

**03** Transfer the template to your MDF or the panel where you're to mount the speakers.

**04** Cut out the MDF with your jigsaw, taking care and with your mask and goggles on for safety (MDF dust is definitely not good for you). With the holes made, mounting the speakers is just a simple drill-and-screw exercise.

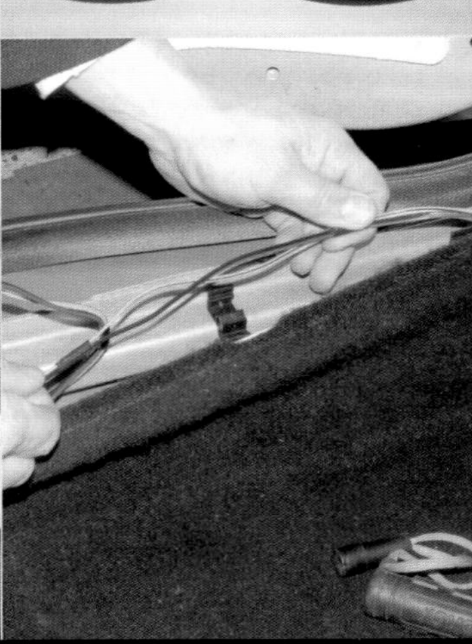

**05** Run the speaker wiring neatly down the car . . .

**06** . . . and connect the 6x9s to the rear speaker wires on the head unit.

**Achtung!**

*MDF dust is nasty stuff to breathe in. Wear a mask when you're cutting, drilling or sanding it.*

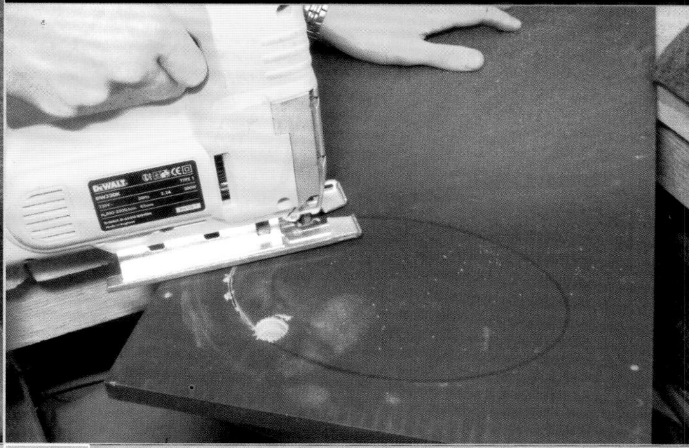

01 First job with a new ready-made shelf is to mark the speaker positions. Not tricky.

02 With a speaker outline marked, remove the wood from the rest of the shelf, and drill a nice big hole somewhere inside the outline... then get busy with the jigsaw.

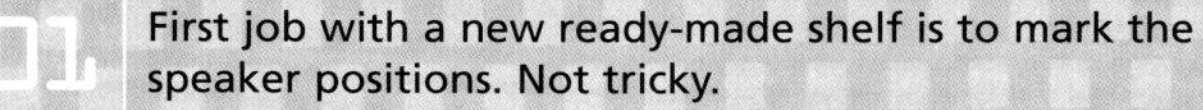

## Stealth shelf 6x9s

03 Use the speaker mounts (or even the speakers themselves) as a template to drill the mounting holes . . .

04 . . . then screw on the speakers themselves. Don't forget that 6x9s can be run off the headset, to provide a little 'rear fill' - if you have them amped-up, you might find that the sound's too biased to the back of the car.

05 Remember that the length of wire to each speaker should be the same (as near as poss), or you might find the speakers run slightly out of phase. Crimp on the right terminals, and connect up your speakers. For max neatness, use P-clips screwed along the edge of the shelf. To remove the shelf more easily, fit some bullet connectors in the speaker wiring, or ask your ICE dealer for a Neutrik connector plug.

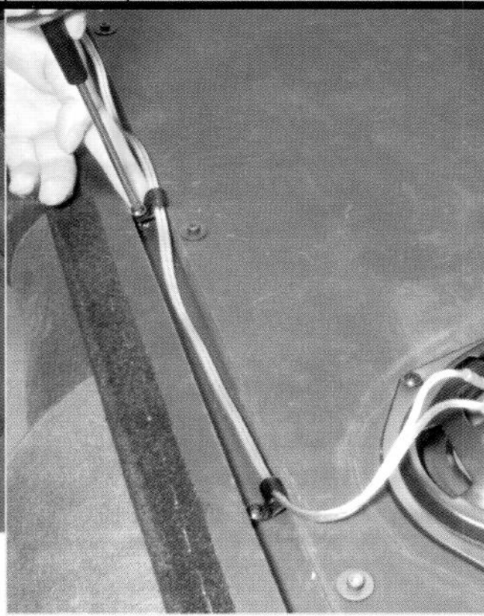

# Amplifiers and subs

**Most people who love their cars love a bit of music in them as well. Actually that's understating the case – we all love our favourite tunes pumping out. To do this we need a good sound system, by which we mean not just something which the manufacturers throw in their models to satisfy the masses. Like we crave more engine power, so we want more watts and more speakers to hear them through.**

So, how many amps do we want in our car? One school of thought says each pair of speakers, and each sub, should have an individual amp - by setting the output from each amp separately, you can control each aspect of the sound, before you even need to think about adding a graphic equaliser. You can also better match your speakers to the level of power they need, to work best. Trouble is, running several amps means doubling-up on wiring, and you could end up drawing a monster amount of power from that battery.

While sophisticated systems can provide the optimum sound pressure and quality, reasonable systems with plenty of punch aren't difficult to put together. Any starter system can be made to seriously kick, using just one 400W four-channel amp - choose the right one carefully (and the components to go with it), and just one will do. With a 'tri-mode' amp, you could run your front components off one pair of channels, bridge the other two for a sub, and run some 6x9s off the head unit. Don't forget that decent modern headsets chuck out fifty-per-channel now, so don't assume you'll need separate amps for everything. Ideally, in any system, the sound shouldn't all come from behind you - ears were designed to work best with sound arriving from in front (and who are we to argue?).

Decide where you'll mount the amps carefully. Any amp must be adequately cooled - don't cover it up so there's no airflow, and don't hang it upside-down from your shelf. The amp we chose is a real show piece - putting it on show will mean it gets cooled enough, automatically.

No system's complete without that essential deep bass boom and rumble. Don't muck about with bass tubes - get the real thing to avoid disappointment. So you lose some of your boot space - so what? Is getting the shopping in an issue? We think not.

Most people opt for the easy life when it comes to boxes, at least until they're ready for a full-on mental install. The 206 at least has a fairly roomy boot, so standard boxes will fit easily. Making up your own box isn't hard though, especially if you were any good at maths and geometry. Oh, and woodwork. Most subs come with instructions telling you what volume of box they work best in, but ask an expert (or a mate) what they think - the standard boxes are just fine, and none are pricey. The only real reason to build your own is if you've got an odd-shaped boot (or want something that looks trick).

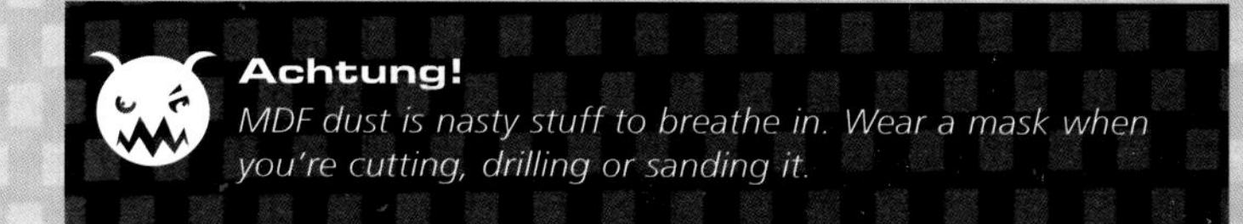


**01** The Boss amp is like small briefcase and, as it glows orange at night, it needs to be put somewhere to show it off. As we were dumping the rear seats in favour of a rear install in MDF, we fitted the amp to our false floor. Here, it's being marked out for position on our boot-floor-shaped MDF panel.

**02** The MDF panel can then be cut. To sink our amp into the floor panel slightly, we chiselled out the shape of the mounting tabs.

**03** Place the amp into position, making sure there's clearance all around. Along the side where the wires connect, make sure you have enough room for the wires to tuck down between the amp and MDF edges. Screw the amp into place, using the rubber washers to insulate the amp from the wood, and minimise vibration from any nearby speakers.

**04** That amp of ours needs a serious power feed - four- or eight-gauge wire at least. It also needs a nice gold-plated ring terminal fitting . . .

**05** . . . which should ideally be soldered to ensure it stays where it's supposed to. Wrap it with insulating tape afterwards to seal it.

**06** The amp power lead needs a permanent 12V source, and in the main fusebox under the bonnet there's a handy 12V connection. You could choose the positive battery terminal, but this nut-and-bolt terminal is neater - take advantage.

>>

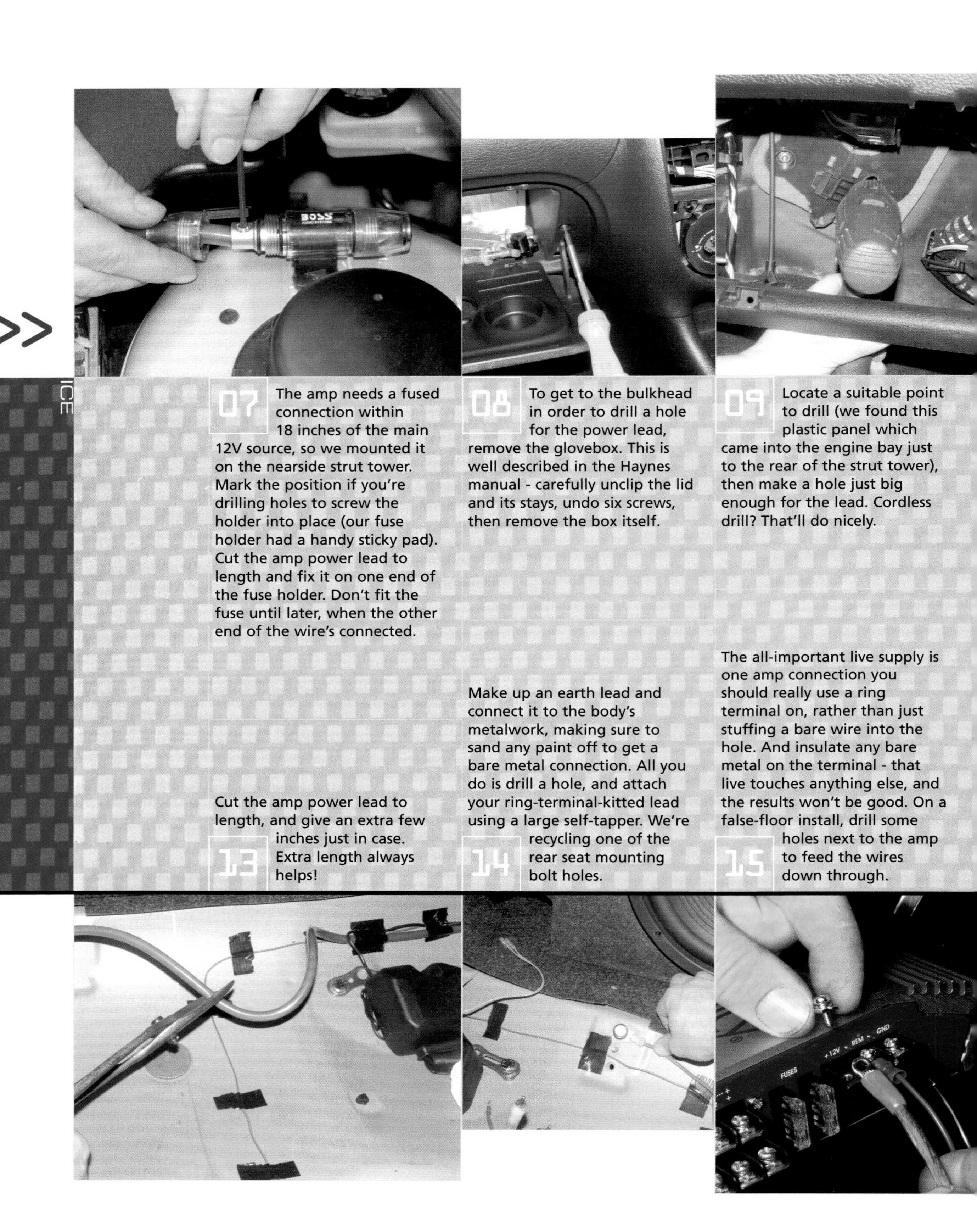


ICE

07 The amp needs a fused connection within 18 inches of the main 12V source, so we mounted it on the nearside strut tower. Mark the position if you're drilling holes to screw the holder into place (our fuse holder had a handy sticky pad). Cut the amp power lead to length and fix it on one end of the fuse holder. Don't fit the fuse until later, when the other end of the wire's connected.

08 To get to the bulkhead in order to drill a hole for the power lead, remove the glovebox. This is well described in the Haynes manual - carefully unclip the lid and its stays, undo six screws, then remove the box itself.

09 Locate a suitable point to drill (we found this plastic panel which came into the engine bay just to the rear of the strut tower), then make a hole just big enough for the lead. Cordless drill? That'll do nicely.

13 Cut the amp power lead to length, and give an extra few inches just in case. Extra length always helps!

14 Make up an earth lead and connect it to the body's metalwork, making sure to sand any paint off to get a bare metal connection. All you do is drill a hole, and attach your ring-terminal-kitted lead using a large self-tapper. We're recycling one of the rear seat mounting bolt holes.

15 The all-important live supply is one amp connection you should really use a ring terminal on, rather than just stuffing a bare wire into the hole. And insulate any bare metal on the terminal - that live touches anything else, and the results won't be good. On a false-floor install, drill some holes next to the amp to feed the wires down through.

**10** Feed the power lead through the bulkhead. Having a mate to help out here is a big plus.

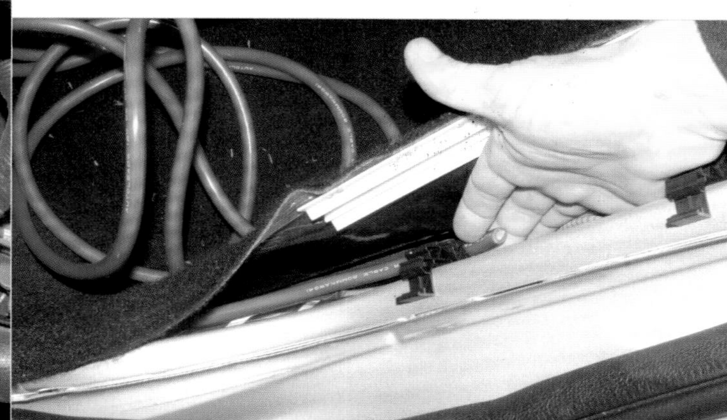

**11** Down the nearside inner sill, there's a factory wiring harness. One more wire won't hurt, so this is an ideal place to run the power cable - you can use all the standard wire clips, as there's enough room.

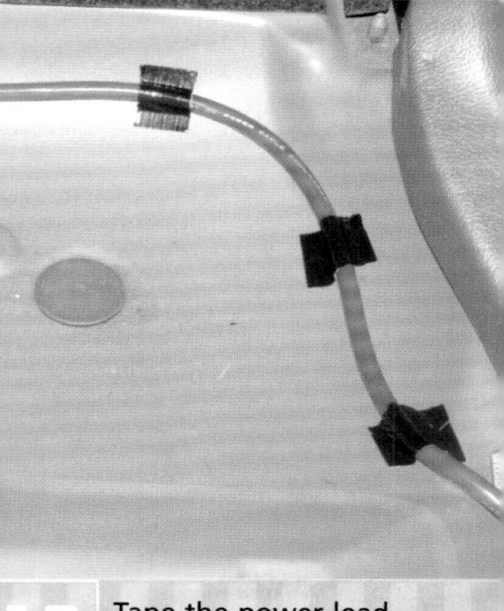

**12** Tape the power lead down with racer's tape (aka carpet tape, duct tape) wherever there's no obvious point to tie it to. Pinning wiring down makes it more reliable, as well as neater.

**16** Read the amp's instruction book carefully when connecting any wires, or you might regret it, especially for bridged or tri-mode. Identify your speaker pos and neg/left and right wires with a piece of tape, and get them screwed on. As with the lives and earths, it's also vital there's no stray bits of wire left poking out.

**17** We had 20ft of RCA lead with sealed ends, meaning we couldn't do any cutting. Bunching-up the RCA leads is a good way to get interference, so we ran the lead neatly around the boot floor and taped it down, before running forward down the driver's side inner sill.

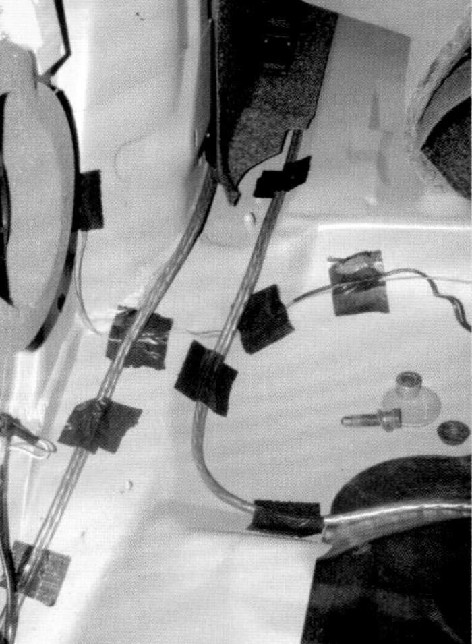

>>

**18** With the trim removed and carpet unclipped from the inner sill, the RCA lead can be run through with the factory wiring harness.

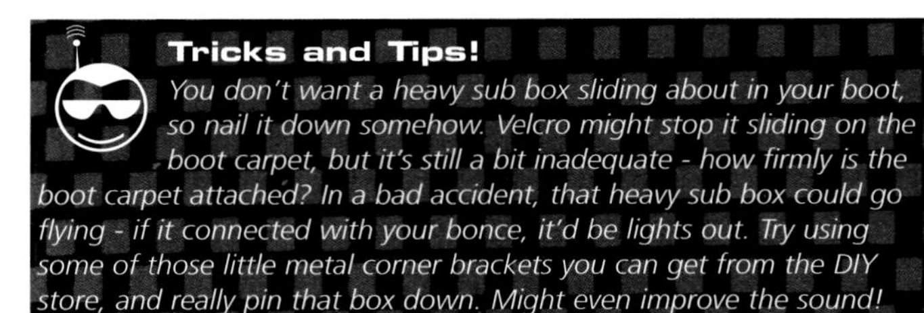

**Tricks and Tips!**

*You don't want a heavy sub box sliding about in your boot, so nail it down somehow. Velcro might stop it sliding on the boot carpet, but it's still a bit inadequate - how firmly is the boot carpet attached? In a bad accident, that heavy sub box could go flying - if it connected with your bonce, it'd be lights out. Try using some of those little metal corner brackets you can get from the DIY store, and really pin that box down. Might even improve the sound!*



**19** Just under the driver's side dash is an ideal place to run the RCAs away from any power leads going to the fusebox, which can cause interference.

**20** The 12-inch Digital Designs (DD Audio) subwoofer can handle 300w RMS, and is all you'll need in the small 206 interior – trust us!

**21** Run the bridged speaker lead from the amp, and connect the wires up at the sub's terminals.

**22** Last thing to do is fit the fuse in your amp's power supply and test it's working.

**23** A good tip is to leave the amps loose until after you've set them up - if you can, leave good access to the gain adjustment (volume) screws after final fitting, too. Starting at normal listening volume, with the amp gain turned down, put on a kicking track, then turn the gain up until the speakers just start to distort. Turn the gain down a tad from there, and you've a good basic setting. Amp gain and headset faders can now be tweaked to give a good balanced sound - or whatever tickles your lugholes.

**Tricks and Tips!**

*Very few systems work 100%, first time. If the amp LEDs don't light up, for instance, are they getting power? Are the p-cont/remote wires connected properly? If the sub doesn't kick, is the amp switch set to bridged or tri-mode, not stereo? Are the low-pass switches in the correct position? RTFM.*

# Wiring-up

For most people, this is the scariest part of an install - just the thought of masses of multi-coloured spaghetti sticking out of your dash might have you running to the experts (or a knowledgeable mate). But - if you do everything in a logical order, and observe a few simple rules, wiring-up isn't half as brain-numbing as it seems.

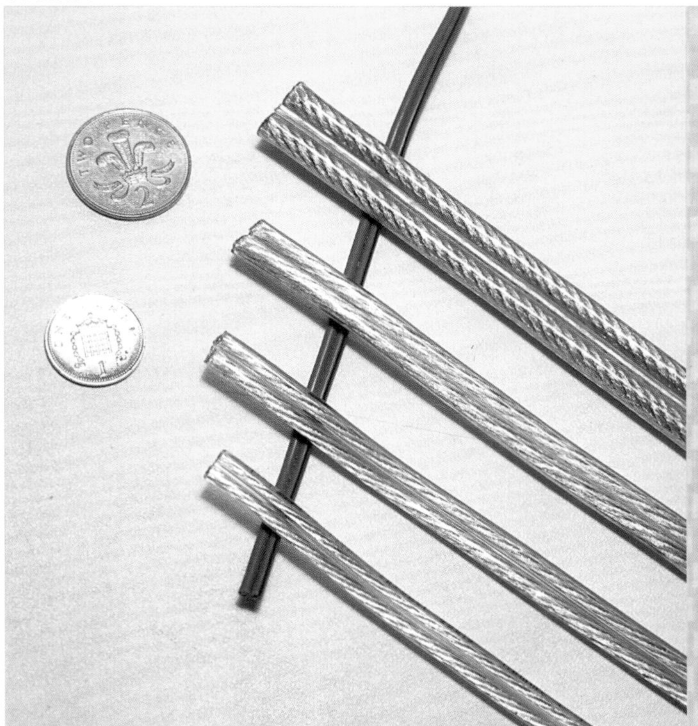

## Live feeds

Although a typical head unit can be powered off the standard Peugeot wiring (the stock wire is good for about 15 amps, tops) running amplifiers means you'll be needing a new live feed, taken straight off the battery. Or in our case, straight off the fusebox.

Get some decent 'eight-gauge' (quite heavy) or 'four-gauge' (getting on for battery cable thickness - serious stuff) wire, and a matching fuseholder. If you're running more than one item off this feed wire, get a distribution block too, which splits the feed up, with a separate fuse for each item - who'd have thought electrical safety can look trick too?

### Pub trivia:

*Hands up, who knows what 'RCA' stands for? We use it every day in ICE-speak, but WHAT does it really mean? Really Clever Amplifier lead? Remote Control Acoustic lead? Well, the answer's a strange one. RCA leads and connectors are also known as 'phono' connectors in the world of TV and hi-fi, and they've been around a long, long time. How long, exactly? We're talking back in the days when you could only get radios - big suckers with valves in them, and long before anyone thought of putting one in a car. RCA actually stands for Radio Corporation of America, who hold the patent on this type of connector and lead. Not a lot of people know that.*

## Speaker and RCA wiring

As with all wiring, the lesson here is to be neat and orderly - or - you'll be sorry! RCA leads and speaker wires are prone to picking up interference (from just about anywhere), so the first trick to learn when running ICE wiring is to keep it away from live feeds, and also if possible, away from the car's ECUs. Another favourite way to interference-hell is to loop up your wiring, when you find you've got too much (we've all been there). Finding a way to lose any excess lengths of wire without bunching can be an art - laying it out in a zig-zag, taping it to the floor as you go, is just one solution.

Another lesson in neatness is finding out what kinds of cable clips are available, and where to use them. There's various stick-on clips which can be used as an alternative to gaffer tape on floors, and then 'P-clips', which look exactly as their name suggests, and can be screwed down (to speaker shelves, for instance). 'Looming' your wiring is another lesson well-learned - this just means wrapping tape around, particularly on pairs of speaker wires or RCAs. As we've already said, don't loom speaker wire with power cables (or even with earths).

The last point is also about tidiness - mental tidiness. When you're dealing with speaker wiring, keep two ideas in mind - positive and negative. Each speaker has a pos (+) and neg (-) terminal. Mixing these up is not an option, so work out a system of your own, for keeping positive and negative in the right places on your headset and amp connections. Decent speaker cable is always two wires joined together - look closely, and you'll see that one wire has writing (or a stripe) on, and the other is plain. Use the wire with writing for pos connections throughout your system, and you'll never be confused again. While we're at it, RCA leads have red and white connector plugs - Red is for Right.

# MDF install

MDF (medium density fibreboard) is a very versatile material which has been used in ICE installs since they started becoming popular in the late 80s. Its beauty is that it's easy to work with, very dense and heavy so it suits speaker applications well. If you have access to a jigsaw (ideally with adjustable-angle blade) and a chisel set, you can work MDF with success. It's not even that expensive, so if you muck it up, it won't cost you loads. Our 8ft by 4ft sheet of 1-inch thick MDF cost just £25, and that was delivered from the local DIY store. You'll need a mate to help carry a sheet this size, and a van to get it home, probably. Do some measuring before you set out, and you could have the massive sheet cut into two or more smaller bits at the store, making life far easier.

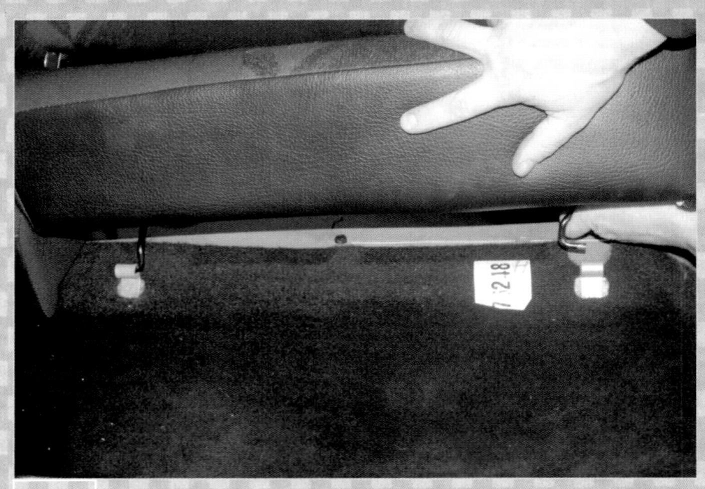

**01** If, like us, you're removing the rear seat in order to create an ICE install, first lift up the seat bases, and unhook the sprung steel retainers. Now the seat bases can be removed completely.

**02** The seat backs are bolted down on a central bracket, so remove the bolts holding it in place.

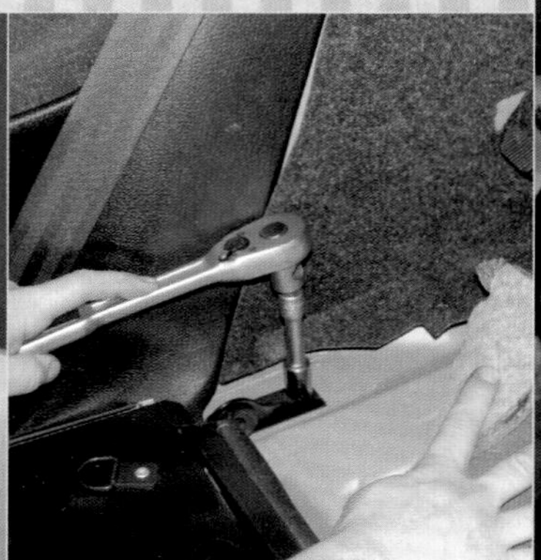

**03** Now fold the backrests forward, and unbolt the brackets either side to release the seats. Remove the seat backs and confine them to storage, with the bases.

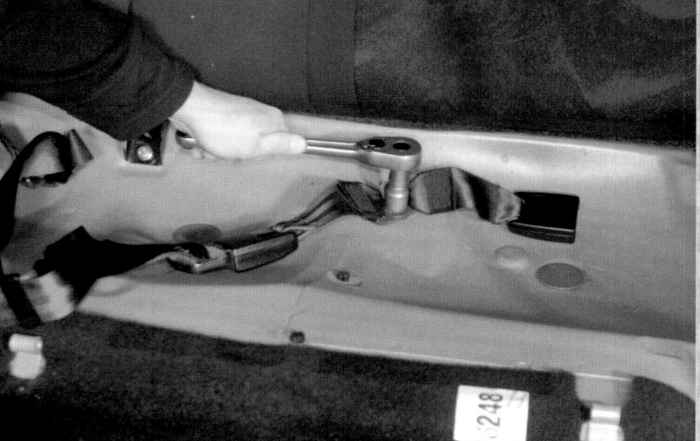

**04** Complete the rear end strip by unbolting the seat belts in the rear - store them too.

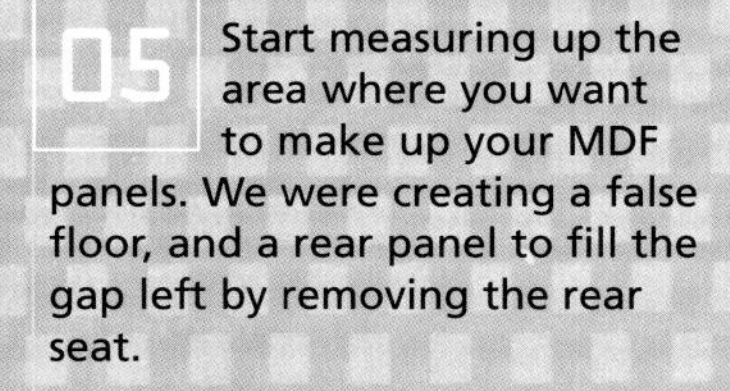

05 Start measuring up the area where you want to make up your MDF panels. We were creating a false floor, and a rear panel to fill the gap left by removing the rear seat.

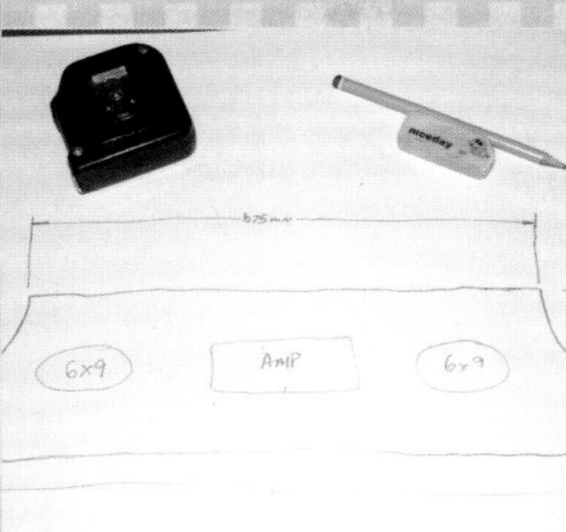


06 A rough sketch allows you to note down your measurements, and gives you a shape and size for your template.

07 Transfer your measurements to a suitably-sized piece of cardboard, then cut it out to make your template. Check the fit of your template, taking into account the MDF is thicker and might not sit exactly the same. Make all the tweaks to your template so it's perfect, then transfer the shape to the wood. This way, you're not continually tweaking the wood - much harder work.

08 Transfer the finished template to your sheet of MDF - make use of the straight edges if at all possible. Cut out the shape with a jigsaw - goggles and a mask are essential, as the dust from the cutting is horrible stuff to breathe in. If possible, do your cutting outside or at least somewhere there's plenty of ventilation.

09 With the floor and back panels finished, you can start adding the speakers and anything else you plan to mount on the MDF. We cut the back panel to allow the subwoofer box to show through into the cabin.

10 The finished install, with the amp mounted centrally, a pair of 6x9s in the rear panel and our interior neons to light up the equipment. All it needs now is trimming up in our choice of carpet/material - the plan is to get some blue seat fabric from Corbeau, to match our front buckets.

# Engines

## Faster, faster!

**So - does your car talk the talk (sounds fast), or does it walk the walk (actually is fast)? There's no shame in just having a fast-sounding car - not everyone can afford mega-performance, which is why bolt-on goodies like induction kits and big-bore exhausts are such big business. Serious engine tuning costs, and not just in the engine parts - your insurance company will throw a wobbly at a gas-flowed head, and might refuse to cover you altogether if you go for that GTI 180 engine conversion.**

The induction kit and sports exhaust are an essential first choice, and usually it's as far as you can really go before your insurance company disowns you. Both mods help the engine to 'breathe' better, which helps when you go for the accelerator initially, improving the response you feel, while you also get a crowd-pleasing induction roar and rasp from the back box, so everyone's happy.

Now for the harsh and painful truth. On their own, an induction kit and back box may not gain you much extra 'real' power. Sorry, but it's a myth. Time and again, people fit induction kits and back boxes, expecting huge power gains, and those 'in the know' have a quiet chuckle. All these things really do is make the car sound sportier, and improve the response - accept this, and you won't be disappointed. Ask yourself why most insurance companies don't generally increase premiums for the likes of a performance rear box or induction kit. The answer is - because (on their own) they don't make enough difference!

The 'bolt-on' performance goodies have more effect as part of an engine 'makeover' package, and setting-up the engine properly after fitting these parts can make a huge difference. If you're halfway serious about increasing the go of your 206, talk to someone with access to a rolling road, so you can prove what's been done HAS actually made a useful gain. If you've spent time and a ton of money on your car, of course you're going to think it feels faster, but is it actually making more power?

Fitting all the performance goodies in the world will be pretty pointless if the engine's already knackered, but it might not be as bad as you think. One of the best ways to start on the performance road is simply to ensure that the car's serviced properly - new spark plugs, filters, and an oil change, are a good basis to begin from. Correct any obvious faults, such as hoses or wiring plugs hanging off, and look for any obviously-damaged or leaking components, too.

# **Breathe** with me...

## Replacement **element**

**One of the simplest items to fit, the replacement air filter element has been around for years - of course, now the induction kit's the thing to have, but a replacement element is more discreet (if you're worried about such things).**

While we're at it, don't listen to anyone who says just take out the air filter completely - this is a really naff idea. The fuel system's air intake acts like a mini vacuum cleaner, sucking in air from the front of the car, and it doesn't just suck in air, but also dust, dirt and leaves. Without a filter, all this muck would end up in the sensitive parts of the fuel system, and will quickly make the car undriveable. Worse, if any of it makes it into the engine, this will lead to engine wear. Remember too, that cheaper performance filters can be of very suspect quality - if your new filter disintegrates completely inside six months, it'll do wonders for the airflow, but it'll also be letting in all sorts of rubbish!

Some performance filters have to be oiled before fitting - follow the instructions provided; don't ignore this part, or the filter won't be effective. If the filter won't fit, check whether you actually have the right one - don't force it in, and don't cut it to fit, as either of these will result in gaps, which would allow unfiltered air to get in.

01 The K&N panel filter is the budget way to better performance, by allowing more air into your engine.

02 To start on the engine, remove the breather pipe clip from the large intake pipe.

03 Undo the Jubilee clip on the main intake pipe where it joins the throttle body.

04 Next, undo the four bolts holding the top of the air box on.

05 Undo the Jubilee clip where the air box joins the main intake pipe.

06 If just fitting a panel filter, this is where you'd exchange it for the stock paper filter and retighten everything. Refit all the bits you took off, making sure that everything's well-tightened, to avoid air leaks.

01 Remove the standard air filter as described in 'replacement element'. Undo the pipe clip underneath the main intake hose.

# Induction kit

You'd either have to be mad or without a pulse not to want more performance from your car, and freeing up your engine's breathing is one way to start. K&N have been at the top of induction and air filtration for many years, because they have a great reputation for producing quality goods. Their filters also last forever if treated correctly and washed/re-oiled every two years or so. What the increased cool air flow from a complete induction kit will do is tell the engine ECU that it needs to add more fuel, which it will do (in small amounts). This will result in a quick-revving, throaty-sounding engine, with (maybe) more power and more torque. So, you're waiting for what exactly?

02 We won't be needing this 'induction kit' any more. You can now remove the bulky intake silencer and intake hose.

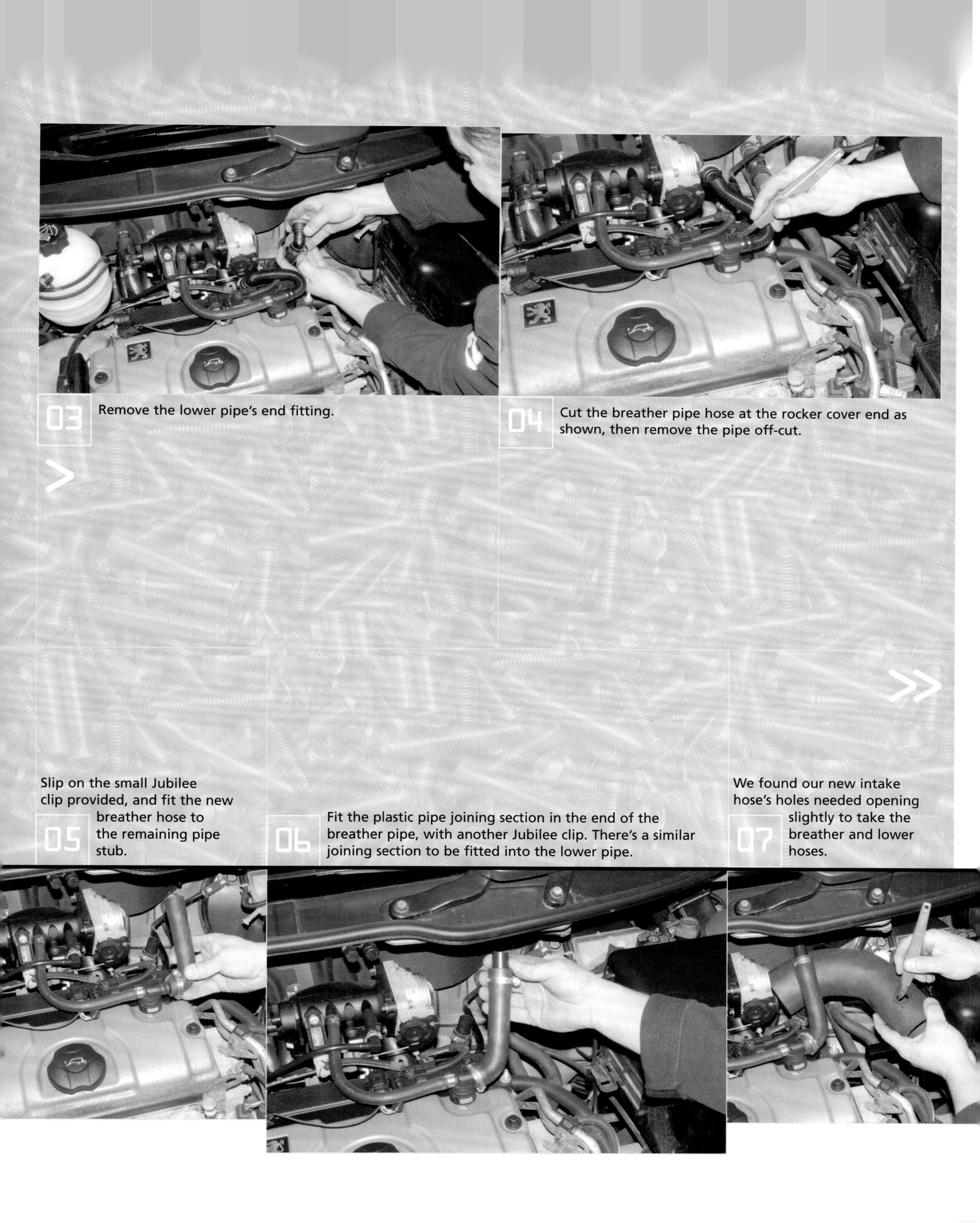

03 Remove the lower pipe's end fitting.

04 Cut the breather pipe hose at the rocker cover end as shown, then remove the pipe off-cut.

05 Slip on the small Jubilee clip provided, and fit the new breather hose to the remaining pipe stub.

06 Fit the plastic pipe joining section in the end of the breather pipe, with another Jubilee clip. There's a similar joining section to be fitted into the lower pipe.

07 We found our new intake hose's holes needed opening slightly to take the breather and lower hoses.

Engines

08 Take the largest Jubilee clip in the box, and slip it onto the large-diameter intake pipe. Now the large pipe can be fitted onto the throttle body.

09 Push the joining section plastic ends from the breather and lower hoses into the large intake pipe. They should be a snug, air-tight fit.

10 Tighten the pipe clip at the throttle body end. It's important this clip is tight - any air leaks at this point could result in frequent stalling (very embarrassing) and high fuel consumption (very expensive).

To mount the essential induction kit filter cone, we need the L-shaped mounting bracket supplied in the kit. This fits using one of the existing engine bolts, at the back of the engine. Do a trial fitting of the cone and bracket, and it'll be obvious which bolt to undo. Fit the bracket, and re-tighten the bolt.

11

Now we've got a bracket, we need something to fit to it. The kit includes a special Jubilee clip with a bolt thread attached - slip this over the large intake pipe, and locate the threaded section into the new bracket.

12

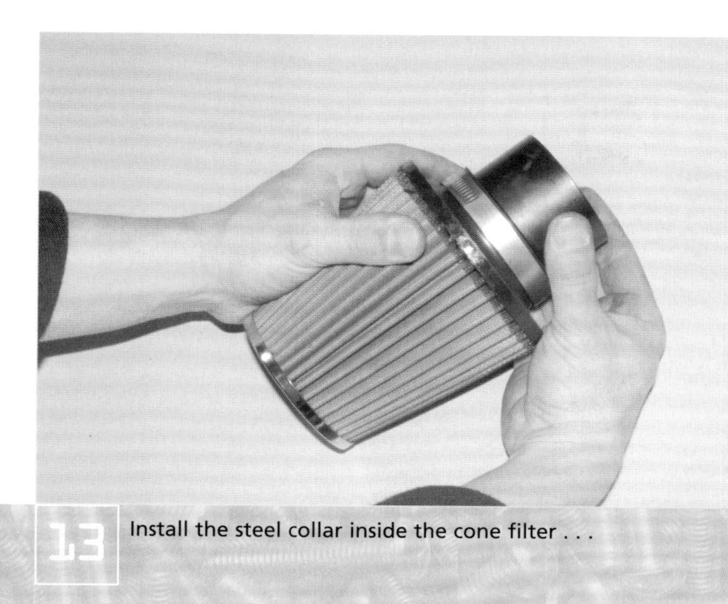

13 Install the steel collar inside the cone filter . . .

14 . . . then push the filter into place and tighten the clips.

15 An induction kit's nothing without a cold-air feed hose, which also gives the ram-air effect you hear bikers going on about. Well, sort-of. Having removed all the other plastic air intake bits, we decided to also rip out the old air box (just pulls free). Not essential to do this, but it'll give you more space and make the engine bay look less cluttered.

16 Assemble the lower air scoop to the cold-air hose . . .

17 . . . then route it downwards, where it can pick up cold air. This might have to be below the bumper, but don't mount it too low, or you'll be sucking up water and small furry mammals. If your 206 is bodykitted-up, try mounting the air scoop behind one of the meshed sections. Fix the scoop in place with cable-ties.

18 Fix the cold-air hose directly beneath the cone filter, to ensure a constant supply of cool air. This too can be tied in place. And that's it! If your 206 doesn't at least sound better for it, you must have done something wrong.

**Finally...**

Once you've fitted your new filter or induction kit, even if you don't take the car to a rolling road for setting up, at least take it to a garage and have the emissions checked - any minor adjustments should ensure that the engine will, if nothing else, still tick over okay, and should ensure an MOT emissions pass.

**Other air filter-type mods**

*One old favourite, if you haven't gone for an induction kit, is drilling holes in the air filter box. Only drill the air filter box below the level where the filter element sits, or the air going into the engine won't be filtered. Making your airbox look like a Swiss cheese won't make the car faster, but it does give you the nice throaty induction roar at full throttle.*

# Adjustable fuel pressure regulator
## (power boost valve)

**These valves allow the fuel system pressure to be increased over the standard regulator valve. Contrary to what you might think, they don't actually provide much more fuel (this is regulated separately by the injection ECU). The effect of increasing the injection pressure is to improve the injector spray pattern, which helps the fuel to burn more efficiently, and has the effect of increasing engine power while actually reducing emission levels.**

To see the true effect of these valves, they must be set up using emission test gear and ideally a rolling road - merely turning the pressure up to the maximum level might not produce the desired effect. Fitting one of these valves involves breaking into the high-pressure fuel line, which is potentially dangerous for the inexperienced - also, if the valve is poorly fitted (or the fuel lines are in poor condition), you could end up with fuel spraying out under pressure onto a hot engine. Make sure you know what you're doing - anything involving petrol requires talent - and watch carefully for any sign of fuel leakage after fitting, even if this is done by a professional.

# No quicker but it looks nice

**Looks are just as important as performance. No hot hatch is 'finished' without making it look sweet. Details to the engine bay as well as your interior and exterior mods are an important factor, especially if you were thinking about getting your motor featured in top magazines. Every one does it, and you're next.**

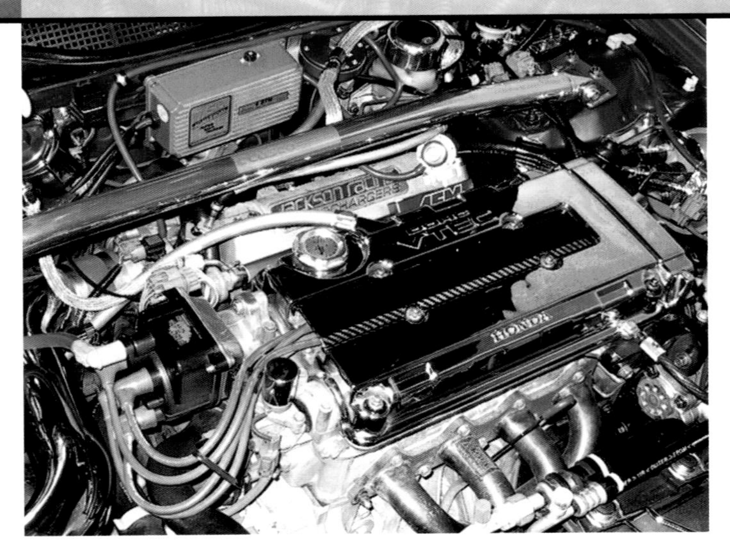


First up - try cleaning the engine, for flip's sake! How do you expect to emulate the show-stopping cars if your gearbox is covered in grot? Get busy with the degreaser (Gunk's a good bet), then get the hosepipe out. You can take it down to the local jetwash if you like, but remember your mobile - if you get carried away with the high-power spray, you might find the car won't start afterwards!

When it's all dry (and running again), you can start in. Get the polish to all the painted surfaces you reasonably can, and don't be afraid to unbolt a few of the simpler items to gain better access. We're assuming you've already fitted your induction kit, but if not, these nicely do away with a load of ugly plastic airbox/air cleaner and trunking, and that rusted-out exhaust manifold cover, in favour of decent-looking product. Take off the rocker cover, and paint it to match your chosen scheme (heat-resistant paint is a must, really, such as brake caliper paint), set off with a funky oil filler cap. A strut brace is a tasty underbonnet feature, especially chromed. Braided hose covers (or coloured hose sets), ally battery covers and bottles, mirror panels - all give the underbonnet a touch of glamour.

# You's a hose

## Engine hose paint

**01** MHW's Tube-It hose paint has been specially developed to stick to rubber surfaces, so is ideal for engine bay hoses which, otherwise, would have to remain boring in black. It only comes in small aerosols, so it may not go as far as you'd like, but you should be able to cover most engine bays with two cans.

**02** First job is to remove the hoses you want to paint. We reckoned our induction kit's intake hose was an ideal candidate. Any others might contain various fluids, so remove them slowly and carefully, and have some rags or a container ready to catch whatever comes out. Give the hose a good clean before even thinking about getting painting.

**03** Spray your hoses, keeping the can shaken as you're painting. Three or four light coats should do the trick. Use a piece of stiff wire up the smaller hoses, to hold them so you can spray them all round.

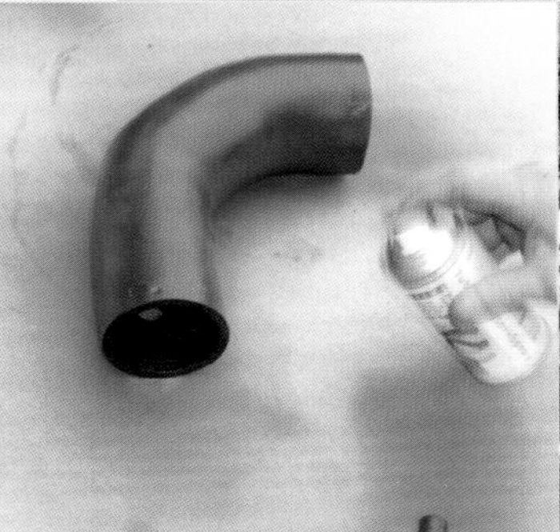

**04** We coated a number of rubber and plastic parts in the engine bay, to improve its looks.

**Achtung!**

*The engine must be completely cold before you start. Even if you've only done a quick lap, it would be dangerous to attempt doing anything with a remotely warm engine, as the fluids inside the pipe are often a lot hotter than they appear. Be warned!*

## Braiding hoses

**01** Unroll your braiding, check the length against your freshly-removed hose, and trim it roughly to length - you might need something heftier than scissors for this.

**02** Now expand the braiding to the right size using a suitable blunt object. Like a screwdriver handle, we mean - what were you thinking of? Once the braiding's roughly the right size, you can slip your pipe in (lovely). Smooth out the braiding round the bends, as it tends to gather up and look naff otherwise, then trim up the ends.

**03** Slide a new Jubilee clip over the braiding at one end, then slip one of the coloured end fittings over the clip. Repeat this process at the other end of your chosen hose, and it'll be ready to fit back on. When you're sure the hose is fully onto its fitting, tighten the hose clip securely to avoid embarrassing leakage.

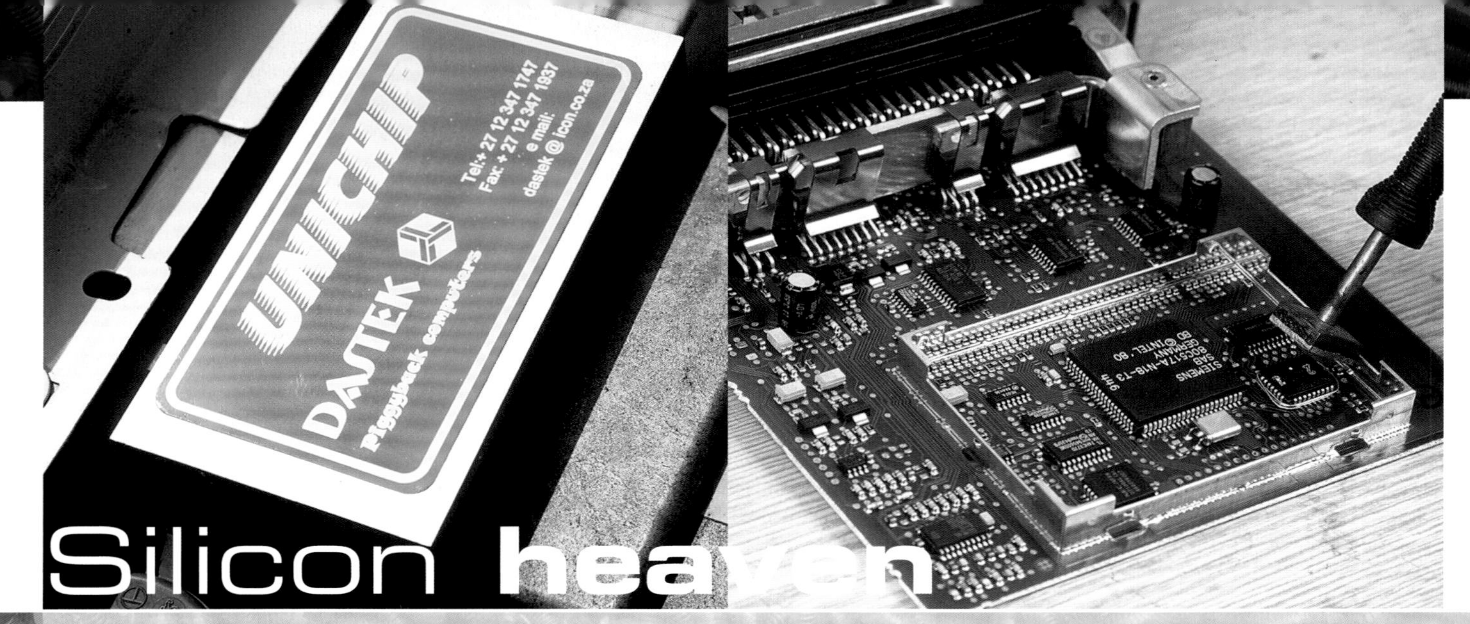


# Silicon heaven

**All 206s have an engine management system with a 'computer' at its heart, known as the ECU, or Electronic Control Unit. The ECU contains several computer chips, at least one of which has programmed onto it the preferred fuel/air mixture and ignition advance setting for any given engine speed or load - this information is known as a computer 'map', and the system refers to it constantly while the car's being driven. Obviously, with the current trend towards fuel economy and reducing harmful exhaust emissions, the values in this 'map' are set, well, conservatively, let's say (read 'boring'). With a little tweaking - like richening-up the mixture, say - the engine can be made to produce more power, or response will be improved, or both. At the expense of the environment. Whatever.**

Companies like Superchips offer replacement computer chips which feature a computer map where driveability and performance are given priority over outright economy (although the company claims that, under certain conditions, even fuel economy can be better, with their products). While a chip like this does offer proven power gains on its own, it's obviously best to combine a chip with other enhancements, and to have the whole lot set up at the same time. By the time you've fitted an induction kit, four-branch manifold, big-bore pipe, and maybe even a fast-road cam, adding a chip is the icing on the cake - chipping an already-modified motor will liberate even more horses, or at least combine it with majorly-improved response. Peugeot tuning specialists are best placed to advise you on the most effective tuning mods.

Chipping is about the best way to extract more horses if your 206 runs on oil, not petrol. Modern turbo-diesel engine management systems control all aspects of fuelling, as you'd expect, but they also control the turbo boost. The more modern your TD is, the more there is to play with, and the more to be gained. Chipping a petrol engine can mean an extra 10 bhp, but turbo-diesels can give three times that gain, from a chip alone - and still with sensible fuel economy

Another feature programmed into the ECU is a rev limiter, which cuts the ignition (or fuel) progressively when the pre-set rev limit is reached. Most replacement chips have the rev limiter reset higher, or removed altogether. Not totally sure this is a good thing - if the engine's not maintained properly (low oil level, cambelt changes neglected), removing the rev limiter and running beyond the red line would be a quick way to kill it. But a well-maintained engine with rally cam(s) fitted could rev off the clock, if the ECU would let it, so maybe not a bad thing after all...

## Now the bad news

Chipping is often thought of as an easy, 'no-tell' route to increased performance and driveability - after all, the ECU is well-buried inside the car, not on show under the bonnet, so who's gonna know? Needless to say, the insurance companies have been wise to this trick for a long time. A sure way to tell whether any 'performance' product does what it says on the tin is to see what it'll do to your premium - telling them you're fitting a sports ROM chip will cost. Big-time. But, in the event of a claim, if they suspect your car's been 'chipped', rest assured, they will make efforts to find out, because if you haven't told them about it, it means they save on paying out. What's an insurance assessor's salary for one day, compared to the thousands you could be claiming in case of an accident or theft? Do it by all means, but at least be honest.

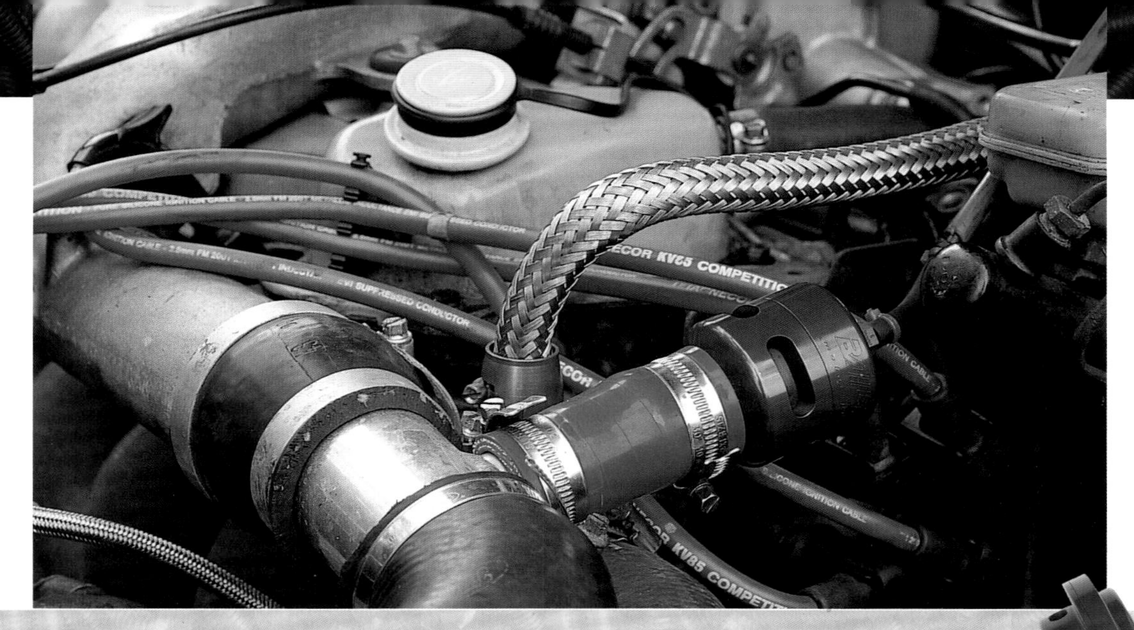

# Engine tuning

**So you've done the filter/induction kit and exhaust box - what's next, short of going for a complete engine swap?**

If you've got a sports back box, try a performance exhaust manifold up front - or better still, a full 'cat-back' system for the best gains. Your 206 is, of course, being strangled all the time you're driving. By a cat - how embarrassing is that? There's the option of a de-cat pipe, which does away with the power-sapping catalytic converter at a stroke, freeing-up as many as 10 or 15 horses on the way (but remember the car's not MOT-able with one of these fitted, so isn't strictly legal for use on the road).

A new camshaft's often a juicy way to pep up a standard motor. Standard cams are pretty good these days, but a fast road cam will still give you more top-end. Once the ECU rev limiter's been disabled (by chipping), swap the cam(s) and you should see more power further up the rev range. Treat your 206 to a skimmed, gas-flowed, big-valve cylinder head as well, and it'll really start to percolate.

As the 1.6 engine's essentially the same unit as used in the Saxo VTR/VTS, turbo and supercharger conversions must be possible - quite a few Saxos out there have them. Maybe a nitrous kit would be simpler, though. Most of the gains on the sportier 206 engines come from cams, cylinder head work and revised throttle bodies - if you added a turbo and/or nitrous on top, we think you'd have all the performance you'd ever need.

## Engine swaps

Most young 206 owners wait 'til they've built up some no-claims bonus on their insurance, and go for a bigger Peugeot engine. Why throw shedloads of cash modding a weenie Peugeot engine, when lots less money spent on fitting a new motor could buy you the same power, with room left for tuning?

If you've "only" got a 1.1 or 1.4 litre lump, a swap for the 1.6 will make a useful difference. The 8-valve 1.6 engine can easily (and cheaply) be tuned to produce as much as the later 1.6 16-valver, and it'll slot straight into the 206 with very little work required. Swapping in a 2.0 litre is a little trickier, but still not half as much work as a 2.0 litre conversion would be on a Nova, say. Specialists such as Pug Performance and L.A.D. Motorsport offer all sorts of tuning assistance to Peugeot owners, and if you're lucky enough to have 2.0 litres already, they can get you anything up to the magic 200 bhp if you've got the funds.

### And finally

And finally tonight - the bad news. Any major engine mods means telling those nice suits who work for your insurance company, and it's likely they'll insist on a full engineer's report (these aren't especially expensive - look one up in the Yellow Pages, under *'Garage Services'* or *'Vehicle Inspection'*).

# Exhausts

**It's gotta be done, hasn't it? Your rusty old exhaust lacks the girth to impress, and doesn't so much growl as miaow. Don't be a wimp and fit an exhaust trim - they'll fool nobody who really knows, and they certainly won't add to your aural pleasure (oo-er). Sort yourself out a decent back box upgrade, and even a timid 206 can begin to cut it at the cruise.**

What a back box won't do on its own is increase engine power - although it'll certainly sound like it has, provided you choose the right one, and fit it properly. Check when you're buying that it can be fitted to a standard system - you'll probably need something called a reducing sleeve for a decent fit, which is a section of pipe designed to bridge the difference between your small-diameter pipe and the larger-diameter silencer. Try and measure your standard pipe as accurately as possible, or you'll have major problems trying to get a decent seal between the old and new bits - don't assume that exhaust paste will sort everything out, because it won't.

Fashion has even entered the aftermarket exhaust scene, with different rear pipe designs going in and out of style. Everyone's done the upswept twin-pipe 'DTM' style pipes, while currently the trend in single pipes is massive Jap-style round exits, or fat oval (or twin-oval) designs. If you must have the phattest 206 on the block,

Know your enemy - this is what your cat looks like inside. Is it any wonder they restrict gas flow?

you can't beat a twin-exit system (from someone like Powerflow), even though it'll probably mean losing your spare wheel in the fitting process. Well, when was the last time you had a puncture? And what are mobiles and breakdown cover for, anyway?

If you've got a capacity-challenged 206, you might need to lightly modify even your standard rear bodywork/bumper to accommodate a bigger rear pipe; if you're going for a bodykit later, your back box will have to come off again, so it can be poked through your rear valance/mesh.

You'll see some useful power gains if you go for the complete performance exhaust system, rather than just the back box. Like the factory-fit system, the sports silencer again will only work at its best if combined with the front pipe and manifold it was designed for! Performance four-branch manifolds alone can give very useful power gains. Watch what you buy, though - cheap exhaust manifolds which crack for a pastime are not unknown, and many aftermarket systems need careful fitting and fettling before you'll stop it resonating or banging away underneath. A sports rear box alone shouldn't attract an increased insurance premium, but a full system probably will.

All 206s are lumbered with a catalytic converter (or 'cat'), which acts like a restrictor in the exhaust, inhibiting the gas flow and sapping some engine power (maybe 5 to 10%). Various specialist exhaust companies market replacement sections which do away with the cat (a 'de-cat pipe'), and get you your power back. Unfortunately, by taking off or disabling the cat, your car won't be able to pass the emissions test at MOT time, so you'll have to 're-convert' the car every 12 months. This fact, arguably, means that the car is illegal on the road with a de-cat pipe fitted - you'd have no defence for this, if questions were asked at the roadside, and potentially no insurance if the unthinkable happens. Sorry, but we have to say it...

One other point to consider, if your 206's been slammed to the floor - will your big new sports system be leaving behind a trail of sparks as it scrapes along the deck? Shouldn't do, if it's been properly fitted, but will the local multi-storey be out-of-bounds for your 206, from now on? And - pub-trivia moment - you can actually be done for causing damage to the highway, if your exhaust's dragging. Well, great.

You probably couldn't give a stuff if your loud system's a very loud major public nuisance, but will that loud pipe start interfering with your sound system? If you rack up many motorway miles, you might find the constant drone of a loud pipe gets to be a real pain on a long trip, too...

# Fitting a **twin-exit system**

Exhausts

**There are loads of manufacturers that supply ready-to-fit back boxes, cat by-passes to full exhaust systems. But what if you want something with a custom feel, perhaps different tail pipes or relocated exits?**

If you do, then Powerflow have the answer! We popped down to our local dealers, Sargents of Yeovil, to find out more about the seemingly-endless possibilities for creating that custom exhaust. Speak to Mike to find out more about exhausts as well as the other car goodies they stock, or visit their website (details at the back of the book). Our bodykit's rear bumper was made for a phat exhaust both sides, and that's exactly what we went for.

First, raise the car - wheel ramps (or a handy four-post lift) are the only sensible option for this procedure. Having an experienced fabricator (that's a welder, not a liar) on hand is a bonus too!

**01** The first part of the process is to remove the original back box. This is carried out in two easy stages. First of all the pipe that connects the centre box to the back box is cut. In our case, cutting the system wasn't required - it was so rusty, twisting the pipes by hand was enough to separate them.

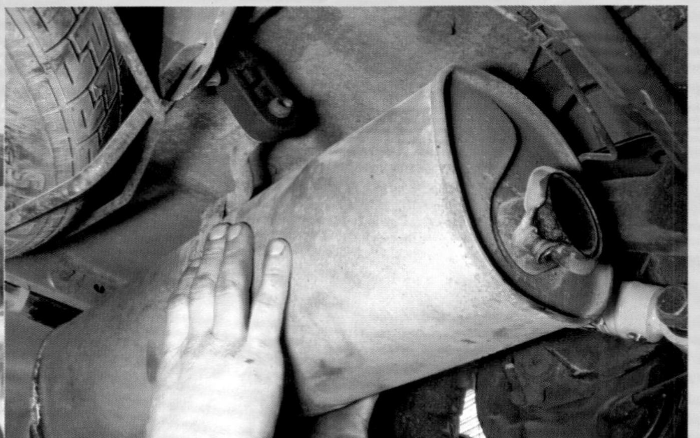

**02** The back box is then unhooked from the rubber clamps (there are two in total) and the box is lifted away from the car.

**03** Next, the centre section of the exhaust is removed. Obviously this is only relevant if you're fitting a full cat-back system. This is done in pretty much the same way as the back box – undo a clamp . . .

**04** . . . and unhook the pipe from the rubber clamp. The complete centre section can then be lowered away from the car.

**05** Next job is to remove the spare wheel cradle, which is hinged at the front, and held up at the back by a long bolt with a hook attached. Use the flat end of the car's wheelbrace to loosen the bolt (inside the boot, at the back). Under the car again, unhook the cradle, and hold it up with one hand while unscrewing the bolt all the way.

**06** Finally, unhook the cradle from the brackets at the front, and remove it and the spare wheel from the car.

**07** Now it's time to commence work on the new, shiny stainless steel system. Our new system isn't having a centre box, so our exhaust chap starts by cutting a length of stainless piping exactly the same length as the original centre section. Then using a special machine, the pipe is bent in exactly the same places as the original. I expect he's heard all the 'bender' gags.

**08** Both ends of the new pipe are extended using a special metal-stretching machine, to create flanges or sleeves. Now the pipes can be joined together to create a full system, using flanges or simply by slotting one pipe inside another (to be clamped or welded). The new centre pipe is offered into place and checked for size - notice the pro exhaust supports holding the rest up.

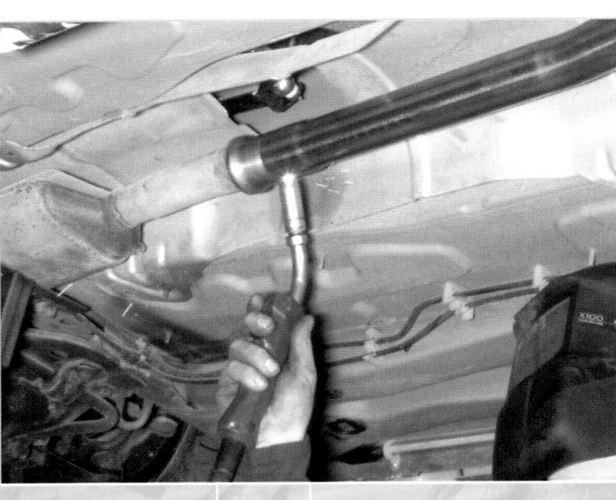

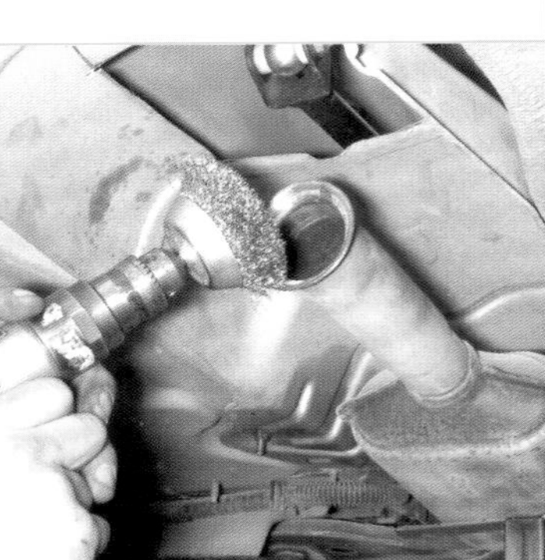

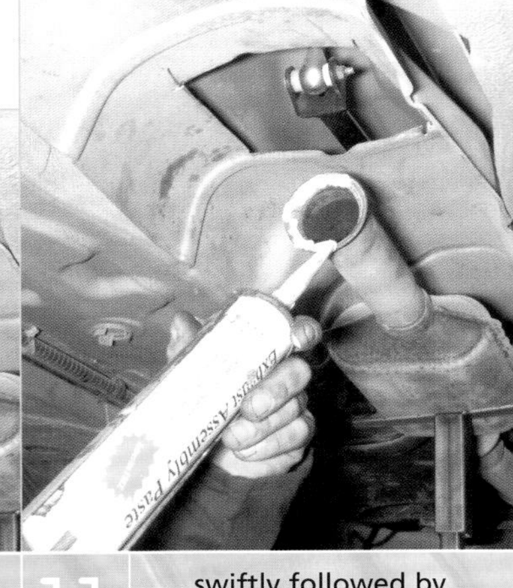


09 Once the pipe has been aligned properly, a metal flange joint is slotted inside the end of the pipe, and tack-welded into place. This flange enables the new centre pipe to be joined to the back of the cat using an exhaust clamp, for easier removal. Not that we're planning on taking it off, you understand.

10 Before the centre pipe is permanently fitted into place, the pipe flange on the cat is given a good clean . . .

11 . . . swiftly followed by a decent bead of exhaust assembly paste.

16 Once the tail pipes are in place, the exhaust tips can be chosen and fitted. The tips are what you'll actually see emerging from your bodykit, so try several before you buy - you're sure to find at least one style you like. Careful positioning will get them in just the right spot, before they're tack-welded into place - this usually requires two people to get it right.

17 The back box is now removed from the car again, and the tail pipes and tips are fully welded into place.

18 With all sections about ready for final fitting, time to think about how the new system's going to stay in place under there. For ease, it's best to use the existing rubber mountings on the car, so brackets now have to be added to the new pipework, to reach them. All in a day's work to our exhaust experts - measure up a sturdy metal strip to reach the rubber mounting . . .

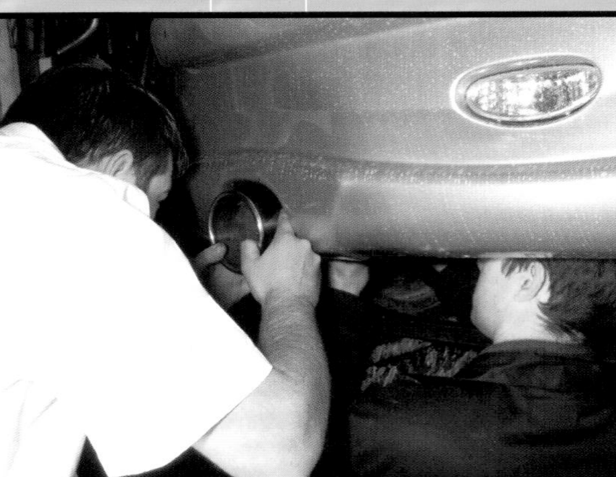

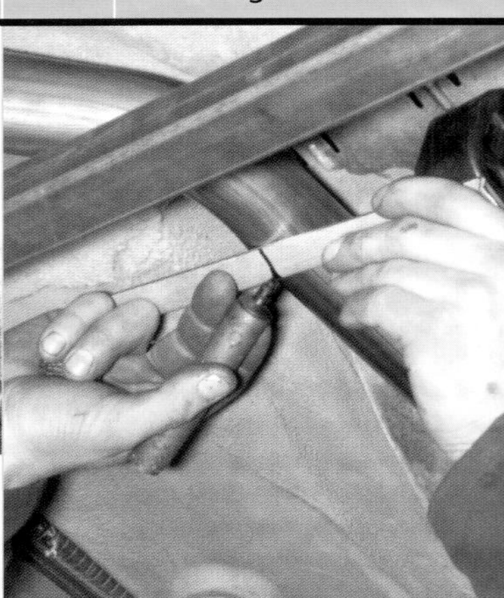

12 Finally the centre pipe is put into place again, lined up, and the exhaust clamp fitted. Tighten the clamp up enough to give a good seal, but don't crush the pipe - this will not result in a free-flowing system!

13 Work now starts on the back box. The exit style you've chosen will determine how time-consuming and difficult this final part is. The back box is positioned across the back of the car and supported in place. Now two sections of pipe are cut and bent into shape - one from the centre section, almost to the box, which gets sleeved and clamped in place . . .

14 . . . whilst a further 'corner' section of pipe is used as the final link to the box itself. Still think creating custom pipework's easy? Only to these guys.

15 Next, the two pipes that exit the back box are cut and bent to shape to create the twin-exit effect. The pipes are offered into place, and any excess pipe is marked with a pen and cut off.

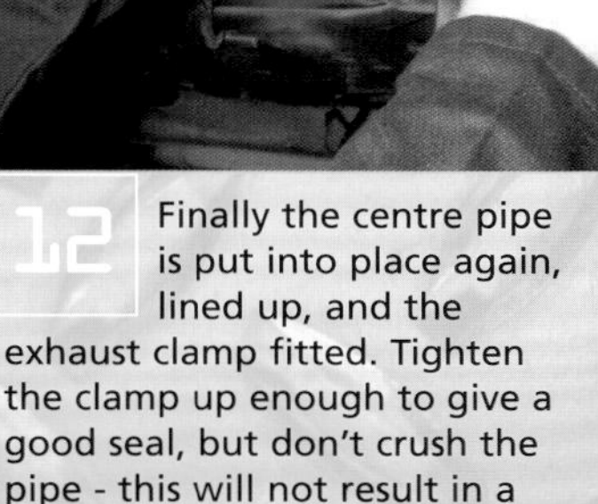

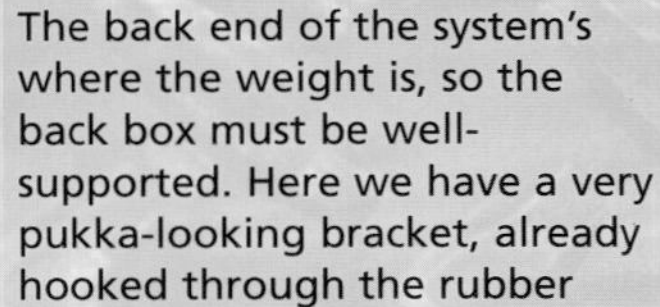

. . . and weld it onto the new pipe. If the strip's made long enough, the end can be bent over as it passes through the rubber 'doughnut', and there's no way it'll fall off.

19

The back end of the system's where the weight is, so the back box must be well-supported. Here we have a very pukka-looking bracket, already hooked through the rubber mounting, about to be welded on. Proper job.

20

You're nearly there! The finishing touch is to lower the car and spray some high-temperature black paint into each tail pipe - this disguises any carbon or other deposits that build up. We're so keen to hear it bark, that paint'll be dry in no time.

21

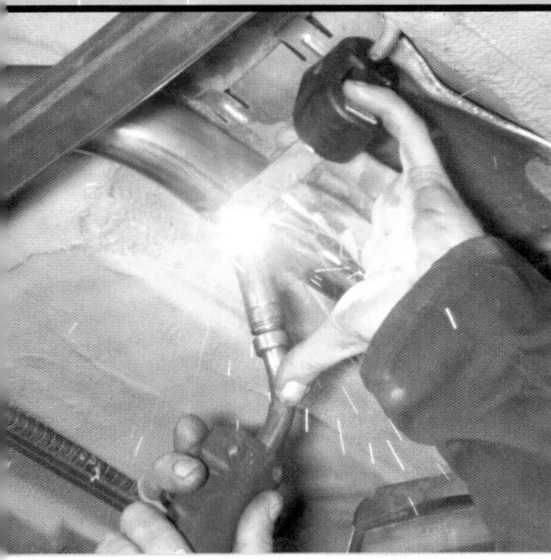

14

# Safety and tools

Reference

## Safety

We all know that working on your car can be dangerous - and we're not talking about the danger of losing your street cred by fitting naff alloys or furry dice! Okay, so you'd be hard-pushed to injure yourself fitting some cool floor mats or a tax disc holder, but tackle more-serious mods, and you could be treading dangerous ground. Let's be honest - we have to put this safety section in to cover ourselves, but now it's in, it would be nice if you read it...

### Burning/scalding

The only way you'll really burn yourself is if your car's just been running - avoid this, and you won't get burned. Easy, eh? Otherwise, you risk burns from any hot parts of the engine (and especially the exhaust - if you've got one, the cat runs very hot), or from spilling hot coolant if you undo the radiator hoses or filler cap, as you might when you're braiding hoses.

### Fire

Sadly, there's several ways your car could catch fire, when you think about it. You've got a big tank full of fuel (and other flammable liquids about, like brake fluid), together with electrics - some of which run to very high voltages. If you smoke too, this could be even worse for your health than you thought.

**a** Liquid fuel is flammable. Fuel vapour can explode - don't smoke, or create any kind of spark, if there's fuel vapour (fuel smell) about.

**b** Letting fuel spill onto a hot engine is dangerous, but brake fluid spills go up even more readily. Respect is due with brake fluid, which also attacks paintwork and plastics - wash off with water.

**c** Fires can also be started by careless modding involving the electrical system. It's possible to overload (and overheat) existing wiring by tapping off too many times for new live feeds. Not insulating bare wires or connections can lead to short-circuits, and the sparks or overheated wiring which results can start a fire. Always investigate any newly-wired-in kit which stops working, or which keeps blowing fuses - those wires could already be smouldering...

#### Crushing

Having your car land on top of you is no laughing matter, and it's a nasty accident waiting to happen if you risk using dodgy old jacks, bricks, and other means of lifting/supporting your car. Please don't.

Your standard vehicle jack is for emergency roadside use only - a proper trolley jack and a set of axle stands won't break the overdraft, and might save broken bones. Don't buy a cheap trolley jack, and don't expect a well-used secondhand one to be perfect, either - when the hydraulic seals start to fail, a trolley jack will drop very fast; this is why you should always have decent stands in place under the car as well.

#### Steering, suspension & brakes

Screwing up any one of these on your car, through badly-fitted mods, could land you and others in hospital or worse. Nuff said? It's always worth getting a mate, or a friendly garage, to check over what you've just fitted (or even what you've just had fitted, in some cases - not all "pro" fitters are perfect!). Pay attention to tightening vital nuts and bolts properly - buy or borrow a torque wrench.

To be absolutely sure, take your newly-modded machine to a friendly MOT tester (if there is such a thing) - this man's your ultimate authority on safety, after all. Even if he's normally a pain once a year, he could save your life. Think it over.

Even properly-fitted mods can radically alter the car's handling - and not always for the better. Take a few days getting used to how the car feels before showing off.

#### Wheels

Don't take liberties fitting wheels. Make sure the wheels have the right stud/bolt hole pattern for your car, and that the wheel nuts/bolts are doing their job. Bolts which are too long might catch on your brakes (especially rear drums) - too short, and, well, the wheels are just waiting to fall off. Not nice. Also pay attention to the bolt heads or wheel nuts - some are supposed to have large tapered washers fitted, to locate properly in the wheel. If the nuts/bolts "pull through" the wheel when tightened, the wheel's gonna fall off, isn't it?

#### Asbestos

Only likely to be a major worry when working on, or near, your brakes. That black dust that gets all over your alloys comes from your brake pads, and it may contain asbestos. Breathing in asbestos dust can lead to a disease called asbestosis (inflammation of the lungs - very nasty indeed), so try not to inhale brake dust when you're changing your pads or discs.

#### Airbags

Unless you run into something at high speed, the only time an airbag will enter your life is when you change your steering wheel for something more sexy, and have to disable the airbag in the process. Pay attention to all the precautionary advice given in our text, and you'll have no problems.

One more thing - don't tap into the airbag wiring to run any extra electrical kit. Any mods to the airbag circuit could set it off unexpectedly.

#### Exhaust gases

Even on cars with cats, exhaust fumes are still potentially lethal. Don't work in an unventilated garage with the engine running. When fitting new exhaust bits, be sure that there's no gas leakage from the joints. When modifying in the tailgate area, note that exhaust gas can get sucked into the car through badly-fitting tailgate seals/joints (or even through your rear arches, if they've been trimmed so much there's holes into the car).

## Tools

In writing this book, we've assumed you already have a selection of basic tools - screwdrivers, socket set, spanners, hammer, sharp knife, power drill. Any unusual extra tools you might need are mentioned in the relevant text. Torx and Allen screws are often found on trim panels, so a set of keys of each type is a wise purchase.

From a safety angle, always buy the best tools you can afford - or if you must use cheap ones, remember that they can break under stress or unusual usage (and we've all got the busted screwdrivers to prove it!).

**DO** Wear goggles when using power tools.

**DO** Keep loose clothing/long hair away from moving engine parts.

**DO** Take off watches and jewellery when working on electrics.

**DO** Keep the work area tidy - stops accidents and losing parts.

**DON'T** Rush a job, or take stupid short-cuts.

**DON'T** Use the wrong tools for the job, or ones which don't fit.

**DON'T** Let kids or pets play around your car when you're working.

**DON'T** Work entirely alone under a car that's been jacked up.

# Legal modding? No such thing!!

### The harsh & painful truth

The minute you start down the road to a modified motor, you stand a good chance of being in trouble with the Man. It seems like there's almost nothing worthwhile you can do to your car, without breaking some sort of law. So the answer's not to do it at all, then? Well, no, but let's keep it real.

There's this bunch of vehicle-related regulations called Construction & Use. It's a huge set of books, used by the car manufacturers and the Department of Transport among others, and it sets out in black and white all the legal issues that could land you in trouble. It's the ultimate authority for modifying, in theory. But few people (and even fewer policemen) know all of it inside-out, and it's forever being updated and revised, so it's not often enforced to the letter at the roadside - just in court. Despite the existence of C & U, in trying to put together any guide to the law and modifying, it quickly becomes clear that almost everything's a "grey area", with no-one prepared to go on record and say what is okay to modify and what's not. Well, brilliant. So if there's no fixed rules (in the real world), how are you meant to live by them? In the circumstances, all we can promise to do is help to make sense of nonsense...

### Avoiding roadside interviews

Why do some people get pulled all the time, and others hardly ever? It's often all about attitude. We'd all like to be free to drive around "in yer face", windows down, system full up, loud exhaust bellowing, sparks striking, tyres squealing - but - nothing is a bigger "come-on" to the boys in blue than "irresponsible" driving like this. Rest assured, if your motor's anywhere near fully sorted, the coppers will find something they can nick you for, when they pull you over - it's a dead cert. Trying not to wind them up too much before this happens (and certainly not once you're stopped) will make for an easier life. There's showing off, and then there's taking the pee. Save it for the next cruise.

The worst thing from your point of view is that, once you've been stopped, it's down to that particular copper's judgement as to whether your car's illegal. If he/she's having a bad day anyway, smart-mouthing-off isn't gonna help your case at all. If you can persuade him/her that you're at least taking on board what's being said, you might be let off with a warning. If it goes further, you'll be reported for an offence - while this doesn't mean you'll end up being prosecuted for it, it ain't good. Some defects (like worn tyres) will result in a so-called "seven-day wonder", which usually means you have to fix whatever's deemed wrong, maybe get the car inspected, and present yourself with the proof at a police station, inside seven days, or face prosecution.

If you can manage to drive reasonably sensibly when the law's about, and can ideally show that you've tried to keep your car legal when you get questioned, you stand a much better chance of enjoying your relationship with your modded beast. This guide is intended to help you steer clear of the more obvious things you could get pulled for. By reading it, you might even be able to have an informed, well-mannered discussion about things legal with the next officer of the law you meet at the side of the road. As in: "Oh really, officer? I was not aware of that. Thank you for pointing it out." Just don't argue with them, that's all...

### Documents

The first thing you'll be asked to produce. If you're driving around without tax, MOT or insurance, we might as well stop now, as you won't be doing much more driving of anything after just one pull.

Okay, so you don't normally carry all your car-related documents with you - for safety, you've got them stashed carefully at home, haven't you? But carrying photocopies of your licence, MOT and insurance certificate is a good idea. While they're not legally-binding absolute proof, producing these in a roadside check might mean you don't have to produce the real things at a copshop later in the week. Shows a certain responsibility, and confidence in your own legality on the road, too. In some parts of the country, it's even said to be a good idea to carry copies of any receipts for your stereo gear - if there's any suspicion about it being stolen (surely not), some coppers have been known to confiscate it (or the car it's in) on the spot!

### Number plates

One of the simplest mods, and one of the easiest to spot (and prove) if you're a copper. Nowadays, any changes made to the standard approved character font (such as italics or fancy type), spacing, or size of the plate constitutes an offence. Remember too that if you've moved the rear plate from its original spot (like from the tailgate recess, during smoothing) it still has to be properly lit at night. You're unlikely to even buy an illegal plate now, as the companies making them are also liable for prosecution if you get stopped. It's all just something else to blame on speed cameras - plates have to be easy for them to shoot, and modding yours suggests you're trying to escape a speeding conviction (well, who isn't?).

Getting pulled for an illegal plate is for suckers - you're making it too easy for them. While this offence only entails a small fine and confiscation of the plates, you're drawing unwelcome police attention to the rest of your car. Not smart. At all.

### Sunstrips and tints

The sunstrip is now an essential item for any modded motor, but telling Mr Plod you had to fit one is no defence if you've gone a bit too far. The sunstrip should not be so low down the screen that it interferes with your ability to see out. Is this obvious? Apparently not. As a guide, if the strip's so low your wiper(s) touch it, it's too low. Don't try fitting short wiper blades to get round this - the police aren't as stupid as that, and you could get done for wipers that don't clear a sufficient area of the screen. Push it so far, and no further!

Window tinting is a trickier area. It seems you can have up to a 25% tint on a windscreen, and up to 30% on all other glass - but how do you measure this? Er. And what do you do if your glass is tinted to start with? Er, probably nothing. Of course you can buy window film in various "darknesses", from not-very-dark to "ambulance-black", but being able to buy it does not make it legal for road use (most companies cover themselves by saying "for show use only"). Go for just a light smoke on the side and rear glass, and you'd have to be unlucky to get done for it. If you must fit really dark tints, you're safest doing the rear side windows only.

Some forces now have a light meter to test light transmission through glass at the roadside - fail this, and it's a big on-the-spot fine.

### Single wiper conversion

Not usually a problem, and certainly not worth a pull on its own, but combine a big sunstrip with a short wiper blade, and you're just asking for trouble. Insufficient view of the road ahead. There's also the question of whether it's legal to have the arm parking vertically, in the centre of the screen, as it obscures your vision. Probably not legal, then - even if it looks cool. Unfortunately, the Man doesn't do cool.

### Lights

Lights of all kinds have to be one of the single biggest problem areas in modifying, and the police are depressingly well-informed. Most people make light mods a priority, whether it's Morette conversions for headlights or Lexus-style rear clusters. If they fit alright, and work, what's the problem?

First off, don't bother with any lights which aren't fully UK-legal - it's just too much hassle. Being "E-marked" only makes them legal in Europe, and most of our Euro-chums drive on the right. One of our project cars ended up with left-hand-drive rear clusters, and as a result, had no rear reflectors and a rear foglight on the wrong side (should be on the right). Getting stopped for not having rear reflectors would be a bit harsh, but why risk it, even to save a few quid?

Once you've had any headlight mods done (other than light brows) always have the beam alignment checked - it's part of the MOT, after all. The same applies to any front fogs or spots you've fitted (the various points of law involved here are too many to mention - light colour, height, spacing, operation with main/dipped headlights - ask at an MOT centre before fitting, and have them checked out after fitting).

If Plod's really having a bad day, he might even question the legality of your new blue headlight bulbs - are they too powerful? Keeping the bulb packaging in the glovebox might be a neat solution here (60/55W max).

Many modders favour spraying rear light clusters to make them look trick, as opposed to replacing them - but there's trouble in store here, too. One of the greyest of grey areas is - how much light tinting is too much? The much-talked-about but not-often-seen "common sense" comes into play here. Making your lights so dim that they're reduced to a feeble red/orange glow is pretty dim itself. If you're spraying, only use proper light-tinting spray, and not too many coats of that. Colour-coding lights with ordinary spray paint is best left to a pro sprayer or bodyshop (it can be done by mixing lots of lacquer with not much paint, for instance). Tinted lights are actually more of a problem in daylight than at night, so check yours while the sun's out.

Lastly, two words about neons. Oh, dear. It seems that neons of all kinds have now been deemed illegal for road use (and that's

interior ones as well as exteriors, which have pretty much always been a no-no). If you fit neons inside, make sure you rig in a switch so you can easily turn them off when the law arrives - or don't drive around with them on (save it for when you're parked up). Distracts other road users, apparently.

#### ICE

Jungle massive, or massive public nuisance? The two sides of the ICE argument in a nutshell. If you've been around the modding scene for any length of time, you'll already know stories of people who've been done for playing car stereos too loud. Seems some local authorities now have by-laws concerning "music audible from outside a vehicle", and hefty fines if you're caught. Even where this isn't the case, and assuming a dB meter isn't on hand to prove the offence of "excessive noise", the police can still prosecute for "disturbing the peace" - on the basis of one officer's judgement of the noise level. If a case is proved, you could lose your gear. Whoops. Seems we're back to "do it - but don't over-do it" again. If you really want to demo your system, pick somewhere a bit less public (like a quiet trading estate, after dark) or go for safety in numbers (at a cruise).

#### Big alloys/tyres

One of the first things to go on any lad's car, sexy alloys are right at the heart of car modifying. So what'll interest the law?

Well, the first thing every copper's going to wonder is - are the wheels nicked? He'd need a good reason to accuse you, but this is another instance where having copies of receipts might prove useful.

Otherwise, the wheels mustn't rub on, or stick out from, the arches - either of these will prove to be a problem if you get stopped. And you don't need to drive a modded motor to get done for having bald tyres...

#### Lowered suspension

Of course you have to lower your car, to have any hope of street cred. But did you know it's actually an offence to cause damage to the road surface, if your car's so low (or your mates so lardy) that it grounds out? Apparently so! Never mind what damage it might be doing to your exhaust, or the brake/fuel lines under the car - you can actually get done for risking damage to the road. Well, great. What's the answer? Once you've lowered the car, load it up with your biggest mates, and test it over roads you normally use - or else find a route into town that avoids all speed bumps. If you've got coilovers, you'll have an easier time tuning out the scraping noises.

Remember that your new big-bore exhaust or backbox must be hung up well enough that it doesn't hit the deck, even if you haven't absolutely slammed your car on the floor. At night, leaving a trail of sparks behind is a bit of a giveaway...

#### Exhausts

One of the easiest-to-fit performance upgrades, and another essential item if you want to be taken seriously on the street. Unless your chosen pipe/system is just too damn loud, you'd be very unlucky to get stopped for it, but if you will draw attention this way, you could be kicking yourself later.

For instance - have you in fact fitted a home-made straight-through pipe, to a car which used to have a "cat"? By drawing Plod's attention with that extra-loud system, he could then ask you to get the car's emissions tested - worse, you could get pulled for a "random" roadside emissions check. Fail this (and you surely will), and you could be right in the brown stuff. Even if you re-convert the car back to stock for the MOT, you'll be illegal on the road (and therefore without insurance) whenever your loud pipe's on. Still sound like fun, or would you be happier with just a back box?

It's also worth mentioning that your tailpipe mustn't stick out beyond the very back of the car, or in any other way which might be dangerous to pedestrians. Come on - you were a ped once!

### Bodykits

The popular bodykits for the UK market have all passed the relevant tests, and are fully-approved for use on the specific vehicles they're intended for. As long as you haven't messed up fitting a standard kit, you should be fine, legally-speaking. The trouble starts when you do your own little mods and tweaks, such as bodging on that huge whale-tail spoiler or front air dam/splitter - it can be argued in some cases that these aren't appropriate on safety grounds, and you can get prosecuted. If any bodywork is fitted so it obscured your lights, or so badly attached that a strong breeze might blow it off, you can see their point. At least there's no such thing as Style Police. Not yet, anyway.

### Seats and harnesses

Have to meet the UK safety standards, and must be securely bolted in. That's about it. It should be possible to fasten and release any seat belt or harness with one hand. Given that seat belts are pretty important safety features, it's understandable then that the police don't like to see flimsy alloy rear strut braces used as seat harness mounting points. Any other signs of bodging will also spell trouble. It's unlikely they'd bother with a full safety inspection at the roadside, but they could insist on a full MOT test/engineer's report inside 7 days. It's your life.

While we're on the subject of crash safety, the police also don't like to see sub boxes and amps just lying on the carpet, where the back seat used to be - if it's not anchored down, where are these items gonna end up, in a big shunt? Embedded in you, possibly?

### Other mods

We'll never cover everything else here, and the law's always changing anyway, so we're fighting a losing battle in a book like this, but here goes with some other legalistic points we've noted on the way:

**a** It's illegal to remove side repeaters from front wings, unless you replace them with Merc-style repeater mirrors. Nice.

**b** All except the most prehistoric cars must have at least one rear foglight. If there's only one, it must be fitted on the right. We've never heard of anyone getting stopped for it, but you must also have a pair of rear reflectors. If your rear clusters ain't got 'em, can you get trendy ones? Er, no.

**c** Fuel filler caps have to be fitted so there's no danger of fuel spillage, or of excess fumes leaking from the top of the filler neck. This means using an appropriate petrol-resistant sealer (should be supplied in the kit). Oh, and not bodging the job in general seems a good idea. Unlikely to attract a pull, though.

**d** Front doors have to retain a manual means of opening from outside, even if they've been de-locked for remote locking. This means you can't take off the front door handles, usually. It seems that rear door handles can be removed if you like.

**e** Tailgates have to have some means of opening, even if it's only from inside, once the lock/handle's been removed. We think it's another safety thing - means of escape in a crash, and all that.

**f** You have to have at least one exterior mirror, and it must be capable of being adjusted somehow.

**g** If you fit new fog and spotlights, they actually have to work. No-one fits new lights just for show (or do they?), but if they stop working later when a fuse blows, relay packs up, or the wiring connectors rust up, you'd better fix 'em or remove 'em.

**h** Pedal extensions must have rubbers fitted on the brake and clutch pedals, and must be spaced sufficiently so there's no chance of hitting two pedals at once. This last bit sounds obvious, but lots of extension sets out there are so hard to fit that achieving this can be rather difficult. Don't get caught out.

**i** On cars with airbags, if you fit a sports wheel and disconnect the airbag in the process, the airbag warning light will be on permanently. Apart from being annoying, this is also illegal.

**j** Pace-car strobe lights (or any other flashing lights, apart from indicators) are illegal for road use. Of course.

**k** Anything else we didn't think of - is probably illegal too. Sorry.

Any questions? Try the MOT Helpline (0845 6005977). Yes, really.

Thanks to Andrew Dare of the Vehicle Inspectorate, Exeter, for his help in steering us through this minefield!

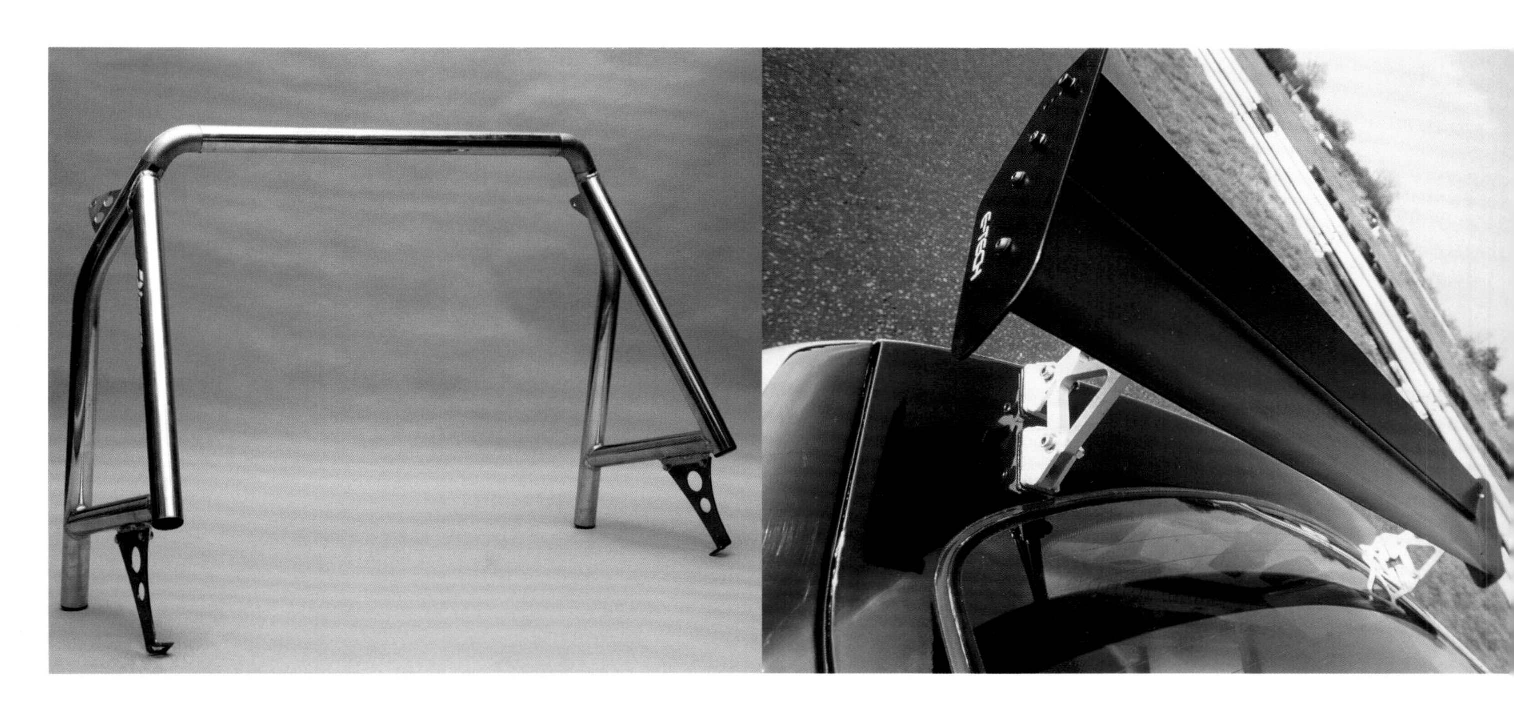

# Thanks to:

We gratefully acknowledge all the help and advice offered from the following suppliers, without whom, etc, etc. Many of those credited below went way beyond the call of duty to help us produce this book - you know who you are. Cheers, guys! Roll the credits...

**ABC Design Autostyling Ltd**
(AutoArt & MHW)
www.abcdesignltd.com

**Auto Inparts Ltd**
(accessories)
01525 382713

**Avon Custom**
(paint and bodywork)
01934 830188
www.avoncustom.co.uk

**Brown & Geeson**
(Momo)
01268 764411
www.brownandgeeson.com

**Corbeau Seats**
01424 854499
www.corbeau-seats.co.uk

**Dash Dynamics** (dash kit)
0870 127 0003
www.dashdynamics.co.uk

**Demon Tweeks** (accessories)
01978 664466
www.demon-tweeks.co.uk

**Draper Tools** (tools)
023 8026 6355
www.draper.co.uk

**Ecosse** (body kit)
01506 516106
www.ecosse-peugeot.co.uk

**Eibach UK**
(B&M Short Shift Kit)
01455 286524

**Eurostyling** (Folia tec)
01908 324950
www.eurostyling.com

**Halfords**
08457 626 625

**House of Kolor** (paint)
01302 341788
www.houseofkolor.com

**K & N Filters** (Induction kits)
01925 636950
www.knfilters.co.uk

**L.A & R.W Piper** (car trimming)
01963 441431
www.trimmers.fsnet.co.uk

**Microscan Alarms**
www.microscanalarms.co.uk

**Mille Miglia (UK) Ltd** (wheels)
01626 832222
www.millemiglia.co.uk

**Planet Line, France** (door mirrors)
00 33 04 74 53 84 00
www.planet-line.com

**Red Dot Racing**
(brake discs & pads)
020 8888 2354
www.reddotracing.co.uk

**Richbrook**
(sport auto accessories)
020 8543 7111
www.richbrook.co.uk

**Ripspeed at Halfords**
0845 609 1259

**Safety Devices** (harnesses)
01353 724201
www.safetydevices.co.uk

**Sargents Performance Centre** (exhaust systems)
01935 427554
www.philipsargent.co.uk

**SPAX**
01869 244771
www.spaxperformance.com

**Toyo Tyres**
01933 411144
www.toyo.co.uk

**A special thank you to:**
Bryn Musselwhite

| | |
|---|---|
| Editorial Director | Matthew Minter |
| Designer | Simon Larkin |
| Page Build | James Robertson |
| Workshop | Paul Buckland<br>Pete Trott |
| Technical Editor | Bob Jex |
| Editor | Ian Barnes |
| Project Co-ordinator | Carole Turk |
| Production Control | Kevin Heals |

HAYNES
MOTOR
MUSEUM
See the
HAYNES MAX POWER
cars in the
flesh!
And over 300 kickin' cars, including, racing, muscle and supercars. All at the Haynes Motor Museum
Sparkford, Yeovil, Somerset BA22 7LH. Tel: 01963 440804 www.haynesmotormuseum.co.uk

Would you call an electrician to change a lightbulb?
Haynes
So why take your car to a garage for the simplest bulb replacement or service?
With a Haynes manual telling and showing you everything you need to know for less than the cost of 30 minutes of a garage mechanic's time*, what have you got to lose? Haynes manuals are available from all good car accessory retailers and bookshops.
For further information or to find your nearest stockist, call 01963 442030 or visit www.haynes.co.uk
Full listing over page
*Average garage labour rate now £40 per hour. Source: Retail Motor Industries Federation

# Haynes Car Manuals

Alfa Romeo Alfasud/Sprint (74 - 88 0292
Alfa Romeo Alfetta (73 - 87 0531
Audi 80, 90 (79 - Oct 86 & Coupe (81 - Nov 88 0605
Audi 80, 90 (Oct 86 - 90 & Coupe (Nov 88 - 90) 1491
Audi 100 (Oct 82 - 90 & 200 (Feb 84 - Oct 89) 0907
Audi 100 & A6 Petrol & Diesel (May 91 - May 97) 3504
Audi A4 (95 - Feb 00 3575
Austin A35 & A40 (56 - 67) * 0118
Austin Allegro 1100, 1300, 1.0, 1.1 & 1.3 (73 - 82) * 0164
Austin/MG/Rover Maestro 1.3 & 1.6 (83 - 95) 0922
Austin/MG Metro (80 - May 90) 0718
Austin/Rover Montego 1.3 & 1.6 (84 - 94) 1066
Austin/MG/Rover Montego 2.0 (84 - 95) 1067
Mini (59 - 69) 0527
Mini (69 - 01) 0646
Austin/Rover 2.0 litre Diesel Engine (86 - 93) 1857
Austin Healey 100/6 & 3000 (56 - 68) * 0049
Bedford CF (69 - 87) 0163
Bedford/Vauxhall Rascal & Suzuki Supercarry (86 - Oct 94) 3015
BMW 316, 320 & 320i (4-cyl) (75 - Feb 83) 0276
BMW 320, 320i, 323i & 325i (6-cyl) (Oct 77 - Sept 87) 0815
BMW 3-Series (Apr 91 - 96) 3210
BMW 3- & 5-Series (sohc) (81 - 91) 1948
BMW 520i & 525e (Oct 81 - June 88) 1560
BMW 1500, 1502, 1600, 1602, 2000 & 2002 (59 - 77) * 0240
Chrysler PT Cruiser (00 - 03) 4058
Citroën 2CV, Ami & Dyane (67 - 90) 0196
Citroën AX Petrol & Diesel (87 - 97) 3014
Citroën BX (83 - 94) A to L 0908
Citroën C15 Van Petrol & Diesel (89 - Oct 98) 3509
Citroën CX (75 - 88) 0528
Citroën Saxo Petrol & Diesel (96 - 01) 3506
Citroën Visa (79 - 88) 0620
Citroën Xantia Petrol & Diesel (93 - 98) 3082
Citroën XM Petrol & Diesel (89 - 00) 3451
Citroën Xsara Petrol & Diesel (97 - Sept 00) 3751
Citroën Xsara Picasso Petrol & Diesel (00 - 02) 3944
Citroën ZX Diesel (91 - 98) 1922
Citroën ZX Petrol (91 - 98) 1881
Citroën 1.7 & 1.9 litre Diesel Engine (84 - 96) 1379
Fiat 126 (73 - 87) * 0305
Fiat 500 (57 - 73) 0090
Fiat Bravo & Brava (95 - 00) 3572
Fiat Cinquecento (93 - 98) 3501
Fiat Panda (81 - 95) 0793
Fiat Punto Petrol & Diesel (94 - Oct 99) 3251
Fiat Regata (84 - 88) 1167
Fiat Tipo (88 - 91) 1625
Fiat Uno (83 - 95) 0923
Fiat X1/9 (74 - 89) 0273
Ford Anglia (59 - 68) * 0001
Ford Capri II (& III) 1.6 & 2.0 (74 - 87) 0283
Ford Capri II (& III) 2.8 & 3.0 (74 - 87) 1309
Ford Cortina Mk III 1300 & 1600 (70 - 76) * 0070
Ford Cortina Mk IV (& V) 1.6 & 2.0 (76 - 83) * 0343
Ford Cortina Mk IV (& V) 2.3 V6 (77 - 83) * 0426
Ford Escort Mk I 1100 & 1300 (68 - 74) * 0171
Ford Escort Mk I Mexico, RS 1600 & RS 2000 (70 - 74) * 0139
Ford Escort Mk II Mexico, RS 1800 & RS 2000 (75 - 80) * 0735
Ford Escort (75 - Aug 80) * 0280
Ford Escort (Sept 80 - Sept 90) 0686
Ford Escort & Orion (Sept 90 - 00) 1737
Ford Fiesta (76 - Aug 83) 0334
Ford Fiesta (Aug 83 - Feb 89) 1030
Ford Fiesta (Feb 89 - Oct 95) 1595
Ford Fiesta (Oct 95 - 01) 3397
Ford Focus (98 - 01) 3759
Ford Galaxy Petrol & Diesel (95 - Aug 00) 3984
Ford Granada (Sept 77 - Feb 85) 0481
Ford Granada & Scorpio (Mar 85 - 94) 1245
Ford Ka (96 - 02) 3570
Ford Mondeo Petrol (93 - 99) 1923
Ford Mondeo Diesel (93 - 96) 3465
Ford Orion (83 - Sept 90) 1009
Ford Sierra 4 cyl. (82 - 93) 0903
Ford Sierra V6 (82 - 91) 0904
Ford Transit Petrol (Mk 2) (78 - Jan 86) 0719
Ford Transit Petrol (Mk 3) (Feb 86 - 89) 1468
Ford Transit Diesel (Feb 86 - 99) 3019
Ford 1.6 & 1.8 litre Diesel Engine (84 - 96) 1172
Ford 2.1, 2.3 & 2.5 litre Diesel Engine (77 - 90) 1606
Freight Rover Sherpa (74 - 87) 0463
Hillman Avenger (70 - 82) 0037
Hillman Imp (63 - 76) * 0022
Honda Accord (76 - Feb 84) 0351
Honda Civic (Feb 84 - Oct 87) 1226
Honda Civic (Nov 91 - 96) 3199
Hyundai Pony (85 - 94) 3398
Jaguar E Type (61 - 72) 0140
Jaguar MkI & II, 240 & 340 (55 - 69) * 0098
Jaguar XJ6, XJ & Sovereign; Daimler Sovereign (68 - Oct 86) 0242
Jaguar XJ6 & Sovereign (Oct 86 - Sept 94) 3261
Jaguar XJ12, XJS & Sovereign; Daimler Double Six (72 - 88) 0478
Jeep Cherokee Petrol (93 - 96) 1943
Lada 1200, 1300, 1500 & 1600 (74 - 91) 0413
Lada Samara (87 - 91) 1610
Land Rover 90, 110 & Defender Diesel (83 - 95) 3017
Land Rover Discovery Petrol & Diesel (89 - 98) 3016
Land Rover Freelander (97 - 02) 3929
Land Rover Series IIA & III Diesel (58 - 85) 0529
Land Rover Series II, IIA & III Petrol (58 - 85) 0314
Mazda 323 (Mar 81 - Oct 89) 1608
Mazda 323 (Oct 89 - 98) 3455
Mazda 626 (May 83 - Sept 87) 0929
Mazda B-1600, B-1800 & B-2000 Pick-up (72 - 88) 0267
Mazda RX-7 (79 - 85) * 0460
Mercedes-Benz 190, 190E & 190D Petrol & Diesel (83 - 93) 3450
Mercedes-Benz 200, 240, 300 Diesel (Oct 76 - 85) 1114
Mercedes-Benz 250 & 280 (68 - 72) 0346
Mercedes-Benz 250 & 280 (123 Series) (Oct 76 - 84) 0677
Mercedes-Benz 124 Series (85 - Aug 93) 3253
Mercedes-Benz C-Class Petrol & Diesel (93 - Aug 00) 3511
MGA (55 - 62) * 0475
MGB (62 - 80) 0111
MG Midget & AH Sprite (58 - 80) 0265
Mitsubishi Shogun & L200 Pick-Ups (83 - 94) 1944
Morris Ital 1.3 (80 - 84) 0705
Morris Minor 1000 (56 - 71) 0024
Nissan Bluebird (May 84 - Mar 86) 1223
Nissan Bluebird (Mar 86 - 90) 1473
Nissan Cherry (Sept 82 - 86) 1031
Nissan Micra (83 - Jan 93) 0931
Nissan Micra (93 - 99) 3254
Nissan Primera (90 - Aug 99) 1851
Nissan Stanza (82 - 86) 0824
Nissan Sunny (May 82 - Oct 86) 0895
Nissan Sunny (Oct 86 - Mar 91) 1378
Nissan Sunny (Apr 91 - 95) 3219
Opel Ascona & Manta (B Series) (Sept 75 - 88) 0316
Opel Kadett (Nov 79 - Oct 84) 0634
Opel Rekord (Feb 78 - Oct 86) 0543
Peugeot 106 Petrol & Diesel (91 - 02) 1882
Peugeot 205 Petrol (83 - 97) 0932
Peugeot 206 Petrol and Diesel (98 - 01) 3757
Peugeot 305 (78 - 89)* 0538
Peugeot 306 Petrol & Diesel (93 - 99) 3073
Peugeot 309 (86 - 93) 1266
Peugeot 405 Petrol (88 - 97) 1559
Peugeot 405 Diesel (88 - 97) 3198
Peugeot 406 Petrol & Diesel (96 - 97) 3394
Peugeot 406 Petrol & Diesel (99 - 02) 3982
Peugeot 505 (79 - 89) 0762
Peugeot 1.7/1.8 & 1.9 litre Diesel Engine (82 - 96) 0950
Peugeot 2.0, 2.1, 2.3 & 2.5 litre Diesel Engines (74 - 90) 1607
Porsche 911 (65 - 85) 0264
Porsche 924 & 924 Turbo (76 - 85) 0397
Proton (89 - 97) 3255
Range Rover V8 (70 - Oct 92) 0606
Reliant Robin & Kitten (73 - 83) 0436
Renault 4 (61 - 86) * 0072
Renault 5 (Feb 85 - 96) 1219
Renault 9 & 11 (82 - 89) 0822
Renault 18 (79 - 86) 0598
Renault 19 Petrol (89 - 94) 1646
Renault 19 Diesel (89 - 96) 1946
Renault 21 (86 - 94) 1397
Renault 25 (84 - 92) 1228
Renault Clio Petrol (91 - May 98) 1853
Renault Clio Diesel (91 - June 96) 3031
Renault Clio Petrol & Diesel (May 98 - May 01) 3906
Renault Espace Petrol & Diesel (85 - 96) 3197
Renault Fuego (80 - 86) * 0764
Renault Laguna Petrol & Diesel (94 - 00) 3252
Renault Mégane & Scénic Petrol & Diesel (96 - 98) 3395
Renault Mégane & Scénic Petrol & Diesel (Apr 99 - 02) 3916
Rover 213 & 216 (84 - 89) 1116
Rover 214 & 414 (89 - 96) 1689
Rover 216 & 416 (89 - 96) 1830
Rover 211, 214, 216, 218 & 220 Petrol & Diesel (Dec 95 - 98) 3399
Rover 414, 416 & 420 Petrol & Diesel (May 95 - 98) 3453
Rover 618, 620 & 623 (93 - 97) 3257
Rover 820, 825 & 827 (86 - 95) 1380
Rover 3500 (76 - 87) 0365
Rover Metro, 111 & 114 (May 90 - 98) 1711
Saab 95 & 96 (66 - 76) * 0198
Saab 99 (69 - 79) * 0247
Saab 90, 99 & 900 (79 - Oct 93) 0765
Saab 900 (Oct 93 - 98) 3512
Saab 9000 (4-cyl) (85 - 98) 1686
Seat Ibiza & Cordoba Petrol & Diesel (Oct 93 - Oct 99) 3571
Seat Ibiza & Malaga (85 - 92) 1609
Skoda Estelle (77 - 89) 0604
Skoda Favorit (89 - 96) 1801
Skoda Felicia Petrol & Diesel (95 - 01) 3505
Subaru 1600 & 1800 (Nov 79 - 90) [illegible]
Sunbeam Alpine, Rapier & H120 (67 - 76) * 0051
Suzuki Supercarry & Bedford/Vauxhall Rascal (86 - Oct 94) 3015
Suzuki SJ Series, Samurai & Vitara (4-cyl) (82 - 97) 1942
Talbot Alpine, Solara, Minx & Rapier (75 - 86) 0337
Talbot Horizon (78 - 86) 0473
Talbot Samba (82 - 86) 0823
Toyota Carina E (May 92 - 97) 3256
Toyota Corolla (Sept 83 - Sept 87) 1024
Toyota Corolla (80 - 85) 0683
Toyota Corolla (Sept 87 - Aug 92) 1683
Toyota Corolla (Aug 92 - 97) 3259
Toyota Hi-Ace & Hi-Lux (69 - Oct 83) 0304
Triumph Acclaim (81 - 84) * 0792
Triumph GT6 & Vitesse (62 - 74) * 0112
Triumph Herald (59 - 71) * 0010
Triumph Spitfire (62 - 81) 0113
Triumph Stag (70 - 78) 0441
Triumph TR2, TR3, TR3A, TR4 & TR4A (52 - 67) * 0028
Triumph TR5 & 6 (67 - 75) * 0031
Triumph TR7 (75 - 82) * 0322
Vauxhall Astra (80 - Oct 84) 0635
Vauxhall Astra & Belmont (Oct 84 - Oct 91) 1136
Vauxhall Astra (Oct 91 - Feb 98) 1832
Vauxhall/Opel Astra & Zafira Diesel (Feb 98 - Sept 00) 3797
Vauxhall/Opel Astra & Zafira Petrol (Feb 98 - Sept 00) 3758
Vauxhall/Opel Calibra (90 - 98) 3502
Vauxhall Carlton (Oct 78 - Oct 86) 0480
Vauxhall Carlton & Senator (Nov 86 - 94) 1469
Vauxhall Cavalier 1300 (77 - July 81) * 0461
Vauxhall Cavalier 1600, 1900 & 2000 (75 - July 81) 0315
Vauxhall Cavalier (81 - Oct 88) 0812
Vauxhall Cavalier (Oct 88 - 95) 1570
Vauxhall Chevette (75 - 84) 0285
Vauxhall Corsa (Mar 93 - 97) 1985
Vauxhall/Opel Corsa (Apr 97 - Oct 00) 3921
Vauxhall/Opel Frontera Petrol & Diesel (91 - Sept 98) 3454
Vauxhall Nova (83 - 93) 0909
Vauxhall/Opel Omega (94 - 99) 3510
Vauxhall Vectra Petrol & Diesel (95 - 98) 3396
Vauxhall/Opel Vectra (Mar 99 - May 02) 3930
Vauxhall/Opel 1.5, 1.6 & 1.7 litre Diesel Engine (82 - 96) 1222
Volkswagen 411 & 412 (68 - 75) * 0091
Volkswagen Beetle 1200 (54 - 77) 0036
Volkswagen Beetle 1300 & 1500 (65 - 75) 0039
Volkswagen Beetle 1302 & 1302S (70 - 72) 0110
Volkswagen Beetle 1303, 1303S & GT (72 - 75) 0159
Volkswagen Beetle Petrol & Diesel (Apr 99 - 01) 3798
Volkswagen Golf & Bora Petrol & Diesel (April 98 - 00) 3727
Volkswagen Golf & Jetta Mk 1 1.1 & 1.3 (74 - 84) 0716
Volkswagen Golf, Jetta & Scirocco Mk 1 1.5, 1.6 & 1.8 (74 - 84) 0726
Volkswagen Golf & Jetta Mk 1 Diesel (78 - 84) 0451
Volkswagen Golf & Jetta Mk 2 (Mar 84 - Feb 92) 1081
Volkswagen Golf & Vento Petrol & Diesel (Feb 92 - 96) 3097
Volkswagen LT vans & light trucks (76 - 87) 0637
Volkswagen Passat & Santana (Sept 81 - May 88) 0814
Volkswagen Passat Petrol & Diesel (May 88 - 96) 3498
Volkswagen Passat 4-cyl Petrol & Diesel (Dec 96 - Nov 00) 3917
Volkswagen Polo & Derby (76 - Jan 82) 0335
Volkswagen Polo (82 - Oct 90) 0813
Volkswagen Polo (Nov 90 - Aug 94) 3245
Volkswagen Polo Hatchback Petrol & Diesel (94 - 99) 3500
Volkswagen Scirocco (82 - 90) 1224
Volkswagen Transporter 1600 (68 - 79) 0082
Volkswagen Transporter 1700, 1800 & 2000 (72 - 79) 0226
Volkswagen Transporter (air-cooled) (79 - 82) 0638
Volkswagen Transporter (water-cooled) (82 - 90) 3452
Volkswagen Type 3 (63 - 73) * 0084
Volvo 120 & 130 Series (& P1800) (61 - 73) * 97010
Volvo 142, 144 & 145 (66 - 74) 0129
Volvo 240 Series (74 - 93) 0270
Volvo 262, 264 & 260/265 (75 - 85) * 0400
Volvo 340, 343, 345 & 360 (76 - 91) 0715
Volvo 440, 460 & 480 (87 - 97) 1691
Volvo 740 & 760 (82 - 91) 1258
Volvo 850 (92 - 96) 3260
Volvo 940 (90 - 96) 3249
Volvo S40 & V40 (96 - 99) 3569
Volvo S70, V70 & C70 (96 - 99) 3573

* = Classic Reprints

Haynes Manuals

Haynes Car Service and Repair Manuals are available from car accessory retailers.
For further information or to find your nearest stockist, call **01963 442030** or visit **www.ha[illegible].co.uk**